ARMENIAN APOCRYPHA RELATING TO ANGELS AND BIBLICAL HEROES

EARLY JUDAISM AND ITS LITERATURE

Rodney A. Werline, Editor

Editorial Board:
George J. Brooke
Esther Glickler Chazon
Kelley N. Coblentz Bautch
Steven D. Fraade
James S. McLaren

Number 45

ARMENIAN APOCRYPHA
RELATING TO ANGELS AND
BIBLICAL HEROES

BY

MICHAEL E. STONE

 **PRESS**

Atlanta

Copyright © 2016 by SBL Press

All rights reserved. No part of this work may be reproduced or transmitted in any form or by any means, electronic or mechanical, including photocopying and recording, or by means of any information storage or retrieval system, except as may be expressly permitted by the 1976 Copyright Act or in writing from the publisher. Requests for permission should be addressed in writing to the Rights and Permissions Office, SBL Press, 825 Houston Mill Road, Atlanta, GA 30329 USA.

Library of Congress Cataloging-in-Publication Data

Names: Stone, Michael E., 1938- author.
Title: Armenian Apocrypha relating to angels and biblical heroes / by Michael E. Stone.
Description: Atlanta : SBL Press, 2016. | Series: Early Judaism and its literature ; 45 | In English; with original Armenian texts translated into English. | Includes bibliographical references and index.
Identifiers: LCCN 2016032651 (print) | LCCN 2016034104 (ebook) | ISBN 9781628371543 (paperback) | ISBN 9780884141891 (hardcover) | ISBN 9780884141884 (ebook)
Subjects: LCSH: Apocryphal books. | Apocryphal books--Translations into Armenian. | Angels.
Classification: LCC BS1696 .S766 2016 (print) | LCC BS1696 (ebook) | DDC 229/.9049--dc23
LC record available at https://lccn.loc.gov/2016032651

Printed on acid-free paper.

Dedicated to my colleagues, the members of the Association Internationale des Études Arméniennes, without whose scholarly devotion and personal friendship my journey would have been far less interesting and enjoyable.

Table of Contents

Preface and Acknowledgments	ix
Signs	x
Abbreviations	xi
Manuscripts Published in This Book	xiii

Part 1: Biblical and Associated Traditions — 1

1.1	Concerning the Twelve Hours of the Night	1
1.2	Concerning the Names of the Twenty-Four Hours of the Day and Night	1
1.3	Concerning the Fifteen Signs of the Judgement, Recension III	4
1.4	The Twelve Gifts Lost by Adam	10
1.5	What Are the Dimensions of the Ark?	16
1.6	The Seven Punishments of Cain	18
1.7	He Counts the Multitude of the Stars	19
1.8	Names of the Jewels of Aaron's Ephod	22

Part 2: Chronological Texts — 25

2.1	Adaptation of Genesis 5:6–28	28
2.2	Chronological Summaries	30
2.3	Concerning Millennia	34
2.4	Concerning the Periods	38
2.5	Generations from Adam to Christ	41
2.6	Concerning the Knowledge of the Times	51
2.7	History of the Forefathers to Abraham and Their Years	55

Part 3: Angelological Texts — 65

3.1	Angelology Text 2	67
3.2	Names of the Angels	70
3.3	Question concerning the Archangels	72
3.4	Concerning the Renewal of Angelic Destruction	76

3.5	The Praise of the Angels	77
3.6	The Ranks of the Angels	81
3.7	Questions concerning Angels	83
3.8	Questions and Answers from the Holy Books	92
3.9	This Is the History of the Discourse (Word)	101
3.10	Ranks of the Angels Who Rebelled	106
3.11	Supplications to Angels	107
3.12	Prayer to the Twelve Guardian Angels	110

PART 4: BIBLICAL STORIES — 113

4.1	Concerning the Tower 1	113
4.2	Concerning the Tower 2	114
4.3	Memorial of the Forefathers Abraham, Isaac, and Jacob	116
4.4	Years and Names of the Forefathers in Order	138
4.5	Short History of the Holy Forefathers	163
4.6	Joseph and Jacob: An Allegory	174
4.7	Third Story of Joseph	176
4.8	The Israelites in Egypt	229
4.9	The Ten Plagues of Egypt	254
4.10	Concerning Jannes and Mambres	258
4.11	Story of the Prophet Asaph	262
4.12	Story of the Prophet Nathan	263
4.13	This Is the Story of Nineveh an[d of Jo]nah	266

Bibliography	277
Subject Index	283
Index of Persons and Places	287
Ancient Sources Index	295

Preface and Acknowledgments

This book presents a further collection of Armenian apocryphal texts, all provided with and drawn from previously unknown manuscript witnesses and nearly all published for the first time. The transmission of biblical and Second Temple period apocryphal traditions from antiquity and their reshaping and function in the communities that nurtured them, forms a significant aspect of their study. I hope that readers and scholars will be as fascinated as I am by the dynamic and responsive forms that such traditions exhibit in Armenian culture.

This book was written under the Israel Science Foundation's personal research grant no. 314/13. Without the support of ISF this book would most likely not have been written. I also acknowledge here the help given to me by several research assistants, primarily Tomer Doitch, whose painstaking assistance contributed much to the documentation of biblical sources of the tradition. Vered Hillel complemented Tomer's work on the difficult text no. 2.7 and my own work on the Jannes and Mambres tradition (4.10). Asya Bereznyak wrote the excursus on the Cainite Lamech (3.8). For the support and for the logistical assistance of Shmuel Rausnitz, my deepest thanks. Prof. Betsy Halpern-Amaru kindly read text 2.7 and helped enrich its annotation.

I express my profound thanks to the Matenadaran, Institute of Ancient Manuscripts in Erevan, Armenia. The vast majority of manuscript texts edited here are drawn from that library by permission. Its directors, the late Sen Arevshatyan and its present director Hrach Tamrazian, could not have been more helpful both in granting me free access to the collection and in providing images of the manuscript texts. Dr. Gēorg Tēr-Vardanean, Curator of Manuscripts in the Matenadaran, and his Department made my work there immeasurably easier. I also express my thanks to His Beatitude, Patriarch Mesrob II of Constantinople for permission to publish the short extracts from Galata manuscript 154; to the editors of *Le Muséon* for permission to publish an extract from Yacoubian 2003, 45–46. The late Archbisop Norayr Bogharian gave me permission to publish the angelological text from Jerusalem, Armenian Patriarchate J1398 (3.1).

Signs

{ }	corruption in text
< >	editor's correction, emendation, or conjecture
[ ]	editor's remarks
( )	additions by the editor for smoothness of style
##/	mark sequential line numbers or section numbers

Abbreviations

AE	the Great Armenian Era, calculated from 551 CE.
AM	anno mundi, i.e., years since creation
ANB	Ačaṙyan, H. Հայոց Անձանունների Բառարան *(Dictionary of Armenian Proper Names)*. Beirut: Sevan Press, 1972
H Arm	the corpus number of Sinai Armenian inscriptions
Arm	(in textual discussions) indicates the Armenian version of the Bible
Bedrossian	Matthias Bedrossian, *New Dictionary Armenian-English*. Beirut: Librairie du Liban, 1985
BL	British Library
ca.	approximately
chap.	chapter
et al.	*et alii/alaiae*
EJL	Early Judaism and Its Literature
Exod. Rab.	Midrash Exodus Rabba
fol., fols.	folio, folios
Gen. Rab.	Midrash Genesis Rabba. *Bereschit Rabba*. Edited by J. Theodor and C. Albeck. Berlin: Akademie Verlag, 1929
hmt	*homoeoteleuton*
Horovitz-Rabin	Horovitz, H. S., and I. A. Rabin. *Mechilta d'Rabbi Ishmael cum variis lectionibus et Adnotationibus*. Repr. Jerusalem: Bamberger & Wahrman, 1969
HTR	*Harvard Theological Review*
IDB	Interpreters Dictionary of the Bible
l. ll.	line, lines
JTS	*Journal of Theological Studies*
LXX	Septuagint or Greek Bible
MH	Մատենագրութիւն Հայոց (Classical Armenian Authors); series cited by volume number
MT	Masoretic Text or Hebrew Bible
NBHL	Նոր բառգիրք հայկազեան լեզուի (New Dictionary of the Armenian Language)
NRSV	New Revised Standard Version
OG	Old Greek

OnaV	Onmoastic Sacra Text Type V
p.m., s.m.	p.m., *prima manu*, text written by the original scribe; s.m., *secunda manu*, text written by a second hand
PVTG	Pseudepigrapha Veteris Testamenti Graece
REArm	*Revue des études arméniennes*
RSV	Revised Standard Version
Stone and Hillel, "Index," no. ##	Indicates the number of the variant in the "Index of Variants" in Michael E. Stone in collaboration with Vered Hillel, *The Armenian Version of the Testaments of the Twelve Patriarchs: Edition, Apparatus, Translation and Commentary*. Hebrew University Armenian Series 11. Leuven: Peeters, 2012
Sus	Susanna
s.v.	*sub vocem*
SVTP	Studia in Veteris Testamenti Pseudepigrapha
Th	Theodotion
UPATS	University of Pennsylvania Armenian Texts and Studies

Points of Procedure

The following procedures have been observed:

I have used the standard English forms of the names in the translation unless the Armenian spelling is very deviant, in which instances I transliterate it in parentheses, using the system of *REArm*.

In citations from Psalms, I have given the Masoretic number and if the LXX and Arm differ, I give their number.

Often, where Armenian has coordinated participles or a participle and a finite verb conjoined by "and," I have rendered into appropriate English, without noting the addition or omission of եւ "and."

Իբրեւ is sometimes rendered "after."

When Armenian numerals are used in the text, I use English numerals in the translation.

Manuscripts are referred to using a sigil for the library in accordance with the system of Association Internationale des Etudes arméniennes; see Bernard Coulie, "Liste des sigles utilisés pour désigner les manuscrits," inavailable in.pdf format on the web site of the *Association internationale des études arméniennes*.

"and throughout x/y" in variants indicates an orthographic variant that is consistent throughout the manuscript being cited.

"preferable" in variants indicates that this reading is better than that preserved in the text.

Manuscripts Published in This Book

Ms Number	Foliation	Title of Work
Galata 154	p. 302	The Ten Plagues of Egypt
Galata 154	p. 303	What Are the Dimensions of the Ark?
J1398	pp. 1–3	Angelology Text 2
M266	90v–91r	Ranks of the Angels
M268	150v	The Ten Plagues of Egypt
M268	150v–151r	Names of the Jewels of Aaron's Ephod
M268	151r	The Seven Punishments of Cain
M268	312r	Names of the Angels
M268	312r–313r	The Praise of Angels
M512	86r–90r	Years and Names of the Forefathers in Order
M537	230v–231r	Names of the Angels
M537	231v–232r	Praise of the Angels
M537	237v	The Ten Plagues of Egypt
M605	25v	The Ten Plagues of Egypt
M682	7r	Praise of the Angels
M682	7r–8r	Questions concerning Angels
M682	7d	Concerning the Tower 2
M682	8v–9r	The Ten Plagues of Egypt and Jannes and Mambres
M682	96r	This Is the History of the Discourse (Word)
M724	178r–180r	Stories of the Prophets Asaph and Nathan
M10320	77v–79r	Concerning the Twelve Hours of the Night
M10720	4v–5r	The Twelve Gifts Lost by Adam
M10320	79r–79v	Ranks of the Angels Who Rebelled
M10320	84v–86v	Concerning the Knowledge of the Times
M10320	87r–87v	Concerning the Twelve Hours of the Night
M1654A	189v–193v	Questions and Answers from the Holy Books
M1665	182v–198v	Memorial of the Forefathers Abraham, Isaac, and Jacob
M2001B	243r	Concerning the Names of the Twenty-Four Hours of the Day and Night
M2001B	243r–243v	Angelology Text 2
M2036	13r	Concerning the Names of the Twenty-Four Hours of the Day and Night
M2036	220r	Concerning Millennia I

M2036	220r, 273r	Concerning the Periods
M2111	219v	Joseph and Jacob: An Allegory
M2111	229v	Joseph and Jacob: An Allegory
M2111	230r–231r	Short History of the Holy Forefathers
M2126	96r–96v	Question concerning the Archangels
M2158	266r	The Ten Plagues of Egypt
M2182	347r–349v	History of the Forefathers to Abraham and Their Years
M2182	350r–350v	The Twelve Gifts Lost by Adam
M2188	242v–243v	Concerning the Fifteen Signs of the Judgement, Recension III
M2188	244r	The Ten Plagues of Egypt
M2242	330r–349v	Third Story of Joseph
M2245	114v	Question Concerning the Archangels
M2245	114v–115r	Fall of the Angels
M2245	116r	Fall of the Angels II
M2245	271r–272r	Generations from Adam to Christ
M4618	126r	Concerning Millennia II
M5690	1r–1v	Concerning the Renewal of Angelic Destruction
M6340	36r–47r	The Israelites in Egypt
M6340	47r–50r	This Is the Story of Nineveh and Jonah
M6617	254v–255r	He Counts the Multitude of the Stars
M6897	413r	The Ten Plagues of Egypt
M6905	1r–1v	Concerning the Renewal of Angelic Destruction
M8076	222r–222v	Chronological Summaries
M8076	223r	Concerning the Millennia III
M8076	273r	Concerning the Millennia II
M8591	82r–82v	Concerning the Tower 1
M8591	82v	What Are the Dimensions of the Ark?
M9100	370v–371r	Concerning the Periods
M9100	372r–373v	Names of the Jewels of Aaron's Ephod
M9121	102r–102v	The Twelve Gifts Lost by Adam
OXBodleian arm c3	322r–329v	Memorial of the Forefathers Abraham, Isaac, and Jacob
OXBodleian arm f 26	333v–334v	Supplication to Angels
OXBodleian arm f 26	334v	Prayer to the Archangel Michael
OXBodleian arm f 26	335r	Prayer to the Twelve Guardian Angels

Part One:
Biblical and Associated Traditions

1.1. Concerning the Twelve Hours of the Night

The text being discussed here gives only the hours of the night. It is to be distinguished from The Hours of the Day and Night, a magical text associated with Apollonius of Tyana, which was published some decades ago from J69 (1728–30) fols. 639r–639v.[1] That document gives names of the hours and coordinates the hours with the conjuration of the talismans most effective in them. The present text is another recension of this writing and it occurs in M10320 (seventeenth century) fols. 87v–89r.[2] Although this Armenian text, which anyway is a torso, is not explicitly connected with Adam, it is a representative of the textual type that other language traditions connected with Adam. The text is entitled Վասն ԺԲ Ժամու Գիշերոյն (Concerning the Twelve Hours of the Night). I published it in 1996 (Stone 1996a, 167–73). It suffices here to give the above information in view of its inherent interest.

1.2. Concerning the Names of the Twenty-Four Hours of the Day and Night

The text published below is quite different from the various versions of The Hours of the Day and Night mentioned directly above, which are related to Adam and to Apollonius of Tyana. The present text gives names of the twenty-four hours that are nearly all comprehensible in Armenian, while the names in The Hours of the Day and Night are incomprehensible. Juliet Eynatyan

---

1. Stone 1982, 39–80. On the manuscript, see Bogharian 1966, 1:224–39.
2. See Eganyan, Zeyt'unyan, and Ant'abyan 1970, 2.1092. There are two sets of numbering on the manuscript's pages I have. The upper gives this text as noted above; the lower is 77v–78r.

published it from M5975 of the fifteenth century[3] and Gohar Muradyan and Aram Topchyan translated it into English.[4]

Here we present further copies of this list, from *Miscellany* M2001B (1373) fol. 243r[5] and *Miscellany* M2036 (seventeenth century) fol. 13r.[6] M2036 does not number the days with Armenian numerals, as M2001B does. In M2036 the names all have the demonstrative/definite –ն at the end, while this is not consistent in M2001B. These above instances are not noted in the critical apparatus. Both these copies of the list have lacunae. In M2001B lines 16 and 21 are missing and M2036 lacks line 24 and a second hand has written Թարեայն in the margin after line 22. The text is that of Eynatyan and translation that of Muradyan and Topchyan, and the variants of the two new witnesses are added in the critical apparatus. I have introduced the numbering system.

It should be observed that this list of names is taken from a different type of literature than the previously published Hours of the Day and Night. It is from the calendarical material that is quite widespread in the Armenian manuscript tradition. On the type of the texts entitled "Calendar," see the remarks of Eynatyan.[7]

Text

0/ ժամք տուընջեան այս է
1/ Ա. Այգ:
Բ. Ծագ:
Գ. Զայրացեալ:
Դ. Ճառագայթեալ:
5/ Ե. Շառաւեղեալ:
Զ. Երկրատես:
Է. Շանթակողմ:
Ը. Հրակաթն:
Թ. Հուրփայլեալ:
10/ Ժ. Թաղանթելն:
ԺԱ. Առագաստն:
ԺԲ. Արփողն:
ժամք գիշերոյն այս է

---

3. Eganyan, Zeytʻunyan, and Antʻabyan 1965, 1:705.
4. Eynatyan 2002, 356–57.
5. See Tēr-Vardanean 2012, 6:961–72.
6. Tēr-Vardanean 2012, 6:1135–42.
7. Eynatyan 2002, 12–23.

Ա. Խաւարակն։
15/ Բ. Աղջամուղջն։
Գ. Մթացեալն։
Դ. Շակաւոտն։
Ե. Կամաւոտն։
Զ. Բաւական։
20/ Է. Խոյթական։
Ը. Գեղական։
Թ. Լուսաճեմ։
Ժ. Առաւոտն։
ԺԱ. Լուսափայլն։
25/ ԺԲ. Փայլածոյն։

Variants

Title վասն գիտելոյ զանուանս ԻԴ ժամուց տուրնջեան եւ գիշերոյ 2001B | այս է] omit 2036

1 Առաջին ժամ տուրնջեան. Այգ 2001B 2 ծայգն 2036 3 զայրացեա 2001B 4 ճառայթ 2001B 4 շառաւիղեալն 2036 7 շնթակողն 2036 9 փայլեալ 2001B 10 թաղանթեալ 2001B 11 Առագատն 2001B 12 արփողըն 2036

Night Title ժամք է] իսկ գիշերոյն 2001B ժամք գիշերոյ 2036 | է] om 2036

14 առաջին պահն Խաւարակն 2001B 16 մրթացեալն 2001B 2036 17 omit 2001B խաղաւօտն 2036 18 Հինզն շատտրատն 2001B կամաւօտն 2036 19 բաւանդական 2001B բաւականըն 2036 20 խուժական 2001B | խու followed by inked out signs 2036 21 գեղական 2001B կիզական 2036 22 omit 2001B 23 լուսափայլն 2001B առաւօտն 2036 24 փայլածուն 2001B լուսայփայլն 2036 25 առաւատուն՝ կամ աշալուշան 2001B փայլածունն 2036

Translation

0/ The hours of the day are the following:
1/ 1. "Dawn"
2. "Rise"
3. "Angry"
4. "Shining"

4   BIBLICAL AND ASSOCIATED TRADITIONS

5/   5. "Sprouting"
    6. "Seeing the Earth"
    7. "On the Lightning's Side"
    8. "Dropping Fire"
    9. "Shining Fire"
10/ 10. "Covered with Pellicle"
    11. "Curtain"
    12. "Bright"
    Then of night, the first watch (is)
    1. "Dark-eyed"
15/ 2. "Twilight"
    3. "Darkened"
    4. Šakawotn
    5. Kamawotn
    6. "Enough"
20/ 7. "With Grim Eyes"
    8. "With Ruptured Eyes"
    9. "Sparkling"
    10. "Morning"
    11. "Light-shining"
25/ 12. P'alacu [Venus]

1.3. Concerning the Fifteen Signs of the Judgement, Recension III

Concerning the Fifteen Signs of the Judgement is quite a widespread text, existing in Latin and many continental vernaculars, as W. Heist has written.[8] The Armenian is the only Oriental version with which I am familiar. The Hebrew translation that I published in 1981 was made from Latin (Stone 1981, 12–13 and 42–57). Therefore, I include the Hebrew with the European vernacular texts. As Heist points out, the Latin and European vernacular versions are quite numerous and Martin McNamara adds details about the Old Irish and other Celtic versions.[9] The content of the text is explicit in its title.

---

8. On the whole work, see Heist 1952 and Stone 1981, 3–40, and sources cited in those two studies.

9. McNamara 1975, 128–38 provides rich information about the Irish text and its reworkings in that language. See further Herbert and McNamara 1990, 153–59, where a translation is given. Fr. McNamara informs me that he is currently working on an expanded treatment of the apocryphon. See further on the Latin version: Lorenzo DiTommaso 2010, 3–11, 14.

PART ONE 5

Such lists of portents were old and already known in ancient Jewish literature of the Second Temple period.[10]

The text of Concerning the Fifteen Signs of the Judgement that I am publishing here is a quite different recension from those I published in 1981 from two Jerusalem manuscripts. The Jerusalem manuscripts are J1729 Theological Texts (1741), p. 320 (Bogharian 1973, 6:40–42) and J1861 *Miscellany* (1669), p. 135 (Bogharian 1973, 6:248–54). It is, apparently translated from an original quite independent of the Jerusalem manuscripts or their ancestors, as will be made evident below. The recension published here, called Armenian Recension III, does not include the attribution to "books of the Jews" found in Recension I. In this publication I use the numbering system and recension designations of my edition of 1981.[11]

Erevan, Matenadaran M2188 is a *Miscellany* of the fifteenth century (Tēr-Vardanean 2012, 7:366–72). It is copied in formal cursive script (bolorgir) and the text of Signs of the Judgement is to be found on fols. 242v–243v. It is written in Ancient Armenian with some medieval features, as are most of the texts published in this book.[12] Armenian numerals in the margins mark each of the fifteen signs. It is not possible to determine the language from which it was translated and I can be no more precise about the dating than to say that it is older than the date of the manuscript. The two preliminary sections, A and B, are quite different from the text of the Jerusalem manuscripts.

Recension 3's relationship with Recensions 1 and 2 is evident from the following list of major similarities and differences:

Signs I, II, VIII are basically the same in all three Armenian texts, though the formulation in M2188 is very distinctive.

Signs III, VI, and XV are quite different.

Sign IV differs, but includes crying out of sea creatures which occurs in Arm Recension 2 and Latin Recension B.

Sign VII concerning the stars may be related to Arm and Latin Sign XII.

Sign X here corresponds reasonably closely to Sign IV of Arm I and II and of Latin B.

Sign XI is Sign V of Arm I and II and Latin B.

---

10. For examples, see Stone 1981, 15–18.
11. Stone 1981, 3–40. On the whole work, compare Heist 1952 and see the sources cited in those two studies.
12. Note that in this manuscript, initial "e" is always written ե.

Sign XII repeats part of Sign IV which does not occur in the other recensions.

Sign XIII, compare Latin Recension B.

Sign XIV may perhaps be compared to the resurrection in the other recensions, which is either Sign XIV or XV.

Text

A/ / fol. 242v / Յաղագս ԵԺ-ան նշանացն. որ[13] լինելոց է յետ սատակման Ներինն նախ քան զզալուստ Քրիստոսի։

B/ Չկնի սատակման Ներինն մասացեն Իս աւուրք մինչեւ ի կատարած աշխարհի եւ ի զալուստն Քրիստոսի. յետ ԻԵ աւուրցն յայլ ԺԵ աւուրսն. սկացին լինել նշանք. յիւրաքանչ / fol. 243r / իւր աւուր նշան մի։

I/ Նշան առաջին աւուրն. այսպէս եղիցի ծովք ի տեղիս իւրեանց բարձրասցին. ԵԺ-ան կանկուն քան զամենայն բարձր լերինս եւ ոչ ելցէ ի տեղոչէ[14] իւրեանց այլ որպէս պարիսպ կանկնեցին շուրքն։

II/ Նշանք երկրորդ աւուրն. ամենայն ծովք խոնարհեցին եւ իջցեն ի խոր այնպէս զի հազիւ կարասցին տեսանել։

III/ Նշան երրորդ աւուրն. ամենայն ինչ յառաջին կերպսն դարձին որպէս ի նախնումա ստեղծաւ։

IV/ Նշան չորրորդ աւուրն. ամենայն կենդանիք եւ որ զեռան ի շուրս ծովուն ժողովին ի վերայ երեսաց ծովուն եւ զօրէն ծնընդականի. ձայն բարձցեն գոչեսցեն եւ մռընչեսցեն գիտելով զվախճանս իւրեանց։

V/ Նշան հինգերորդ աւուրն ամենայն թոչունք երկնից ժողովեցին ի մի վայր եւ լացեն եւ ոչ կերիցեն եւ ոչ արբցեն. գիտելով զի հասեալ է վախճան իւրեանց։

VI/ Նշան վեցերորդ աւուրն. գետք հրեղէնք յարեւմնից յարիցեն ընդդէմ երեսաց հաստատութեան մինչեւ յարեւելս ընթանալով։

VII/ Նշան եօթներորդ աւուրն. ամենայն մոլորականք եւ անմոլար աստեղք սփռեցեն {լինք}[15] լինքեանց հրեղէն վրանս։

VIII/ Նշան ութերորդ աւուրն. շարժեցից երկիր մեծապէս. այնպէս զի ոչ ոք ի մարդկանէ կարիցէ կեալ եւ ոչ կենդանի ինչ. / fol. 243v / այլ անկցին ամենեքեան ի գետին։

---

13. Armenian ներն *nern*.
14. Note phonetic confusion չ/ջ; see Stone and Hillel, "Index," no. 424.
15. Corrupt dittography.

IX/ Նշան իններորդ աւուրն. ամենայն քարինք մեծամեծք եւ փոքունք պատառեսցին ի չորս մասունս. եւ իւրաքանչիւր մասն բախեցի ի միւս մասն:

X/ Նշան տասներորդ աւուրն. ամենայն ծառք անտառի եւ բանջար խոտոյ գող արեան հեղցեն:

XI/ Նշան մետասան‹երորդ›¹⁶ աւուրն. ամենայն {կենդանիք երկրի}.¹⁷ լերինք եւ ամենայն մարդկային շինածք փլցին եւ փոշի դարձին:

XII/ Նշան երկոտասան‹երորդ› աւուրն. ամենայն կենդանիք երկրի ժողովեցին ի դաշտս մռնչեցեն եւ ոչ կերից[են] եւ ոչ արբցեն:

XIII/ Նշան երեքտասան‹երորդ› աւուրն. ամենայն գերեզմանք յարեւելից մինչեւ ի մուտս արեւու բացցին եւ դիակունք կանկնեցին յափն գերեզմանացն:

XIV/ Նշան չորեքտասան‹երորդ› աւուրն. ամենայն մարդկային ազգ որ կենդանիք իցեն ի տեղեաց եւ ի բնակութեանց իւրեանց. ելեալք շրջեսցին ընթանալով որպէս յիմարք:

XV/ Նշան հնգետասան‹երորդ› աւուրն. ամենայն մարդիկք մեռցին զի ընդ առաջին մեռելա ելցեն: Յայնժամ եկեսցէ Քրիստոս եւ ամենայն հրեշտակք ընդ նմա եւ տեսցեն զնայ ուրացողքն եւ հրեայքն եւ ասասցեն այս է Քրիստոսն, զոր մեք խաչեցաք յԵրուսաղէմ. այժմ ճշմարտապէս ճանաչեմք զսայ եւ տեսանեմք զնշան բերռացն. եւ կոծեցեն զանձինս իւրեանց մեծապէս ի վերայ նորա:

Translation

A/ Concerning the 15 signs that are going to take place after the destruction of the Antichrist before the coming of Christ.

B/ After the destruction of the Antichrist there will remain 40 days until the end of the world and the coming of Christ.¹⁸ After 25 days, on 15 other days signs will commence, one sign on each day.

I/ The sign of the first day will be thus: the seas in their places will rise

---

16. The editor has added ordinal endings in accordance with the preceding numerals.
17. Dittography from Sign XII marked with erasure points.
18. The number forty is typological, to be compared with the forty days of the flood (Gen 7:4), Moses' forty days on Sinai (Exod 24:18); and Christ's forty days in the desert (Matt 4:2 and parallels). Lent lasts forty days and in Armenian ecclesiastical custom this is the length of the time of mourning, and also of a priest's self-isolation after consecration.

8   BIBLICAL AND ASSOCIATED TRADITIONS

> up 15 cubits (higher) than the highest mountains and will not go forth from their place, but the waters will stand like a wall.[19]

II/ The signs of the second day: all the seas will become low and they will descend to the depths so that they will be barely able to see them.[20]

III/ The sign of the third day: everything will return to its first[21] form, as it was created formerly.

IV/ The sign of the fourth day: all animals[22] and those things which swarm in the sea's waters assemble upon the face[23] of the sea, and like (a woman) in childbirth, they will raise up their voices, they will call out and bellow, having apprehended their end.[24]

V/ The sign of the fifth day: all the birds of the heavens shall gather in one place and weep and neither eat nor drink, knowing that their end has come.[25]

VI/ The sign of the sixth day: fiery rivers will rise up from the west running over against the face of the firmament, as far as the east.[26]

VII/ The sign of the seventh day: all the planets and the fixed stars will be scattered through their fiery tent.[27]

VIII/ The sign of the eighth day: the earth will shake mightily, so that no

---

19. Two themes are evoked here. Despite the differences in measurements, this is clearly an eschatological repetition of Noah's flood, Gen 7:19-20. The description of the waters standing like a wall is from the Crossing of the Red Sea, Exod 14:22, 29.

20. This is a reversal of Sign I. In addition, the drying up of the waters is a sign of theophany, see Josh 2:10, 4:23; Isa 50:2, 51:10; Ps 66 (65):6, etc. Similar is a sign of the eschaton in 4 Ezra 6:24.

21. I.e., former.

22. Or: living things.

23. I.e., surface.

24. This is the sign of Day III in the other recensions and in the Latin versions plotted in Stone 1981, 9-10. The signs speak of the created beings perishing step by step, in roughly the order in which they were created according to Gen 1.

25. They act in a fashion exactly parallel to the marine creatures in Day IV. The birds do not feature in Recensions I and II.

26. This sign does not occur in Recensions I and II. Fire as a portent appears in 4 Ezra 5:8, but that verse is not comparable with the statement about fire here; Recensions I and II have fire burning sea and earth as Sign VII. This fire might be compared with Joel 2:30, "And I will give portents in the heavens and on the earth, blood and fire and columns of smoke."

27. Prof. David Runia gracious communicated the following (9 March 2015): "I think that the reference is a combination of Greek and biblical thought. Plato uses the image of the tent for the heavens in the Timaeus, but it seems predominantly biblical to me. That the heavens consist of fiery objects and can itself be called fiery is common in Greek philosophy. See, for example, the Placita of Aëtius 2.11." A striking instance of the heavens as a tent or curtain is Isa 40:22.

human will be able to stand nor any living creature, but all will fall onto the ground.[28]

IX/ The sign of the ninth day: all very great and small stones will be split into four parts and each part strike against the other.[29]

X/ The sign of the tenth day: all forest trees and green grasses shall drip bloody dew.[30]

XI/ The sign of the 11<th> day: all the {living beings of the earth},[31] mountains and all human buildings will crumble and turn into dust.[32]

XII/ The sign of the 12<th> day: all the animals[33] of the earth shall assemble in the field. They shall bellow and neither eat nor drink.[34]

XIII/ The sign of the 13<th> day: all the graves from the east to the west[35] will be opened and the corpses will be stood up at the edge of the graves.[36]

XIV/ The sign of the 14<th> day: all the human race who will be alive in (their) places and in their dwellings, having gone forth shall go around running like madmen.[37]

XV/ The sign of the 15<th> day: all men shall die so they may go forth to greet the dead. Then Christ shall come and all angels with him and the deniers and the Jews[38] and they shall say, "This is the Christ whom we crucified in Jerusalem. Now we truly know him and see the sign of the nails." And they shall smite themselves greatly because of that.

---

28. Compare 2 Sam 22:8 = Ps 18(17):8, Ps 68:8 (67:9), Ezek 38: 20, Joel 2:10 all relating to theophanies, some like Joel 2:10 in anger. See also 4 Ezra 6:14, 2 Apoc Bar 70:8, Matt 24:7.

29. See Sign VI of Recensions I and II. See Nah 1:6, Matt 27:51, and T. Levi 4:1. Compare Stone 2007, 1:24.83 and 86 (p. 250). Many of the signs in these lists appear in one or another context in Adamgirkʻ.

30. 4 Ezra 5:5.

31. The phrase, "living beings of the earth" seems strange here, and is a dittography from Day XII below.

32. The destruction of human buildings is the sign of Day V in Recensions I and II. Compare 4 Ezra 10:53–54.

33. Or: living things.

34. կերից is corrupt for կերիցեն. According to the sign of Day V, the birds neither eat nor drink. Here it is the living beings or animals who act in the same way.

35. Literally "rising of the sun" and "setting of the sun."

36. Sign XIII is Sign XI in the other two recensions. The last phrase "and the corpses ... graves" simply talks of the corpses falling out of their graves. As a specific sign, see Matt 27:52 and compare, Adamgirkʻ, 1.24.87 (p. 250).

37. This sign is a shorter form of Sign X in the other two recensions. No parallels to the running around are known.

38. This sign is not found in Recensions I and II. It is, however, the sign of Day XIV in Latin Recension C, the Historia Scholastica of Petrus Comestor. This is another indication that Armenian Recension III is independent of Recensions I and II.

1.4. The Twelve Gifts Lost by Adam

In 1959, H. S. Anasyan noted the existence of this text in a *Miscellany* M9100 (1686) (Anasyan 1959, 1:246, no. 4) and Narineh Yacoubian first published it in 2003 (Yacoubian 2003, 45–52). Here we reproduce her edition and translation of M9121 *Miscellany* (1732–1733), fols. 102r–102v and add the witness of M2182 Sermons of Gregory of Tatʻew (1674), fol. 350r–350v (Tēr-Vardanean 2012, 7:339–44). The character of this witnesses is discussed in the notes below. The text in M9121 is an example of the numerous lists of biblical events, persons, and objects that circulated in Armenian. A strong tradition of lists of such biblically related objects existed and such texts are very abundant in the Armenian tradition.[39] After it, we publish another text with a similar title, but different content, taken from M10720 *Miscellany* (eighteenth century), fols. 4v–5r (Malkhasyan 2007, 3:175–77). Not all the gifts are explicit in the text of Genesis, and certain of them are dependent on exegetical and legendary traditions, with which that story was embroidered.[40]

1.4.1. M9121, fols. 102r–102v

Text

1/ Յաղագս Ադամայ ժԲան պարգեւք զոր ունէր մարդն առաջին
եւ կորոյս․
Նախ՝ առողջութիւն առանց հիւանդութեան։
Երկրորդ՝ մանկութիւն առանց ծերութեան։
Երրորդ՝ յագեցումն առանց տաղտկութեան։
5/ Չորրորդ՝ ազատութիւն առանց ծառայութեան։
Հինգերորդ՝ գեղեցկութիւն առանց տգեղութեան։
Վեցերորդ՝ անշարշարութիւն ենթակայ անմահութեան։
Եօթներորդ՝ առատութիւն առանց կարօտութեան։
Ութերորդ՝ խաղաղութիւն առանց խռովութեան։
10/ Իններորդ՝ անհոգութիւն թարց երկիւղի։
Տասներորդ՝ ճանաչումն թարց տգիտութեան։
Մետասաներորդ՝ փառք առանց անարգութեան։
Երկոտասաներորդ՝ ուրախութիւն առանց տրտմութեան։

---

39. See Stone 1996b, 611–46 cited from the reprint in Stone 2006a, 2:105–37, esp. 131–34.
40. On Armenian embroideries of the Adam traditions, see Stone 2013.

Translation

1/ Concerning Adam. The 12 Gifts which the First Man had and lost.
First, health without sickness.
Second, childhood without (old) age.
Third, satiety without tediousness.
5/ Fourth, freedom without slavery.
Fifth, beauty without ugliness.
Sixth, impassibility subject to immortality.
Seventh, abundance without lack.
Eighth, peace without turbulence.
10/ Ninth, freedom from care without fear.
Tenth, knowledge without ignorance.
Eleventh, glory without dishonor.
Twelfth, happiness without grief.[41]

1.4.2. A Different Text with a Similar Title

This text, preserved in M10720, fols. 4r–4v (eighteenth century), is preserved in Grigor Tatʻewacʻi's *Book of Questions*. Since Grigor Tatʻewacʻi lived in the fifteenth century (1344?–1409), his work precedes the late manuscript M10720, which dates from the eighteenth century. The manuscript is a rich *Miscellany* containing many documents related to biblical history (see Malkhasyan 2007, 3:176–77). Grigor's *Book of Questions* was written at a time of polemics between the Armenian Apostolic Church and the Roman Catholic Church. It is a theological compendium, parts of which were often copied into manuscripts without attribution, as they were relevant to particular concerns. In the present volume, such copied texts are the document presented here and 3.2. Names of the Angels; 3.5. The Praise of the Angels, and 4.9.1. Concerning the Ten Plagues of Egypt.

I have filled in lacunae from the printed edition of *The Book of Questions* and enclosed them within pointed brackets, that is, < > (Tatʻewacʻi 1993, 278–79). Variants are noted below the Armenian text.

Text

1/ Երկոտասան պարգեւք էին ի դրախտին զոր կորոյս Ադամ։

---

41. Compare Gen 3:16–17.

Նախ. տեսութիւն Աստուծոյ:
Երկրորդ. խոսակցութիւն:
Երրորդ. անմահութիւն:
5/ Չորրորդ. լուսեղէն պատմուճան:
Հինգերորդ. ան<աղտ> կեանք.
Վեցերորդ. անձերանելի հասակ:
Եօթներորդ. վայելչ<ութիւն անաշխատ>. փափկութեան
դրախտին:
Ութերորդ. մշակութիւն Աստուծոյ. <այսինքն> անմահ տնկոյն
<երկրագործ եւ պահապան>:
10/ Իններորդ. սէր եւ զուր Աստուծոյ ի վերայ մարդոյն
հնազանդութեամբ պատուիրանին զի զայր առ նա:
Տասներորդ. թագաւորութիւն ի վերայ ամենայն ձեռակերտաց:
Մետասաներորդ. քահանայութիւն:
Երկոտասաներորդ. մարգարէութիւն:
Ջայս ԲԺ պարգեւ եհան ի մէնջ Եւայ:
15/ Նախ ի տեսութիւն Աստուծոյ. զի նչ եւս յաւել տեսանել զերեսն
Աստուծոյ.
Ի խոսակցութենէն. զի մինչ ի Յորդանան այլ / fol. 4v / նչ ասի
խոսիլ հօր Աստուծոյ ընդ մարդկան:
Ի յանմահութենէն. զի վճիո եհատ հող էիր եւ ի հող դարձցիս:
Ի լուսաւոր պատմուճանէն. յորժամ կերան ի պտղոյն եւ
ծանեան. զի մերկ էին եւ արարին իւրեանց գաւածանելին.
Ի յանախտ կենացն. տրտմութեամբ եւ քրտամբք երեսացն
կերիցեն զհացն.
20/ Ի յանձերանելի հասակէն. փուշ եւ տատասկ բուսցի քեզ.
Իսկ ի պահպանութենէն. յորմէ պատուիրեցի քեզ չուտել.
կերար արդեօք ի նմանէ.
Ի վայելչութենէն. Ասէ եհան զնա եւ բնակեցոյց ընդդէմ
դրախտին փափկութեան:
Իսկ ատելութիւն ցոյցք. զուցէ ձգիցէ զձեռն եւ առնիցէ.
Իսկ թագաւորութենէն. մարդ ի պատուի էր եւ նչ իմացաւ:
25/ Ի քահանայութենէն. զի նչ իշխեաց պատարագս մատուցանել
ի կեանս իւր.
Իսկ ի մարգարէութենէն. լրեաց զի նչ եւս երեւի բան մի
յիշատակ շնորհաց նորայ:

Variants

In these variants, the lemma is the text of M10720 and variant is the printed edition.

2 տեսութիւնն 3 խօսակցութիւնն 7 անծերանելի] անծերանալի 8 վայելչո‹ւթիւն անաշխատ›[42] 9 Աստուծոյ] աստուծոյ այսինքն | տնկոյն] տնկոցն երկրագործ եւ պահապան 14 եհան | եւա 15 տեսութիւն] տեսութենէն | զերեսն] զերեսս 16 հօր Աստուծոյ խոսիլ 17 ի1°] իսկ | եհատ] եհատ ասելով 18 կերան] կերին | իւրեանց] om] զսփածանելին] սփածանելիս 19 քրտամբ 20 բուսցի քեզ] բուսցին ի քեզ 21 քեզ] om | կերար] կերեր 22 ի] իսկ ի | եհան] գնա] գնասա 23 գոյց | իւր] + եւ առնիցէ 24 իմացաւ] + հաւացարեաց անասնոց անբանից 26 նորա

Translation

1/ There were 12 gifts in the Garden, which Adam destroyed.[43]
First, the vision of God.
Second, conversation (i.e., with God).
Third, immortality.
5/ Fourth, a luminous garment.
Fifth, un‹blemished› life.
Sixth, unageing status.
Seventh, enjoy‹ment without toil› of the Garden of Delights.
Eighth, cultivation of God, ‹that is the agriculture and guarding› of the immortal tree.
10/ Ninth, love and pity of God upon mankind through the obedience of the commandment that was coming to him.
Tenth, kingdom over all the things made by hand.[44]
Eleventh, priesthood.
Twelfth, prophecy.
These 12 gifts Eve took away from us.

---

42. This reading in pointed brackets is drawn from the printed edition.
43. Or: lost.
44. Apparently by the hand of God, i.e., creatures. This is somewhat unusual, for often Adam is referred to the one created by God's hand (see Gen 1:27, 2:7 His hand is not explicit here), while the stress is on the rest of creation being by speech. See Stone 2013, 12, citing Agathangelos, Life and History of St. Gregory §§2, 17. Later sources are cited in Stone 2013, 40, 86, 130, and 155. Similar views are found in Jewish sources.

15/ First, in the vision of God, for he no longer saw the face of God.
From the conversation—for up to the Jordan, God the Father is not said to speak with man.[45]
From immortality—for he passed the sentence: you were dust and you will return to dust.[46]
From the luminous garment—when they ate of the fruit and realized that they were naked, they made the loincloths for themselves.[47]
From the life without blemish—through sadness, and sweat of the brow you shall eat bread.[48]
20/ From the unageing status—it will bring forth thorns and thistles for you.[49]
Then from the observance of that which I commanded you not to eat,[50] —you indeed ate of it.
From the enjoyment—it says, "he sent him forth and made him dwell over against the Garden of Delight."[51]
Then the demonstrations (of) hatred—perhaps he will stretch forth (his) hand and do (it).[52]
From the kingdom—man was in honor and he did not discern (it).
25/ From the priesthood—for he could not offer sacrifices during his life.
Then he was silent from the prophecy—for no further thing does appear as a memory of his grace.[53]

1.4.3. M2182, fols. 350r–350v

In M2182, fols. 350r–350v an incomplete form of the preceding text occurs, based on the same section of Grigor Tatʻewacʻi's *Book of Questions*. We have treated it in the same way as that text. Instead of the fully written ordinal

---

45. I.e., up to the Baptism, see Matt 3:17, Mark 1:11, Luke 3:22.
46. Gen 3:19.
47. Gen 3:7.
48. Gen 3:19.
49. Gen 3:18.
50. Gen 2:17.
51. Gen 3:23–24.
52. Gen 3:22.
53. Kingdom, priesthood, and prophecy were three qualities which Adam was said to have in Eden. These qualities are attributed to Adam singly and as a group by various Armenian authors. They are presented as a group by Grigor Tatʻewacʻi, Mxitʻar Ayrivanecʻi, and Yovhannēs Erznkacʻi Corcorecʻi: See Stone 2013, 135 and sources referred to there. Of course, they are also attributed to Christ as the New Adam.

numerals, from item 2 to item 9 the text uses Armenian cardinal numerals. Moreover, the preserved text stops at the end of the ninth gift, so it is incomplete. M2182 is a copy of works by Grigor, including excerpts from *Book of Questions* (see Tēr-Vardanean 2012, 7:339–44).

Text

1/ Քանի պարգեւք էին ի դրախտի եւ գիտելի է զի ԲԺ-ան պարգեւք էին ի դրախտին:
Նախ՝ տեսութիւն Աստուծոյ.
Բ. խօսակցութիւն.
Գ. անմահութիւնն.
5/ Դ. լուսեղէն պատմուճան.
Ե. անախտ կեանքն.
Զ. անծերանալի հասակն.
Է. վայելչութիւն անաշխատ փափկութիւն դրախտին.
Ը. մշակութիւն Աստուծոյ ի վերայ անմահ տնկօցն երկրագործ.
/ fol. 350v /
10/ Թ սէր եւ փոյթ եւ պահպանութիւնն Աստուծոյ ի վերայ մարդոյն հնազանդութիւն պատճանին զի զայր առ նա:

Variants

In these variants, the lemma is the text of M2182 and variant is the printed edition.

1 The title line is quite different 2 տեսութիւնն 3 խօսակցութիւնն 6 կեանք 8 փափկութեան 9 ի վերայ] այսինքն 10 եւ պահարան 11 փոյթ] գոյթ | հնազանդութեամբ | պատճանին] պատուի բանին | որ] զի

Translation

1/ How many gifts were there in the Garden? And it is to be known that there were 12 gifts in the Garden.
First, vision of God
2. Conversation (i.e., with God).
3. The immortality.
5/ 4. A luminous garment.
5. Life without blemish.
6. An unageing status.

7. Enjoyment of the Garden's delight without labor.
8. Cultivation of God—upon the immortal plants, agriculture.
10/ God's love and care and protection of man, obedience to ...[54] for it/he was coming to him.

1.5. What Are the Dimensions of the Ark?

This brief text occurs on fol. 82v of M8591, a *Miscellany* of the fifteenth century (see Eganyan et al. 1970, 2:766). It is a restatement of Exod 25:10. This document is preceded on fols. 82r–82v by a text on the Tower of Babel. A section resembling the present document is also embedded in a longer document in Galata manuscript 154, p. 303 apparently of the seventeenth century (Kiwleserian 1961, 975-90). That manuscript is now housed in the Patriarchal Collection in Istanbul and we publish it by permission of H. B. Patriarch Mesrop II Mutafyan. The passage parallel to M8591 was published in §12 of our edition of Genealogy of Abraham (Stone 2012, 78–85, see §12). Here, for convenience we add a copy of our edition and translation of the Galata manuscript following the text of M8591. It will be observed that the dimensions are followed in Galata 154, p. 303r–303v by details about the Tent of Witness, which do not occur in M8591 in which this text is followed by the Story of Father Abraham that we published elsewhere (Stone 2012, 36–50).

Text

Բ կանկուն եւ կէս երկայն. կանկուն եւ կէս լայն. կանկուն եւ կէս բարձր. եւ եդին ի ներս. զտախտակ պատգամացն Աստուծոյ. եւ սափորն ոսկի, լի մանանիւ. եւ գաւազան Ահարոնի, կանանչ տերեւով եւ Գ ընկուզով. եւ բուրվառն որ ի ձեռն Ահարոնի դարձաւ ոսկի. եւ զարկղն կտակարանացն:

Translation

Two cubits and a half long, a cubit and a half wide, a cubit and a half high.[55] And they placed in it: the Tablet of God's commandments,[56] and the golden[57]

---

54. Unknown word.
55. Exod 25:10. These biblical references are not repeated in the notes in Galata 154 below.
56. Exod 25:21. The Bible says "testimony" (Arm վկայութիւնն), not "Tablets etc."
57. That the urn was golden is a detail added in the list of these objects as found in Heb 9:4,

urn full of manna,[58] and Aaron's staff, green and leafy, and three nuts,[59] and the censer that turned into gold in Aaron's hand,[60] and the ark of the testaments.[61]

Galata 154 Text

12. Թէ ո՞ր չափ էր տապանակ ուխտին: Երկայն. Բ կանգուն եւ կէս: Լայնն կանգուն եւ կէս: Բարձր կանգուն եւ կէս:
Եւ կայր ի մէջն տապանակ օրինացն. սափորն ոսկի լի մանանայիւ. ցաւազանն Ահարոնի որ ծաղկեցաւ. բուրվառն պղնձի որ եղեւ ոսկի ի ձեռն Ահարոնի:
Խորանն վկայութեան յետ ելիցն. Ե ամսոյ սկսան. եւ Է ամիսն կատարեցաւ. խորհուրդ է աւուր արարչութեանն. եւ կանգնեցաւ սկիզբն երկրորդ ամին:

Translation

12. Of what measure was the Ark of the Covenant? Two and a half cubits long, a cubit and a half wide and a cubit and a half high.
And there was inside: the tablet of the Law, a golden urn full of manna, Aaron's staff which flowered, the bronze censer which became golden in Aaron's hand. The Tent of Witness after the exodus: they began in the fifth month and the plan was completed on the seventh month, it is an allegory of the seven days of creation, and it was set up at the beginning of the second year.[62]

---

which text says, "the ark of the covenant covered on all sides with gold, which contained a golden urn holding the manna, and Aaron's rod that budded, and the tables of the covenant."
    58. Exod 16:32–34.
    59. See Num 17:8 and compare this statement with Heb 9:4, cited above. The number of nuts is not specified in Num 17:8.
    60. The incident with the censer referred to here is not biblical.
    61. Or: "covenants." This is not in the Galata manuscript and is superfluous, since the tablet of the Law was already mentioned at the beginning of this paragraph. It is introduced, however, in accordance with Heb 9:4, which has been utilized in the latter part of this sentence.
    62. See Exod 40:2. The origin of the preceding dates is unclear. In Lev 8:35 the process of anointing the sons of Aaron is said to continue for seven days. In the next verse, the offering of sacrifices and the divine descent on the Tabernacle are related, cf. the dedication in Lev 9:34.

1.6. The Seven Punishments of Cain

This short text occurs in a *Miscellany*, M268 (1697) on fol. 151r.[63] It is based on the biblical verse in Gen 4:15. It is a list of Cain's seven punishments, one of a number of differing such lists, and it may derive from an ambiguity in the Septuagint of Gen 4:15. W. Lowndes Lipscomb treated this theme at some length.[64] The number seven comes from an interpretation of Gen 4:24. The idea of Cain's seven punishments is widely attested in Jewish, Christian, and Gnostic sources (see Lipscomb 1990, 86–92). The content and order of the list given here are the same as in Abel and Cain §§38–45. The fifth punishment is unclear. In *The Book of Questions* by Grigor Tatʻewacʻi there is a different list of Cain's seven punishments, and he prefixes a list of Cain's seven sins to it (Tatʻewacʻi 1993, 287).

Text

1/ Այս է Կայինի է պատիժն:
Առաջին՝ կոտոշն:
Երկրորդ. կոտոշին ձայնելն:
Երրորդ. թողումս մարմնոյն:
Չորրորդ. անյագ ուտելն:
5/ Հինգերորդ. ըստ վայր փոխելն:
Վեցերորդ. անքուն լինելն:
Եւթներորդն. անմահ լինելն:

Translation

1/ These are the seven punishments of Cain.
First, the horn.[65]
Second, the crying out of the horn.[66]

---

63. Eganyan, Zeytʻunyan, and Antʻabyan 1984, 1:1131–34.
64. Lipscomb 1990, 86–92. He discusses Gen 4:15 particularly on pp. 86–87. The idea of seven punishments of Cain is widespread in both Jewish and Christian sources.
65. Cain received a horn according to Midrash Tanḥuma on Genesis. This is a comment on the ambiguity of the sign God gave him according to Gen 4:15. It is also an important motif in the legend about the Cainite Lamech killing Cain, see *Tanḥuma Berešit* 10–11. The legend is discussed below; see the introductory remarks to 3.8.
66. Cain's horn appears also in Gen. Rab. and it is connected with "If they will not believe you or heed\hear the first sign..." (Exod 4:8). Thus it is possible that the crying out of the horn is inspired by the notion that a sign should be heard.

Third, shaking of the body.
Fourth, insatiable eating.[67]
5/ Fifth, moving from place to place.[68]
Sixth, being sleepless.
Seventh, being undying.

1.7. HE COUNTS THE MULTITUDE OF THE STARS

M6617 (1618) (Eganyan et al. 1970, 2:357–58) is a *Miscellany* containing a number of interesting texts relating to biblical and allied traditions. Such are *From the Wisdom of Solomon, Miracles (Wonders) of Solomon's Temple, Concerning the Weights*—perhaps Epiphanius's work (Stone and Ervine 2000), *Concerning the Chariot of the Divinity* (cf. Ezek 1),[69] and *Concerning the Bones of Adam and Eve*.[70] The text published here is found on fol. 254v–255r. The running head in the manuscript attributes this writing and some others to Marutha. *The Bones of Adam and Eve* from the same manuscript is also attributed to Marutha, and I remarked in the introduction to that work: "It seems most likely that this was not Marutha of Maipherkat, a Syrian bishop who died before 420, some of whose writing was translated into Armenian (see Thomson 1995, 69). A better candidate is the writer of this name mentioned by H. Ačaṙean (1972, 3:270). He was the author of Բանք ի վերայ զանազան Նիւթոց հին եւ նոր Կտակարանաց, այլ եւ ի վերայ ժողովոց եւ հերձուածողոց նմանց եւ յայտնութեան Մահմետի եւ բաժանման Վրաց եւ Հայոց "Discourses concerning various subjects of the Old and New Testaments, and also concerning Councils and certain heretics and the appearance of Mohammed and the division between the Georgians and Armenians" (Stone 2000, 242, repr. Stone 2006a, 1:142).

Text

1/ Թուէ զբազմութիւն աստեղաց

---

67. This is probably a commentary on Gen 4:12a: "When you till the ground, it shall no longer yield to you its strength."
68. See Gen 4:12 and compare with Abel and Cain §43. The list in Repentance of Adam and Eve §§50–58 is different, though it shares some punishments with that published here. However, even when they share punishments, the two lists are in a quite different order.
69. See Stone and van Lint 2000, 144–58. This might be the same work.
70. Stone 2000, 241–45, repr. Stone 2006a, 1:141–45.

/ fol. 254v / բանգի զհտէ զհւրաքանչիւր[71] hոգի թէ իւրոյ մարմոյ են. եւ կոչէ զհւրաքանչիւր ոք եւ նոքայ լսեն արարչին եւ ոգին ընթանա առ մարմին. իբրեւ զառն՝ ի մայր իւր.

2/ Եզեկիէլ ասէ եթէ ի տեղիս ուրեմն հաստատութեանդ դեգերեալ մման մարմոյն ոգիքն. զի իբրեւ զաւանդ եւտուն երկրի զմարմինան եւ առնելոց են ի յարութեանն:

3/ Ասէ սուրբն Յոհան Ուկէբերան. թոչուն արագաթեւ է ողորմութիւնն. եւ հանապազ / fol. 255r / առաջի արքունական աթոռոյն կայ. եւ յորժամ տանջիմք յանկարծակի սլանայ եւ թափեալ պահէ ի տանջանացն եւ ամփոփեալ պահէ ընդ ամրածածուկ ընդ թեւաւքն իւրովք:

4/ Նոյնպէս եւ սուրբն Սահակ ի տեսլեանն տեսանէր. ծառ մի ճիթենի վարսատուր պտղալից յոյժ[72] զոր եւ հրեշտակն մեկնէր նմայ ասելով թէ երեւումն քեզ սքանչելի ճիթենոյն: Ջտուրս եւ զողորմութիւնն եւ զվէր մարդկան առ միմեանս եցոյց քեզ բարձրեալն:

5/ Չի մաւտ եւ առաջին եւ պատուական աստուածութեանն: աղքատ սիրութիւնն է. յամենայն բարեզործութիւնս: Որով առաջին սուրբքն ընդիրք երեւեցան: Աբրահամ. Յոբ. Կոռնելիոս եւ նմանք ոցա:

6/ Առանց որոյ եւ կուսանացն արհամարհեալ զվաստակ կուսութեանն. արտաքոյ հարսանեացն դիպեցան: Սովաւ ճանաչի յանձինս մարդկան. կնիք արդարութեանն Աստուծոյ.

7/ Որ ասաց յայսմ ծանիցեն ամենեքեան թէ իմ աշակերտք էք. եթէ սիրիցէք զմիմեանս.

8/ Զոր եւ սուրբն Բարսեղ ասէ թէ Ճշմարտագոյն շնորհք. եւ մեծագոյն ի կաթողիկէ եկեղեցի[73] չիք այնքան որպէս զաղքատացն դարմանատրութիւնն:

9/ Չիք այնպիսի որ ուրախ առնէ զԱստուած. Որպէս զողորմութիւնն քանգի թագաւորն եւ քահանայքն եւ մարգարէքն նովաւ աւծանէին:

10/ ընդէ՞ր զի Աստուծոյ մարդասիրութիւնն. նշանակ առնուին յանձինս զաւծութիւնն եւ ցուցանէին եթէ հոգին սուրբ ի մարդիկ ողորմութեամբ է զալոց.

11/ եւ քանզի Աստուած ողորմի մարդկան եւ մարդասիրութիւնն ցուցանէ. Վասն այնորիկ ի նովաւ ծանին. քանգի եղոյ անուն եւ

---
71. ւl° above line.
72. յl° above line.
73. եկ above line.

ողորմութիւնն մի է ըստ յունարէն լէզուոյ եւ քանզի աշխարհս
ողորմութեամբ Աստուծոյ հաստատեալ կայ եւ պահի:

Translation

1/ He counts the multitude of stars.⁷⁴ Because he knows that each soul belongs to its body, and he summons each of them and they hearken to the Creator and the soul runs to the body like a lamb to its mother.

2/ Ezekiel says that in a certain places of the/this firmament the souls of the body stay wandering.⁷⁵ For they gave their bodies to the earth like a deposit and they will receive (it back) in the resurrection.⁷⁶

3/ Saint John Chrysostom says: mercy is a swift-winged bird, and it stands always before the royal throne. And when we are punished, suddenly it soars, and being poured out it protects (us) from the punishment and having gathered us in, it preserves (us) under its powerfully concealing wings.⁷⁷

4/ In this same fashion St. Sahak also saw in the vision:⁷⁸ a leafy olive tree very full of fruit,⁷⁹ which indeed the angel explained to him saying, "The appearance to you of the wondrous olive tree⁸⁰ (means that) the Most High showed you grace⁸¹ and mercy and the love of men for one another."

5/ For the love of the poor is close⁸² and first and (most) honored of (by)

---

74. Citation of Ps 147(146):4. The stars are commonly identified with the righteous in Late Antique religious thought: compare Dan 8:10–12, 25; 1 En. 43:4, 46:7; T. Levi 18.3; LAB 33:5. The classic work on this is Cumont 1960; see also Stone 1990a, 244–45.

75. Compare Job 12:10.

76. This is perhaps related to Ezek 37. The soul as a deposit is to be found in 1 Tim 6:20; 2 Tim 1:12. Cf. Stone 1990a on 4 Ezra 4:42 (p. 99), which uses this banking metaphor. Here, however, it is the body that is viewed as a deposit in the earth. That is less widespread. The idea of the souls wandering in the air is found in several Armenian sources, in various contexts. See, e.g., Ques. Ezra B6.

77. For the image of hiding under wings, compare Ps 91(90):4. It is quite common. The personification of mercy is striking and can be compared with the Rabbinic idea of the hypostases of the divine mercy and justice.

78. On the Vision of St. Sahak see the articles by Gohar Muradyan 2014, 313–25, and concerning the Greek version Garitte 1958, 255–78. This vision is to be found in ch. 16 of Łazar Pʻarbecʻi's *History of the Armenians*.

79. Compare Ps 52:8(51:10).

80. Pʻarbecʻi, *History* 16:8, 17.

81. Or: gift.

82. I.e., nearby, at hand, easily accessible.

the Deity of all benefactions,[83] by which the former saints were shown to be elect: Abraham, Job, Cornelius,[84] and those like them.

6/ Without it, also the reward for virginity is despised even by the virgins; they are to be considered[85] outside of marriage. With it, the seal of God's righteousness is recognized in the souls of men.[86]

7/ It said: "By this all shall know that you are my disciples, if you love one another."[87]

8/ Saint Basil also says this: There is no truer and greater grace/merit in the catholic church than the nourishing of the poor."

9/ There is nothing which so makes God happy as mercy, because the kings and the priests and the prophets were anointed with it.

10/ Why? Because they were to receive into themselves the anointing as a token of God's philanthropy, and to demonstrate that the Holy Spirit is going to come with mercy to human beings.

11/ And because God has mercy on men and shows (his) philanthropy, for that reason they are known through it. Because the name of oil and mercy is one in the Greek language[88] and because this world is established and preserved through God's mercy.

1.8. Names of the Jewels of Aaron's Ephod

This text, found in M268, a *Miscellany* of the year 1697, fols. 150v–151r is a list of the twelve stones on the breastplate of Aaron, the high priest.[89] This manuscript also preserves a list of The Seven Punishments of Cain (see 1.6 above), which precedes the present text. Before that, there is The Ten Plagues of Egypt, also published in the present volume (4.9 below).

The discussion about the gems on Aaron's breastplate originates from Exod 28:17–20. It was developed in the Greek patristic tradition, notably by

---

83. Compare Prov 14:20–21.
84. Acts 10.
85. ղհոլհմ means "to happen, suit."
86. My thanks are extended to Prof. Abraham Terian, who made important suggestions about the translation of this section and of §10.
87. John 13:35.
88. The reference is to the similar, but unrelated, Greek words, ἔλαιον "olive oil" and ἔλεος "pity, mercy." The same word play stands behind the expression *oleum ligni misericordiae* in LAE 41:2, 42:3. It is also reflected in the wording of the other versions of that work in the same pericope.
89. Eganyan, Zeyt'unyan, and Ant'abyan 1984, 1:1131–34.

Epiphanius of Salamis in his treatise, *De gemmis*. The *De gemmis* survives in Armenian, both in long and in epitomized forms, which I have discussed elsewhere.[90] The present text is a mere list of the gems, with none of the typological correlations or gemmological details found in the *Epitomes* and in the fuller text of the *De gemmis*. The names of gems and their order are compared with M9100, *Miscellany* of 1686, fols. 372–373v and differences are recorded in the notes. I published the text of M9100, with a study, in 1989.[91] In general, however, though the two texts are intimately connected, M9100 is a much longer and more developed version.

The list of gems on the High Priest's ephod is found quite frequently in Armenian manuscripts in a shortened or a fuller form. Thus copies have been observed in M6483, *Miscellany* (1757); M6897, *Miscellany* (1317); M7020, *Miscellany* (1787); M7250, *Miscellany* (sixteenth century); M8075, *Miscellany* (1709); M9100, *Miscellany* (1686); M10430 (1662); a different work on precious stones occurs in a medical manuscript M10484, *Medical Texts* (1831); other copies in various text forms also exist.

Text

Այս է Ահարոնի Վակասին ԺԲ-ն ականց անունքն:
Կարգ առաջին.
    Սարդիոն. եւ տապզիոն. եւ զմրուխտ:
Կարգ. երկրորդ.
    կարկեհան. եւ շափիղայ. եւ յասպիս:
Եւ կարզն երրորդ.
    սուտակ. եւ դճաղմ.[92] / fol. 151 / եւ ատակ:
Եւ կարզն Չորրորդ.
    Ոսկեակն.[93] եւ եղունգն. եւ բիւրեղ:

Translation

These are the Names of the twelve Jewels of Aaron's Ephod.
The first row:

---

90. Blake (1934) edited many forms of this work. See also Stone 1989, 467–76. A much longer text belonging to this corpus survives in M266, fols. 91v–93v.
91. See note 90, above.
92. In M9100 դճաղմ.
93. In M9100 we read a quite different word: ակինդն "hyacinth."

Cornelian and topaz and emerald.[94]
(The) second row:
Ruby and sapphire and jasper.[95]
And the third row:
Amethyst and turquoise and agate.[96]
And the fourth row:
Chrysolite and onyx and beryl.[97]

---

94. In M9100 the emerald is first in this row; see Exod 28:17.
95. Compare Exod 28:18.
96. In M9100 turquoise is first in this row; compare Exod 28:19.
97. This word is corrupt in M9100. Here it is accurate; see Exod 28:20.

Part Two: Chronological Texts

Lists of the generations, summaries of the number of years of periods of past history, and other writings exhibiting concern with chronology are widespread in the Armenian manuscript tradition. We have remarked above on the partiality of the Armenian learned tradition for catalogues and lists and the chronological lists form part of this.[1] A selection of such lists is published here, and they seem to have taken the chronographic tradition, of which Eusebius of Caesarea's *Chronicle* (Aucher 1818) is an early representative, as a starting point. Such lists and summaries may be found, for example, in the fragments of the *Chronographiae* by Sextus Iulius Africanus (ca. 180–ca. 240 CE) and the *Chronography* by George Cedrenus (eleventh century)[2] and similar lists also occur in *History of the Armenians* by Movsēs Xorenacʻi (Thomson 2006, 71–73 and 100–101). Lists that are based on data in the Bible are not surprising. Although starting from the details given in the Bible, many Armenian lists have calculations that accord neither with the dates in the Septuagint nor with those in the Masoretic Hebrew text. Below, the lists' spans of time have been compared with those in these two biblical versions and notes added at the appropriate junctures.

A substantial part of the material in this second part of our book, which is edited from later manuscript copies, derives from works resembling and including extracts from the *Chronography* of Pʻilon (Philo) of Tirak, a seventh-century Armenian author.[3] This chronography was published by Fr. B. Sargisean under the title "Anonymous Chronicle" and attributed to the seventh century, while H. Bartikian attributed it to Anania Širakacʻi, also of the seventh century.[4] It is, in fact, the only seventh-century chronography surviving. There are six manuscripts of the work and the edition in MH is based

---

1. See the introductory remarks to text 1.4, above.
2. Walraff and Adler 2007, 27–31; Adler and Tuffin 2002, §§9–11, §§20–30, etc.
3. See Hakobyan 2009, 5:899–969. At least, this is the case as far as surviving texts are concerned. There might, of course, have been other sources as well.
4. Sargisian 1904. Hrach Bartikian published a recent introductory essay on its ascription in MH 5:899–900. A further introductory essay by Alexan Hagopian follows in the same work on pp. 900–902.

on M2679 (981 CE) while another prime, early witness, the extracts from the *Chronography* in M5245 (1280) sometimes preserves a better text. We consulted the work in the edition of Alexan Hakobyan in MH, see note 3 above. Naturally, the role of Philo of Tirak's *Chronography* as a source for medieval scholastic texts needs to be further investigated. Moreover, it is noteworthy that it is the only work of its genre that survived from the seventh century. Here, however, the above remarks must suffice.

The texts published here are select representatives of this robust tradition. Doubtless, many more documents exist than we have edited here. Our principle has been, in general, to select texts that concern individuals in the biblical tradition from Adam to Christ. For most of this period, the sequence and life spans of the leaders, patriarchs, and kings are based on the biblical text, which has been consulted in both the Septuagint and the Masoretic forms. The figures in some of the lists, as we have noted, have no parallels in biblical sources and quite often totals given as such do not agree with the sum of the years actually set out in detail.

Lists of Patriarchs, Kings, and Leaders

In 1981, I published a text titled The Generations from Adam from M8076, a seventeenth-century *Miscellany*, fols. 221r–222r (Stone 1981). This is a list of patriarchs, kings, and emperors from Byzantine times. It concludes its list of individuals with Heraclius and his two sons, Heraclius Constantinus and Constans (642–688), apparently the Kostandin of the text, of whose reign only two years were recorded. This would yield the date of 644 CE. In 1981, when I published this text, I was of the view that this indicated that the work was composed in the seventh century. Moreover, I observed that several names appear as transliterations from Greek, instead of in their Armenian forms, thus suggesting that the list might have been translated from Greek. However, it is possible that the reason that the list stops when it does is that it ceases with the Arab conquest of Armenia. The first Arab incursion was in 640 and in 654 a Moslem governor of the capital Dvin was appointed.[5]

P'ilon's *Chronicle* opens with the attribution of the following to "Movsēs Xorenac'i and Andreas" and then immediately gives chronological entries very similar to those in text 4.5 and which continue in §17–29 down to Noah. A somewhat different formula is found in its list of the descendants of Shem

---

5. Tēr-Ghewondyan 1976, 19–20, 179. If this view is correct, then this list might have been composed later. non liquet.

(§§40–47). It is clear that such chronological lists existed in Armenian from at least the seventh century.

The list of *Seventy-Two Languages or Nations*, is directly drawn from P'ilon Tirakac'i §§57–60. I published it from a late copy in 1996 and further copies exist (Stone 1996a, 158–63). Following it come lists of the descendants of the sons of Noah and lists of their countries. In 1981, I published an analogous text under the title *Peoples of the Sons of Noah* (Stone 1981, 222–23, 228–41). Lists of the literate nations are also found in P'ilon §§68 (Japhethites), §89 (Hamites), and §103 (Shemites). A later, reformulated list exists enumerating twelve literate nations and it is transmitted in quite numerous copies (Stone 1996a, 159, 163).

Chronological Summaries

Chronological summaries often come at the end of detailed lists of generations, such as that referred to above, or at breaks in texts that retell biblical stories. The format usually is usually something like the following:

From Adam to the flood   xxx years
From the flood to Abraham   xxx years, and so forth.

I published one such list from J1529 (1684) and compared it with W313 (1697), 201r–202r under the title *Chronological Summary down to Christ* (Stone 1996a, 81–82, 98–99). I published a second summary, which I entitled *Dates* from W422 (ca. 1661), p. 13 (Stone 1996a, 99–100), and yet another similar list included in *Biblical Paraphrases* (Stone 1982, 120). In those publications, I adduced similar summaries, occurring in the Latin *Acts of Pilate*[6] and the Greek *Hypomnesticon of Josephus*.[7] In addition to these, a similar list exists in the Suda, s.v. "Adam" (ed. Adler, 1:45) and the same sort of summary lists occur in many Armenian manuscripts. We observed such in M451, *Miscellany* (1692), 15v (Eganyan et al. 2004, 2:741–44); BL ms or 2621, *Homilies and Miscellany* (1600), 206v–208r (Conybeare 1913: 249–52). This genre was widespread and further examples are given below. Due to their character, it is difficult to limn the relationships between them.

However, older lists, such as the twelfth century one published by Eynatyan from M1999 (twelfth century; Eynatyan 2002, 80–81), must underlie the various later texts giving summaries of years between significant bibli-

---

6. Recension A, chap. 12; James 1924, 145.
7. Apud Fabricius 1722, 332. For these texts, see Stone 1982, 82–83.

cal events. Eynatyan's list is much shorter than the texts given here, but their totals are, on the whole, the same, though there are very often discrepancies between the numbers.

2.1. ADAPTATION OF GENESIS 5:6–28

In Stone 1996a, 82–83, I gave a translation of an extract from Vardan Arewelc'i's *Commentary on Genesis* (thirteenth century).[8] It was, in fact, drawn by A. Zeyt'unyan from three manuscripts of the *Ritual* (*Maštoc'*). I did not reproduce the Armenian text then, an omission that I rectify below. The text is adapted from Gen 5:6–28, which it follows closely in part, omitting some phrases and introducing some few sentences, mainly synchronisms.

Text

1/ Սէթ երկերիւր եւ հինգ ամաց ծնաւ զԵնովս։ Եւ եկեաց այլ եւս ամս եւթն հարիւր եւ եւթն եւ ամենայն ժամանակ նորա իննհարիւր եւ երկոտասան ամ։

2/ Ենովս լեալ ամաց հարիւր եւ իննսուն, ծնաւ զԿայնան։ Եւ եկեաց այլ եւս եւթն հարիւր հնգետասան մինչեւ ցիւսուն եւ երեք ամս Մաթուսաղայի։

3/ Կայնան ամաց հարիւր եւ եւթանասուն ծնանի զՄաղաղիէլ։ Եւ եկեաց այլ եւս ամս եւթն հարիւր եւ քառասուն մինչեւ ցկաթուցն ամս Ղամեքա։

4/ Մաղաղիէլ լեալ ամաց հարիւր եւ վաթսուն եւ հինգ, ծնանի զՅարեդ։ Եւ եկաց այլ եւս ամս եւթն հարիւր եւ երեսուն մինչեւ ցկաթուցն եւ մի ամս Ղամեքայ։

5/ Յարեդ լեալ ամաց հարիւր վաթսուն եւ երկու, ծնանի զԵնոք։ Եւ եկեաց այլ եւս ամս ութ հարիւր մինչեւ ցերկերիւր վաթսուն եւ մի ամս Նոյի։

6/ Ենոք լեալ ամաց հարիւր վաթսուն եւ հինգ ծնանի զՄաթուսաղա։ Եւ եկեաց այլ եւս ամս երկերիւր մինչեւ ցհինգ հարիւր եւ քսան եւ եւթն ամս Յարեդի։ Եւ հաճոյ եղեալ Աստուծոյ ոչ ուրեք գտանէր, քանզի փոխեաց զնա Աստուած։

7/ Մաթուսաղա լեալ ամաց հարոյր ութսուն եւ հինգ ծնաւ զՂամեք։ Եւ եկեաց այլ եւս ամք ութ հարոյր եւ երկու։

---

8. Zeyt'unyan (1985, 165–66) published this fragment.

8/ Ղամէք լեալ ամաց հարյր ութսուն եւ ութ, ծնանի զՆոյ: Կացեալ այլ եւս հինգ հարյր վաթսուն եւ հինգ մինչեւ չհինգ հարյր վաթսուն եւ հինգ ամ Նոյի, որում ասաց հայրն Ղամէք, կոչեցեալ զանուն նորա Նոյ:

Translation

1/ Seth at 205[9] years begot Enosh. And he lived a further 707 years, and all of his time was 912 years.[10]
2/ Enosh was 190 years old; he begot Kenan (Kaynan). And he lived a further 715 (years),[11] until the 53rd year of Methusaleh.
3/ Kenan (Kaynan) at 170 begot Mahalelel. And he lived a further 740 (years),[12] until the 60th year of Lamech.
4/ Mahalelel was 165 years old; he begot Jared. And he lived another 730 years, until the 61st year of Lamech.[13]
5/ Jared was 162 years old; he begot Enoch. And he lived a further 800 years[14] until the 261st year of Noah.
6/ Enoch was 165 years old; he begot Methusaleh. And he lived another 200 years until the 527th year of Jared. And he was pleasing to God and was not to be found, for God transferred him.[15]
7/ Methusaleh was 185 years old; he begot Lamech. And he lived another 802 years.[16]
8/ Lamech was 188 years old; he begot Noah. He lived a further 565 years until the 565th year of Noah, to whom his father Lamech said that he called his name Noah[17]

---

9. So the LXX. Hebrew has 105. There are similar differences throughout this passage, with Arm agreeing with LXX against Hebrew.
10. Gen 5:6-7.
11. Gen 5:8-11.
12. Gen 5:12-14.
13. Gen 5:15-17.
14. Gen 5:18-20.
15. Gen 5:21-24.
16. Gen 5:25-27.
17. Gen 5:28-31.

2.2. Chronological Summaries

Chronological summaries have been discussed in the introductory remarks to this section. The first list given below is drawn from a *Miscellany* of M8076 (seventeenth century), fols. 222r-222v.[18] A text from the *Miscellany* M2001B (fourteenth century; Tēr-Vardanean 2012, 6:961-72), fol. 37r runs parallel to lines the text of ll. 26-37 of M8076's text, but with some substantial differences. Similar summaries, but briefer than those given here and drawn from M1999 (twelfth century) are published by Eynatyan.[19] The last span in the text she published is from Nicea to the Council of Ephesus: contrast here below. In M8076, the summary itself concludes at line 42 and a polemical passage on calendar follows.

We have assigned numbers to each statement of a date rather than to lines of the text. The text commences on fol. 222r and concludes on 222v.

Text of M8076

1/	/ fol. 222r / Ադամայ ի փոխելն Ենովքայ, ամք	ՌՆՉԷ:
	Ի փոխմանէն Ենովքայ մինչեւ ի ջրհեղեղն, ամք	ՇՁԵ:
	Յադամայ մինչեւ ի ջրհեղեղն, ամք	ՍՍԽԲ:
	Ի ջրհեղեղէն մինչեւ յաշտարակն, ամք	ՇԻԵ:
5/	Յադամայ ի յաշտարակն, ամք	ՍՁՒԷ:
	Ի ջրհեղեղէն ի ծնունդն Աբրահամու, ամք	ՋԽԲ:
	Անտի ի յելն Եգիպտոսի, ամք	ՇԵ:
	Անտի ի Սողոմոնի Դ ամս եւ ցտաճարին շինումս, ամք	ՆՁ:
	Անտի ի նորոգումս տաճարին Զորաբաբէլի եւ ի Դարեհի երկրորդ ամս, ամք	ՇԺԲ:
10/	Անտի ի ծնունդն Քրիստոսի, ամք	ՇԺՑ:
	Միանգամայն ծնունդն Քրիստոսի, ամք	ՐՃՀՐ:
	Ի ծնընդենէն ի դիր Շ-եկին, ամք	ՇԿԲ:
	Ի մկրտութենէն ի Ի ամս Կոստանդիանոսի, ամք	Յ:
	Անտի / fol. 222v/ ի հայ թվականն, ամք	ՄԻԴ:
15/	Որք ասեն ի լինելութենէ աշխարհի մինչեւ ի ծնունդն Քրիստոսի ամք ՐՆԻ լինել, մեծապէս սխալեցան յաւելով գտգիտութիւն առանց ճշմարտութեան. վասն զի յարարչութենէն զժամանակա

---

18. Eganyan et al. 1970, 2:667-668. Dr. Gohar Muradyan most graciously aided me on some points of calendarical learning.
19. Eynatyan 2002, 98-101 and 166-67; see Tēr-Vardanean 2012, 6:945-56.

PART TWO

ոչ որ կարասցէ զիտել ի մարդկանէ։ Բայց միայն արտաքսելոյն
Ադամայ ի դրախտէն։

16/ Ի Ի ամէն Կոստանդիանոսի մինչեւ ի դիր Մ-եկին, ամք ՒԳ.ՁԱ
թվականին Հռոմոց։

ՅԲ ամին Փիլիպոսի մինչեւ ի յամս Կոստանդիանոսի, <>։
Եւ անտի ԻԳ լինի ՃԴ.Մ Անդրիասին։
Միանգամայն մինչեւ ի հայ թուականն, ամք ՅԴ։

20/ ի ծննդենէն Քրիստոսի մինչեւ ի սուրբն Գրիգոր, ամք ՅԴ։
Ի սրբոյն Գիրգորէն[20] ի սուրբն Սահակ, ամք ՃԲ։
Ի սրբոյն Գրիգորէն ի հայ թվականն, ՄՕԲ։
Ի յԱդամայ ի հայ թվականն, ամք ՐՇՕԲ։

25/ Ի ջրհեղեղէն ի հայ թվականն, ամք ՎՇԺ։
ՅԱբրահամէ ի հայ թվականն, ամք ՍՇԿԵ։
Ի Մովսիսէ ի հայ թվականն, ամք ՍԿԳ։
Ի Սողոմնէ ի հայ թվականն, ԴՇԿԳ։
Ի յերկրորդ շինութենէն ի հայ թվականն ՌՁԸ։
Ի ծննդենէն Քրիստոսի ի հայ թվականն ամք ՇՕԳ։

30/ Ի ծննդենէն Կոստանդիանոսի ի հայ թվականն, ամք ՄՕ.ԺԳ։
Ի յառաքելոյն Թաթէոսէ ի սուրբն Գրիգոր, ամք ՄԿԶ։
Ի ծննդենէն Քրիստոսի ի Նիկիոյ ժողովա, ամք ՀԴ ՅԻԲ։
Անտի ի Կոստանդնուպօլսի ժողովա, ՀԴ։
Անտի յԵբեսոսի առաջին ժողովա, Օ։

35/ Անտի ի Քաղկեկոնի ժողովա, ԻԷ ամք։
Անտի ի Դվայ ժողովա ի հայք, ԼՁ։
Անտի ի բղբոյ ժողովա ի սուրբ Կաթուղիկէն, ամք Դ։
Յորում որոշեցին գՅոհան Տիկորեցին, եւ էր
թուականն հայոց ՃԶԳ։
Իսկ յելիցն ի վիրապէն սրբոյն Գրիգորի, ամք ՆԼԳ։

40/ Եւ թարքմանութենէն հայ գրոյս, ամք Յ։

Translation of M8076

1/ From Adam to the translation of Enoch,   1,487 years.
From Enoch's translation to the flood,   555 years.
From Adam to the flood,   2,242 years.[21]

---

20. Ի հայ crossed out.
21. This subtotal differs from the sum of the preceding lines, which is 2,042.

	From the flood to the Tower,	525 years.
5/	From Adam to the Tower,	2,767 years.[22]
	From the flood to the birth of Abraham,	942 years.
	Thence to the exodus from Egypt,	505 years.
	Thence to the fourth year of Solomon and to the building of the temple,	380 years.
	Thence to the renovation of the temple by Zerubbabel and to the second year of Darius,	512 years.
10/	Thence to the birth of Christ,	518 years.
	Altogether, to the birth of Christ,	5,198 years.[23]
	From the Nativity to the establishment of the 532 years period[24]	562 years.
	From the Baptism to the 20th year of Constantine,	300 years.[25]
	Thence to the (inception of) the Armenian era,	224 years.[26]
15/	Those who say that from the coming into being of the world to the birth of Christ (were) 5,420 years erred greatly, by increasing ignorance without truth. For no one human can know the time from creation, but only from the expulsion of Adam from the Garden.	
16/	From the 20th year of Constandianos[27] until the establishment of the 200 year period	23.81 years of the Byzantines.[28]
	In the 2 year of Philip up to the year of Costandianos[29]	
	And thence 23 is 104.200 of Andrias,[30]	

---

22. As in the previous note, the subtotal is two hundred years more that the sum of the preceding lines.

23. This figure is discussed below in note 194. The subtotal 5,198 is 226 years less than the actual sum of the elapsed periods, which is 5,425.

24. See Eynatyan 2002, 471–72 concerning the 532 years period. The same is to be found in her book on pp. 166–67.

25. Cf. Eynatyan 2002, 166.

26. The Great Armenian Era commences in 551 CE. Reckoning that Christ was baptized at the age of 30 and adding 300 (line 13) and 224 (line 4) we reach a total 554. This difference of three years between 551 and 554 occurs in other chronological texts.

27. This refers to Constantine I (306–337 CE). Thus the twentieth year of Constantine is 336 CE. By the way, Eusebius's *Ecclesiastical History* reaches the twentieth year of Constantine, and this is mentioned in the titles of some editions (remark by G. Muradyan).

28. Unclear.

29. This might be Emperor Philippicus Bardanes, an Armenian by origin, who ruled for two years 711–713 CE. He held Monothelite views, engendering a doctrinal controversy with Rome.

30. Who this Andrias was is somewhat unclear. From an article by H. S. Anasyan on "Andeas of Byzantium" (1974, 1:393) we learn the following. Andreas of Byzantium (or of Athens) is dated to the fourth century and is said to be an expert on calendar and astronomy. He was credited with a bicentenary Paschal list the inception of which was in the year 352–353. See

	Altogether up to the Armenian era,	304 years
20/	From the birth of Christ up to St. Gregory,	304 years.
	From St. Gregory to St. Sahak,	108 years.
	From St. Gregory to the Armenian era,	252.
	From Adam to the Armenian era,	5,552 years.
	From the flood to the Armenian era,	3,510 years.
25/	From Abraham to the Armenian era,	2,565 years.
	From Moses to the Armenian era,	2,063 years.
	From Solomon to the Armenian era,	1,563 years.
	From the second building to the Armenian era,	1,088 years.
	From the birth of Christ to the Armenian era,	553 years.
30/	From the birth of Costandianos to the Armenian era,	250.13 years.[31]
	From the sending of Thaddeus to St. Gregory,	266 years.
	From the birth of Christ to the Council of Nicea,[32]	74.322 years.
	Thence to the Council of Constantinople,	<74>.[33]
	Thence to the First Council of Ephesus,	50 years.
35/	Thence to the Council of Chalcedon,[34]	27 years.
	Thence to the Council of Dvin in Armenia,	36 years.[35]

Thence from the Council of Պղպոյ[36] to the holy Kat'ołikē, 90 years in which they separated John Tikorec'i, and it was 173 of the

---

further on him, and particularly on his writings, many still only known in manuscript, Anasyan 1959, 1:854–64. On the 200-year lists see Eynatyan 2002, 471 (Armenian on p. 462). So "200 of Andrias" is possibly the bicentenary list of Andreas. On this point the gracious assistance of G. Muradyan is acknowledged. The date indicated by "thence 23 is 104.200 of Andrias" remains obscure. If Constandinos is Constantine the Great, then this line makes no sense for he preceded Philip and did not follow him. So, one of the identifications is incorrect.

31. Perhaps this means 263 years. The year 551 (start of the Armenian Era) less 272 (birth of Constantine the Great, would yield 279 years. This is, however, uncertain and the reason for the notation employed is unknown.

32. The interpretation of ՀԴ = Հոոմնց դար, "Byzantine millennium" or "era" was suggested by Dr. Sergio LaPorta. It is, as he notes in his communication, a conjecture. However, we have chosen not to follow him in this and to read as the number 74. Compare this number with those in lines 16 and 30 above.

33. Since the Council of Nicea was in 325 CE and the first Council of Constantinople was in 381, i.e., a span of fifty-six years. The three-year difference in the calculation of from the birth of Christ to Nicea is also found in note 26 above.

34. K'ałkekon in Armenian is corrupt for K'ałkedon, i.e., Chalcedon.

35. The First Council of Dvin took place in the year 506, and the second in 554.

36. It is unclear what this might be, but the event referred to in the next line is apparently the expulsion of the Catholicossal locum tenens John Tikorec'i in 724 at the Council of Vałaršapat (the "Kat'ołikē" of the text): see Ačařean, ANB 3.553 (Sergio La Porta). The text gives this as AE 173, i.e., 551 + 173 CE = 744, which is considerably off the mark.

Armenian era.
And after St. Gregory's coming out of the pit, 433 years.
40/ And from the Armenian translation of the Book 300 years.

2.3. Concerning Millennia

2.3.1. Concerning Millennia I

Eynatyan published two versions of this text previously, from M1999 (twelfth century; Tēr-Vardanean 2012, 6:961–64) and M5975 (fifteenth century; see Eganyan et al. 1970, 2:225) and they were translated into English by Muradyan and Topchyan (Eynatyan 2002, 98–101, 352–54). Here we give an additional copy of the text type found in M5975, as well as some associated texts. The text printed below is drawn from M2036 *Miscellany* (seventeenth century), 220r (Tēr-Vardanean 2012, 6:1135–42). The only substantial difference between it and M2036 is the addition of line 9 in the latter. The usual chiliastic enumeration puts the Nativity at the middle of the sixth millennium and the Parousia at the beginning of the seventh so corresponding to the Sabbath of the world-week. It usually does not have an eighth millennium.[37]

Text

1/ / fol. 220r / վասն դարուց
Առաջին դարըն ենովք փոխեցաւ:
Երկրորդ դարն ջրհեղեղն եկ աշխարհի:
Երրորդ դարն աշտարակն շինեցաւ:
5/ Չորրորդ դարն գալն Աստուծոյ առ Աբրահամ:
Հինկերորդ դարն ելքն եղեւ յեգիպտոսէ:
Վեցերորդ դարն եղեւ մարդեղութիւն Բանին Աստուծոյ:
Եօթներորդ դարն եղիցի կատարած կենցաղոյ. եւ մուտ ընդ
ութերորդին յարութիւն ամենայն մարդկան:

Translation

1/ Concerning Millennia.

---

37. See Stone 1996a, 87–89. See succinctly also art. "Millenarianism," in Cross and Livingstone 1974, 916.

In the first era, Enoch was translated.[38]
In the second era, the flood came to the earth.[39]
In the third era, the Tower was built.[40]
5/ In the fourth era, God's coming (to) Abraham.[41]
In the fifth era, the exodus from Egypt took place.[42]
In the sixth era, the incarnation of the Word God took place.[43]
In the seventh era will be the completion of life and at the inception of the eighth, the resurrection of all humans.

2.3.2. Concerning Millennia II

This document resembles the preceding text[44] and here the last line is quite clear. M5975 edited by Juliet Eynatyan seems to lack the words "the resurrection of all humans." This text is drawn from M4618, fol. 126r, a *Miscellany* of the seventeenth century.

Text

1/ Դարձեալ. Այս են դարք որ գրեցան յիմաստնոց որ եղեն մեծամեծ հրաշք։
Առաջին դարն Ենովք փոխեցաւ անմահութեան։
Երկրորդ չրհեղեղն։
Երրորդն աշտարակն շինեցաւ։
5/ Չորրորդն աւետիքն Աբրահամու։
Հինգերորդն Սողոմոն գտաճարն շինեաց։
Վեցերորդն Տէրն մեր մարմնացաւ ի սուրբ կուսէն։
Ի լնուլ է դարուն եւ ի մտանելն ի Ը-ն յարութիւն բնութեանս մարդկան։

---

38. Gen 5:22–24. The line about Adam found in Millennia II is omitted.
39. Gen 6–9.
40. Gen 11:1–9.
41. Gen 12:1–3.
42. The story of the exodus from Egypt begins in the first chapter of Exodus and continues through to the conquest of the land of Israel in the book of Joshua. Reference here is probably to Exod 12:30–42, which relates the actual exodus.
43. "The Word" refers to Christ.
44. I print it from a transcription I made in the Matenadaran some years ago.

Translation

1/ Again: these are the eras which were written down by the wise, in which very great miracles took place.
In the first era, Enoch was translated to immortality.[45]
The second, the flood.[46]
The third, the Tower was built.[47]
5/ The fourth, the annunciation to Abraham.[48]
The fifth, Solomon built the temple.[49]
The sixth, Our Lord took on flesh from the Holy Virgin.[50]
At the fulfilment of the seventh era and at the beginning of the eighth is the resurrection of the body (or: nature) of humans.[51]

2.3.3. Concerning Millennia III

A different recension of this text occurs in M8076, *Miscellany*, seventeenth century, fol. 223r. Because the differences in wording are so considerable, we give its text in full.

Text

1/ / fol. 223r / Յառաջին դարուն ենովք յերկինս փոխեցաւ։
Յերկրորդ դարուն. ջրհեղեղն եղեւ։
Յերրորդ տարուն բաժանումն լեզուացն. ուստի ՀԲ ազգ սփիւռեցան ընդ ամենայն երկիր։
Չորրորդ աւետիքն Աստուծոյ լինին առ Աբրահամ. որով փրկեցան ամենայն տիեզերք։
5/ Եւ Հինգերորդ. Սողոմոն տաճարն անուան Աստուծոյ շինէր։
Իսկ վեցերորդին Տէր մեր Յիսուս Քրիստոս մարմնեցաւ ի սուրբ եւ յանարատ կուսէն Մարիամայ։
The ensuing chronological summary by millennia reads:

---

45. Gen 5:22–24.
46. Gen 6–9.
47. Gen 11:1–9.
48. Gen 12.1–3.
49. 1 Kgs 6:1–9.
50. Matt 1:18, Luke 2:6–7, John 1:14.
51. Compare art. "Millenarianism," in Cross and Livingstone 1974, 916. The view that there were eight millennia was less current in antiquity than that the world week of seven thousand years.

ՅԱդամայ մինչեւ ցԽ ամս Յաբեթի   Ռ ամ:
եւ ի Խ ամէն Յաբեթի մինչեւ ՅՇԸ ամս Նոյի.   Ռ ամ:
եւ ՅՇԸ ամէն Նոյի մինչեւ ՂԵ ամս Սերուքայ.   Ռ ամ:
10/ եւ ՂԵ ամէն մինչեւ Սերուքայ[52] ԺԹ ամս Յայիրայ   Ռ ամ:
եւ ի ԺԹ ամէն Յայիրայ մինչեւ ԻԳ ամս Պտղմեայ.
եւ ԻԴ Անտիոքու մեծի.   Ռ ամ:
եւ ի չորրորդ ամէն Պտղմեայ. եւ ԻԴ ամացն Անտիոքու մինչեւ
ԼԵ ամս Խոսրովու Յորգքտեան.   ՊԻԵ ամ:
եւ պիտոյ է լրումս 8-իս ՃՀԳ ամ:
Իսկ զ.Է-երորդ դարն եթէ շաբաթ հանգստեան արասցէ
կատարած աշխարհիս. կամ թէ ի թիկանց աշխարհիս. / fol.
223v / խառնեցցէ Աստուած գիտէ. եւ ոչ այլ ոք:
Իսկ ԳԺ-երեակն եւ կես Ժ-երեկին ի տեսիլ սրբոյն Սահակայ.
ԳՃՅ ամ է եւ է փոխումս նորա յառաջին ամս երկրորդ
Յազկերտի. որդոյ Վռամայ թագաւորին Պարսից. որդոյ
յիշատակն աւրհնութեամբ եղիցի. եւ աղօթիւք նոցա Տէր մեզ
ողորմեցցի:

Translation

1/ In the first era, Enoch was translated to heaven.[53]
    In the second era, the flood took place.[54]
    In the third era, the division of the languages, whence 72 nations were scattered over all the earth.[55]
    In the fourth era, God's annunciation to Abraham took place, by which the whole universe was saved.[56]
5/ And the fifth, Solomon built the temple of the Name of God.[57]
    Then in the sixth our Lord, Jesus Christ took on body in the holy and immaculate Virgin Mary.[58]
    The ensuing chronological summary by millennia reads:
    From Adam to the 40th year of Japheth, years   1,000.
    And from the 40th year of Japheth until the 358th year of Noah,

---

52. This word is transposed and should precede մինչեւ.
53. Gen 5:22–24.
54. Gen 6–9.
55. Gen 11:1–9.
56. Gen 12:1–3. The resulting universal salvation is likely produced by the typology seeing Abraham's Annunciation foreshadowing that to the Virgin.
57. 1 Kgs 6:1–9.
58. Matt 1:18, Luke 2:6–7, John 1:14.

38   CHRONOLOGICAL TEXTS

                     1,000 years.
And from the 358th year of Noah until the 95th year of Serug,
                        1,000.
10/ And from the 95th year of Serug until the 19th year of Jair,
                     1,000 years.
And from the 19th year of Jair until the 23rd year of Ptolemy, and the 24th year of Antiochus the Great,[59]   1,000 years
And from the fourth year of Ptolemy and the 24th year of Antiochus until the 35th year of Xosraw son of Hormizd,[60]   827 years
And to complete this 7,000 (years), 173 years lack.
Then, in the seventh era, whether he will make a Sabbath of rest, a completion of this world, or whether he will confuse the rear side of this world,[61] God knows and none other.
Then thirtyfold and half tenfold in the vision of St. Sahak (is) 350 years,[62] there is his change in the first year of Yazdekert the Second, son of Vahram king of the Persians,[63] whose (Sahak's) memory be blessed and through their prayers our Lord will have mercy upon us.

2.4. Concerning the Periods

A different but similar work, enumerating seven eras, was published in Stone 1996a, 138–39 from the *Miscellany* M9100 (seventeenth century), fols. 370v–371r. Here we give the version occurring in the seventeenth-century *Miscellany*, M2036 on fol. 273r. That manuscript is another seventeenth-century *Miscellany*. This text has also been published previously from M5975 (fifteenth century; see Eganyan et al. 1970, 2:22570) by Juliet Eynatyan, and translated by Gohar Muradyan and Aram Topchyan (Eynatyan 2002, 352–53). We have here transcribed and translated the text of M2036, fol. 273r, but have not given

---

59. The fourth year of Ptolemy V Epiphanes was 200 BCE; the twenty-fourth year of Antiochus III the Great was 198 BCE.
60. This is Khosrow II of Iran (ruled 590–628 CE). By the calculation implied by the text, the end of that millennium is 629 CE, showing a small discrepancy.
61. Perhaps meaning "the end" or "the state of affairs at the end."
62. The vision of St. Sahak and its suggested interpretations are discussed by Muradyan (2014); see also Garitte 1958. Muradyan discusses the 350 years referred to in the vision, to which our text also refers, on pp. 329–331. Ultimately it goes back, of course, to Dan 12:7 which gives the basis for 350 years rule of the wicked ("a time, two times, and half a time"). Similar but not identical, are Dan 9:27 about the times and 11:31 about the "abomination of desolation." Daniel's prophecy is taken up by Mat 24:15, in connection with the "abomination of desolation."
63. He was king of Persia (420–438 BCE).

the material of a different character following line 12. The text of M5975 is virtually identical with it, bar a few minor variants. Another form of this text occurs in V879 (Čemčean 1996, 6:26).

Text

1/ / fol. 273r / Յաղագս շրջանց
Առաջին շարցանին էլ Ադամ ի դրախտէն:
Երկրորդ շարցանին. Ենովք անմահութեան փոխեցաւ:
Երրորդ[64] շրցանին. Մեկնեաց Աստուած զազգն Սէթայ յազգէն Կայենի:
5/ Չորրորդ շրցանին. կազմեաց Նոյ գտապանն:[65]
Հինգերորդ շրցանն.[66] լեզուքն բաժանեցան:[67]
վեցերորդ շրցանն. եղեն ծնունդքն Աբրահամու:
Եօթներորդ շրցանն. էլ Իսրայէլ Էգիպտոսէ:
Ութերորդ շրցանն. Սողոմոն գտաճարն շինեաց:
10/ Իններորդ շրցանն. Զորաբաբէլ նորոգեաց գտաճարն:
Տասներորդ շրցանն. ծնաւ Քրիստոս:
Մետասներորդ շրցանին. եղաւ թվական Հայոց:[68]

Translation

1/ Concerning the Periods.
In the first period, Adam went forth from the Garden.[69]
In the second period, Enoch was translated to immortality.[70]
In the third period, God separated the family (race) of Seth from the family (race) of Cain.[71]
5/ In the fourth period, Noah formed the Ark.[72]

---

64. Երրորդ Eynatyan 2002 and M5569.
65. գտապանակն M5569.
66. From here to line 11 Eynatyan 2002 reads շրցանին, correctly; however M5569 reads like the text above.
67. So M5569, Eynatyan 2002.
68. M5569 adds three lines of text relating to the birth of the Virgin and the baptism of Christ.
69. Gen 3:23–24.
70. Gen 5:22–24.
71. See Gen 4:16–26.
72. Gen 6–9.

(In) the fifth period, the nativity of Abraham took place.[73]
<(In) the sixth period>
(In) the seventh period, Israel went forth from Egypt.[74]
(In) the eighth period, Solomon built the temple.[75]

10/ (In) the ninth period, Zerubbabel renewed the temple.[76]
(In) the tenth period, Christ was born.[77]
(In) the eleventh period the calendar of the Armenians was set.[78]

In M2036, fol. 273r and Eynatyan (2002) from line 11 on we read:

Թվական եւ[79] Ե-երեակն հռոմայեցոց. ՇԶ էր շրջանն, Ե-երեակ Դ եղեւ յղութիւն Եղիսաբեթ.
ՇԷ[80] Ե-երեակ[81] Ե Աւետիք սուրբ կուսին եղեւ
ՇԸ Ե-երեակ զէ եղեւ ծնունդն Քրիստոսի.
Դարձեալ կրկնեցաւ շրջանն եւ եղեւ Ձ թիւ Ե-երեակն Բ մկրտութիւն Քրիստոսի
Թ թիւ Ե-երեակն գԶ եղեւ խաչելութիւն Քրիստոսի:

Translation

The Roman date of the period and the septenary[82] were 506 and four (Wednesday) respectively, when Elizabeth conceived.[83]
In the 507th year [of the period], when the septenary was five (Thursday[84]) the Annunciation to the Virgin took place.[85]
In the 508th year [of the period], when the septenary was seven (Saturday), Christ was born.

---

73. Gen 11:26.
74. The story of the exodus from Egypt begins in the first chapter of Exodus and continues through the conquest of the land of Israel in the book of Joshua.
75. 1 Kgs 6:1–9.
76. Ezra 3.
77. Matt 1:18, Luke 2:6–7, John 1:14.
78. The cycle of the Great Armenian Era (AE) starts in 551 CE.
79. էր M2036.
80. om M2036.
81. երեկն M2036.
82. Eynatyan 2002, 469: "Septenary (եօթներակ)—the day of the week (Monday and so on) coinciding with the last day of a given year is the septenary of the next year."
83. Luke 1:24.
84. Eynatyan 2002 has "Tuesday."
85. Luke 1:30–36.

The period was repeated again; it was the sixth year and the septenary was four, when Christ was baptized.[86]
The ninth year: the septenary was six (Friday), when the crucifixion of Christ took place.[87]

2.5. GENERATIONS FROM ADAM TO CHRIST

This text, found in M2245, fols. 271r-272r, a *Miscellany* of 1689 (see Tēr-Vardanean 2012, 7:619-28), commences with a genealogy of Jesus drawn principally from Matt 1. However, at points where information from the Hebrew Bible is available, it draws on it for details. The genealogy runs down to Jesus in §15. In §§16-19 a text on six Marys ensues. This is followed by genealogical notes on Jacob's sons, details about the descent of Moses, about Pharaoh's daughter, etc. (§21). Following this, the descendants of Abraham from Hagar and Keturah are set forth, including a claim anchoring the Arcasid dynasty in Abraham's genealogy (§22). Then an enumeration of the Judges and their activities follows (§§23-28) and finally a summary of Jewish rulers after the Exile and down to the birth Christ (§§29-30).

Overall, the lifespans in the early part of the genealogy accord, as we would expect, with the LXX chronology. Occasionally they stray, often through the common corruption of the Armenian numerals for 5 and 7.[88] Some of the details, such as the name of Pharaoh's daughter, Mari, and the name of a queen of Ethiopians, T'esbi, are not biblical, but are apparently developments of certain Greek and Hebrew traditions.[89] According to Jub. 47:5 the name of Pharaoh's daughter was Tarmuth,[90] and in Syncellus it is Thermuthis (Adler and Tuffin 2002, 173). However, Eusebius of Caesarea calls Pharaoh's daughter Merris (*Praep. ev.* 27) and Artapanus calls her Meroïs;[91] see Ginzberg 1909-1938, 5:398. Here there is also T'esbi, Queen of the Ethiopians.

---

86. Mark 1:9, etc.
87. Matt 27:35, Mark 15:24, Luke 23:33, John 19:18.
88. See Stone and Hillel, "Index," no. 222.
89. The names are also found in the text *History of Moses* published by Sargis Yovsēpʻianc' (1896, 199-206, on p. 201). A not totally satisfactory English translation is to be found in Issaverdens 1934, 133-40, with the names on 135. The text is drawn from hagiographical collections called Ճառընտիր "Collections of Homilies."
90. VanderKam (1989, 306) gives some versions of this name, but none of them resembles T'esbi in particular. The name of Pharaoh's daughter, Mari is probably derived from the name of his sister, Miriam.
91. See Ginzberg 1909-1938, 5:398. Ginzberg cites various names attributed to Pharaoh's daughter mainly by Hellenistic Jewish sources.

Text

1/ Ազգահամար սկսեալ յԱդամայ մինչեւ ի Քրիստոս:
Ադամ ՋԼ ամ ապրեցաւ:
Սէթ ՋՃԲ:
Ենովս ՋԵ:
Կայինան ՋՃ:
2/ Մադադիէլ ՊՂԵ:
Յարեդ ՋԿԲ:
Ենովք ՅԿԵ:
Մաթուսաղա ՋԿԹ:
Ղամէք ՁՕՂ:
3/ Նոյ ՋՕ:
Սեմ Ո:
Արփաքսադ ՇՃԵ:
Սաղայ:
Երեր:[92]
4/ Փաղէգ ՅԽՂ:
Ռագաւ:
Սերուք ՅԼ:
Նաքովր:
5/ Թարայ:
Աբրահամ ՃՀԵ:
Իսահակ ՃՁ:
Յակոբ ՃԽԵ:
Յուդայ:
6/ Փարէզ:
Եզրոն:
Արամ:
Ամինադաբ:
Նայասոն:
7/ Սաղմոն:
Բոյոս:
Ովբէթ:
Յեսսէ:
Դաւիթ:
8/ Սողոմոն:

---

92. This and the preceding name have no year span, nor do most of the following.

Րոբոյամ:
Աբիայ:
Ասափ:
9/ Յովսափաթ:
Ուրամ:
Զայս երիս թագաւորս:
զՈքոզիայ:
10/ եւ զԳոթողիայ, մայրն: եւ զՈւաս:⁹³ եւ զԱմասիայ:
Ոչ է գրեալ ազգահամարն. աւետարանիչն: Վասն լինելոյ
դուստր: Թոռունք:
Ապայարու: Ոզիայ: Ուաթամ:
Աքազ:
Եզեկիայ:
11/ Մանասէ:
Ամովս:
Յովսիայ:
Յեքոնիայ:
12/ Սաղաթիէլ:
Զորաբաբէլ:
Աբիութ:
Եղիայկիմ:
13/ Ազովր:
Սադովկ:
Ի Սադովկա առաջի ամին: Աղեքսանդր Մակեդոնացի
յայտնեցաւ:
Աքին:
Եղիուղ:
14/ Եղիազար:
Մաթան:
Յակոբ:
Յովսեփի:
15/ Յիսուս Քրիստոս. ծնանի ի Բեթղահէմ Հրէաստանի:
16/ Վասն Մարիմանցն:
Նախ Մարիամ սուրբ Աստուածինն:
Երկրորդ. Մագդաղենացին. յորմէ է դեւքն ելին:
Երրորդ՝ միւս Մարիամ Մագդաղենացին:⁹⁴

---

93. Matthew 1 serves as the source.
94. It seems that Magdalene here is the result of a confusion.

Չորրորդ՝ Մարիամա, Յակոբայ եւ Յովսեա մայրն. որ էր կին կոչեցեալ Աստուածահօրն:

17/ Հինգերորդ. Մարիամս. Կղեոպեանն. որ կայր ատ խաչին: Կղեոպայոս եղբայր էր Յովսեփիայ: Եւ / fol. 271v / Մարիամս այս դուստր էր նորա. եւ վասն այսչափ ազգականութեանցս, քոյր Աստուածամօրն կոչեցաւ:

18/ Վեցերորդ՝ Մարիամ. քոյրն Ղազարու. որ օծ զՏէրն իւղով: Իսկ Մարիամս, քոյրն Փիլիպպոսի:
Բայց Մարիամանք որ օծին զՏէրն: Կարձիս կա ի մէջ վարդապետաց. զի Յոհան Ոսկիբերանն. եւ Իգնատիոս Բ ասին զմինն պոոնիկ. եւ զքոյրն Ղազարու. կին պարկեշտ:

19/ Իսկ լատինացիք մի ասին. բայց կրկին անգամ օծեալ. որում մեոք թողաւ. եւ մի վասն եղբօրն յարութեան:

20/ Որդիքն Յակոբայ: Ռուբէն: Շմաւոն: Ղեւի: Յուդայ: Իսաքար: Զաբողոն: Դան: Նեփթաղիմ: Գաթ: Ասեր: Յովսէփ: Բենիամին: Եւ ծնաւ դուստր մի Լիա. անուն նորա Դինայ:

21/ Յաբրահամու ի Մովսէս: Աբրահամու. Իսահակ: Յակոբու. Ղեւի: Կահաթ. Ամրամ: Մովսէս: Եւ մայրն Մովսէսի. Յոզաբէթ: Եւ դուստր փարաւոնի. որ որդեգիր արար զՄովսէս Մարի: Եւ Թեսբի Եթովպացոց թագուհին է:

22/ Եւ Աբրահամու որդի. աղախնոյն ի Հազարայ, Իսմայէլ: Եւ ի Քետուրա կնոջէն. եղեն. Զ որդիք Աբրահամու. Եմրան, Յեկտան, Մադան, Մադիան, յորմէ մադիանացիք, Եսբոկ, Սովիւ է. ուստի բազմացեալք. ցին զարեւելս. ի պահել. յորմէ թագաւորք Պարսից. եւ Հայոց. Արշակունիք կոչեցեալք:

23/ Դատաւորք: Եւ յետ Յեսուա որ տիրեցին: Առաջին՝ Գոդոնիէլ. եւ յետ սորա. Աւող. սա երկոցունց ձեռաց յաջողակ. եւ արար սուր երկսայրի. թզաւ երկայն. եւ սպան զեղոմ արքայ Մովաբու ճախ ձեռօքն:

24/ Եւ յետ սորա Սամեգար որ մաճին. ՋՃ այր եսպան: Եւ յետ սորա Բարակ. սա եսպան զՍիսարա եւ զԱբէն. ի ձորն Կիսոնի:
Եւ յետ սորա Գեդեհոն. սա եւտես զզեղմա իմանալի. յորժամ ծեծեր զցորեանն ի կալն. որ ի չուր ըմպելն ընտրեաց զօրսն, եւ թագուցեալ սափորոթ. զվառեալ լապտերսն. եւ եհար ԳՃ արամբք ՃԻՌ յարսն. սա եսպան զՈվրէբն. / fol. 272r / զԶէբն, զԷբէէ, զՍաղմանայ, եւ զայլսն:

25/ Եւ յետ սորա Աբիմելէք հարճ որդին Գեդեհոնի. որ եսպան Հ եղբայրս իւր. ի վերայ վիմի մոյ:

Եւ յետ սորա Թովդայ:
Եւ յետ սորա Յայիր. եւ եղեն նորա որդի ԼԲ:
Եւ յետ սորա Յեփթայի. սա գդուստրն իւր Աստուծոյ զոհեաց,
եւ ոչ հաճեցաւ Աստուած:

26/ Եւ յետ սորա Յեսերոն. եւ եղեն նորա ուստերք Լ, եւ դստերք Լ:
Եւ յետ սորա Էլոն:
Եւ յետ սորա Աբդոն որդի Էլլէքայ. եւ եղեն որդիք նորա Խ եւ Լ,
որդիք որդւոց նորա:

27/ Եւ յետ սորա Սամսոն, որդի Մանուէի. սա կալաւ ԹԾ ադուես եւ
կապեաց ի նոսա ջահս, եւ այրեաց զանդաստանս այլազգեաց.
Եւ ծնօտիւ իշոյն. եհար զհազարսն. եւ ի նոյն ծնօտէ եհան ջուր
եւ արբ, եւ զախեալ դուռն քաղաքին եղեալ յուսն. եւ եհան ի
գլուխ լերինն:

28/ Եւ յետ սորա Հեղի քահանայն. եւ ապա Սամուէլ, եւ Սաուղ
թագաւորն. եւ այլն ըստ կարգի մինչեւ գերութիւնն:

29/ Եւ յետ գերութեանն քահանայք իշեցին ժողովրդեանն: Չի
երեք կարգ էին իշխանութիւնն Հրէից: Առաջին դատաւորք,
մինչեւ ի Սաուղ: Երկրորդ, թագաւորքն մինչեւ ի Զորաբաբել
եւ Յեսու քահանայն:

30/ Եւ աստի քահանայք մինչ ի Յիսուս Քրիստոս փրկիչն
ճշմարիտ: Եւ անդ դադարեցան առաջնորդք. օծեալքն. յորում
երեւեցաւ ճշմարիտ օծեալն Քրիստոս:

Translation

1/ Enumeration of the generations starting from Adam up to Christ.
Adam lived 930 years.[95]
Seth,   912.[96]
Enos,   907.[97]
Kenan (Kaynan), 910.[98]
2/ Mahalelel,   897.[99]

---

95. See Gen 5:5. This is Adam's age at the time of his death according to the genealogical list in Gen 5. This text follows Gen 5 down to Shem (Gen 6:10). From that point the ages are drawn from Gen 11:10–27. When figures occur other than in these two sources, they will be noted.
96. Gen 5:6.
97. According to Gen 5:11, Enosh lived for 905 years. This is most likely an instance of the common confusion of the Armenian notation for 5 (Ե) and 7 (Է). See Stone and Hillel, "Index," no. 222.
98. Gen 5:14.
99. This figure does not match Gen 5:17, which says that Mahalalel died at the age of 895. We

	Jared,	962.[100]
	Enoch,	365.[101]
	Methusaleh,	969.[102]
	Lamech,	753.[103]
3/	Noah,	950.[104]
	Shem,	600.[105]
	Arpachshad,	517.[106]
	Shelah.[107]	
	Eber.	
4/	Peleg	343.[108]
	Reu.	
	Serug	330.[109]
	Nahor.	
5/	Terah.	
	Abraham,	177.[110]
	Isaac,	180.[111]
	Jacob,	145.[112]
	Judah.	
6/	Perez.[113]	

---

find 890 in 2.5. Enumeration of the Generations, and 897 in 4.4. Years and Names of the Forefathers in Order. The 5/7 variant, therefore, does not originate in the present copy. On this variant see the preceding notes 87 and 97.

100. Gen 5:20.
101. Gen 5:23.
102. Gen 5:27.
103. This figure does not match Lamech's age at death according to MT Gen 5:31 which is 777. However, it agrees with the LXX.
104. Gen 9:29.
105. Gen 11:10-11.
106. Arpachshad's life span is 438 in the MT, 465 in the LXX (Gen 11:12-13).
107. The text skips Kenan (Kaynan) son of Arpachshad, in that respect resembling the MT of Genesis, while the LXX includes him.
108. Peleg's age at death according to MT Gen 11:18-19 is 239, and 339 in the LXX. Neither agrees with Concerning the Times.
109. The Hebrew of Gen 11:22-23 yields 230 years.
110. Abraham's age at death in Gen 25:7 is 175. Again the variation of 5 and 7 is to be noted: compare notes 87 and 97. The genealogy from Abraham to Joram is drawn from several sources: Gen 46:12, Ruth 4:18-22, 1 Chr 2, Matt 1, Luke 3:23-38, etc. Yet none of these sources contains lifespans, but only the sequence of the names.
111. Gen 35:28.
112. According to Gen 47:28 Jacob's age at death was 147: another instance of the 5/7 variant: compare notes 87 and 97.
113. A genealogical list from Perez to David is found in Ruth 4:18-22; for the birth story of

PART TWO 47

Hezron.
Aram.¹¹⁴
Aminadab.
Nahson.
7/ Salmon.
Boaz.
Obed.
Jesse.
David.
8/ Solomon.¹¹⁵
Rehoboam.¹¹⁶
Abijah.
Asaph.¹¹⁷
9/ Jehoshaphat.
Joram.
These three kings
Ahaziah,¹¹⁸
10/ and Athalia (Gotoliah) his mother,¹¹⁹ and Uzziah (Ozias).¹²⁰
and Amaziah.¹²¹
The Evangelist does not record (in) the genealogy the existence of a daughter. His grandsons: Ahaiab,¹²² Uzziah, Jotham.¹²³

Perez see Gen 38:29.

114. Probably Ram: see Ruth 4:19 and 1 Chr 2:9. The LXX have Ἀρραν and the Armenian Bible has Արամ, "Aram," as does the text here.

115. A genealogical list of kings from David to Salathiel is found in 1 Chr 3, Matt 1:6–15; for the birth of Solomon see 2 Sam 12:24.

116. 1 Kgs 11:43.

117. Probably Assa: see 1 Kgs 15:8, 1 Chr 3:10.

118. According to the Bible in 2 Kgs 8:25, 1 Chr 3:11 Ahaziah is indeed the son of Joram. Matt 1:8 reads "Joram the father of Uzziah." The two names and, apparently the two kings, are confounded.

119. Gotʻoliah is Athaliah, mother of Ahaziah, see 2 Kgs 11:1–3. She ruled the land for six years according to 2 Kgs 11:3. Gotʻolia is the form of her name found in the LXX, where other instances of transliteration of Hebrew ʻayin by Greek gamma are found, perhaps most notably Gaza and Gomorrah, both of which have initial ʻayin in Hebrew.

120. Again, Matt 1 dominates the genealogy. According to 2 Kgs 11:12 Joash became king after Athaliah.

121. Uzziah is the son of Amaziah and father of Jotham, see 2 Kgs 15:3 and 2 Chr 26:1.

122. The name Ahaiab is unclear. No such a person is to be found in the Hebrew Bible, nor in the genealogy in Matt 1.

123. Armenian Ovatʻam = Jotham, son of Uzziah, was king of Judah, compare 2 Kgs 15:7, Matt 1:9.

Ahaz.
Hezekiah.
11/ Manasseh.
Amos.[124]
Josiah.
Jechoniah.[125]
12/ Salathiel.[126]
Zerubbabel.[127]
13/ Azor.[128]
Zadok.
In the first year of Zadok, Alexander of Macedon appeared.[129]
14/ Eleazar.
Achim.
Eliud.
Mattan.
Jacob.
Joseph.
15/ Jesus Christ was born in Bethlehem of Judea.
16/ Concerning the Marys.
The first Mary is the Holy Mother of God.[130]
The second is Magdalene from whom seven demons went forth.[131]
The third is the other Mary Magdalene.[132]
The fourth Mary is the mother of James and Joses.[133]
17/ The fifth is Mary the Cleopite,[134] who was near the cross. Cleopas was

---

124. Probably Ammon, see 1 Chr 3:14, Matt 1:10.
125. Again Matt 1:11 dominates the genealogy. According to 1 Chr 3:16 Jechoniah is the son of Jehoiakim, who was omitted from this list as were a number of the other monarchs mentioned by Kings and Chronicles.
126. Son of Jechoniah, see 1 Chr 3:17, Matt 1:12.
127. According to Matt 1:12; Luke 3:27, Zerubbabel is the son of Salathiel, this is not the case in 1 Chr 3:19 where he appears as the son of Pedaja, yet the books of Haggai, Ezra, and Nehemiah also have him as the son of Salathiel, see Hag 1:1, 12; Ezra 3:2, 8; Neh 12:1, etc.
128. According to Matt 1:13 Azor is great grandson of Zerubbabel, his grandfather was Abiud and his father was Eliakim. The name Azor is not present in the Hebrew Bible, and rest of this list is taken from Matt 1.
129. This note puts Zadok in the fourth century BCE.
130. Matt 1:16.
131. See Mark 16:9 and Luke 8:2.
132. The repetition of "Magdalene" could be a scribal error, still it is unclear who this "other Mary" might be; cf. Matt 27:61, 28:1; Luke 24:10; Acts 12:12.
133. See Mark 8:3, 15:40, also for the form Joses.
134. See Infancy Gospel of Ps.-Matthew §42: Elliot 1993, 98.

PART TWO 49

Joseph's brother. This Mary was his daughter and because of this genealogy, she was called the sister of the Mother of God.

18/ The sixth Mary is the sister of Lazarus who anointed the Lord with oil.[135] Then Mary, sister of Philip. But (as for) the Marys who anointed the Lord, there are (varying) opinions among the doctors, for in John Chrysostom and Ignatius it is said that one was a prostitute, and the sister of Lazarus was a chaste woman.

19/ But the Latins say (that there was) one, but she was anointed a second time; once when her sins were forgiven, and once because of her brother's resurrection.[136]

20/ The sons of Jacob:[137] Reuben, Simeon, Levi, Judah, Issachar, Zebulun, Dan, Naphtali, Gad, Asher, Joseph, Benjamin. And Leah bore one daughter whose name was Dinah.[138]

21/ From Abraham to Moses: Abraham, Isaac, Jacob, Levi, Kohath, Amram, Moses. And Moses's mother was Jochebed.[139] And the daughter of Pharaoh who adopted Moses (was called) Maři.[140] And Tʻesbi[141] was queen of the Ethiopians.

22/ And Abraham (had) a son from his maidservant Hagar, Ishmael.[142] And from his wife Keturah Abraham had six sons: Emran (Zimra), Jektan (Joshkan), Medan (Matan),[143] Midian (Madian) from whom are the Midianites, Esbok (Ishbak) and Shua (Soviw). From them they became numerous; they filled the East. From them are the Arcasid kings of the Persians and the Armenians.

23/ Judges: And after Joshua those who ruled (were): first, Othniel (Godoniel),[144] and after him, Ehud. He was skilled with his two hands and he made a two-edged sword a palm wide. And he killed Edom, king of Moab with his left hand.[145]

---

135. See John 11:2.
136. John 11:2, 12:3.
137. Gen 35:22–26.
138. Gen 30:21.
139. Exod 6:16–20, Num 26:59.
140. This is apparently connected with the name of Moses' sister: see part 4, note 1025. On these names, see the discussion in Sargisian 1898, 228.
141. See the introductory remarks, above.
142. Gen 16:15.
143. 1 Chr 1:32.
144. This was Othniel, who is Γοθονιηλ in the LXX. See Josh 15:17, Judg 3:9, etc.
145. Judg 3:15–30.

24/ And after him Shamgar.[146] With a handle, he killed 100 men.[147]
And after him Barak. He[148] killed Sisera and Jabin in the valley of Kishon.[149]
And after him Gideon. He saw the intelligent fleece,[150] when he was pounding the wheat in the threshing floor.[151] He chose his force by the drinking of water.[152] He also hid burning torches in jars,[153] and with 300 men, he smote 120,000 men.[154] He killed Oreb, Zeeb, Zēbēē, Zalmunna, and the others.[155]

25/ And after him, Abimelech,[156]
And after him was Tola,[157]
And after him was Jair. And he had 32 sons.[158]
And after him was Jepthah. He sacrificed his daughter to God and God was displeased.[159]

26/ And after him was Ibzan.[160] And he had 30 sons and 30 daughters.
And after him was Elon.[161]
And after him was Abdon the son of Hillel. And his sons were 40, and the sons of his sons (were) 30.[162]

---

146. The Armenian has a corrupt form, "Samēgarar."
147. Compare Judg 3:31.
148. According to the narrative in Judg 4:17–22 as well as the Song of Deborah (Judg 5:24–27), Jael and not Barak, killed Sisera.
149. Armenian = Kishon, see Judg 4:13. Armenian Abēn = Jabin, king of Canaan, concerning whose death see Judg 4:24.
150. See Judg 6:37–39. The fleece was "intelligent" or "intelligible" in that it provided a sign according to God's will.
151. Judg 6:11. The biblical text speaks of a winepress rather than a threshing floor.
152. Judg 7:4–7.
153. Judg 7:16–21.
154. For three hundred, see Judg 7:6; for the numbers smitten, see Judg 8:10.
155. Judg 7:24–25 where Zēb = Zeeb; while Zēbēē = Zebah and Saɫmana = Zalmunna whom Gideon captured according to Judg 8:5–12.
156. Judg 8:29–9:56.
157. Tʻovɫa is Tola son of Puah, see Judg 10:1.
158. Yayir is Jair; according to Judg 10:3–4 he had thirty sons.
159. Judg 11:1, 34–40. God's displeasure is not explicit in the biblical text.
160. On Ibzan, see Judg 12:8–10. In the Armenian Bible he is "Esebon," following the LXX Εσεβων. Our text has "Hesebon."
161. Judg 12:11–12.
162. Judg 12:13–15. According to the LXX, the name of his father was Sellēm, but in the MT it is Hillel. In our text he is son of Ēllēkʻ, which is closer to MT. Arm Bible has the same as our document, while the Peshitta has hlyn. Conceivably the Armenian translator at some point read the Syriac final yn as a plural and so put an Armenian plural ending kʻ on hl. This would not

PART TWO 51

27/ After him was Samson son of Manoah.[163] He caught 300 foxes and tied torches to them and burnt the fields of the foreigners.[164] And with an ass's jaw, he smote thousands. And he brought forth water from[165] that same jaw and drank (it).[166] And he put the locked gate of the city on his shoulder and took it forth to the top of the mountain.[167]

28/ And after him was Eli the priest, and then Samuel, and king Saul,[168] and other(s) in their order until the Exile.

29/ And after the Exile, priests ruled the people, for the Jews had three orders of authority. First, judges down to Saul; second, kings up to Zerubbabel and Joshua the priest.

30/ And from that point priests up to Jesus Christ, true saviour. And there anointed rulers ended, when Christ, the true Anointed One appeared.

2.6. Concerning the Knowledge of the Times

This text occurs in M10320, fols. 84v–86v. The manuscript in a *Miscellany* of the seventeenth century (Eganyan et al. 1970, 2:1092). A marginal ornament and a line of red script mark the text's beginning. The list has two parts. The first runs from Adam to Christ, and the second deals with the period from Mohammed on. According to §12, the composition was written in AE 851 which is 1402 CE.

It should be observed that a clear seam occurs in §9. Not only is a different word used for "year" from that point on,[169] but the author also departs from the strict formulaic genealogy of the preceding sections and uses a narrative style. This seems to suggest that he took the passage from §1 and up to the first part of §9 from a preexisting list, earlier than the fifteenth century, and the second part is, perhaps, his own addition.

---

be the only case where the Armenian Bible preserves a Syriac form of a name, rather than the Greek, which is usually dominant.
163. Armenian Manuē = Manoah, see Judg 13:24.
164. Judg 15:4–5.
165. Or "with," taking the ablative in an agentive meaning.
166. Judg 15:15–19; that the water flowed from or by means of the jawbone is one possible exegetical inference from Judg 15:19. Another reading might refer to a place name *Leḥi* (compare the LXX with the Targum for these two readings.)
167. Judg 16:3.
168. The stories about Eli the priest, Samuel and Saul are written in the book of Samuel.
169. See note 196 below.

Text

1/ / fol. 84v / Վասն Ժամանակաց Գիտելոյ զոր ընենեն
2/ Ադամա մինչեւ ի ջրհեղեղ են ամք ՍՄԻԳ, որք են ժամանակք Ժ:
Սէթ, Ենովս, Կանայն, Մաղախիէլ,[170] Արետ, Ենովք, Մաթուսաղա, Ղամէք, Նոյ:
3/ Իսկ ի ջրհեղեղէն մինչեւ ի ծնունդն Աբրահամու են ամք ՁԽԲ, որք են ժամանակ[171] Ժ, մարդու:
Սեմ, Արփաքսա/ fol. 85r/թ, Կայնան, Սաղդայ: Եբեր: Փաղեկ. Ռագաւ, Սերուք, Նաքովր, Թարայ, Աբրահամ:
4/ Իսկ ի յԱբ<ր>ահամէ[172] մինչեւ ի Մովսէս. եւ ելանելն եգիպտոսի են ամք ՇԷ, որք են ժանամակք է մարդոյ՝
Աբրահամ, Իսահակ, Յակոբ, Ղեւի, Կահաթ, Ամրամ, Մովսէս.
5/ Իսկ ի Մովսեէէ մինչեւ ի Սողոմոնի Դ ամ. եւ ի տաճարին շինութիւն ՆՁ,[173] որք են ժամանակք է մարդոյ՝
Նայասեն. Սաղդայ, Բոյոս, Յովբէթ. Յեսսէ. Դաւիթ մարգարէ, Սողոմոն:
6/ Իսկ ի Սողոմոնէ մինչեւ ի նորոգել տաճարին ի Զորաքաբելէ են ամք ՇԺԲ որ ժամանակա ԺԲ մարդոյ է.
Ռոբովամ, Աբիայ, Ասափ, Յովս/ fol. 85v/այթափի,[174] Յովրամ, Ոզիայ, Յովայթամ, Յեքոնիա:
7/ Իսկ ի գերութենէն մինչեւ ի ծնունդն Քրիստոսի: ամք ՇԺԸ. որք են ժամանակք ԹԺ. մարդոյ:
Սաղաթիայ, Զարաբաբել, Աբիութ, Եղիակիմ, Ազովրն, Սաղովկ, Աքին, Եղիուդ, Եղիազար, Մատթան, Յակոբ, Յովսէփի:
8/ Արդ զամենայն եւ լինի յԱդամայ մինչեւ ի Քրիստոս. ամք ՐՃՂԸ:
Իսկ ի Քրիստոսի մկրտութենէ մինչեւ ի Կոստանդինոսի հաւատալն. են ամք Յ.
9/ Ի Քրիստոսէ մինչեւ ի հայ թուականն են ամք[175] ՇԾԴ:
ի Քրիստոսէ մինչեւ յերեւել սուտ մարգարէին, Մահմետին. են ամք ՈԺԳ. Եւ ի Մահմետ/ fol. 86r /է ի մեզ ՉՂԱ տարի.

---

170. On this spelling see Stone and Hillel, "Index," no. 317.
171. ժամանակք would be expected, see part 3, note 36 below.
172. Correction mark over the second ր, which has been emended to ր.
173. Probably the word ամք has been lost.
174. This is taken as Jehosaphat, with a transposition of the last two consonants.
175. Ամք was written first, and then an erasure mark placed over ք.

10/ Եւ այն որ այլազգիք Պ ասեն եւ այլ օելի, սուտ են զի պակաս
 հաշուին. {նք}¹⁷⁶ քան զի նռպայ գտարին ՅՕՂ որ համարին, զի
 լուսնոյ տարին է. իսկ մեք. տարի զարեգականն օրն հաշուինք.
 որ է ՅԿԵ օր որ ժ{Պ}¹⁷⁷ որ օելի քան զՏաճիկներուն,¹⁷⁸ զի
 լուսնին տարին ՅՕՂ օր է: Վասն այն նոցա հաշուովս օելի¹⁷⁹
 գայ. Եւ մերս պակաս:
11/ Արդ ժողովեա յԱդամայ մինչեւ ի մեզ ամք ՅՈՂ. Իսկ այս որ
 ասացի թուի թէ պակաս է ի կատարեալ համարեն:
12/ Չի թարքմանիշքն, ի յԱդամայ մինչեւ ի Հայ թվականն ճումլա
 ՐՋԶՋ տարի ասեն: Եւ Հայ թուական հիմա ՊՕԱ է, ի վերայ
 աձ լինի յԱդամայ մինչեւ ի մեզ գՊԻՂ տարի.
13/ Եւ այս աւելի¹⁸⁰ վասն այն է: / fol. 86v / որ Ջհուտն ի տարին.
 Օ<Բ>.¹⁸¹ աւր պակաս կու բռնէ. Այսինքն ի շաբաթին Ա օր.
 վասն զի շաբաթ օրն Աստուծոյ էր անուած քան¹⁸² մարդոյ
 աւուրք չհին հաշուիլ. եւ ասի համարով, ՄԻԲ տարի պակաս է
 նոցա հաշիւնքն. զթարգմանացն. եւ Քրիստոս փարք: Այսքան
 վասն ժամանակաց:

Translation

1/ The Knowledge of Times which are examined:¹⁸³
2/ From Adam up to the flood are 2,223 years which are ten generations,¹⁸⁴
 Seth, Enosh, Kenan (Kaynan), Mahalalel (Malaxiēl), (J)ared, Enoch,
 Methusaleh, Lamech, Noah.
3/ Then, from the flood up to the birth of Abraham are 942 years, which
 are ten human generations.¹⁸⁵
 Shem, Arpachshad, Kenan (Kaynan),¹⁸⁶ Shelah, Eber, Peleg, Reu,
 Serug, Nahor, Terah, Abraham.

---

176. Ք surmounted by erasure mark.
177. See note 197.
178. Postclassical form.
179. լ above line.
180. Correction mark above this word.
181. See note 197.
182. Taking զան as զայն.
183. The verb is actually an impersonal 3rd pers. pl.
184. Literally: times, and so in §§2–7. In text 2.7 the word ազգ is used for "generation."
185. Compare Matt 1:17, which served the author, since he has Kenan (Kaynan), who is not found in Hebrew Genesis.
186. Not in Gen 11 and it makes an eleventh name. Perhaps comparable with Kenan (Kaynan),

4/ Then, from Abraham up to Moses and the exodus of Egypt are 507 years, which are seven human generations.
Abraham, Isaac, Jacob, Levi, Kohath, Amram, Moses.

5/ Thence from Moses to the fourth year of Solomon and to the building of the temple (were) 480 years,[187] which are seven human generations. Nachshon, Shelah, Boaz, Joad, Jesse, the prophet David, Solomon.[188]

6/ Then, from Solomon up to the renewal of the temple by Zerubbabel are 512 years, which are 12 human generations.
Rehoboam, Abijah, Asaph (Asa), Jehosaphat,[189] Jehoram,[190] Uzziah, Jotham, Jechoniah.[191]

7/ Then, from the Exile up to the birth of Christ is 518 years, which are 12 human generations: Sałat‘iay,[192] Zerubbabel, Abiud, Eliakim, Azor, Zadok, Achin, Eliud, Eleazar, Matthan, Jacob, Joseph.[193]

8/ Now all the years from Adam to the birth of Christ were 5,198.[194]
Then, from Christ's baptism up to the conversion of Constantine is 300 years

9/ From Christ up to the Armenian era is 554 years.[195]
From Christ up to the appearance of the false prophet Mohammed is 613 years, and from Mohammed to us is 791 years.[196]

---

fourth from Adam in above lists. The genealogy in Luke has Kenan (Kaynan) or Cainan (Luke 3:36) as son of Arpachshad as does Jub. 8:1.

187. See 1 Kgs 6:1.

188. Although twelve generations are mentioned, only seven names occur in the following list.

189. The Armenian is apocopated, reading Jōasayt‘ap‘, with transposition of the last two consonants. The text gives the preceding name as Asaph, but it should be Asa. The best-known Asaph was a reputed author of Psalms, and other individuals of this name occur in the Hebrew Bible. On the psalmist Asaph, see the work published below 4.11 Story of the Prophet Asaph.

190. Armenian: Yovram.

191. This is likely Jechoniah, father of Salathiel (Matt 1:12). The following names down to Achin are taken from Matt 1. As in §6 above, all twelve names are not listed, but only eight.

192. This should be Սաղաթիէլ "Salathiel."

193. The text speaks of twelve generations and it follows Matt 1 exactly.

194. The total here agrees with 2.2 §10; Stone 1982, 82–83, and Adam and His Grandsons §23 (Stone 1996a, 99). Thus this figure is quite widespread in Armenian texts. Other totals are found elsewhere: 2.2 §15 polemicizes against a number of 5,420; 4.4 §48 has 5,138. In the Acts of Pilate Latin A, chap. 12, the figure is 5,430 or 5,500.

195. This is usually reckoned at 551. Compare part 2, note 78 above.

196. This means that the author lived in 613 + 791 years after Christ, i.e., 1404. If this is calculated from Christ's birth that is the date. If it is calculated from Christ's baptism, it would be somewhat earlier. The Hegira is usually set in 620 which + 791 yields 1411 CE. According to either calculation this document was composed in the early fifteenth century. Observe the use of

PART TWO   55

10/ And that the Muslims say it is 800 (i.e., instead of 791) and even more, is false, for their calculation is short, because they reckon the year to 354 days, for it is a lunar year, while we reckon the year by the solar day, which is 365 days, which is 1<2>[197] days more than that of the Muslims. For the lunar year is 354 days. For that reason by their reckoning there are[198] more (i.e., years), and by ours, less.

11/ Now, altogether[199] from Adam up to us is 6,604 years. But this which I said seems to be less than the perfect reckoning.

12/ For the Translators say (that) from Adam up to the Armenian era is altogether 5,976 years. And the Armenian date now is 851. Add to the total from Adam to us the 824 is 6,824 years.

13/ And what is more, because the Jews have 52 days less in their year, that is one day a week,[200] because the Sabbath days was called God's they are not reckoned as human days,[201] their reckoning I also said (to be) short by 222 years by their reckoning. Glory to Christ and the translators.

Thus much concerning the times.

2.7. History of the Forefathers to Abraham and Their Years

This text, like the preceding, gives lifespans and generations of the various patriarchs from Adam to Abraham. It is included in a manuscript of Grigor Tat'ewac'i's Book of Sermons, M2182 on fols. 347r–349v. The manuscript was copied in 1674 (Tēr-Vardanean 2012, 7:339–44).

Throughout, spaces have been left for colored initials that were never entered. We do not note them. There are Armenian numerals in the outer margins, which we have replaced by Western numerals marking the sections. This text is, in fact an expansion on Gen 5:5–32, including some apocryphal

---

the word տարի for "year" from this point on, where ամ, which means the same, has been used exclusively down to this point.

197. An apparent confusion of the labials, b and p. We have emended the translation. The texts reads 10,800, which makes no sense.

198. Taking քայ as կայ.

199. Literally: gather together.

200. I.e., not counting.

201. There seems to be no basis for this in Jewish tradition, and the Jewish calendar is lunar, with the basic year being 354 days, but it is adjusted to the solar year by intercalation. The word անուած is taken as deriving from անուանել "to name" and քան as a medieval spelling of քայն.

traditions. Overall, as one would expect, M2182 follows the Septuagint for ages and spans of life. However, there are many discrepancies between those totals that recur and, clearly, the calculation is corrupted. The names of the wives of the patriarchs are given in separate lists, ultimately going back to Jubilees.[202] In Stone 1996a, 90–91, a table is given of the names as they are found in five different sources. We do not remark on the variant forms of these names here.

M2182 seems to have utilized two sources: (1) Dominant is a Greek biblical text, which agrees with the LXX Vaticanus, as well as Eusebius's *Chronicle* on the dating from Adam to the flood and to the birth of Abraham; and (2) particularly in the generations from Shem to Abraham, it used a source with affinities to the Hebrew Bible. Moreover, §9 refers explicitly to two sources. The gross dates are calculated from the year of the flood, which is given in §12, and not by inner calculations of the years of the individual patriarchs. For example, Adam to Abraham is calculated by adding 942, the number of years from the flood (2,242) to Abraham equalling 3,184 (§24).

Table of Gross Dates

	M2182	LXX Vat.
Adam to flood	§12 2242	2242
Adam to Transfer of Enoch (birth of Methusaleh)	§8 1285	1287[a]
Adam to Abraham	§24 3184	3184

[a] The discrepancy is due to the common confusion between the numbers 5 and 7 in Armenian.

Table of Comparison of the Genealogy and Lifespans Following Gen 5[203]

Name	MT	LXX	M2182[a]
Adam	0–930	0–930	0–930
Seth	130–1042	230–1142	230–1142
Enosh	235–1140	435–1340	435–1340
Kenan	325–1235	625–1535	625–1535

---

202. See the discussion of the names of the antediluvian Patriarchs' wives in Stone 1996a, 89–91 and in VanderKam 1989, 31.

203. This table was prepared by Tomer Doitch. It was fine-tuned by Vered Hillel. I am indebted to their careful work. The figures are all calculated as *anno mundi*, i.e., year 1 is the year of creation of the world.

Mahalalel	395–1290	795–1690	795–1690[b]
Jared	460–1422	960–1922	960–1922
Enoch	622–987	1122–1487	1122–1487[c]
Methusaleh	687–1656	1287–2256	1287–2256[d]
Lamech	874–1651	1454–2207	1454–2177[e]
Noah	1056–2006	1642–2592	1642–2592[f]
Shem, Ham, Japheth	1556–	2142–	2142
FLOOD	1656	2242	2242[g]

[a] *History of the Forefathers to Abraham and Their Years* M2182, fols. 347r–349v.
[b] There is a minor incompatibility in the text. Mahalalel begot Jared at 165 and lived for 730 years more, so in total his lifespan should be 895, yet the text has him dying at 897. This can again be explained by the common confusion between the numbers 5 and 7 in Armenian.
[c] Here as well, is an incompatibility in the text that can be explained by the confusion of 5 and 7. For clarification of the dates concerning Enoch, see note 215.
[d] Another instance of the confusion of the numbers 5 and 7.
[e] On the lifespan of Lamech, see note 220 below.
[f] Noah's lifespan is drawn from Gen 9:29.
[g] The date of the flood agrees with the LXX Vat. and Eusebius's *Chronicle*.

Table of Comparison of the Genealogy following Genesis 11

Name		Begot offspring at	Years lived after first offspring
Shem	MT	100	500
	LXX	100	500
	M2182	100	500
Arpachshad	MT	35	403
	LXX	135	430
	M2182	135	403
Kenan	MT	-	-
	LXX	130	330
	M2182	-	-
Sela	MT	30	403
	LXX	130	330
	M2182	130	406
Eber	MT	34	430
	LXX	134	370
	M2182	134	433
Peleg	MT	30	209
	LXX	130	209
	M2182	134	209

Reu	MT	32	207
	LXX	132	207
	M2182	135	207
Serug	MT	30	200
	LXX	130	200
	M2182	130	200
Nahor	MT	29	119
	LXX	79	129
	M2182	79	119
Terah	MT	70	135 (Gen 11:32)
	LXX	70	135 (Gen 11:32)
	M2182	70	135

Text

0/ / fol. 347r / Պատմութիւն Նախահարցն. մինչեւ gԱբրահամ եւ զամս նոցա:

1/ Նախ ...[204] Ադամ յելանելոյն ի դրախտէն. լեալ ամաց ՍԼ ծնանի զղՍէթ յետայէ կեայէ կնոջէ իւրմէ. եւ եկաց այլ եւս ամս Ձ եւ ծնանի այլ եւս ուստերս եւ դստերս, մինչեւ ի ՃԼԵ ամս Մադադիելի. եւ մեռանի ՋԼ ամաց:

2/ Սէթ լեալ ամաց ՄԵ ծնանի զԵնովս յԱզովրայ կնոջէ իւրմէ. եւ եկաց այլ եւս ամս ՁԷ, մինչեւ ի քսաներորդ ամն Ենովքայ, եւ ծնաւ ուստերս եւ դստերս. եւ մեռաւ ՋԺԲ ամաց:

3/ Ենովս լեալ ամաց ՃՂ ծնանի զԿայինան ի Նուենայ կնոջէ իւրմէ. եւ եկաց այլ եւս ամս ՉԺԵ մինչ ՕԳ ամս Մաթուսաղայի, եւ ծնաւ ուստերս եւ դստերս. եւ մեռաւ[205] ՋԵ ամաց:

4/ Կայինան լեալ ամաց ՃՀ ծնանի զՄադադիէլ ի Մադադեդա կնոջէ իւրմէ, եւ եկաց այլ եւս ամս ՉԽ, մինչեւ ի ութսուն Ա ամս Ղամեքայ. եւ ծնաւ ուստերս եւ դստերս. եւ մեռաւ ՋԺ ամաց:

5/ Մադադիէլ լեալ ամաց ՃԿԵ ծնանի զՅարետ ի Դինայ կնոջէ իւրմէ, եւ եկաց այլ եւս ամս ՁԼ մինչեւ / fol. 347v / ի ԽՐ ամս Նոյի. եւ ծնաւ ուստերս եւ դստերս. մեռաւ ՊՂԵ ամաց:

6/ Յարետ լեալ ամաց ՃԿԲ ծնանի զԵնովք ի Բառաքայ կնոջէ իւրմէ, եւ եկաց այլ եւս ամս Պ մինչեւ ի ՄՁ ամս Նոյի. եւ ծնաւ ուստերս եւ դստերս. եւ մեռաւ ՋԿԲ ամաց:

---

204. Illegible word, perhaps crossed out.
205. In margin p.m.: deletion in text.

7/ Ենովք լեալ ամաց ՃԿԵ ծնանի զՄաթուսաղա ի Յադներայ կնոջէ իւրմէ, եւ եկեաց այլ եւս ամս Մ, եւ հաճոյ եղեալ Աստուծոյ. փոխեցաւ ԼԳ ամին Ղամեքայ. ծնանելով ուրտերս եւ դստերս. եւ փոխեցաւ ՅԿԵ ամաց:
8/ Ժողովին յԱդամայ մինչեւ ի փոխիլն Ենովքայ ազգ Է ամք ՌՆՁԷ:
9/ Մաթուսաղայ լեալ ամաց ՃԿԵ ծնանի զՂամեք ի յեղնայ կնոջէ իւրմէ, եւ եկեաց այլ եւս ամս ՊԲ. ամայ անցանել զջրհեղեղաւն ամօք. ԺԴ որ զկենաց նորա թիւ յայտ առնէ: իսկ եթէ որպէս յայլ օրինակս կայ. բայց եկեաց այլ եւս ամս ՉՁԲ եւ ծնաւ ուստերս եւ դստերս. եւ մեռանի ՋԿԹ ամաց:
10/ Ղամեք լեալ ամաց ՃՁՑ ծնանի զՆոյ ի Բեդնայ կնոջէ իւրմէ, եւ եկաց այլ / fol. 348r / եւս ամս ՇԼՑ եւ ծնաւ ուստերս եւ դստերս. եւ յառաջագոյն քան հայր իւր զՄաթուսալա վաղճանեցաւ Ղամեք ի ՇԼԵ ամացն Նոյի ՉԻԳ. ամաց:
11/ Նոյ լեալ ամաց Ղ. ծնաւ զՍեմ զՔամ եւ զՅաբեդ ի Նոյեմզարայ կնոջէ իւրմէ, եւ եկաց այլ եւս ամս Ճ. եւ եկն ջրհեղեղն. եւ յետ ջրհեղեղին ամս ՅՌ. եւ մեռաւ. ՋՌ ամաց:
    Ժողովին ամք ի փոխմանէն Ենովքայ մինչեւ ցջրհեղեղն ամս. ՋՌԵ. եւ ազգ Գ.
12/ Իսկ յԱդամայ. ազգ Ժ եւ ամք ՇՄԽԲ է զիարդ յետ ջրհեղեղին գրեն. եւթանասունքն ի Սեմայ մինչեւ յառաջին ամս Աբրահամու:
13/ Սեմ լեալ ամաց Ճ. ծնանի զԱրփաքսադ յերկրորդ ամի յետ ջրհեղեղին, Ի Դիզայկղիքադայ կնոջէն իւրմէ, եւ եկաց այլ եւս ամս Շ. ծնաւ ուստերս եւ դստերս եւ մեռաւ Ո ամաց:
14/ Արփաքսադ լեալ ամաց ՃԼԵ ծնանի զՍադա Ի Յաաքուրիայ կնոջէ իւրմէ, եւ եկաց այլ եւս ամս ՆԳ. ծնանի ուստերս եւ դստերս. եւ մեռաւ ՇԼՑ ամաց: / fol. 348v /
15/ Սադայ լեալ ամաց ՃԼ ծնանի զեբեր ի Մուքայ կնոջէ իւրմէ, եւ եկաց այլ եւս ամս ՆՁ մինչէ է ամս Սերուքայ. ծնանի ուստերս եւ դստերս. եւ մեռաւ ՇԼՁ ամաց:
16/ Եբեր լեալ ամաց ՃԼԴ ծնանի զՓաղեկ ի Ջուքայ կնոջէ իւրմէ, եւ եկեաց այլ եւս ամս ՆԼԳ մինչէ ԼԸ ամս Նաքովրայ. եւ ծնաւ ուստերս եւ դստերս. եւ մեռաւ ՇԿԵ ամաց:
17/ Փաղեկ լեալ ամաց ՃԼԴ ծնանի զՌագաւ ի Ջիուրայ կնոջէ իւրմէ, եւ եկեաց այլ եւս ամս ՄԹ մինչէ ի Հե ամս Սերուքայ. եւ ծնաւ ուստերս եւ դստերս. եւ մեռաւ ՅԽԳ ամաց:

18/ Յալուր<ս>²⁰⁶ Փաղեկայ բաժանեցաւ երկիր զՓաղեկն բաժանիլ ասի. եւ սա առաջ քան զհայր իւր վաղճանի. առ սովաւ աշտարակին գործութիւն եղաւ եւ լեզուաց բաժանումն:
19/ Եւ գումարին ի ջրհեղեղէն մինչեւ ցաշտարակին ազգ Ե եւ ամք ՇԻԵ յԱդամայ ազգ ԺԵ եւ ամք ՎՁԿԷ:
20/ Իսկ յետ Փաղեկայ, Ռագաւ լեալ / fol. 349r / ամաց ՃԼԵ, ծնանի զՍերուք²⁰⁷ ի Սուրայ կնոջէ իւրմէ, եւ եկաց այլ եւս ամս ՄԷ մինչեւ ՀԷ ամս Նաքովրայ. ծնաւ ուստերս եւ դստերս. եւ մեռաւ ՅԻԲ ամաց:
21/ Սերուք լեալ ամաց ՃԼ, ծնաւ զՆաքովր ի Մեղքայ կնոջէ իւրմէ, եւ կեցեալ այլ եւս ամս Մ մինչեւ ՇԱ ամս Աբրահամու, ծնաւ ուստերս եւ դստերս. եւ մեռաւ ՅԼ ամաց.
22/ Նաքովր լեալ ամաց ՀԹ ծնանի զԹարայ ի Եսբքայ կնոջէ իւրմէ, եւ կեցեալ այլ եւս ամս ՃԺԹ մինչեւ ի ԽԹ ամս Աբրահամու, ծնաւ ուստերս եւ դստերս. եւ մեռաւ ՃՂՇ ամաց:
23/ Թարայ լեալ ամաց Հ ծնաւ զԱբրահամ յԵղնայ կնոջէ իւրմէ, եւ կեցեալ մինչեւ ԼԵ ամս Իսահակայ, այլ եւս ամս ՃԼԵ. եւ ծնաւ ուստերս եւ դստերս. եւ մեռաւ ՄԵ ամաց:/ fol. 349v /
24/ Ժողովին ամք ի ջրհեղեղէն մինչեւ յառաջին ամս Աբրահամու ՋԽԲ եւ ազգու Թ. իսկ յԱդամայ ազգու ԺԲ, եւ ամս ՎՃՁԴ:
25/ Աբրահամ լեալ ամաց ՀԵ, երեւի նմայ Աստուած եւ ասէ́. ել յերկրէ քումմէ: Որով եկեալ բնակեցաւ ի Խառան եւ անդի պանդրխտեցաւ ի քանանացւոց²⁰⁸ երկրի: Եւ ՁՁ ամաց լեալ ծնանի զԻսմայէլ ի Հագարայ, եւ զԹ ամաց լեալ թլփատի ինքն, եւ ամենայն ընտանոծին արուք ի տան իւրոյ. եւ Ճ ամաց լեալ ծնանի զԻսահակ. Իսահակ լեալ ամաց Կ. ծնանի զՅեսու. եւ զՅակոբ:
26/ Այս ըստ եօթնասնից թարգմանութեան:

Translation

0/ The Story of the Forefathers down to Abraham and their Years.
1/ First…²⁰⁹ Adam at the going forth from the Garden was 230 years

---

206. This is emended to յալուրս, a plural locative.
207. Unclear sign follows q.
208. Sic.
209. Illegible word, perhaps crossed out.

old.[210] He begot Seth from his wife, Eve.[211] And he lived another 700 years and he begot more sons and daughters, up to the 135th year of Mahalalel.[212] And he died at 930 years.

2/ Seth at 205 years begot Enosh from Azovra his wife. And he lived another 707 years, up to the twentieth year of Enoch, and he begot sons and daughters. And he died at 912 years.

3/ Enosh, being 190 years old begot Kenan (Kaynan) from Nuena[213] his wife. And he lived another 715 years until the 53rd year of Methusaleh. And he begot sons and daughters and died at 905 years.

4/ Kenan (Kaynan), being 170[214] years old begot Mahalalel from Małałeda his wife. And he lived another 740 years until the eighty first year of Lamech. And he begot sons and daughters and died at 910 years.

5/ Mahalalel, being 165 years old begot Jared from Dina his wife. And he lived another 730 years, until the 48th year of Noah. And he begot sons and daughters and died at 897 years.

6/ Jared, being 162 years old begot Enoch from Barakʻa his wife. And he lived another 800 years, until the 280th year of Noah. And he begot sons and daughters and died at 962 years.

7/ Enoch, being 167 years old begot Methusaleh from Yadnera[215] his wife. And he lived another 200 years and was pleasing to God. And he was transferred at 365 years.

8/ Altogether from Adam to the transfer of Enoch were seven generations and 1,285 years.[216]

9/ Methusaleh, being 165 years old begot Lamech from Edna his wife.

---

210. The Bible does not mention the year in which Adam and Eve were cast out of the Garden. Compare with Jub. 3, which has Adam and Eve being cast out after seven years. The statement that Adam begot Seth in AM 230 agrees with LXX rather than MT. This seems to be the case for most of the rest of the text as well.

211. The genealogical list in Gen 5 does not contain the names of the forefathers' wives or mothers, except in the case of Eve, of whom Gen 4:25 says she is the mother of Seth. Footnotes on the names of the wives were added only where there is notable information available. For more on this subject see Lipscomb 1978, 149–63.

212. In Armenian Małałiēl. This paradigm of "He lived another XXX years, up to the XXX year of XXX" repeats throughout the Armenian text and does not appear in the Bible. It seems to be based on calculations from the biblical information and the text itself.

213. Nuena is to be identified as Noam, the wife (and sister) of Enosh, according to Jub. 4:13. This is a variant of the Armenian form of the name, see Stone 1966, 90–91 for details.

214. See Jub. 4:14 for a variant of Kenan (Kaynan)'s wife's name.

215. The name was Edni in Jub. 4:27. Armenian "Yadnera" is a variant of the same.

216. The number 1,285 refers to the sum of years from Adam to the birth of Methusaleh, not to the transfer of Enoch.

And he lived another 802 years. From this, he passed beyond the flood by 14 years,[217] which the number of his life makes evident. But if it is as in the other copy,[218] he still lived another 782 years. And he begot sons and daughters and he died at 969 years.

10/ Lamech, being 188 years old begot Noah from Bedna his wife. And he lived another 535 years, and he begot sons and daughters. And Lamech died 535 years[219] before his father Methusaleh, in Noah's 723rd year.[220]

11/ Noah, being 500 years old begot Shem, Ham, and Japheth from Noyem Zara[221] his wife. And he lived another 100 years and the flood came, and after the flood <he lived> for 350 years and died at 950 years.

Taken together the years from the translation of Enoch up to the flood numbered 755 and three generations.

12/ So it was ten generations and 2,242 years from Adam just as the Septuagint wrote. After the flood, from Shem up to Abraham's first year—

13/ Shem, being 100 years old begot Arpachshad[222] in the second year after the flood, from Dizeykłibad(a)[223] his wife. And he lived another 500 years and he begot sons and daughters and died at 600 years.

14/ Arpachshad,[224] being 135 years old begot Sela from Ysaburia[225] his wife. And he lived another 403 years.[226] He begot sons and daughters and died at 538 years.

---

217. This number does not fit the chronological calculations of the individual patriarchs within the text. However, it does fit the statement in §12, that there were 2,242 years from Adam to the flood.

218. It seems that the author used two sources in writing this text, which might explain a number of the errors and peculiarities in its calculations.

219. This is the first of many numbers given in M2182 that do not accord with calculations within the text, nor with any known source. Where such instances occur, they are briefly noted.

220. The 723 years is actually the total number of years Lamech's lifespan.

221. Noah's wife's name is not mentioned in Genesis, nor does any similar name occur in the Hebrew Bible. Yet in Jub. 4:33 Noah's wife is named Emzara and she is named Amzara in Genesis Apocryphon (1Q20) 6:7. In rabbinic literature she is named Naama and she is commonly recognized as the daughter of Methuselah: see Gen. Rab. 23.3 (Theodor-Albeck 224) on Gen 4:22. Armenian might combine these two traditions: see Stone 1996a, 89–91.

222. See Gen 7:10, 11:10 and 9:24. offspring.

223. According to Jubilees her name was Sedeqtelebab (7:16).

224. According to Jub. 8:1, Arpachshad's son Kenan (Kaynan) was born in AM 1375 and according to Jub. 8:5 Kenan (Kaynan)'s son Sela was born in AM 1432, when Arpachshad was sixty-four years old.

225. Rasueya according to Jub. 8:1.

226. M2182 follows the chronology of the primary source for Arpachshad's age at the birth of his son, but seems to follow the secondary source in the length of years he lived after his son's birth.

PART TWO 63

15/ Sela, being 130 years old begot Eber from Mukʻa his wife. And he lived another 406 years, until the seventh year of Serug; he begot sons and daughters and died at 538 years.[227]

16/ Eber, being 134 years old begot Peleg from Zuba his wife. And he lived another 433 years, until the 38th year of Nahor and he begot sons and daughters. And he died at 567 years.

17/ Peleg, being 134 years old begot Reu from Ziura[228] his wife. And he lived another 209 years, until the 75th year of Serug. He begot sons and daughters and died at 343 years.

18/ In Peleg's days the earth was divided up. Peleg means "to be divided." [229] And he died before his father. In his time the work of the Tower took place and the division of the tongues.[230]

19/ And summed up, from the flood to the Tower were 5 generations and 525 years. From Adam it was 15 generations and 3,767 years.[231]

20/ Then, after Peleg, Reu being 135 years old, begot Serug from Sura his wife. And he lived another 207 years, until the 75th year of Serug. He begot sons and daughters and died at 342 years.

21/ Serug, being 130 years old begot Nahor from Milcah his wife. And he lived another 200 years, until the 51st year of Abraham. He begot sons and daughters and died at 342 years.

22/ Nahor, being 79 years old begot Terah from Iscah his wife.[232] And he lived another 119 years, until the 49th year of Abraham. He begot sons and daughters and died at 138 years.

23/ Terah, being 70 years old begot Abraham from Edna his wife. And he lived until the 35th year of Isaac, another 135 years. He begot sons and daughters and died at 205 years.

24/ The years from the flood up to the first year of Abraham total 942 and nine generations. But from Adam 12 generations and 3,184 years.

25/ When Abraham was 75 years old, God appeared to him and said, "Go forth from your land."[233] Through this he came and dwelt in Haran. And thence (he went and) sojourned in the land of the Canaanites.

---

227. The figures in our text are problematic. They may be an inaccurate conflation of the author's two sources.
228. In Jub. 10:18, the name is Loma.
229. The name Peleg is indeed derived from the Hebrew root with the meaning of "divided."
230. See Gen 11:3–9.
231. The total number of years from the flood to the Tower presented in our text does not agree with any known ancient source, nor with the inner calculations of the text itself.
232. According to Gen 11:29, Iscah was Nahor's daughter, and his wife was Milcah.
233. Gen 12:1.

And when he was 86 years old he begot Ishmael from Hagar,[234] and when he (Ishmael) was nine years old he (Abraham) circumcised himself and all the male domestics in his house.[235] And when he was 100 years old, he begot Isaac.[236] Isaac at the age of 60 begot Esau and Jacob.[237]

26/ This is according to the Septuagint translation.[238]

---

234. Gen 16:15.
235. Gen 17:11.
236. Gen 21:1-3.
237. Gen 25:25-26.
238. See the introductory remarks to this section.

Part Three: Angelological Texts

Armenian angelological texts focus around a limited number of themes. This is evident not only in the documents published here, but also from previously published documents. Although this volume presents a number of texts, they constitute only an illustrative sample. Therefore, here I shall not attempt either a synchronic or a diachronic presentation of angelology among the Armenians. Those are subjects deserving of a major monographic study.[1] My aim here is more modest: to give some examples of the extensive textual material that exists still in manuscripts. Naturally, one should remark, the study of angelology can barely, if at all, be studied in isolation from the magical, medical, and apotropaic ideas current among Armenian Christians. One focus of angelological texts is lists of angelic names, sometimes making explicit the domain over which each named angel has authority. Many of these lists bear the characters of "omnibus" lists of incantations. Such lists are found below in sections 3.1 from J1398 (*Miscellany*, seventeenth century), 3.3.3 from M537 (Lexicological, 1673), and M286 (Gospels, sixteenth century). See further J1130 (*Miscellany*, bolorgir), p. 240.[2] On the one hand, the angels and their functions form part of cosmological speculation and teaching. On the other, such knowledge usually serves apotropaic ends, designed to instruct in the use of angelic powers for beneficial purposes. There are numerous variants of the forms of the names included in such lists, variation in the names themselves, and in number of angels and archangels specified. Some such are illustrated in the following table:[3]

---

1. Much information is to be found in the following works, and the list is at best indicative: Feydit 1986; Loeff 2002; Stone, 1992, 147–57; Harutyunyan 2006; Stone 2006b, 427–35; Russell 2011, 5–47. Moreover, there exist printed apotropaic works, such as The Book of Cyprians, and many details are included in some manuscript catalogues, such as those of the Jerusalem Patriarchate, Chester Beatty Library, and others. These details are usually relevant to the amulet books and scrolls such as those described by Loeff and Russell, cited above.
2. See Bogharian 1971, 5:45; Stone 1992, 1996b.
3. The numbers preceding the names indicate their order in the source cited.

M2001B	M537	J1398
1 Michael	2 Michael	1 Michael
2 Gabriel	1 Gabriel	2 Gabriel
3 Uriel	5 Uriel	3 Nuriel
4 Zitʻayel		4 Zitʻayel
5 Raphael	3 Raphael	5 Raphael
6 Bovatʻael		6 Putʻayēl
7 Dakuel	6 Daksuel	7 Mdasayēl
	4 Anael	
	7 Barakʻael	
	8 Adoniel	
	9 Phanuel	

The first, third, and fourth columns are clearly variants of a single list. That list is also embedded in the nine-angels list of M537, the second column, which is influenced by lists of nine angelic classes, some of which we will discuss below in section 3.3, 5, 6, and 7.

The influence of the nine classes of angels enumerated by pseudo-Dionysius Areopagiticus is pervasive in the Armenian traditions. This is clear in the texts given below, enumerating the nine classes of angels.[4] In addition, as we shall see in the remarks on those texts, this organization of angels was also widespread in other Christian circles, being evident already in such Paleo-Christian works as Ascension of Isaiah and Testament of Adam. They are also specified in Cave of Treasures[5] and in Testament of Adam among many other works.[6]

Another dimension of Armenian angelographic lore is the story of the Fall of the Angels. This is an ancient and widespread theme, found as early as the prophet Isaiah chap. 14 and equally drawing on the famous passage on Gen 6:1–4.[7] This story recurs in the Armenian tradition, both in connection

---

4. See the discussion in the introductory remarks to texts 3.5, 3.6, and 3.7 below.
5. See Bauckham, Davila, and Panayotov 2013, 1:540. The list in Cave of Treasures specifies eight names of classes and adds one general class. This work does not exist in Armenian.
6. A similar but different list of the nine angelic classes is to be found in M2245, fols. 148r–148v.
7. On the generative character of these passages see Stone 2015, 342–57. This article does not pretend to exhaust this broad topic, but it provides current bibliography and discussion of the Genesis and Isaiah passages. See further the recent volume of essays: Harkins, Bautch, and Endres 2014.

with the Lucifer tradition in Isa 14:12–15 and the Sons of God tradition in Gen 6:1–4. The New Testament's texts about the fall of Lucifer and about the Dragon were also influential on the Armenians. Luke 10:18 reads: "I watched Satan fall from Heaven like a flash of lightning." The fall of Satanic figures, such as the Dragon is described in Rev 12:9: "The great dragon was thrown down, that ancient serpent, who is called the Devil and Satan, the deceiver of the whole world—he was thrown down to earth, and his angels were thrown down with him." This subject is discussed further in the introductory remarks to text nos. 3.2, 7, and 8 below.

3.1. Angelology Text 2

This text (see Stone 1992 and 2006b) was published first in Armenian in 1969 from p. 1 of J1398, a seventeenth-century *Miscellany* and for a second time, with an English translation, in 1992.[8] Here the published text has been collated against another copy found in M537 fol. 243v.[9] It provides information both about the names of the archangels and their apotropaic functions. Moreover, in addition to the list of seven archangels in §2, it lists other angels, specifying the realm over which each has authority.

Text

1/ / p. 1 / Անուանք սրբոց հրեշտակապետացն Աստուծոյ, զոր խնդրեաց յԱստուծոյ սուրբ եւ սքանչելագործ այրն Աստուծոյ, եպիսկոպոսն Գրիգորիոս, զի ցուցցէ նմա զկարգ սրբոց հրեշտակապետացն, եւ առաքեցաւ հրեշտակ ի Տէր,[10] եւ ասաց նմա իմաստութեամբ, եւ են այսրիկ:

2/ Միքայէլ, Գաբրիէլ, Նուրիէլ, Չիթայէլ, Ռափայէլ, Բութայէլ, Սդասայէլ:

3/ Սոքա են որ կան շուրջ զաթոռովն Աստուծոյ, եւ ունին իշխանութիւն ի ‹Տեառնէ› բժշկել զախտս մարդկան:

4/ Որ յիշեսցէ զմի յեւթանց հրեշտակապետացն, եղիցի ընդունելի առաջի Աստուծոյ խնդրուածք նորա, եւ փրկեսցէ

---

8. Bogharian 1969, 5:45 from J1398, p. 1; Stone 1992.
9. The sequential number in the text's title relates to its position in the series of angelological texts published in Stone 1992 and 2006b.
10. We read Տեառնէ as in M2001B.

Տէր զնա յաւուր յայնմիկ յամենայն նեղութենէ զինչ եւ ի վիշտ անկանիցի:
5/ Ջանուն Ռափայէլ հրշտակին յիշեսցէ, անվաաս ապրի ի նեղութենէն.
6/ Որ ի վերայ բնոյ ունի իշխանութիւն, Յովէլ է անուն հրեշտակ- ին. սա է ճրագն որ լուսատուրէ յերկրի զիաւատացեալս. սա զարթուցանէ զազգս մարդկան փառաբանութիւն Աստուծոյ. որ զզեցեալ ունի զսա ապրի ի խաւարային դիւացն:
7/ Որ ի վերայ ծովու եւ չուրց եւ գետոց ունի իշխանութիւն, Մեղքիսն¹¹ է անուն հրեշտակին: սա է որ ապրինեաց զաղբիւրս շրոց. սա է որ աստէ ճայն բարբառոյ. սա է որ էջն յերկնիցն եւ ապրինեաց զՅորդանան.
8/ Որ ի վերայ ցաւոց ունի իշխանութիւն, Հարգեղ կոչի անուն հրեշտակին: Յորժամ որք ի ցաւս հասանէն եւ ի նեղութիւն, եւ յիշեսցէ զանուն նորա, նոյն ժամայն յաղնակնութիւն հասցէ նմա:
9/ Որ ի վերայ մեղաւորացն է պահապան հրեշտակն՝ Ազարիէլ է անուն նորա: Որ զզեցեալ ունի զանուն նորա, ապրի ի մեղաց՝ եւ հասանէ ապաշխարութեան:
10/ Որ ի ջերման ունի իշխանութիւն, Սրայէլ է անուն նորա՝ որ յիշէ զանուն նորա ոչ մեծենա ի նա ջերմ:
11/ Որ մայրից եւ անտարից ունի իշխանութիւն, Սադամանոս է անուն նորա: Որ զնա ընդ անտառաս՝ եւ յիշէ զանուն նորա, ապրի ի թշնամեաց՝ յերեւելեաց եւ յաներեւութից: Քրիստոսի փառք յ[աւիտեանս]:

In M2001B the text continues with the following lines to the end of fol. 243v, but apparently a leaf has fallen out, for present fol. 244r starts with the middle of a calendarical text.

12 (M2001B) Որ ի վերա յաղթութեան ունի իշխանութիւն. Միքայէլ եւ Նաթանայէլ են անուանք նոցա: Սրա են որ յաղթեն թշնամն[

Apparatus

The lemma is from M537 and the variants are drawn from M2001B, 243r–243v for sections 1–11.

1 հրեշտակապետացն] հրեշտակացն |Աստուծոյ] om | սուրբ եւ

---

11. Perhaps a typographic error in Bogharian for Մելքիոն "Melk'ion."

սրանչելագործ]սրանչելագործնեւսուրբն|այրն—եպիսկոպոսն] om | Գրոգորիոս] Գրիգոր | զի — հրեշտակապետացն] om | Տէր] տեառնէ | իմաստութեամբ] ատուզութեամբ 2 Նուրիէլ] Ուրիէլ | Բութայէլ] Բովաթաէլ | Մդասայէլ] Դակիէլ 3 որ] որք | <տեառնէ>] տէր J1398 : cf. §1 4 որ1°] եւ ով որ | յեօթանց | հրեշտակապետացն] հրեշտակապետացս | Տէր զնա] ~ | Աստուած] om | նեղութեէ] փորձութեէ | անկանիցի — 5 qu-] illegible | անվ-] illegible 6 քրնոյ | սա] այս | ճրրագն | զազզս — դիւացն] ով յիշէ զանուն նորա "he who remembers his name" 7 ծովուն | ունի իշխանութիւն] precedes եւ չորոց | սա1°] սայ | սա էլ1° — qЗորդանան] om 8 Հարզեդ] Արզէլ | որ ի գաւս — նեղութիւնն] գաւ հասանի ումէք կամ նեղութիւն | յիշեցէ] յիշէ | յաղնականութիւն հասցէ նմա] հասանի յաղնութիւն նոցա 9 մեղաւորացն | միայնատրաց "solitaries" | զգեցեալ ունի] յիշէ | ապրի ի] եւ զրով առ ինքն պահէ՝ փրկի ի "and in writing keeps it with him is saved from" 10 ի] ի վերայ | Սռայէլ] Սուքայէլ Suk'ayēl | որ] որ որ | յիշէ] յիշեցէ 11 որ] որ ի վերայ | Սադմանիս Saḷmanis | նորա] հրեշտակին | ընդ1°] + մայրիս եւ ընդ | յաներեւելեաց եւ յաներեւելեաց] om : *the concluding doxology is omitted*

Translation

1/ The names of the holy archangels of God, which Bishop Gregory, the holy and wonderworking man of God,[12] besought of God, that he show him the rank of the holy archangels, and an angel was sent by God and wisely said (them) to him, and these are they.
2/ Michael, Gabriel, Nuriel, Zitʻayēl, Raphael, Butʻayēl, Mdasayēl.[13]
3/ These are those who stand around God's throne, and they have authority <from> God to heal the afflictions of humans.
4/ Whoever mentions one of the seven archangels, his requests will be acceptable before God, and the Lord will save him on that day from every affliction and suffering into which he will fall.

---

12. This refers, perhaps, to Gregory Thaumaturgus or "the Miracle-worker" and may be a translation of his attribute. He lived in the third century and was a student of Eusebius of Caesarea.
13. Instead of Mdasayēl, M2001B has Dakuēl, which may be compared with Daksuel in M537 in the list tabulated above.

5/ (When) he mentions the name of the angel Raphael, he will live unharmed by distress.
6/ The name of the angel who has authority over sleep is Yovēl. He is the lamp which illuminates the faithful on earth. He arouses the praise of God by the race of men. He who invokes him is saved from the dark demons.
7/ The name of the angel who has authority over sea and waters and rivers is Melkisn.[14] He is the one who blessed the springs of water. He it is who pronounces the sound of speech. He is the one who descended from the heavens and blessed the Jordan.[15]
8/ The name of the angel who has authority over pains is called Hargel. When someone has pains and distress and mentions his name, immediately help comes to him.[16]
9/ The angel who is guard over the sinners[17] has the name Azariel. He who invokes his name is saved from sin and achieves penitence.
10/ Sokʻayēl is the name of him who has authority over fever. Fever will not come near to him who mentions his name.
11/ Salamanos is the name of him who has authority over woods and forests. He who goes through forests and mentions his name will be saved from enemies visible and invisible. Eternal glory to Christ.
12/ M2001B: Michael and Natʻayēl are the names of those who have authority over success. They are those who overcome enem[

3.2. Names of the Angels

This is another, less elaborate form of the list of nine angels, which is also included in the table above.[18] This particular list appears in two Miscellanies, M268 of the year 1697 on fol. 312r and M537 of the year 1673 on fols. 230v–231r. This list also appears in Grigor Tatʻewacʻi's *Book of Questions* (Tatʻewacʻi 1993, 144) and it is quite possible that the manuscripts extracted it from that source. The text given below is taken from M537, fol. 312r. M286 is literatim identical with it in this short document. To each name an etymological explanation is added, thus rendering them in the onomastic form also current in

---

14. Or, perhaps, Melkʻion. He is called Elkʻos in 3.12 §10.
15. Apparently at the Baptism. This idea also appears in 3.12 §10.
16. Or: he comes to him for help, i.e., the angel to the suppliant.
17. For "sinners," M2001B has մխատորաց "solitaries" and that reading may be preferable.
18. See my introductory remarks, above.

Onomastica Sacra.[19] Such uses of etymologies are widespread and they even occur embedded in narrative texts.[20]

Text

1/ / fol. 230v / Վասն անուանց հրեշտակաց. հարց.
Քանի հրեշտակապետի անուն ասի եւ մեկնի:
Պատասխանի.
Առաջին Գաբրիէլ. որ է պատկեր Աստուծոյ:
5/ Երկրորդ: Միքայէլ. որպէս զԱստուած կամ հզօր:
Երրորդ.Ռափայէլ. բժշկութիւն:
Չորրորդ. Անայէլ. / 231r / լրումս Աստուծոյ:
Հինգերորդ. Ուրիէլ. տեսումս Աստուծոյ:
Վեցերորդ. Դակսուէլ. ինքն աստուածային:
10/ Եւթներորդ.[21] Բարաքայէլ. սկիզբն աստուածային:
Ութներորդ Ադոնիէլ. Տեառն իմոյ Աստուծոյ:
Իններորդ. Փանուէլ. յայտնութիւն Աստուծոյ.

Translation

1/ Concerning the name of angels. Question:
How many names of the archangels are spoken and interpreted?
Answer:
The first is Gabriel, which[22] is "image of God."
5/ Second – Michael, "like God" or "strong."[23]
Third – Raphael, "healing."
Fourth – Anayel, "God's fullness."[24]

---

19. On Armenian onomastic texts, see Wutz 1915 and Stone 1982. On the Armenian lexicographic tradition, see Amalyan 1975 and earlier, 1971.
20. See, e.g., below, Third Story of Joseph §54, 4.5. Short History of the Holy Forefathers.
21. In M268 the scribe started to write Ութներորդ, realized his error, and wrote Եւթներորդ over that word.
22. Or: who.
23. Presumably the explanation of Michael includes, by confusion, the explanation of Gabriel "strong." The explanation given for Gabriel has no basis in the meaning of the name but could definitely be given as the explanation of "Michael." Note that Gabriel precedes Michael, as occurs sometimes in Armenian documents. The reason for the present oddity is that the explanations of the first two names are transposed.
24. The basis of this interpretation is unclear.

Fifth – Uriel, "seeing of God."²⁵
Sixth – Daksiel, "his divine self."²⁶
10/ Seventh – Barakʻiel, "divine beginning."²⁷
Eighth – Adoniel, "of the Lord my God."
Ninth – Phanuel, "Revelation of God."²⁸

3.3. Question concerning the Archangels

This text, entitled in the manuscript Հարցումն հրեշտակից²⁹ Question (about) the Angels occurs in M2126, a *Miscellany* of 1697, fols. 96r–96v; in M2242, a seventeenth-century *Miscellany*, fol. 268v; and in M2245, a *Miscellany* of 1689, fols. 114v–115r. In M2126 Question about the Archangels is followed by a series of questions and answers on biblical topics that continue down to fol. 98v. In M2245 the pages following Question about the Archangels record questions about humans, Christ, etc. M2242 also follows this first question with more questions and answers, but I do not have images of the continuation of this manuscript at my disposal. We must regard the document as part of the extensive Armenian literature of questions and answers, which was particularly cultivated in educational or polemical contexts. Very many of such questions focus around problems arising in exegesis of the Bible.

In M2245, fol. 116r there occurs a question about the dwelling of the angels above the firmament, which is not found in the corresponding position in M2126 and M2242. Then there is a discussion of the Fall of Satan, which is also dealt with by Grigor of Tatʻew in *Book of Questions* (Tatʻewacʻi 1993, §1.3.7, 152–53). However, the present text does not occur in that great theological compendium and its section dedicated to the angelic fall commences, Ո՞րքան է անկումն սատանայի։ պատասխանի։ Չանկումն սատանայի երակի է իմանալ, "Of what measure is the fall of Satan? Answer: The fall of Satan is to be understood in three ways."

---

25. The basis of this interpretation is unclear, unless it comes from *ūr* "light" which was then associated with "seeing."
26. The basis of this interpretation is unclear. This name is usually found in such lists.
27. Presumably not taken from Hebrew *baraq* = "lightning" or *bērēk* = "blessing," but somewhat inaccurately from *bārāʾ* meaning "create."
28. Either derived exegetically from Gen 32:30 or, anyway, from "God's face." Alternatively, it could be taken as a hybrid Greek-Hebrew φαίνω + ʾel.
29. Sic.

The theme of the fall of angels occurs in different contexts.[30] One form of it derives ultimately from interpretation of Gen 6:1–4. The scholarly literature on this incident, which features already in texts from the third century BCE and from then on, is extensive. The third-century BCE source is the pseudepigraphon called 1 Enoch and the tradition developed extensively in other ancient extrabiblical works.[31] Its further growth may be traced throughout biblically influenced cultures, including the Armenian.[32]

In some Byzantine sources the incident is treated Euhemeristically and interpreted as the Cainite women seducing the Sethite men, who are called "sons of God."[33] This form of the tradition also occurs in Armenian, particularly in the Apocryphal Adam Books and see below in the text 4.5. Short History §§28–29 (see Lipscomb 1990).

The present text, like Grigor Tatʻewacʻi's *Book of Questions* mentioned above, draws upon a variant of the Fallen Angels tradition,[34] according to which Satan, an angel of highest rank, rebelled against God before creation of the world or in the wake of the creation of Adam and was expelled from heaven with his host. This tradition, with a biblical source in Isa 14:12–15, occurs in the Armenian version of the primary Adam book, known as *The Penitence of Adam*, which seems to be a quite early translation from Greek. It recurs in Armenian literature in a variety of contexts over the centuries.[35]

I have chosen to give a diplomatic edition of M2126 and record the variants of the other two manuscripts in a critical apparatus. In the apparatus, the manuscripts are designated by their shelf numbers. On occasion, one or both of the other manuscripts has a reading that is clear while that of M2126 is very difficult. When I consider such variants superior, I have introduced them into the text within pointed brackets. When M2126 can be construed, but nonetheless one or both of the other manuscripts seems to preserve a better reading, I have left M2126 in the text and added ": preferable" following the

---

30. See also the introductory remarks to this section.
31. See Nickelsburg 2001, 165–73; a most recent collection of studies is Harkins et al. 2014. See also Stone 2015.
32. The history of the Fall of the Angels in later traditions is traced by Reed 2005.
33. See Adler 1989, 113–16. For more instances of the Armenian reading of this, see, for example, *Sermon concerning the Flood* (Stone 1996a, §§2–6, 176–78), *Question* (§§4–6, 119–20), and *The Sethites and the Cainites* (§§10–11, 205–6). Further details are to be found in the notes to these passages in Stone 1996.
34. On this general taxonomy of the Angelic Fall traditions, see Stone 2015 and see further Anderson 2000, 83–110.
35. Stone 2013. See particularly the appendix, "Satan and the Serpent."

variant. This brief document has been designated, following the manuscripts, Question about the Archangels.

Text

0/ Հարցումն հրեշտակապետից.
1/ / fol. 96r / Զինչ պատճառ է որ հրեշտակք³⁶ մեղանչեցին. Աստուած զմարդն փրկեաց հրեշտակն ոչ. Պատասխանի. Նախ վասն զի հրեշտակք յորժամ ըստեղծան յակաւն թօթափելն. ճանաչեցին զփառսն իւրեանց եւ զԱստուած. թէ որպէս է մեծ եւ ամենայկարող. յայնժամ առանց միջնորդի, յապրստամբեցան յԱստուծոյ որ ոչ ով չխափիեաց զնուա.
2/ Եւ մարդն յորժամ ըստեղծաւ. ոչ շանաչեաց³⁷ զինքն. եւ իմացաւ <հաստատ թէ> վասն այս մեղացս արտաքսէ <զիս> Աստուած. եւ միջնորդ եղեւ օձն եւ կինն եւ խափեցին:
3/ վասն այն պարտ էր մարդոյն փրկիլ. զի բազում պատճառ ունէր խափէութեանն. եւ հրեշտակք ոչ զոք ունէին պատճառ. ոչ <qoծ>³⁸ եւ կին. այլ ինքն ընդ ինքն ապըստամբեցաւ Աստուծոյ.
4/ երկրորդ պատճառ. վասն զի մարդկային սեռս մի մարդ էր ըստեղծեալ. թէ ոչ փրկեալ, բնութիւնն³⁹ եւ բազում խափանեալ էր. բայց հրեշտակաց սեռն բոլոր ըստեղծեալ էր. թէ կէսն անկաւ կէսն մացին վասն այն հրեշտակք ոչ փրկեցան:

Variants

0/ Հարցումն] + է վասն 2242 | հրեշտակապետից] հրեշտակաց 2242 հրեշտակ 2245
1/ հրեշտակք] հրեշտակ 2242 2245 | հրեշտակն] զհրեշտակն 2242 զհրեշտակ 2245 | հրեշտակք 2°] հրեշտակ 2242 զհրեշտակացն 2245 | զփառսն] զփառատրութիւն 2242 2245 | մեծ եւ] մեծ | ամենայկարող] ամենակարող 2242 2245 | յապըստամբեցան]

---

36. On the common phonetic variant կք > կ, see Stone 1990b, 11–12 and Stone and Hillel, "Index," no. 333. The same variant recurs below.
37. For this phonetic variant, շ/ճ see Stone and Hillel, "Index," no. 437.
38. For this phonetic variant oծ/og, see Stone and Hillel, "Index," no. 408.
39. This phrase is somewhat unclear. The word բնութիւնն means "nature," but in medieval texts may also mean "body."

ապստամբեցան 2242 ապրստամբեցան 2245 | ով] ով որ 2245 |
չխափեաց] չի խափեաց 2242 2245 : preferable
2/ չանաչեաց] ճանաչեաց 2242 2245 : preferable | <հաստատ թէ>]
հաստատութեան 2216 : corrupt | <qհu>] omit 2216 | խափեցին
] + զնա 2242
3/ խափէութեանն] խաբէութեան 2242 2245 | հրէշտակք]
հրէշտակ 2242 | <qoծ>] 2242 2245 qog 2216 : corrupt | եւ կին]
եւ ոչ կին 2242 | ապրստամբեցաւ] ապստամբեցաւ 2242 2245 |
Աստուծոյ] յԱստուծոյ 2242 2245
4/ պատճառ] պատճառն 2242 | սեռս] սեռս 2242 2245 | բազում]
բազումք 2245 | սեռն] սեռն 2242 սեռս 2245 | ստեղծեալ 2242 |
հրէշտակք] հրէշտակս 2242

Translation

0/ Question about[40] Archangels
1/ What reason is there that the archangels sinned (and that) God saved the human and not the angel? First, because the angels, when they were created in the blink of an eye recognized their glory and God, how great He is and omnipotent. Then, without an intermediary, they rebelled against God, they whom no one deceived.
2/ And man, when he was created did not recognize himself and he discerned <that, "It is certain> that on account of this sin God is expelling <me>." And the serpent was the intermediary, and the woman, and they deceived (i.e., him).
3/ For this reason it was necessary for man to be saved. For he had many excuses[41] for being deceived. And the angels did not have any one as an excuse,[42] not the serpent and not a woman. But they rebelled against God on their own.
4/ A second reason: because humankind was created as one man. If he were not saved, nature and many (people) also would have been prevented (from coming into being), but angelic kind were all created. If half fell, half remained. Because of that the angels were not saved.

---

40. M2242 has "It is a question about the angels;"
41. Or: reasons.
42. Or: cause. This is a reference to Gen 3:12–13.

3.4. Concerning the Renewal of the Angelic Destruction

This brief text occurs in M5690, fols. 1r–1v. A mention of Augustine is found as well as two citations from "Albert," probably Albertus Magnus. I have not been able to locate them precisely. The manuscript was copied in the nineteenth century and contains writings of Andreas of Cappadocia.[43] It relates to two aspects of angelology. It is presumably of Armenian Catholic origin.

Text

0/ յաղագս նորոգման հրեշտակային կործանման
1/ Կործանումն հրեշտակաց նորոգեցի փրկեցելովքն:
2/ Եւ Օգոստինոս ասէ թէ այնքան մարդիկք փրկեցին. որչափ անկեալք են դեւքն: Իսկ Գրիգոր ասէ. այնքանք փրկեցին որքանք հրեշտակք մնացին:
3/ Նա եւ ումանք ասացին թէ երկու որմունք լինիցին յերկինս. մինն մարդկան. եւ միւսն հրեշտակաց. իսկ կործանումն հրեշտակաց նորոգեցի կուսանօր:
4/ Եւ ի մի որմս այսպէս մարդկանց փրկելոց այնքանք լինիցին. որքան են հրեշտակք. եւ կուսանք ի միւս կողմս[44] Ալպերթ երկրորդ գիրք ԻԴ գլուխ:
5/ Դաս հրեշտակաց են ինն: իւրաքանչիւր դաս ունի զիւրաքանչիւր գունդ արդ՝ մի գունդն հրեշտակաց ունի զմիութիւն 6666.[45] իսկ այնքան են՝ ի յիւրաքանչիւրս դասս գունդք. որքան միութիւնք են յիւրաքանչիւր գունդս. Ալբերթ երկրորդ գիրք ԻԳ գլուխ.

Translation

0/ Concerning the Renewal of the Angelic Destruction
1/ The destruction of angels will be renewed by saved ones.[46]
2/ And Augustine says that as many humans will be saved as demons

---

43. Eganyan et al. 1970, 2:165.
44. Written over another word.
45. Note the Western numerals in the text. It is, of course, a very late manuscript.
46. That is, redeemed humans will make up the full complement of angels, in the place of those who fell.

(that) fell. But Grigor[47] says (that) as many will be saved as angels remained.

3/ Behold, some said that there will be two walls in heaven,[48] one for humans and the other for angels. But the perishing of angels will be renewed by virgins.[49]

4/ And in one wall there will be as many saved as there are angels, and as virgins in the other wall. Albert, book 2, chapter 24.

5/ The ranks of angels are nine. Each class has it own band. Now, one band of angels has 6666 units. Now, there are as many bands in each of these classes as there are units in each rank. Albert, book 2, chapter 24.

3.5. THE PRAISE OF THE ANGELS

This document deals with the praise pronounced by the angels in heaven. This picture of the angels ranked in heaven singing God's praises of is rooted in the heavenly visions of the prophet Isaiah (Isa 6), of Micaiah b. Imla (1 Kgs 22:19), and Daniel (Dan 7:10). It is greatly developed in Jewish and Christian apocalyptic literature, such as 1 En. 14:18–23 and Mart. Ascen. Isa. chaps. 9–10.

The present text, found M286, fols. 312r–313r, is composed of two parts. The first is an enumeration of the classes of angels, together with their praise, which in every case but one is a verse from the Bible. The verses are often apocopated at the end of the line, so the scribe can start each angelic class on a new line. The enumeration is drawn from Grigor Tat'ewac'i's list in *The Book of Questions* (Tat'ewac'i 1993, 144), which is itself drawn from Grigor's presentation of the *Celestial Hierarchy* of Ps. Dionysius. However, the order of the angelic classes is reversed and Ps. Dionysius does not set forth the verses pronounced by each angelic class. This reversed order also occurs in the second copy of the list, found in M537, fols. 231r–232r. We give the text of M286 and the variants occurring in M537 are in the apparatus. Differences in apocopation of biblical citations are not noted.

One segment of the text also appears in M682, another seventeenth-century *Miscellany* on fol. 7r, as part of a composite text titled, *Short Questions Selected and Assembled from Books*. The part parallel to *The Praise of the Angels* is reproduced below the text of M286.

---

47. Perhaps Tat'ewac'i.
48. Apparently "walls" refers to "enclosures."
49. The virgins will make up the numbers of the angels who fell.

The second part of the text is a list of nine classes of biblical holy leaders, concluding with the վարդապետք "the Doctors," the only ecclesiastical group mentioned. These are typologically correlated with the nine angelic classes. This correlation does not appear in Tatʻewacʻi's *Book of Questions* in the section associated with angelic praise.[50]

Text

1/ / fol. M268, 312r / Վասն փառաբանութեանց հրեշտակաց հայրց.
2/ Զի՞նչ է փառաբանութիւն թ. դասուց հրեշտակաց։
3/ Պատասխանի. Նախ եւ առաջին դաս, Աթոռոցն. եւ փառաբանութիւն է նոցա այն զի ասեն. Աթոռ քո Աստուած յաւիտեանս յաւիտենից։
4/ Երկրորդ դաս, Քերովբէիցն. եւ փառաբանութիւն է նոցա այն զի ասեն։ Ալիելաւ են փառք Տեառն ի տեղոջէ իւրմէ։ / fol. 312v /
5/ Երրորդ[51] դաս, {Քերովբէիցն}.[52] եւ փառաբանութիւն[53] է նոցա այն զի ասեն։ Սուրբ սուրբ սուրբ Տէր զօրութեանց. լի են երկինք եւ երկիր փառօք քո։
6/ Չորրորդ դաս, Տէրութեանցն. եւ փառաբանութիւն է[54] նոցա այն զի ասեն. Արքայութիւն քո արքայութիւն յաւիտենից. եւ տերութիւն քո ազգէ։[55]
7/ Հինգերորդ դաս, Զօրութեանց. եւ փառաբանութիւն է նոցա. այն զի ասեն։ Զի սուրբ[56] դու ես քահանայապետ յաւիտենից. եւ Տէր ընդ աջմէ քումէ։[57]
8/ Վեցերորդ դաս, Իշխանութեանցն. եւ փառաբանութիւն է

---

50. See further on the nine classes of angels in the introductory remarks to this section.
51. Երրորդ "third": the abbreviation mark has been omitted over this word.
52. Սերովբէիցն "of the Seraphs" in M537, correctly.
53. In the ending -ութիւն, which is abbreviated to -ութի, the թ and ի are ligatured, and this happens throughout the text.
54. է is written over another letter p.m.
55. Two variants from the Bible occur. First the Bible reads ամենայն "all" following the second occurrence of արքայութիւն "kingdom" and second, the two last words of the verse are omitted. They should be մինչեւ յազգ "to generations."
56. Սուրբ is above the line p.m.
57. Instead of this verse, M537 has Տացին քեզ հեթանոսք ի ժառանգութիւն քեզ. եւ իշխանութիւն (Ps 2:8). See further note 64 below.

նոցա. այն զի ասեն: Տէր հզօր զօրութեամբ իւրով. Տէր կարող ի պատերազմի:
9/ Եւթներորդ դասք, Պետութեանցն. եւ փառաբանութիւն[58] նոցա այն զի ասեն.[59] [այս՝ հինգերորդին է. միտք չէր վերայ] տացին քեզ հեթանոսք ի ժառանգութիւն քեզ. եւ իշխանութիւն:
10/ Ութերորդ դասք, Հրեշտակապետացն. եւ փառաբանութիւն է նոցա. այն զի ասեն: Ողորմեա դու ստեղծեր մի կորուսաներ. եւ զգործս ձեռաց [բոլ]:
11/ Իններորդ դասք հրեշտակացն, եւ փառաբանութիւն[60] է նոցա այն զի ասեն. զոր ասացին ի / fol. 213r / ծնունդն փրկչին. Փառք ի բարձունս Աստուծոյ[61]:
12/ Քահանայապետք. ի նմանութիւն Աթոռոցն:
13/ Արինադիրք. ի նմանութիւն Քերովբէիցն:
14/ Քահանայք. ի նմանութիւն Սերովբէիցն:
15/ Դատաւորք. ի նմանութիւն Տէրութեանցն:
16/ Թագաւորք. ի նմանութիւն Զօրութեանց:[62]
17/ Մարգարէք. ի նմանութիւն Իշխանութեանցն:
18/ Առաքեալք. ի նմանութիւն Պետութեանցն:
19/ Աւետարանիչք. ի նմանութիւն Հրեշտակապետացն:
20/ Վարդապետք. ի նմանութիւն Հրեշտակացն:

Translation

1/ Question: Concerning the praises of the angels:
2/ What is the praise of the nine classes of angels?
3/ Answer: The first class of all (is) of the Thrones. And their praise is that, that they say, "Your Throne, God, is forever and ever." [63]
4/ The second class (is) of the Cherubs. And their praise is that, that they say, "Blessed be the glory of God from his place."[64]

---

58. + է M537.
59. To end: Զի դու ես քահանայապետ յաւիտենից. եւ տէր ընդ աջմէ քումմէ, "For you are holy, eternal high priest and the Lord is at your right hand" Ps 110(109):1, 4–5 in M537. In M286 this verse is recited by the powers, see §7. However, this is an error that was noticed by the scribe, who wrote ք above the first word of the quotation in §7 and ա over the first word of the quotation in §9 to indicate the transposition.
60. փ over another letter, p.m.
61. M537 adds the rest of the verse: եւ երկիր խաղաղութիւն ի մարդիկ.
62. զօրութեանցն M537.
63. Ps 45:6(44:7) picking up the name of the angelic class Աթոռք "Thrones."
64. Ezek 3:12.

5/ The third class (is) of the {Cherubs}.⁶⁵ And their praise is that, that they say, "Holy, holy, holy is the Lord of Hosts. The heavens and the earth are full of your glory."⁶⁶

6/ The fourth class (is) of the Dominions. And their praise is that, that they say, "Your kingdom is an eternal kingdom and your dominion is from generation (to generation, i.e., forever.)"⁶⁷

7 The fifth class (is) of the Powers. And their praise is that, that they say, "For you are holy, eternal high priest, and the Lord is at your right hand."⁶⁸

8/ The sixth class (is) of the Princedoms. And their praise is that, that they say, "Lord, mighty through his power; Lord, victorious in war."⁶⁹

9/ The seventh class (is) of the Rulers. And their praise is that, that they say, [this belongs to the fifth (i.e., class); my mind was not on (it)]⁷⁰ "The gentiles were given to you as a heritage for you and princedom."⁷¹

10/ The eighth class (is) of the Archangels. And their praise is that, that they say, "Be merciful! You created, do not destroy the works of [your] hands."⁷²

---

65. This is erroneous as remarked in note 52 above. It should read "Seraphs."

66. The citation is from Isa 6:3. It differs from the text of Isaiah, however, and is in the form in which it occurs in the Liturgy. For լի է ամենայն երկիր "all the earth is full" it reads լի են երկինք եւ երկիր "the heavens and earth are full."

67. See note 79. The citation is of Ps 145(144):13. Observe the reprise of the word "dominion" in the selected verse.

68. The quotation is from Ps 110(109):4–5. It is adapted to the context here, however, by omission of a phrase, "after the order of Melchizedek" and by the substitution of "high priest" for "priest." The connection to "Powers" is through the phrase "at your right hand." This evokes Matt 26:64 and parallels, where the Son of Man is said to be seated, in the future, ընդ աջմէ զաւրութեանն "at the right hand of the Power." Compare also verses 1 and 5 of this psalm.

69. This is a quotation from Ps 24(23):8. For կարող here the Psalm has հզօր. The existence of this variant is not noted by Zohrab.

70. This is a scribal note, relating to the displacement of the verses mentioned above. The mark p.m. above ու of the word տուցին "were given" signals the start of the scribe's comment, which extends to վերայ. Following that word is a sign to mark the end of the insertion. Even if the adjustment implied by this insertion is made, the verses still do not accord with the names. The scribe has discovered the problem, but not the solution. The problem is that most of the verses cited do not evoke the name of the angelic class which pronounces them. The verse cited is from Ps 2:8, but is corrupted. The original reads տուց քեզ զհեթանոսս etc. "I will give you the gentiles, etc."

71. Ps 2:8.

72. Zech 1:12. The same quotation is set in the mouths of the nine classes of angels in Feydit, Text no. LX (pp. 214–15). The word png has been omitted at the end of this section, which is also the end of a line in the manuscript and is very crowded.

11/	The ninth class (is) of the angels. And their praise is that, that they say what they said on the birth of the Saviour, "Glory to God on high."[73]
12/	The high priests, in the likeness[74] of the Thrones.
13/	The lawgivers, in the likeness of the Cherubs.
14/	The priests, in the likeness of the Seraphs.
15/	The judges, in the likeness of the Dominions.
16/	The kings, in the likeness of Powers.
17/	The prophets, in the likeness of the Princedoms.
18/	The apostles, in the likeness of the Rulers.
19/	The evangelists, in the likeness of the Archangels.
20/	The doctors, in the likeness of the Angels.

3.6. The Ranks of the Angels

This text occurs in M266, a *Miscellany* of the seventeenth century, on fols. 90v–91r. It is intimately connected with the next document and notes on the main topics are given there. "Dionysius" is of course Pseudo-Dionysius whose writing about the angelic orders in the work entitled *Celestial Hierarchy* was very influential.

Text

1/	/ fol. 90v / Դիոնեսիոսի ասացեալ է. / fol. 91r / Առաջին դաս Հրեշտակաց որ են պատգամաւոր. եւ փառաբանութիւն է նոցա այս qop[75] առ հովիւսն ասեն Փառք:
2/	Երկրորդ դաս ի վերայ նոցա. Հրեշտակապետացն. եւ փառաբանութիւն է նոցա այն զոր Զաքարիա լուաւ թէ մինչեւ յերբ ոչ ողորմեցցիս Տէր:
3/	Երրորդ դաս ի վերայ Աթոռացն. եւ փառաբանութիւն է նոցա այս. աթոռ քո Աստուած յաւիտեանս յաւիտենից:
4/	Չորրորդ դաս ի վերայ նոցա Տէրութեանցն. եւ փառաբանութիւն (է նոցա). արքայութիւն քո արքայութիւն յաւիտեանս:
5/	Հինգերորդ դաս. Պետութեանցն. եւ փառաբանութիւն (է նոցա) քահանայութեան. դու ես քահանայ յաւիտեանս:

---

73. Luke 2:14.
74. "as the type of."
75. Read the relative pronoun որ, and not որ "might." For the variation of n/o, see Stone and Hillel, "Index," no. 408.

6/ Վեցերորդ դաս Զաւրութեանցն. եւ փառաբանութեամբ. Տէր hզաւր եւ կարող. ի պատերազմի:
7/ Եւթներրորդ դաս. Իշխանութեանցն. եւ փառաբանութիւն (է նոցա). տուան քեզ հեթանոսք ի ժառ[անգութիւն] իշխա[նութեան]:
8/ Ութերորդ դաս. Սերովբէիցն. Եւ փառաբանութիւն (է նոցա) երեք սրբենի զոր լուաւ Եսայի. երեքկին սրբասցութիւն.
9/ Իններորդ Քերովբէիցն. որ լսին վարք իմաստութեան Աստուծոյ, եւ փառաբանութիւն է նոցա. լի են երկինք եւ երկիր փառաւք նորա.

Translation

1/ Dionysius said that:
The first class (is) of the Angels who are messengers. And their praise is this, <that> to the shepherds they say, "Glory …"[76]
2/ The second class (is) above them, of the Archangels. And their praise is what Zechariah heard, "How long will you withhold mercy, O Lord."[77]
3/ The third class (is) above the Thrones. And their praise is this, "Your throne, God, is forever and ever."[78]
4/ The fourth class, the Dominions (is) above them. And (their) praise (is), "Your kingdom is an eternal kingdom."[79]
5/ The fifth class, is of the Principalities. And (their) praise (is) of the priesthood, "You are a priest forever."[80]
6/ The sixth class is of the Powers. And through their praise, "The Lord is mighty and powerful."[81]
7/ The seventh class is of the Princedoms. And (their) praise (is), "The nations are given to you as an inheritance of princedom."[82]
8/ The eighth class is of the Seraphs. And (their) praise (is) three sanctities[83] which Isaiah heard, a three-fold sanctification.[84]

---

76. Luke 2:14.
77. Zech 1:12.
78. Ps 45:6(44:7).
79. Ps 145(144):13.
80. Ps 110(109):4.
81. Ps 24(23):8.
82. Ps 2:8.
83. Probably a plural form, analogous to the Cilician Medieval plural in -նի and earlier -անի: see Karst 1901, §§237–244.
84. I.e., the Trishagion in Isa 6:3.

9/ The ninth (class) is of the Cherubs who heard the conduct of God's wisdom and their praise is, "The heavens and the earth are full of his glory."[85]

3.7. Questions concerning Angels

The texts published in this section deal with a series of issues about angels, incorporating also versions of texts discussed above. The document occurs in *Miscellany* M682 copied in 1679 on fols. 7r–8r. It is part of an elenchic composition and deals with a range of subjects found in Genesis, including the creation story. The text concludes with sections on the Tower of Babel and Abraham (7d–8r).[86] Here we publish the parts of this elenchic disquisition that deal with angels. The other material relevant to the biblical stories follows the angelology. It is written on a large format paper in a cramped hand in a single column. For this reason, we have divided it up into nine sections and we give not just the folios, but also the line spans of the different sections. We have introduced paragraph divisions within the sections.

"Dionysius" refers to (pseudo)-Dionysius the Areopagite, whose *Heavenly Hierarchy* serves, as we observed above, as a source for much angelic lore. The document enumerates the angelic classes or ranks in ascending order. Its formulation is much abbreviated and many words are elided. Words required in the translation to clarify the sense are supplied in round brackets. This text is followed by a section of the same folio enumerating the various ecclesiastical ranks

Section 1: The Ranking of the Angels

Text

1.1/ / fol. 7r ll. 1–12/ Հարցումս կարճառօտ ընտրեալ եւ հաւաքեալ ի գրոց:
1.2/ Նախ եւ առաջին հարցումս թէ որպէս են հրեշտակաց կարգաւորութիւնքն:

---

85. A variant form of Isa 6:3b found in the Divine Liturgy; see Nersoyan 1984, 66–67.
86. The original numbering of the folios is used. The numbers are confused since in turning over folio 7, apparently an additional folio was turned. The numbers thus run: 7a, 7b, 7c, 7d, 8a, 8b, 9a, etc. The texts dealing with Adam, the Tower of Babel, and Abraham will be published elsewhere.

1.3/ Պատասխանի: Առաջինն Աթոռոց դասք. և փառաբանութիւն է նոցա այս. Աթոռ քո Աստուած յաւիտեանս յաւիտենից:

1.4/ Երկրորդ Սերովբէք, և ասեն. սուրբ սուրբ սուրբ Տէր զօրութեանց:

1.5/ Երրորդ Քերովբէքն, և ասեն. Օրհնեալ են փառք Տեառն ի տեղւոջ իւրում:

1.6/ Չորրորդ Տէրութեանց, և ասեն. Տէր հզօր զօրութեամբ իւրով. տէր կար[ող]:

1.7/ Հինգերորդ Զօրութիւնք, և ասեն. Արքայութիւն քո արքայութիւն յաւիտենից. և տէր:

1.8/ Վեցորորդ Իշխանութիւնք, որք ասեն. Տացին քեզ հեթանոսք ի ժառանգութիւն և իշխանութիւն:

1.9/ Եօթներորդ Պետութիւնքն, և ասեն. Դու ես քահանայապետ յաւիտենից և Տէր ընդ աջմէ քումմէ:

1.10/ Ութերորդ Հրեշտակապետքն, և ասէ. Ողորմեա դու ստեղծեր մի կորուսաներ:

1.11/ Իսկ դաս Հրեշտակն, ներքին քան զամենեսեան. և հույս առ մարդիկ. որք ասեն փառք ի բարձունս և երկիր խաղաղութիւն և ի մարդիկ:

Translation

1.1/ Short Question(s), selected and assembled from books.
1.2/ The first and foremost question: Of which sort are the orderings of the angels?
1.3/ Answer: The first (are) the ranks of the Thrones and their praise is, "Your throne God is forever and ever."[87]
1.4/ The second, Seraphs and they say, "Holy, holy, holy is the Lord of Hosts."[88]
1.5/ The third, Cherubs and they say, ""Blessed is the glory of the Lord in His place."[89]
1.6/ The fourth, the Dominions and they say, "The Lord (is) strong through his might, the Lord (is) mighty."[90]

---

87. Ps 45:6(44:7).
88. Isa 6:3.
89. Ezek 3:12.
90. Ps 24(23):8.

1.7/ The fifth, the Powers and they say, "Your kingdom is an everlasting kingdom, and Lord." [91]

1.8/ The sixth, the Rulers, who say, "The gentiles will give you for a heritage and rule."[92]

1.9/ The seventh, the Principalities and they say, "You are High Priest forever and the Lord is by your right hand."[93]

1.10/ The eighth, the Archangels and they say, "Have mercy, Lord, you created, do not destroy."[94]

1.11/ The ninth, the Angels lower than all and close to men, who say, "Glory on high to God, and <on> earth peace for men."[95]

Section 2: Angels and Prophets

Text

2.1/ / fol. 7r ll. 12–18 / Են եւ այլ զանազան օրհնութիւնք վերնոցն որպէս Դանիէլ ասաց թէ հազար հազարաց պաշտէին եւ բիւրք բիւրոց կային առաջի նորա:

2.2/ Եւ եզեկիէլ ասէ զքառբառ նոցա խուռն արձակեալ ահք ....[96] թնդմամբ իբրեւ զջուրց ջոր[...]ութիւն[97] եւ ձայնք նոցա իբրեւ զձայն Սադայի. եւ [...] անիւքն զեղգեղել աղաղակէին:

2.3/ Եւ Զաքարիաս լուաւ զաղօթելն նոցա առ Աստուած զի ասեն. Տէր մինչեւ յերբ ոչ ողորմիս Երուսաղէմի. այս Հ ամ է:

2.4/ Եւ Գաբրիէլ Դանիէլի ասէր. Ի սկիզբն աղօթից քոց ելի պատգամ. եւ թէ ես եմ որ մատուցանեմ զաղօթս քո առաջի Աստուծոյ.

2.5/ Եւ այլք ալելուիա երգէին որպէս ետես Յովհաննէս ի տեսեանն: Եւ ի նուագելն նոր ի նորոյ հնչեցուցանէին զձայն օրհնութեան:

Translation

2.1/ There are also various blessings of the celestial ones, such as Daniel

---

91. Ps 145(144):13.
92. Ps 2:8.
93. Ps 110(109):4–5.
94. Zech 1:12.
95. Luke 2:14.
96. Seven illegible letters.
97. Partly illegible.

said, "A thousand thousands were serving and a myriad myriads were standing before him."[98]

2.2/ And Ezekiel said, "Their sound was of a rushing confusion [illegible] through the sound like that of waters [illegible], and their sounds (were) like the sound[99] of the Almighty and [unclear] the wheel, singing pleasantly, they were supplicating."[100]

2.3/ And Zecharias heard their praying to God, that they were saying, "Lord, how long will you not have mercy on Jerusalem, it is 70 years."[101]

2.4/ And Gabriel said to Daniel, "At the beginning of your prayer a pronouncement went forth and I am he who brings your prayers to God."[102]

2/5 And the others were singing Halleluia, as John saw in (his) vision. And in the singing of new, anew they were uttering the sound of blessing.[103]

Section 3: Nine Ranks of Angels and Humans

Text

3.1/ /fol. 7r lines 18–20/ Ընդ այսորիկ եւ զազգս մարդկան յորդորեաց Աստուած. Թ դասուք աւրհնել զԱրարիչն իւրեանց:

3.2/ Ի նահապետան նմանութիւնք Աթոռցն:
Օրհնադիրք՝ Քերովբէից:
Դատաւորք՝ Սերովբէից:
Քահանայք՝ տերութեանց:
Թագաւորք՝ զօրութեանց:

3.3/ Մարգարէք՝ իշխանութեանց:
Առաքեալք՝ պետութեանց:
Աւետարանիչք՝ հրեշտակապետաց:
Վարդապետք՝ հրեշտակաց:

Translation

3.1 / According to this, God exhorted the race of humans to bless their Creator in nine ranks:

---

98. Dan 7:10.
99. Or: voice.
100. The preceding text is quite illegible in places. The reference is to Ezek 1:24.
101. Zech 1:12.
102. A quotation based on Dan 8:16 and 9:21–24.
103. Compare Rev 14:2–3.

Among the patriarchs, the likenesses of the Thrones.
　　　The Lawgivers, of the Cherubs.
　　　The judges, of Seraphs.
　　　Priests, of Dominions.
　　　Kings, of Powers.
3.2/　Prophets, of Rulers.
　　　Apostles, of Principalities.
　　　Evangelists, of Archangels.
　　　Teachers, of Angels.

Section 4: Nine Ranks of Angels and Ecclesiastics

Text

4.1/　/ fol. 7r, lines / Այսպէս եւ նորա ս[ուրբ] եկեղեցի կարգեցաւ.
　　　Կաթողիկոսն՝ ի նմանութիւն Աթոռոցն:
　　　Եպիսկոպոսն՝ Քերովբէից:
　　　Քահանայն՝ Սերովբէից:
　　　Սարկաւագն՝ Տէրութեանց:
　　　Կիսասարկաւագն՝ Զօրութեանց:
4.2/　Ջահընկեայն՝ Իշխանութեանց:
　　　Երդմեցուցիչն՝ Պետութեանց:
　　　Ընթերցօղք՝ Հրեշտակապետաց:
　　　Դռնապացք՝ Հրեշտակաց:
　　　որք եղեն աղհնաբանիչք Աստուծոյ:

Translation

4.1/　Thus also his holy Church was ordered.
　　　The Catholicos, in likeness of the Thrones.
　　　The bishop, of Cherubs.
　　　The priests, of Seraphs.
　　　The deacon, of Dominions.
　　　The sub-deacon, of Powers.
4.2/　The acolytes, of Rulers.
　　　The exorcist, of Principalities.
　　　The readers, of Archangels.
　　　The doorkeepers, of angels.
　　　They were glorifiers of God.

Section 5. Another Ordering of Angels and Ecclesiastics

Text

5.1/ / fol. 7r lines 20–23 / Դարձեալ այլ խորհուրդ. զի թէպէտ կաթողիկոս եւ եպիսկոպոս ասաիճանոք զանազանեն. բայց հասարակ քահանայական կարգ կոչի.
Քահանայք նման աթոռոց:
Սարկաւագն. Քերովբէից:
Կիսասարկաւագ. Սերովբէից:
Ջահընկալ. Տերութեանց:
Ընթերցող. Զօրութեանց:
5.2/ Դռնապաց. իշխանութեանց:
Կրօնաւոր՝ Պետութեանց:
Մկրտեալքն՝ հրեշտակապետաց:
Երախայքն՝ Հրեշտակաց:
Այսպէ[ս] կարգեաց մեծ Դիոնեսիոս ուսեալ ի Պօղոսէ առաքելոյ ի փառս Քրիստոսի Աստուծոյ մերոյ:

Translation

5.1/ Again, another secret (mystery): just as a Catholicos and a bishop are distinguished by rank, but are called equal in the priestly order.
Priests (are) like Thrones,
The deacon, to the Cherubs.
Subdeacon, to Seraphs.
5.2/ Acolyte, to Dominions,
Reader, to Powers.
Doorkeeper, to Rulers.
Monks, to Principalities.
The baptised, to Archangels.
Catechumens, to Angels.
Thus the great Dionysius ranked (them), having learned from the apostle Paul[104] for the glory of Christ, our God.

---

104. Eph 3:10, 6:12, 1 Pet 3:22.

Section 6. On Which Day Were the Angels Created?

Text

6.1/ 7r l. 28–7v l. 1 / Հարց: թէ որ օր ստեղծան հրեշտակք:
Պատասխանի: Առաջինն օր կիրակին՝ որ միաշաբաթ ասի. ստեղծ Աստուած է իրք. Ա հրեղէն երկինք. եւ Բ հրեշտակք. եւ Գ լուսաւորք որ յօդս. եւ Դ. տարերք. այսինքն հող. եւ ջուր. օդ եւ հուր. եւ ժամանակն որ լինի ութ:

6.2/ Իսկ երկրուշաբթի՝ զկէս ջրոյն փետեկտել ի Զ դիմացյայսկոյս եւ յայնկոյս. եւ այլ հաստատութիւնն արար որ է կապոյտ երկին:

6.3/ երեքշաբթի՝ ասաց ժողովեցին ջուրքն ի ծովս. եւ երեւեցի ցամաքն. եւ բուսան ծառք եւ բոյսք ամենայն պտղաբերք. ի խորհուրդ <մրգիցն>:¹⁰⁵

6.4/ Իսկ չորեքշաբթի՝ արեգակն եւ լուսին եւ աստեղք. որք ցիր եւ ցան էին. եղ յամանի եւ սահման եղ կալ իւրաքանչիւր կարգի. յօրինակ Աստուածածնին:

6.5/ Իսկ հինգշաբթին ասաց. բխեցեն ջուրք գեռունս եւ գթտ/ fol. 7v /չունս. որք թռեան յօդս. օրինակ առաքելոցն. որք ի ծովէ կոչեցան եւ յերկինս ելան:

6.6/ Իսկ ի վեց<երորդ> աւուր ուրբաթի, ստեղծ զմարդն եւ այլ չորքոտանիք:

Translation

6.1/ Question: on which day were the angels created?
Answer: On the first day, Sunday, which is called the first of the week, God created seven things: 1/ fiery heavens, and 2/ angels, and 3/ the luminaries which are in the atmosphere,¹⁰⁶ and 4–8/ the four elements, that is earth and water, air and fire; and time, which is eight.¹⁰⁷

6.2/ Then, on Monday having divided half of the water into 6 aspects,

---

105. See note 110.
106. These luminaries are distinct from the sun, moon, and stars, the creation of which is attributed to Wednesday; see §6.4 below. In Gen 1:3 the creation of light is recounted.
107. This is clearly based on a particular exegesis of Gen 1:1–3, that included various other items in the list of the first day's creations. On the four elements' creation, a common idea in Armenian tradition, see Stone 2013, index s.v. "elements." Time almost seems to be added as an afterthought.

hither and thither,[108] and also he made the firmament, which is the blue heaven.[109]

6.3/ On Tuesday he said "Let the waters be gathered into the seas, and let the dry land be seen." And all fruit-bearing trees and plants sprang up for the mystery of the <fruits>.[110]

6.4/ Then, on Wednesday the sun and the moon and the stars,[111] which were scattered. He set (them) in a vessel and he set a limit for each order to remain, as a type of the Mother of God.[112]

6.5/ Then, on Thursday, he said, "Let the waters bring forth crawling things and birds that fly in the air," as a type of the Apostles, who were summoned from the sea and ascended to the heavens.[113]

6.6/ Then on the sixth day, Urbat (Friday) he created man and also the quadrupeds.[114]

Section 7. Where Did He Create Humans?

Text

7.1/ / fol. 7v ll. 2–5 / Հարց: թէ ո՞ւր ստեղծ զԱդամ:

2/ Պատասխանի: ի վայրս դրախտին ստեղծ. եւ յետ աւուր եղ ի դրախտին. յայտ է որ ասէ գիրն, թէ էած Աստուած զամենայն կենդանիս առ Ադամ կոչել նոցա անուանս. ուրեմն ոչ էր դրախտն տեղիք անասնոց եւ զազանաց. այլ արտաքոյ էր:

3/ Եւ ումանք Երուսաղեմ ասեն ստեղծեալ զմարդն. ըստ այնմ թէ Սիովնի ասի մայր. եւ մայրդ ծնաւ ի նմա. բայց զի Մովսէս ոչ գրեաց Աստուծոյ է գիտելի:

---

108. Observe Pseudo-Zeno 1.0.1 which talks of six positions, an idea developed in 1.1.0–1.6.18: see Stone and Shirinian 2000. The number six plays a major role in this work.
109. Gen 1:6–8.
110. The word is abbreviated to մգրէիցն; we suggest that this is a mistake for մրգից "of the fruit" or its abbreviation մրգցն. See Gen 1:11–12.
111. The sun, moon, and stars are represented by ideographs.
112. Gen 1:14–18. The vessel in which He put the luminaries was like the Theotokos, in whom Christ was put. Alternatively, perhaps a reference to the iconography of the Virgin, standing on the moon, among the stars.
113. Gen 1:20–22.
114. Gen 1:24–25.

Translation

1/ Question: Where did he create Adam?
2/ Answer: He created (him) in the environs of the Garden. And after a day, he put (him) in the Garden.[115] That which Scripture says is clear, that God brought all the animals to Adam to call them names.[116] Therefore, the place of the animals and beasts was not the Garden, but outside (it).
3/ And some say that man was created in Jerusalem according to that Zion was called mother,[117] and this mother gave birth in it. But because Moses did not write (about this), it is knowable to God (alone).

Section 8. On Which Day Did Sadayēl Fall from the Garden?

Text

8.1/ / fol. 7v, lines 7–8 / Հարց: թէ Սադայէլ որ օր անկաւ ի դրախտէն: Պատասխանի: Ասեն թէ ի հինգշաբաթի օրն անկաւ. վասն որոյ ուրբաթի մարդն ստեղծաւ զի լցցէ զտեղին նորա. յաղագս որոյ մախացաւ:

Translation

8.1/ Question: On which day did Sadayēl[118] fall from the Garden?
Answer: They say that he fell on Thursday, because of which on Friday man was created, so that he might fill his place.[119] On account of this he was envious.[120]

---

115. Gen 2:8, 15.
116. Gen 2:19–20.
117. See, for example, Isa 66:8.
118. This is a name for Satan, whom some traditions also name Satanael.
119. For the idea that humans fill the place of the fallen angels, see Stone 2013, 46–47.
120. See Stone 2013, 358. There this is said to be the view of Zak'aria Kat'ołikos (ninth century).

3.8. QUESTIONS AND ANSWERS FROM THE HOLY BOOKS

This text occurs in M1654A, a *Miscellany* (1336), fols. 189v–193v (Eganyan 2009, 5:763–79). It covers a considerable range of biblical topics and we have transcribed and translated it all. The particular tradition of Lamech, Cain's grandson (§14), is rather distinctive and most of the other sections contain material of interest.

Excursus: The Lamech Tradition mentioned in §14.
by A. Bereznyak

The biblical story of Cain ends with his being driven away from God's presence. Genesis does not tell the reader what befell the first murderer after that (Gen 4:11–17). However, Jewish and Christian exegetes attempted to provide some answers to this question and were particularly concerned with the question of Cain's death. This was an issue because the curse of Cain included the words, "Then the LORD said to him, 'Not so! If any one slays Cain, vengeance shall be taken on him sevenfold.' And the LORD put a mark on Cain, lest any who came upon him should kill him (Gen 4:15)." How then did Cain die?

According to one of the apocryphal traditions Cain's grandson,[121] Lamech, was responsible for Cain's death.[122] In the rather ambiguous verses in Gen 4:23–24, known as "Lamech's Song," Lamech seems to be telling his wives that he had murdered a man and a boy.[123] This is interpreted as a confession,[124] and the man Lamech had supposedly killed is identified as his own grandfather, Cain. This reading is buttressed by verse 4:24 "If Cain is avenged sevenfold, truly Lamech seventy-sevenfold" which introduces Cain's name and also a seventy-sevenfold punishment.

On this basis, both Jewish and Christian sources relate a similar story: blind Lamech, assisted by a young boy (sometimes identified as his grandson), inadvertently kills Cain while hunting, and after he realizes what he has done, Lamech accidentally kills the boy as well.[125] There are some variations within this tradition. The Conflict of Adam and Eve with Satan contains a

---

121. He is to be distinguished from the Sethite Lamech, Enoch's grandson (Gen 5:25).
122. Compare the version in Jub. 4:31, where a house falls on Cain.
123. Of course, if the two clauses are parallel, then the man and the young man or boy are one and the same. However, this is not the way it was read by the apocryphal tradition being discussed.
124. See Kugel 1990, 93–94 for possible interpretations of these verses.
125. E.g., Cave of Treasures, in Bauckham 2013, 1:546–47; *Palaea Historica*, 604–5; Midrash Tanḥuma on Gen 11.

slightly different and more elaborate version of the story. In its version, blind Lamech accompanies his grandson, who tends sheep, in order to protect him from robbers. Mistaking Cain for a robber, Lamech kills him with an arrow. As in other versions, when Lamech finds out whom he has killed, he claps his hands and accidentally kills his grandson as well (Malan 1882, 121–23). Ethiopian biblical commentaries cited by Cowley contain a slight deviation from the standard story according to which, Lamech kills Cain with a stone, rather than an arrow.[126]

1/ Հարցմունք եւ պատասխանիք ի գրոց սրբոց:
[Մ]ինչ ոչ էին ստեղծեալ հրեշտակք եւ մարդիք. զաստուածութիւնն ո՛վ փառաւորէր:
Պատասխանի: Հայր յՈրդոյ փառաւորի. եւ Որդի ի Հաւրէ. եւ Սուրբ Հոգին ի նոցունց. փառաւորէին զմիմեանս:

2/ Հարց: Չի՞նչ յանցեաւ սատանա:
Պատասխանի: զի նման Բարձրելոյն խորհեցաւ լինել:

3/ Հարց: հրեշտակք կա՞ն ի նոյն երկեղի. եթէ զուցէ անկան:
Պատասխանի: Այո՛ կան ի նոյն երկեղին հանապազ. վասն այնորիկ կան անդադար ի փառաբանութիւն:

4/ Հարց: Մարդն՝ Աստուծոյ պատկեր իւ՞ կոչեցաւ. յորժամ ոչ էր նման պատկերի նորա:
Պատասխանի: մարդն պատկեր Աստուծոյ. վասն անձնիշխանութեանն կոչեցաւ:

5/ Հարց: Սա/ fol. 190b /տանա գիտէր. եթէ քանի ծառ հրամանեց Աստուած ուտել Ադամա:
Պատասխանի: գիտէր. վասն այնը զի լուաւ ի Տեառնէ զասացելն առ Ադամ. վասն այնմիկ[127] եդ բանս ընդ կնոջն:[128]

6/ Հարց: Ադամ եւ կինն ի դրախտն ստեղծան եթէ արտաքո ստեղծան.
Պատասխանի: արտաքո ստեղծան. վասն զի գրեալ է. թէ եդ անդ զմարդն զոր ստեղծ:

7/ Հարց: քանի ժամանակ եկաց Ադամ ի դրախտին. զի զիրք բազում ասեն. եւ այլք ոչ աւր մի:

---

126. Cowley 1988, 78. For a detailed overview of the topics raised by the biblical text, including possible interpretations of Cain's punishment, Lamech's song, the sources of Lamech's blindness, Lamech's guilt or lack thereof, see also Kugel 1990; Byron 2011, 106–65; further Aptowitzer 1922.
127. This should, by standard grammar, be այնորիկ.
128. Observe the orthography.

Պատասխանի: Վասն զի ի դրախտին ոչ տիւ կայր. եւ ոչ գիշեր. այլ հանապազ լոյս էր. վասն այնր ոչ որ զիտաց գսահմանս կենացն Ադամայ:

8/ Հարց: Աւձն մարդկային բարբառով խաւսեցաւ, ընդ ոչն. եթէ իւր բարբառով: Պատասխանի: ցանկայր աւձն մարդկային բարբա/fol. 190r/ռոյս. վասն այնորիկ էմուտ ի նա սատանա: եւ խաւսել ետ մարդկային բարբառով:

9/ Հարց: Սատանա ունէ՞ր իշխանութիւն մտանել յաւձն թէ ոչ: Պատասխանի: ունէր. վասն զի թոյլ ետ Աստուած մտանել. յաղագս փորձելոյ զմարդն:

10/ Հարց: Բոցերէն սուրն դեռ եւս պահէ՞ զդրախտն. եթէ ոչ: Պատասխանի: Ի ձեռն խաչին բարձաւ սուրն ի միշտ. եւ բացաւ մեզ ճանապարհի ծառոյն կենաց:

11/ Հարց: Եթէ Ադամ չէր յանցել ի դրախտին կայր հանապազ թէ ոչ:
Պատասխանի: Այո՛. փոխելոց էր որպէս թագ յապարանից յապարանս:

12/ Հարց: Ապաշխարեց Կաեն թէ ոչ:
Պատասխանի: Ապաշխարեց ստոյգ զի վասն նորա եկն չրիեղեղն. եւ ապրեցաւ ի չրիեղեղէն:

13/ Հարց: Կաեն յինչ պատճառի եսպան զԱբէլ: / fol. 191r /
Պատասխանի: Զի իւր գործքն չար էին. եւ եղբաւրն բարիք:

14/ Հարց: Եւ Ղամեք յի՞նչ պատճառի եսպան զԿաեն.
Պատասխանի: Վասն նախատանաց ազգին իւրո:

15/ Մաթուսաղա է՞ր ապրեցաւ շատ քան զայլ մարդիկ:
Պատասխանի: Վասն առաքինութեն[129] հաւրն իւրո Ենովքայ:

16/ Հարց: եւ զի՞նչ էր առաքինութիւնն Ենովքայ:
Պատասխանի: զի ի պտղ աշխարհիս ոչ ճաշակեցաւ:

17/ Հարց: Քանի ամ կուսութեամբ եկաց Նո:
Պատասխանի: Շ ամ:

18/ Հարց: Եւ զի՞նչ պատճառի եկաց զայնչափ ժամանակս:
Պատասխանի: Վասն զի երկեւ ի չար ծնընդոց ժամա<նա>կին.[130] զի իւր ծնունդն էլ[131] չար չլինէր:

19/ Հարց: Յո՞րժամ առ զկինն:
Պատասխանի: Յորժամ առ հրաման գտապանական շինելո:

20/ Եւ քանի ամ շինեց գտապանն Նո:

---
129. The use of the ablative is bizarre.
130. ժամակին, which is probably corrupt.
131. Postclassical form.

Պատասխանի: գձ ամ:
21/ Հարց: եւ քանի աւր եկն ջրհեղեղն.
/ fol. 191v / Պատասխանի: Խ աւր:
22/ Հարց: եւ ո՞ւր եղին գտապանն:
Պատասխանի: ի լերինն Սարարադա յազատ Մազիս:
23/ Հարց: եւ Նո վասն է՞ր անիծեց զորդին որդո իւրո, եւ ոչ իւր որդին որ յանցեաւ:
Պատասխանի: Վասն զի Աստուած աւրհնեալ էր զանդրանիկն. վասն այնորիկ ոչ կարաց զաւրինութիւն Աստուծոյ ընդ անիծաւք արկանել:
24/ Հարց: զաշտարական յերկինս ելանելը պատճառաւ շինեցին թէ յայլ պէտոս:
<Պատասխանի:> Բ պատճառի շինեցին. մինն յաղագս այնր եթէ դարձել ջրհեղեղն լինելոց է. եւ միուսն այլ պատճառի վասն զի կարի անհոգաց ելէին:
25/ Հարց: Մի՞ս յԱդամայ եղեւ սկիսբն ուտելո:
Պատասխանի: ոչ յԱդամա. այլ ի Նոէ հրամաեցաւ ուտել. նոյնպէս եւ գինին:
26/ Հարց: Չի՞նչ խորհուդ էր զի զՄովսէս թաքուցին ծնողքն:
Պատասխանի: Վասն զի ի ձեռն նորա էր լինելոց փրկ/ fol. 192r/ութիւն Իսրայելդի:
27/ Հարց: Մովսէսի գիր ետ Աստուած էթէ պատուիրան:
Պատասխանի: զերկուսն. գիր եւ պատուիրան:
28/ Հարց: Չի՞նչ պատճառաւ հրամաեց Աստուած ժողովրդենն խաբէութեամբ կողոպտել զեգիպտացիսն զզանձս իւրեանց: մինչեւ ինքն հրամաեաց ամենեցուն Տէրն. զարդար վաստակա վաստակեչ:
Պատասխանի: Ո՛չ էթէ կողոպտեր. այլ չորէք ծ ամին դարն եւ խիստ ծառաութեանն զոր ծառեցին էգիպտացիոցն:
29/ Հարց: Մովսէսի ընդէ՞ր ոչ հրամաեց առնուլ:
Պատասխանի: վասն զի ոչ էր աշխատել ի կանն եւ յաղիւսարկութիւնն:
30/ Հարց: Չքառասուն ամ ընդէ՞ր կացոյց զժողովուրդն յանապատին:
Պատասխանի: Վասն զի էգիպտական մոլորութեամբն թաւլեալ էր / fol. 192v / ժողովուրդն. վասն այնորիկ զխ ամ յանապատ սրբեց զնոսա: եւ ապա հրամաեց մտանել յերկիրն աւետեաց:

31/ Հարց: Եւ ի ցամաքն ընդէ՞ր ոչ սատակեց զփարաւն այլ ի ծովփա:
Պատասխանի: Վասն զՀ ամ զհրայելացոց զծնունդն ջրահեղեցոյց արար: Վասն այնորիկ նովին ջրովս եւ ինքն սատակեցաւ:

32/ Հարց: Խոզն ի սկզբանէ էր պիղծ. եթէ Մովսէս ասաց զնա պիղծ:
< Պատասխանի >: Վասն զի զոր ինչ ուտէին եզիպտացիքն. զայն պեղծ համարեցաւ. եւ զոր ոչն ուտէին զայնսիկ հրամեց ուտել:[132]

33/ Հարց: վեմս որ երթայր զհետ յԻսրայէլի. կենդանի՞ էր եթէ անշունչ:
Պատասխանի: Այն՝ կենդանի էր. վասն զի վէմս էր ինքն Քրիստոս:

34/ Հարց: Եւ զհետ Իսրայէլի զիա՞րդ երթայր. տանի՞ն էթէ ինքն երթայր:
Պատասխանի: ոչ տանէին այլ ինքն երթայր:

35/ Հարց: / fol. 193r / Ընդէ՞ր ոչ էթող Աստուած Դաւթի շինել զտաճարն. մինչ նա սուրբ էր քան զՍողոմոնն:
Պատասխանի: Վասն պատերազմացն չիրամեցաւ Դաւթի:

36/ Հարց: ԵւզՍողոմոնիզգալուրսնընդէ՞ր լիացոյցեւ խաղաղացոյց:
Պատասխանի: Վասն շինե[լ]ո զտաճարն:

37/ Հարց: Եւ Սողոմոնի [յ]անցանացն եղեւ թողութիւն թէ ոչ:
Պատասխանի: Ոչ եղեւ թողութիւն:

38/ Հարց: Յունան ի Տեառնէ առաքեցաւ ի Նինվէ. ընդէ՞ր եղեւ փախստական յԱստուծոյ:
<Պատասխանի>: վասն զի գիտէր զԱստուծոյ մարդասէրութիւնն որ խափանելոց էր զմարգարէութիւն նորա:

39/ Հարց: Յովաննէս ի ծնունդս կանայց յինչպէս պատճառս անուանեցաւ մեծ:
Պատասխանի: Վասն զի յորովայնէ երկրապազեց Քրիստոսի. զոր ոչ այլ ոք ի ծնունդս կանաց արար:

40/ Հարց: Եւ փոքրիկն յարքայութեանն մեծ ո՞վ է:
Պատասխանի: Ինքն Բանն Աստուած որ եկն եւ վասն մեր փո/ fol. 193v /քր կացաւ. զի զմեծ մեծս արասցէ:

41/ Հարց: Հրեշտակքն որ ասէին ո՞վ է այս որ դիմել գայ Յեդովմա. ի կուսէ ծնընդեանն չէին տեղեակ. եթէ ի հօրէ:
Պատասխանի: Ի կուսէ ծնընդենն միայն չէին տեղեկ:

---

132. Corruption of հրամայեաց.

42/ Հարց: Սատանա մինչեւ ցոյր վայր ոչ զիտաց զորդի Աստուծոյ. ի մկրտութեանն. եթէ ի փորձութեանն. թէ ի խաչելութեանն։ Պատասխանի: հանապազ կայր ի կասկածի: բայց ի խաչելութեանն յորժամ ի ձեռս Հաւր աւանդեց զհոգին յայնժամ ապա զիտաց եթէ Աստուած էր, որդի Աստուծոյ:

43/ Հարց: Ի զալուստեն Տեառն անցանէ՞ երկիրս. եթէ նորոգի: Պատասխանի: Ո՛չ եթէ անցանէ. այլ նորոգի. ո՛չ եթէ վասն մեղաւորացն. այլ վասն արդարոցն. զի երեսնաւոր լինելոց են որպէս եւ ասաց Քրիստոս. եւ կարզեցէր երեսնաւոր զերկիրս. եւ կամաւոր[end of photograph.

Translation

1/ Questions and Answers from the Holy Books.
[U]ntil angels and humans were created, who glorified the Godhead? Answer: The Father was glorified by the Son, and the Son by the Father, and the Holy Spirit by them. They were glorifying one another.

2/ Question: How did Satan transgress?
Answer: Because he thought to become like the Most High.[133]

3/ Question: Were the angels always in that very fear, lest they fall?
Answer: Yes, they were always in that very fear. On account of this they were ceaselessly glorifying.

4/ Question: Why was man called the image of God when he was not like His image?
Answer: Man was called the image of God on account of (his) free will.[134]

5/ Question: Did Satan know of how many trees God commanded Adam to eat?
Answer: He knew on account of that, that he heard the Lord's speech to Adam.[135] On account of that he spoke with the woman.

6/ Question: Were Adam and Eve created inside the Garden or outside?
Answer: They were created outside (it), because it written that he put there the man whom He created.[136]

7/ Question: How long did Adam remain in the Garden, for some books say a lot and others, not one day?

---

133. See Isa 14:13–14.
134. Or: autonomy. See Stone 2013, index s.v. "free will." See Gen 1:26.
135. I.e., Gen 2:16–17.
136. Gen 2:8.

Answer: Because in the Garden there was no day and no night but it was always light, therefore no one knows the limits of Adam's life.

8/ Question: Did the serpent speak with human speech or not? Or with its own speech?
Answer: The serpent spoke with this human speech. For that reason Satan entered into it and caused it to speak with human speech.[137]

9/ Question: Did Satan have the authority to enter the serpent, or not?
Answer: It did have, because God gave it permission to enter for the sake of testing man.

10/ Question: Does the fiery sword still guard the Garden or not?[138]
Answer: The sword is removed by means of the Cross for always, and the way to the tree of life is open for us.[139]

11/ Question: If Adam had not transgressed, would he have remained in the Garden always or not?
Answer: Yes. Like a king he would have moved from palace to palace.

12/ Question: Did Cain repent or not?
Answer: He surely repented, since the flood came on his account and he was saved from the flood.[140]

13/ Question: For which reason did Cain kill Abel?
Answer: Because his own works were evil and his brother's, good.

14/ Question: And for which reason did Lamech kill Cain?
Answer: Because of the dishonor of his family.[141]

15/ Question: Why did Methusaleh live longer than other humans?
Answer: On account of his father Enoch's virtue.

16/ Question: And what was Enoch's virtue?
Answer: That he did not taste of the fruit of this world.[142]

17/ Question: How many years did Noah live in virginity?
Answer: 500 years.[143]

18/ Question: And for what reason did he live (thus) for so long?

---

137. This is based on the idea of demonic possession: Satan possessed the serpent: see Stone 2013, 177–210.
138. Gen 3:24.
139. Compare 4 Ezra 8:52.
140. I.e., had he not repented, he would not have been saved from the flood. The view that Cain survived the flood, however, is unusual. This conflicts with the legend to which §14 refers.
141. Lamech's story is discussed in the Excursus at the end of the Introductory Remarks to this document.
142. Stone 2010, 517–30. See further in Lipscomb 1990, 62–68.
143. Gen 5:32.

Answer: Because he feared the evil offspring of that time, lest his offspring also be evil.

19/ Question: When did he take a wife?
Answer: When he received a command to build the Ark.

20/ Question: And for how many years did Noah build the Ark?
Answer: For 100 years.

21/ Question: And for how many days did the flood come?
Answer: 40 days.[144]

22/ Question: And where did they put the Ark?
Answer: In the mountain of Sararad,[145] in high Mazis.[146]

23/ Question: And why did Noah curse his son's son and not his own son who transgressed?
Answer: Because God had blessed the firstborn. For that reason he could not expel God's blessing with a curse.

24/ Question: Did they build the tower for the reason of climbing to heaven, or for some other need?
<Answer:> They built for two reasons. The first, because of this,[147] if again a flood will take place, and the second other reason, because they climbed most hopelessly.

25/ Question: Was the beginning of eating meat from Adam?
Answer: Not from Adam, but from Noah was it commanded to be eaten. Likewise, wine.[148]

26/ Question: Which idea[149] was it that brought Moses' parents to hide him?
Answer: Because the redemption of Israel was going to take place through him.

27/ Question: Did God give Moses a book or a commandment?[150]
Answer: Both, a book and a commandment.

28/ Question: Why did God command the people to plunder the Egyptians

---

144. Gen 7:4, 12, 17.
145. See P'awstos Buzand 3:10, who has "Sararat" and the discussion in Garsoïan 1989, 252–53.
146. The higher of Masis's two peaks. On the mountain's identification, see Stone, Amihai, and Hillel 2010, 307–11.
147. Literally: that. See Concerning the Tower 1 and 2 (4.1 and 4.2) for this reason.
148. This is evident from the commandment concerning blood that was first given to Noah (Gen 9:4–5) and from Noah's planting of the vine (Gen 9:20–21).
149. Or "plan, mystery."
150. I.e., an oral commandment.

of their treasures by a ruse, while[151] the Lord himself commanded all of them to work honest labor?
Answer: It is not that he plundered (them), but they served the Egyptians for four hundred years of bitter and hard service.[152]

29/ Question: Why did he not command Moses to take (i.e., the treasure)?
Answer: Because he had not labored in the clay and in the brick-laying.

30/ Question: Why did the people remain in the desert for forty years?
Answer: Because due to the Egyptian sin,[153] the people was topsy-turvy. For that reason he purified them in the desert for 40 years. And then he commanded (them) to enter the Promised Land.[154]

31/ Question: And why did he not slaughter Pharaoh on dry land, but in the sea?[155]
Answer: Because for 70 years they drowned the Israelite offspring.

32/ Question: Was the pig originally unclean, or did Moses say (proclaim) it unclean?
Answer: Because whatever the Egyptians ate, that was reckoned unclean. And that which they did not eat, he commanded (i.e., the Israelites) to eat.

33/ The rock that went after Israel, was it alive on inanimate?[156]
Answer: Yes, it was alive, because the rock was Christ Himself.[157]

34/ Question: And how did it go after Israel? Did they lead (it) or did it come of itself?
Answer: They did not lead it but it came of itself.

35/ Question: Why did God <not> permit David to build the temple, since[158] he was holier than Solomon?
Answer: Because of (his) wars, David was not commanded.

36/ Question: Why did he fill Solomon's days and make (them) peaceful?
Answer: On account of the building of the temple.

37/ Question: And was there forgiveness of Solomon's sins, or not?

---

151. Until.
152. Exod 3:21–22. This reason is also advanced in a number of Jewish Hellenistic and Rabbinic sources as well as by Patristic authors; see Ginzberg 1909–1938, 5:436.
153. I.e., the sin that they learned from the Egyptians or in Egypt.
154. See Deut 1:8, 31:7, etc.
155. Exod 15:19, Deut 11:4.
156. Was the rock of Exod 17:6 assumed to be the same as that of Num 20:8, 10 and to have travelled with the Israelites? This seems to be behind 1 Cor 10:4.
157. 1 Cor 10:4 is the direct source of this text.
158. Literally: while. See 1 Kgs 5:3.

Answer: There was no forgiveness.[159]

38/ Question: (If) Jonah was sent to Nineveh by the Lord, why did he flee from God?
<Answer>: Because he knew God's love of men which would obstruct his pro[phe]cy.[160]

39/ Question: For what sort of reason was John, born of woman,[161] called "great?"
Answer: Because from the womb he worshipped Christ, which no one else born of women did.

40/ Question: And which infant is great in the kingdom?
Answer: The Word God himself, who came, became small for our sake, for he will make the great great.[162]

41/ Question: The angels who were saying, "Who is this who comes from the direction of Edom,"[163] were they not informed that He born of the Virgin is from the Father?
Answer: They were not informed only about the birth from the Virgin.

42/ Question: Up to which place did Satan not know the Son of God, His baptism, His temptation, or His crucifixion?
Answer: He (Satan) was always in doubt, but in the crucifixion, when He (Christ) yielded up his spirit (soul) to the hands of the Father, then he knew (realised) that He was God, the Son of God.

43/ Question: Will the earth pass away at the Lord's coming, or will it be renewed?
Answer: It will not pass away but be renewed, not for the sake of the wicked but for the sake of the righteous. For they are going to become thirtyfold[164] as Christ said. And[end of photograph.

3.9. THIS IS THE HISTORY OF THE DISCOURSE (WORD)

The full title of this work is: This is the History of this Discourse (Word) which reveals to us that which took place. It occurs in manuscript M682 on fol. 96r.

---

159. The question of Solomon's sins and repentance received a different answer in Armenian Solomon apocrypha. See Stone 1978, 1–19.
160. See 4.12. This Is the Story of Nineveh an[d of Jo]nah below.
161. Literally: "women." This is based on Matt 11:11, Luke 7:28.
162. If մեծ մեծս is taken to be corrupt for մեծամեծս, one might translate "do very great things." This may be preferable.
163. Isa 63:1 taken as a Messianic prophecy.
164. Thus taking it from երեսունն and see Matt 13:8, 23.

ANGELOLOGICAL TEXTS

This manuscript is discussed above in the introductory remarks to texts 1.12, 3.7, etc.

The section given here deals with two questions: the fall of Satanayēl and his angels in §§1–5 and Adam's fruit in §§6–10. It has some distinctive ideas, as has been observed in the notes on §7.

Text

0/ Այս է պատմութիւն բանիս որ յայտնէ մեզ գեղեալն:
1/ Ընդէ՞ր թօթափեցաւ յերկնից զդասս[165] հրեշտակացն Սաղանայէլի:
   Չի մեծ հրեշտակ էր քան զամենայն, վասն այն նախատեաց եւ թօթափեցգնուաս. զի բազմագործնակլիցիզիմիհպարտեցին այլ հրեշտակքն. վասն այն խրատ առեալ են ամենայն զունդք հրեշտակաց. որք կան առաջի Աստուծութեանն դողան եւ սարսեալ անդադար աւհինեն եւ փառաբանեն:
2/ Եւ ասեն. սուրբ սուրբ սուրբ Տէր զօրութեանց. գոչեն եւ աղաղակեն. բայց յահէ Աստուածութեանն ոչ կարեն հայիլ ի տեսութիւն փառացն Աստուծոյ: Դարձեալ մեզ խրատ լիցի զի մի հպարտայաք եւ կորիցուք. զի տեսէք եւ ի մից առեք. զի այն որ ի վեր եւ բարձր էր քան զամենայն հրեշտակս երբ հպարտեցաւ ի վայր անկաւ:
3/ Իսկ մեք որ այնչափի մեղք ունիմք. որ սատանային միայն չէ գործել. այն մեղքն որ մեզ ունիմք. սատանայ միայն հպարտութիւն գործեաց ի լույսն մերկեցաւ. եւ ի խաւար մատնեցաւ: Իսկ մեք շնութիւն պոռնկութիւն պղծութիւն գողութիւն զմարդասպանութիւն եւ զմատնելութիւն. եւ այլ բազում չարաչար մեղք որ ոչ բերէ զերես մարդոյ յիշել զնա. թէ ի հպարտութիւն այլ ի վերայ ամենայն մեղաց գործեալք փրկիլ ի դժոխոցն:
4/ Դարձեալ զի Թ դաս հրեշտակացն որ մաքուր են ի մեղաց. ամենեւին զքնութիւն մեղաց ոչ գիտեն. այնպէս սարսափին եւ զարհուրին. եւ դողան եւ սասանին յահէ փառաց նորա. աւհինեն եւ աղաղակեն. որ ոչ մեղք. ոչ մահ. ոչ դատաստան. եւ ոչ տանջանք:
5/ Իսկ մեք ապա որչափի պարտիմք լալ եւ ողբալ որ քան զբարձր

---

165. The use of the nota accusativi here is late, when its function became enfeebled.

լերներ[166] ծանր մեղք եմք գործել. կամ որշափ պիտիմք դողալ եւ սարսափել յահէն Աստուծոյ. լալով եւ ցաւագին {կակծելով}[167] հոգի ունիմք տալոյ. վայ մեր մեղացն կամ որշափ պիտիմք աղօթել եւ աղաղակել. ալրինել եւ գովել. լալ եւ կոծել խոստավանալ եւ ապաշխարեալ. որ չնշէ զզիր մեղաց մերոց օրն դատաստանին կամ ազատել զմեզ ի հրոյն յաւիտենից. եւ ի վիշապաց հրեղեաց։

6. Դարձեալ Մեկնութիւն պտղոյն Ադամա
գի ոչ թէ պտուղն շար էր որ կերաւ Ադամ. գի շար պտուղն ի մէջ դրախտին ինչ կանէր. շարն այն էր որ Աստուած պահք եդ Ադամայ թէ մի ուտեր ի ծառոյդ գի տեսցէ եւ փորձեցէ[168] զԱդամ. թէ պահէ զպատուիրանն եւ գիւսքն Աստուծոյ։

7/ ապա հրամանի տայր. յայնժամ ուտեր ի պտղոյն ոչ ինչ փասեր այլ մանաւանդ ի վերինն Երուսաղէմ բարձրանայր. երբ կերաւ զպա<հ>քն եւ մոռացաւ զխորհուրդն. վասն այն բարկացաւ ի վերայ Ադամայ եւ Եւայի. ի դրախտէն ի դուրս հանեաց։

8/ Իսկ այժմ նոյն օրինակաւ բերանօք սրբոց առաքելոցն եւ հայրապետացն[169] պահքն եւ պատուիրանն ետ մեզ. գի որ պահեն նման Եղիայի եւ Ենովքա, արքայութիւնն վերանան. իսկ որք քակեն զպահքն եր[ան]եալ հայրապետաց. Ադամայ նման ի դրախտէն ելանեն։

9/ Դարձեալ ընդէ՞ր հարցաներ Ադամայ թէ ու՞ր ես. գի ինքն գիտեր որ անդ էր նա։ Վասն այն հարցաներ. գի թէ Ադամ մեղայ էր ասացեալ, թողութիւն գտաներ եւ ոչ ելաներ ի դրախտէն. Ապա մեղայ ոչ ասաց. այլ գիւր մեղաց պատճառն ի յԱստուած ձգեաց, եւ ասաց. կինս զոր դու ստեղծեր սա ետ ինձ եւ կերա զպտուղն. վասն այն բարկացաւ Աստուած գի ոչ ասաց մեղայ Ադամ։

10/ Դարձեալ ընդէ՞ր Եւայի ասաց. զայդ ինչ գործեցեր կին դու. միթէ եւ կինն մեղայ ասեր. եւ կինն ուսեալ ի Ադամայ պատճառն ի յԱստուած եհան ասելով. զայդ օձդ որ դու ստեղծեր նա խաբեաց գիս եւ կերա։ Իբրեւ ետես Աստուած որ մեղայ ոչ ասացին. այլ պատճառ ի յինքն հանին. վասն այն արտաքսեաց[end of photo

---

166. Postclassical form.
167. Perhaps read կոծելով "bewailing." See further on in this section for the expression լալ եւ կոծել.
168. ձ over g p.m.
169. g over p p.m.

Translation

0/ This is the History of this Discourse (Word) which reveals that which befell us.

1/ Why was Satanayēl's rank of angels cast out of the heavens? Because he was a greater angel than all, therefore he was jealous.[170] And He[171] cast them out that there might be an example for many, lest the other angels be proud. On account of that, all the groups of angels were rebuked,[172] who stand before the Godhead. Trembling and shaking unceasingly, they blessed and praised.

2/ And they say, "Holy, holy, holy is the Lord of hosts."[173] They call out and supplicate, but from fear of the Godhead they are unable to look upon the vision of the glory of God. Again, let it be a rebuke[174] for us, lest we be proud and perish. For, see and take to mind that when he who was superior and higher than all the angels was proud, he fell to earth.

3/ But we who have such great sins, (like) which Satan did not do alone, those sins which we have. Satan only acted with pride. He was stripped of the light and delivered over to darkness. But we (have committed) adultery, fornication, abomination, theft, murder, and treachery, and many other very wicked sins, which the human countenance cannot bear recalling. That (is) for pride—but for all sins which were done, to be saved from Hell.[175]

4/ Again since nine ranks of angels[176] who are clean of sins, do not apprehend the nature of sins altogether, thus they are dismayed and astounded and shake and shudder from the fear of His glory. They bless and beseech those who (have) no sins, no death, no judgment, no punishment.[177]

5/ But we then, how much are we obliged to weep and mourn, who have

---

170. Concerning Satanael's jealousy, see Stone 2013, 27, 65, 197, and 203–7. Grammatically this might also mean "He (God) was jealous and cast them out...." This seems inherently less likely an interpretation.

171. I.e., God.

172. Or: counselled.

173. Isa 6:3. The Trishagion came to play a major role in Jewish and Christian liturgy, as well as in Manichean texts.

174. Or: counsel.

175. The last sentence in this section is somewhat unclear.

176. Nine is a standard number of angelic classes in Christian texts.

177. I.e., the angels.

done sins heavier than the high mountains, or how much should we shake and shudder from the fear of God, weeping and <bewailing>, we must give up our soul. Alas, our sins! or how much should we pray and beseech, bless and praise, weep and bewail, confess and repent, so that he annihilates the book of our sins[178] (on) the day of judgement or frees[179] us from eternal fire and from the fiery dragons.[180]

6/ Again a Commentary on[181] Adam's Fruit
For (it was) not that the fruit which Adam ate was bad, for how was there bad fruit in the Garden? That was the evil, that God gave a fast[182] to Adam, "Do not eat of this tree," so that he might see and test Adam, whether he observes the commandment and the directive of God.

7/ Then He gave a command. At the hour he ate of the fruit there was no harm, but he particularly ascended to the upper Jerusalem.[183] When he ate the fast[184] he also forgot the mystery; on account of that He was angry with Adam and Eve. He expelled them from the Garden.

8/ So now, in the same way he gave us fasts and a commandment by the mouth of holy apostles and patriarchs, since those who fast go up to the kingdom like Elijah and Enoch,[185] but those who break the fasts of the bl[ess]ed patriarchs, go forth from the Garden like Adam.[186]

9/ Again, why did He ask, "Adam, where are you?"[187] for He himself knew that he was there. He asked for the (following) reason, that if Adam were to say, "I sinned," he would find forgiveness and would not go forth from the Garden.[188] Then he did not say, "I sinned," but cast the cause of his sin upon God and said, "This woman whom you cre-

---

178. Cf. Col. 2:14.
179. Literally: to free.
180. Cf. Isa 66:24.
181. Or: explanation of.
182. God's prohibition of the fruit is often called "a fast," and the protoplasts are accused of breaking their fast.
183. This idea is unusual.
184. I.e., the forbidden fruit.
185. Here there is the common interpretation of Gen 5:24 and 2 Kgs 2:11 as the assumption of Enoch and Elijah.
186. Gen 3:23.
187. Gen 3:9.
188. A common theme in homiletic literature: see Stone 2013, 74–75. This interpretation of Gen 3:9 is current from the mid-first millennium on.

ated gave the fruit to me and I ate (it)."[189] On account of that God was angry, that Adam did not say, "I sinned."[190]

10/ Again, why did He say to Eve, "Why did you, woman, do that," perchance the woman would say, "I sinned." And the woman, having learned from Adam, laid the blame on God, saying, "That serpent, which you created deceived me and I ate."[191] When God saw that they did not say, "I sinned," but laid the blame on Him himself, for that reason he expelled [end of photo

3.10. Ranks of the Angels Who Rebelled

This text, in manuscript M10320, fols. 79r–79v[192] enumerates sundry biblical numbers and measures, starting from the number of the rebellious angels, who are discussed above, see the introductory remarks to this section.[193]

Text

1/ / fol. 79r / Դասք հրեշտակաց որք[194] ապստամբեցօ. Լ գլխորք էին. ու ամէն մէկ / fol. 79v / ԼԲ ԼԲ ի գլխորք էին. եւ դասն Դ էին. Գ դասն երկիր անկեալ. եւ մին մացեալ.
Տրդատ.[195] Ձ տարի խոզ կեցօ.
Փարօն որ ընկղմեցօ ի ծովւ. ԹՃԲ մարդ էր.
Մովսէս. ժողովուրդն ՃԻ բիւր էր.
5/ Խ ամ անապատն կեցան:

Translation

1/ The classes of angels who rebelled. There were 30 chief ones,[196] and

---

189. Gen 3:12.
190. This section, and the following one on Eve, follow the standard Armenian interpretation of Gen 3:12–19.
191. Gen 3:13.
192. See the introductory remarks to 2.6.
193. Above pp. 66–67.
194. ք surmounted by erasure mark.
195. Trdat (Tiridates) III, King of Armenia (ca. 287–300), like Nebuchadnezzar in Dan 4:31–32, was changed into an animal, a wild boar. His reversion to human form was presided over by St. Gregory, and as a result he converted to Christianity. See Agathangelos §212.
196. The number is two hundred in 1 En. 6:6.

each / fol. 79v / one was 30,000 chief ones, and there were four ranks.
Three ranks fell to earth and one remained.
Trdat: he lived for six years as a pig.
Pharaoh: those who were drowned in the sea were 900,000 men.[197]
Moses: the people were 120,000.[198]

5/ They lived (in) the desert for 40 years.

3.11. Supplications to Angels

Bodleian Arm f 26, 333v–335r contains three short texts concerning various angels. They are of interest since they show how angels are invoked.

Text 1 Supplication

1/ Պաղատանք ընդդէմ հրեշտակաց եւ հրեշտակապետաց, Քերովբէից եւ Սերոբէից. աղաւթք.
2/ / fol. 333v / Անկանիմ առաջի քո ամենայն դասակցութեանց երկնաւոր զօրացդ հրեշտակացդ, անճառելի հրեշտակապետացդ, անիմանալի զօրութեանց, անքննել Սերովբէից ահաւորի՝ Քերովբէիցդ անակնարկելի. աթոռոցդ անհետազօտելի, եւ այլ ամենայն զօրութեանց վեհագունից անքաւից ծածկելոց ի հոգոց մտաց մեր ասերիգս[199] հրեղինացդ եւ հոգեղինացդ. լուսեղինացդ՝ որ անհաս բարձրութեամբ անակնարկելի տարածգութեամբ, յանիմանալի յաշխարհդ մի՛ա/ fol. 334r /ցեալ էք անկարօտ փառօք ի սէր ճշմարիտ միայնոյ բարոյն վառեալ ի հուր աստուածութեան.
3/ եւ անփոփոխ ի բարերարիսն. աստուածայսերբք[200] եւ մարդասերբք իմանիք[201] անուանիք. սակս որով երեւեցուցեալ սուր հատանող հրանիւթիցդ՝ ներքք՝ եւ ոչ կիզուք զարժանիսն կորստեան. վասն որոյ եւ ես հասեալս ի ծայրս ամենայն չարեաց.
4/ աղաղակեմ առ սրբութիւնդ սրբոց՝ եւ ունիմ աղերս եւ

---

197. Exod 12:37 speaks of six hundred picked chariots and all the other chariots of Egypt.
198. The numbers in Exodus are larger; see Exod 12:37 and 38:26.
199. There is a sublinear flat arc below –աս-. The element սեր may mean "genus, γένος» and it is in an oblique case, in the plural, with the suffixed demonstrative -ս-. The meaning is unclear.
200. –սեր– above line p.m.
201. In marg p.m.

բարեխօս զձեզ առ ինքնական զօրութիւն Երրորդութեանդ՝ եւ միահեծան աստուածութեանդ զկարզս երանաւէտ պաշտամման ձեր եւ զվէր առ ամենեսեան ի սուրբս եւ յամենից կարօղն՝ եւ հաստատօղն՝ միաբան հայցեցէք ի Տեառնէ զփրկութիւն իմոյ բազմամեղ անձինս նմանակից արարչին ձերոյ. որ ի խաշին կալով սպանողացն հայցէր թողութիւն.

5/ եւ մի զագրիք յանքիւ անօրէնութեանց. լերուք պահապան հոգոյ եւ մարմնոյ իմոյ. յայսմհետէ եւ մատուցող աղօթից իմոց. առաջի արարչին բնու/ fol. 334v /թեանցս. Աստուած յաւիտենական եւ անհաս անիմանալի. Երրորդութիւն սուրբ՝ յիշեա զփառս սուրբ կուսին. եւ զզօրութիւն սուրբ խաշին. զնահատակութիւն ճգնութիւն ամենայն սրբոց. եւ զվէր բոլոր երկնային զօրութեանցն՝ եւ վասն յիշատակի նոցա թող զմեղս իմ բազում. եւ ընկալ զմաղթանս աղօթից իմոց. որ ալրինեալդ ես այժմ եւ միշտ.

Translation

1/ Supplication (directed) towards angels and archangels, Cherubs and Seraphs. A prayer.

2/ I fall before you,[202] all participants of the heavenly hosts of Angels, you indescribable Archangels, you incomprehensible Powers, you fearsome unsleeping Seraphs, you Cherubs who cannot be regarded, you Thrones who cannot be investigated, and all other sublime powers, infinite, hidden from our minds' spirits, …,[203] you fiery ones and you earthen ones, you luminous ones who are inconceivable in height, unseeable in extent,[204] you incomprehensible ones in the world, you unite by full glory in true love of the single Good, burning in the fire of the Godhead,

3/ and unchanging in these benefices. Lovers of God and lovers of humans, you are named noetic on account of which you have made appear a cutting sword of a fiery element,[205] excuse and do not burn those worthy of destruction, on account of that I having reached the edges of every evil.

4/ I beseech the sanctity of your holinesses, and have you as prayers and

---

202. This pronoun is single, despite it specification as a series of angelic ranks.
203. Incomprehensible word, see note 199.
204. Taking տարածզրութեամբ as derived from տարածիչ "shot to a distance."
205. Or: substance.

intercessors to the very power of the Trinity and to the absolute Divinity, the ranks of your blessed service and the love towards all the saints and the One more powerful and more certain than all. Together ask my salvation of the Lord, me the sinful person, sharer of the likeness of your Creator, who being on the cross begged for the forgiveness of those who were killing Him.

5/ And do not reject (me) for innumerable acts of lawlessness. Be guardians of my soul and body, and henceforth (be one who) offers my prayers before the Creator of this nature (body) of mine. God, eternal and boundless, inconceivable holy Trinity, remember the glory of the Holy Virgin and the power of the holy cross, the valor, the ascesis[206] of all saints, the love of all the heavenly hosts, and for the sake of their memory, forgive my many sins, and accept my prayerful beseeching,[207] you who are blessed now and forever.

3.11.2. Prayer to the Archangel Michael

This text is preserved in the same manuscript OXBodleian ms arm f.26 on fol. 334v. It is another example of an apotropaic prayer directed to angels.

/ fol. 334v / Աղօթք հրեշտակապետի Միքայէլ
Երկնային զօրութեանցն նախազօրավար. եւ այժմ աղաչեմք զքեզ անարժան քո ծառայս, որ քոյին աղաչանօրդ պատսպարեցես զմեզ ընդ հովանաւորութեամբ թեւոց քոց՝ աննիւթ քոց փառացդ պահապանեալպս, առաջի քո անկանիմք՝ եւ հաւատով գոչեմք. յանձկութենէ փրկեա զիս՝ որ ես կարապետ վարին զօրացն որ եստեղծն զքեզ ճշմարիտն Աստուած նմա փարք յաւիտեանս յաւիտենից ամէն:

Translation

Prayer to the Archangel Michael
First commander of the heavenly hosts, now we beg you, (I) your unworthy servant, who beseeches you, shelter us under the shadow of your wings,[208] guardians of your immaterial glory. Before you we fall down and call faithfully. From straitness save me, because you are the

---

206. Perhaps this word should be in the genitive, yielding the meaning "the valor of the ascesis ..."
207. Literally: "the beseeching of my prayer."
208. Compare Ps 91(90):1, 4. The shifts in number are not highly significant.

precursor of the conduct of the hosts, you whom the true God created, to Him is glory forever and ever.

3.12. Prayer to the Twelve Guardian Angels

This document also occurs in OXBodleian ms arm f.26 on fol. 335r and it is the third of the angelological prayers we are publishing from that manuscript. This Armenian text was published previously from J1130, *Miscellany* (Prayers), p. 240 by N. Bogharian in 1969 and I republished it with an English translation in 2006 (Bogharian 1969, 4:201; Stone 2006a, 1:420–22). An analogous text is no. 69 in Feydit 1986, 223–24.

Here we give the text of OXBodleian arm f.26 (A), comparing it with our 2006 edition of J1130 (J). The variants are given in the apparatus below. We have kept the section numbering of the 2006 edition.

1/ Աղօթք Անուանք ԲԺ հրեշտակացն որ յամենայն ժամ կան մեզ պահապան։

2/ / fol. 335r / Յիշեա զՍարագիէլ հրեշտակն՝ եւ ապրիս ամենայն նեղութենէ։

3/ Յիշեա զՍարսիէլ հրեշտակն՝ եւ զոր ինչ ուզես Աստուծոյ տա քեզ։

4/ Յիշեա զՅովիէլ հրեշտակն եւ հալածին դեւք եւ դիւական ազանդք։

5/ Յիշեա զՄիքայէլ հրեշտակն եւ զԳաբրիէլ. եւ անփասա կաց ուր երթիցես։

6/ Յիշեա զՌափայէլ հրեշտակն եւ ոչ մերձենայ ի քեզ ցաւք եւ տրտմութիւնք։

7/ Յիշեա զսուրբ Սուքայէլ հրեշտակն. զի ի վերայ չերման ունի իշխանութիւն եւ որ յիշէ զսա. չերմն ոչ մերձենա ի նա։

8/ Յիշեա զՍարագիէլ հրեշտակն՝ որ ի վերայ ծնընդոց ունի իշխանութիւն. որ յիշէ ոչ փասի.

9/ Յիշեա զՂուկիէլ հրեշտակն. եւ ազատիս ամենայն նեղութենէ։

10/ Յիշեա զԵլքոս հրեշտակապետն ի վերայ չորց ունի իշխանութիւն. սա էշ երկնից եւ ի Յորդանան. եւ արհնեաց զորդին Աստուծոյ։

11/ Յիշեա Չիկայէլ հրեշտակն՝ եւ զՆուրիէլ ամեն։

Variants

1 Աղօթք] այս են J 2 յիշեա] յիշեալ J 3 ուզես] խնդրես J | յԱստուծոյ J 4 յիշեա] ի վերայ քնոյ յիշեալ J 5 հրեշտակն] հրեշտակս follows Գաբրիել J | ուր եւ J 6 յիշեա J | տրտմութիւն J 7 յիշեալ J 8 ծննդոցն J 9 յամենայն J | զիթայել J | ամէն] om J

Translation

1/ A Prayer, Names of the 12 Angels who Protect us at Every Hour
2/ Mention[209] the angel Saragiēl and you will be saved from every distress.
3/ Mention the angel Sarsiēl, and whatever you wish of God, he will give you.
4/ Mention the angel Yoviēl, and the demons and demonic magic will be put to flight.
5/ Mention the angel Michael, and Gabriel, and be unharmed wherever you go.
6/ Mention the angel Raphael and pains and sadness shall not approach you.
7/ Mention the holy angel Suk'iēl, for he has authority over fever and fever does not approach the one who mentions him.
8/ Mention the angel Saragiēl who has authority over births. The one who mentions (him) is not harmed.
9/ Mention the angel Łukiēl and you will be freed from every distress.
10/ Mention the archangel Elk'os.[210] He has authority over the waters. He descended <from> heavens to the Jordan and blessed the Son of God.[211]
11/ Mention the angel Zikayēl, and Nuriēl. Amen.[212]

---

209. Or "remember" and thus throughout this text.
210. It is unclear why Elk'os is titled "archangel" and the archangels Michael and Gabriel are called "angels"; see §5 above.
211. An unusual interpretation of the descent of the Holy Spirit on Christ in the Baptism. It is usually represented as a dove. Compare Mark 1:10 "the Spirit descending like a dove on him"; cf. Matt 3:16, Luke 3:22, John 1:32. The same function is found in text 3.1 §10 and in Feydit 1986, 223–24, where the angel is called Melqos. The other names are quite similar to those in Feydit 1986, no. 69 (223–25), which list is more extensive.
212. This line makes the impression of being an addition.

Part Four: Biblical Stories

4.1. Concerning the Tower 1

Manuscript M8591, which transmits this text on fols. 82r–82v, also contains *Story of Father Abraham*, published elsewhere (Stone 2012, 36–50), and *What Are the Dimensions of the Ark?* (above, text 1.5). The story of the Tower of Babel as it is found in M8591 recurs in *Biblical Paraphrases* with nearly identical details (see Stone 1982, 91–93). Both Genesis and *Biblical Paraphrases* are silent as to the measurements of the Tower. The text here appears to be an extract from a larger work. As to its contents, the confusion of tongues is not discussed nor anything else but the building itself. This incompleteness strengthens the idea that the text is excerpted from a larger document.

Text

Վասն աշտարակին

Եւ ՀԲ տանուտէրքն միաբանեցան. եւ սկսան շինել թրծեալ աղիւսին ընդդէմ հրոյ. եւ կուպրն ի շաղախի տեղ ընդդէմ ջրոյ. եւ բարձրացուցին Ժ ամսոյ ճանապարհին (լ)213 ելն եւ ընդ էջն. թանձրութիւն պարըսպին. Դ կանկուն. էջն Ծ կանգկուն Խ ամս շինեցին. ամառն եւ ձմեռն. եւ իշխանք վերակացու դրածոյն. Լամուր ի Սեմա ազգէն. Հայկն, Յաբեթի. եւ Բէլն, ի Քամա. եւ յետ Շ ԻԵ ամաց ջրհեղեղին էր սկիզբն շինուածոյ աշտարակին. յաշխարհին Բաբիլոնի:

---

213. Unclear sign.

Translation

Concerning the Tower

And 72 family heads[214] agreed and began to build with baked brick (as a protection) against fire and with pitch in the place of mortar (as a protection) against water.[215] And they elevated it to the height of ten months' travel, in ascent and descent. The thickness of the walls was 90 cubits. The descent (was) 50 cubits. They built for 40 years in summer and in winter. And the princes supervising the building[216] (were) Lamur of the family of Shem, Hayk of Japheth[217] and Bēl of Ham. And 525 years after the flood was the beginning of the building in the land of Babylon.[218]

4.2 Concerning the Tower 2

As noted in 1.5 above, fol. 7d M682 contains a brief text on the Tower of Babel.[219] This manuscript is discussed above in the introductory remarks to texts 1.12, 3.5, and 3.7. While 4.1 dealt with the dimensions of the Tower, this short text is narrative and also discusses the question of the division of the languages.

Text

1/ Վասն աշտարակի շինել. [Թ]է[220] ինչ պատճառս շինեցին:
2/ Զի յետ Նոյի ՇԻԵ ամին դարձեալ ամբարշտեցան մարդիկք. եւ յիշեցին զզրհեղեղն թէ վասն մեղաց եղեւ. բայց դրախտն Ադամայ ոչ եհաս ջուրն զի բարձր է լեառն դրախտին. եւ մօտ ի լուսնական գօտին. վասն այսորիկ ասեն եկայք շինեցցուք

---

214. See 4.2, Concerning the Tower 2 below on the number seventy-two. The incident is retailed in Gen 11:1–9. The confusion of tongues is not mentioned here.

215. Gen 11:3. Note the similar train of thought regarding the choice of materials for the two stelae: see *History of the Forefathers* §41; see Stone 1996a, 198–200 and below 4.5 §16. The Bible mentions baked bricks and bitumen.

216. դրած seems to be a participial form of the verb դնեմ "to put." Perhaps this means the building activity, which is what is called for in context.

217. Note this rooting of Armenian self-understanding in biblical tradition.

218. Above in several of the *Chronological Summaries* in part 2, 525 is the number of years from the flood to the Tower of Babel.

219. See part 1, part 3, note 86.

220. The colored and enlarged initial of this word was omitted. We conjecture թ, as above.

աշտարակ եւ բարձրացուցցուք մինչեւ գօտին լուսնական ի
չափ դրախտին. զի թէ այլ գայցէ. ոչ հասցէ անդ։
3/ Եւ բարձրացուցին մինչեւ Ժ ամսոյ ճանապարհի. Ե ամիս ի
գնալն: Եւ տեսեալ Աստուծոյ զչար միաբանութիւնն. հնչեաց
հողմ սաստիկ եւ եղեւ շարժումն խիստ եւ փլոյց զաշտարակն.
եւ յահէ ցրուեցան մարդիկքն. եւ ապա ուշաբերեալ սկսան այլ
եւ այլ լեզուս խօսել. եւ բաժանեցաւ մի լեզուն ՀԲ վասն որոյ
ցրուեցան իւրաքանչիւր աշխարհի եւ խաղաղացան:

Translation

1/ About the Building of the Tower. For which reasons did they build (it)?
2/ Because 525 years after Noah[221] again men acted impiously. And they remembered that the flood took place on account of sins. However, the water did not reach Adam's Garden for the mountain of the Garden is high,[222] and close to the lunar zone.[223] For this reason, they said, "Come, let us build a tower and let us raise it up to the lunar zone in the same measure[224] as the Garden, so that if it (i.e., the flood) comes again, it will not reach there."[225]
3/ And they raised it up to tenth months' travel, five months in going.[226] And God seeing the evil agreement, raised up a fierce wind and a strong earthquake took place[227] and destroyed the Tower and the men were scattered through fear. And then, their sense returned and they began to speak various languages and one language was divided into 72, on account of which each was scattered to his own land and they lived in peace.[228]

---

221. See part 2, note 231.
222. That the Garden was on a mountain or a height was a common tradition: see Stone, 2013, 15, 51–52 and sources cited there. See also 1QGenApoc 2.23, Cave of Treasures 18:13, 19:4 (Bauckham et al. 2013, 1:554) and other sources.
223. Based on Gen 11:4. Here a cosmology is reflected in which the seven planets, including the moon, were seen as occupying an ascending order of "spheres" of which the lowest is the lunar. Below this zone, the earth and visible sky form the sub-lunar zone. The biblical cosmology is simpler, reading "with its top in the heavens."
224. Meaning "height."
225. This is an expanded form of Gen 11:4, which is interpreted by 4.2 in terms of later cosmology as the lunar zone.
226. I.e., each way, ascending and descending. See preceding text for this matter.
227. The wind and earthquake are additions to the biblical account in Gen 11.
228. The text of the list of seventy-two languages exists in quite numerous manuscript copies. One form of it was published in Stone 1996a, 161–63. It is already found in P'ilon Tirakac'i's

4.3. Memorial of the Forefathers Abraham, Isaac, and Jacob

This document is an expansive retelling of the stories of the Patriarchs. It is known to me in four manuscript copies, and doubtlessly more exist. The copies known to date are:

M	M1665	1445	*Miscellany*	Taušał, Vaspurakan
B	OXBod Arm c 3	1632	*Lectionary*	New Julfa
Y	M6092	17th c.	*Miscellany*	
E	BL Egerton 708	17th c.	*Miscellany of Biblical Stories*	

The sections of this text dealing with Abraham were published in Stone 2012, 55–77 from M1665 (M). The material found in OXBodleian Arm c 3, that is, ms B, 222r–229v is another copy of this document which was not available when I edited §§1–48 and encompasses nearly all the material published there. In preparing the edition of §§1–48, I had three other manuscript copies at my disposal, those in M2012, M6092 (Y) and BL Egerton 708 (E).[229] As noted in the edition of sections 1–48, the Vorlage of Y had suffered displacements, and the section published here is not extant in that manuscript. Ms E is not presently at my disposal.

The text of §§49–101 occurs in M (M1665) on fols. 182v–198v and in B (OXBod Arm c 3) on fols. 325v–329r. Textually B is very close to M, even to the extent of shared orthographic details: see, for example, note 246. The text following the present document in manuscript M is Joasaph and Barlaam, which starts on fol. 190r of the manuscript. It is written in two columns and by a different hand. Ms M's text of §§49–§101 is published here.[230] Its beginning is marked by an enlarged word and a line of colored writing. Section divisions below are numbered sequentially following those in the previously published Abraham material. All the text published here is presented for the first time.

Chronography (seventh century); see p. 27 above. Rabbinic sources talk of seventy languages and peoples, while early Christian sources talk of seventy-two languages. This has been suggested to reflect the difference in the numbers of Noah's grandchildren in Gen 10, seventy according to the MT and seventy-two according to the LXX. However, it must be remarked that a variation of seventy/seventy-two is found elsewhere, as in the numbers of translators of the Septuagint and in the number of Christ's disciples. See on the text about seventy-two languages, Stone 1996a, 158–63.

229. See Eganyan et al. 2009, 5:815–20; Baronian and Conybeare 1918, 140–49; Eganyan et al. 1970, 2:248–49; Conybeare 1913, no. 90, 218–25.

230. Since B was not collated in Stone 2012, it is worth noting that in it, sections §§14–26, published there, are abbreviated in B.

PART FOUR

Although the present edition of §§49–101 is based on a diplomatic transcription of Ms M as the text, the image of fols. 183v–184r, that is, one opening of manuscript M, is missing from the microfilm at my disposal. For that section I have used ms B as the text. Into M's text, I have introduced a small number of clearly preferable readings of B and corrections of corruptions and marked them by pointed brackets < >. The scribe of M has proofread the text and introduced a number of interlinear corrections, which I noted. An apparatus of variants of B from M is found following the text.

The document is a retelling of the biblical story and though it is clearly Christian, the sort of exhortative expositions found, for example, in The Third Story of Joseph (see 4.7 below) are absent. Some comparisons are made with earlier Christian and Jewish exegesis and recorded in the notes to the translation.

Text

49/ / fol. 325v / Եւ իբրեւ եհաս Յակոբ ի հուն Յորդանանու ՚տասանորդեաց գխաշինսն իւր. Եւ եհան ԴԽ յամենայնէ գտասանորդսն. եւ առաքեաց եսաւայ եղբօրն իւրում: Եւ զայլն արար յերկուս բանակս եւ անցոյց ընդ գետն: Եւ պատուիրեաց ամենեցուն ասել հարցողաց. թէ Յակոբայ ենք[231] ծառային եսաւայ: Եւ ինքն ի վաղիւն երթայր կաղալով. եւ այն վասն Գ պատճառաց:

50/ Նախ՝ զի մի թուեսցի <երագ> նմա՝ գօտեկրին լինել ընդ Տեառն Աստուծոյ:
Եւ երկրորդ. զի որք կամիցին Աստուած պաշտութեամբ կեալ ի Քրիստոս Յիսուս. ի հալածանս կացցեն. եւ ամենայն որ խոնարհեցուցանէ զանձն բարձրասցի:

51/ Եւ երրորդ. զի տեսցէ եսաւ՝ զկաղալն Յակոբայ. եւ ողորմ անկցի ի սիրտ նորա:

52/ Եւ ի գնալն Յակոբայ՝ կաղալով միայն. եւ ահա եսաւ գայր ընդ առաջ նորա. ԴԽ արամբք ճիատրոք:
Իբրեւ ետես գՅակոբ եսաւ. զի գայր, վաղվաղակի էջ եսաւ ի ձիոյն: Ընդ նմին եւ ամենայն զաւրքն ճիաթափի եղեն:

53/ Եւ գիրկս արկեալ եղբարքն լացին ի վերայ միմեանց պարանոցի: Եւ ապա հեծեալ ի ձիս գնացին: Եւ բերեալ Յակոբ զկանայսն. եւ զորդիսն իւր՝ յերկրպագութիւն եսաւայ. եւ

---

231. Postclassical form in both manuscripts.

խնդրեաց Յեսաւայ մաղ անդէն. մինչեւ հաստատեցին մանկունքս:
Չի խոնճեալ էին ի ճանապարհին. եւ զի խաշանցն ծնունդն հասեալ էր. վասն այսորիկ մաղցին անդէն: Եւ եսաւ գնաց ի տուն իւր ի լեառն Սէիր. այն է էդոմ: Եւ յետ աւուրց չուեաց Յակոբ ի գնալ. եւ հասեալ մերձ ի Բեդղահէմ. անդ՝ / B fol. 326r / ծնաւ Հռաքէլ զԲենիամին. եւ մեռաւ ի ծնունդն:

54/ Եւ կոչեաց Յակոբ զանուն տղային. Բենիամին: որ ասի որդի աջոյ: / M end of fol. 183r /[232] Եւ ապա հասեալ առ Իսահակ հայրն իւր ի Մամբրէ. մերձ ի Քեբրոն: Եւ եդեն Իսահակայ ամք կենաց Ճ եւ Ձ: Եւ մեռաւ Իսահակ ի բարիոք ծերութեանն. եւ թաղեցին զնա որդիքն իւր Յակոբ՝ եւ Եսաւ. եւ եդին յայրին Սիկիմա. ուր էին Աբրահամ եւ Սառա՝ ի Քեբրոն. անդ եդին եւ զԼիա՝ զմայր որդոցն Յակոբայ:

55/ Եւ զՅովսէփ սիրէր Յակոբ առաւել քան զեղբարսն. եւ արարեալ էր նմա՝ պատմուճան ծաղկեայ: Եւ յաւուր միում ետես Յովսէփ[233] երազ. եւ ասաց Յակոբայ հաւր իւրոյ. թէ ես եւ եղբարք իմ. ի դաշտի որայ կապեաք: Եւ իմ որայն կանգնեցաւ ուղորդ. եւ եղբարց իմոց որեայքն եկեալ երկիր պագանէին որային իմոյ:

56/ Իբրեւ լուան եղբարքն. սկսան ատել զՅովսէփ՝ եւ Յակոբ սիրէր զնա: Եւ յետ աւուրց ինչ. ետես Յովսէփ միւս եւս երազ: Եւ ասաց Յակոբայ. թէ արեգակն եւ լուսինն եւ աստեղք մետասան. եկեալ երկիր պագանէին ինձ:

Իբրեւ լուան եղբարքն. եւս յաւելին ատել զնա. եւ ասին. մի թէ թագաւոր լիցիս դու՞. եւ մեք զամք երկիր պագանել քե՞զ:

57/ Եւ եդեւ յետ աւուրց. եւ էին եղբարքն Յովսեփայ ի ծնունդ[234] ոչխարացն ի Սիքիմ: Եւ Յակոբ առաքեաց զՅովսէփ ի ծործորոյն Քեբրոնի. առ եղբարսն ի տեսանել զողջունէ նոցա. եւ բերել նմա զրոյց: Եւ եկեալ Յովսէփ. ոչ եգիտ զեղբարսն ի Սիւքեմ:

58/ Եւ շշեալ անդ՝ որոնէր զեղբարսն: Եւ ետես զնա այր մի մոլորեալ ի դաշտին. եւ եհարց թէ՝ զի՞նչ խնդրես. եւ նա ասաց զեղբարսն իմ: Ասէ այրն. երեկ չուեցին աստի՝ եւ լուայ զի ասէին թէ երթամք ի Դովթայիմ:

59/ Եւ գնաց Յովսէփ ի Դովթայիմ. եւ եգիտ զնոսա անդ: Իբրեւ

---
232. The image containing the next two pages is missing from Ms M. The text is drawn from B.
233. n over ե B.
234. Erasure.

տեսին եղբարքն Յովսեփի զի զայր. ասեն եկայք սպանցուք զնա՝ եւ տեսցուք թէ յին՟չ կատարին երազք²³⁵ նորա: Եւ Ռուբէն ոչ եթող սպանանել զնա. այլ ասաց թէ ընկեցուք ի գուբ մի յանապատի աստ. եւ մի մեղիցուք յարիւն նորա:

60/ Զայս ասաց Ռուբէն. զի գերծուսցէ զմանուկն. եւ հասուցանէ զնա առ հայրն իւր. եւ առեալ ընգեցին զնա մերկ ի գուբ մի դարտակ: Չի հանին զձաղկեայ պատմուճանն յանձնեն:

61/ Եւ ինքեանք նստեալ ուտէին գհացն. զոր տարաւ նոցա Յովսեփի. եւ մաց Յովսեփի ի խորն զալուրս Գ: Եւ ահա՝ Մադիանացիք՝ արք վաճառականք. / M resumes here with fol. 184v / եկեալ անցանէին:

62/ Ասաց Յուդա՝ ընդէ՟ր սպանեմք զեղբայրն մեր. եկայք վաճառեսցուք զսա Իսմայէլացոցս. եւ մի մեղիցուք յարիւն նորա: Եւ վաճառեցին զՅովսէփի Լ դահեկան. Գաղ. եւ Դան. եւ զժ գողացան. եւ զԻ ցուցին եղբարցն իւրեանց:

63/ Եւ զծաղկեա շապիքն Յովսեփա թաթաւեցին յարիւն ուլուն. զոր զէնին եւ կերեան: Եւ զայն արեան թաթախի ի հայրն ուղարկեցին. ասելով թէ զպատանեակն քո զազան չար եկեր: Եւ Յակոբ իբրեւ ետես զայն. պատառեաց զհանդերձս իւր. եւ յոյժ զզացաւ. եւ լայր անմխիթար՝ թէ զազան չար եկեր զիմ տղայն:

64/ Եւ գնացեալ հասին մադիանացիքն. յԵգիպտոս. եւ վաճառեցին զՅովսեփի. Պետափրեա դահճապետին փարաւոնի: Եւ եզիտ Յովսեփի շնորհս առաջի Պետափրեայ. եւ զամենայն ինչ զոր ունէր ետ ի ձեռս Յովսեփա: <Եւ ամենայն ինչ յաջողէր դահճապետին. ի ձեռն Յովսէփայ:> զի Տէր էր ընդ նմա:

65/ Եւ եղեւ տարփալ կնոջն Պետափրեա. <չար ցանկութեամբ վասն մեղաց ընդ Յովսէփիայ>: Եւ շատ ջանաց ազգի ազգի դեղոք եւ հնարիւք՝ եւ ոչ կարաց ձգել զՅովսէփի ի մեղս: Վասն որոյ չարախաւսեաց զՅովսէփի. առ այրն իւր Պետափրեա: Եւ արկին զՅովսէփի ի բանտն փարաւոնի:

66/ Եւ ետ նմա Տէր շնորհս առաջի բանդապետին. եւ ամենայն բանտարգելոցն. զի Տէր էր ընդ / fol. 185r / Յովսեփա: Եւ էր յաչս ամենայն մարդկան <հա>ճելի:

67/ Եւ եղեւ զի բարկացաւ փարաւոն՝ խոհարարին իւրոյ՝ եւ տակառապետին. եւ արկ ի բանդ զերկոսինն: Եւ Յովսէփի կայր ի սպասու նոցա. եւ ի միումէ գիշերի տեսան էրազ երկոքինն.

---

235. No plural ending, as is fairly common with nominatives and accusatives.

BIBLICAL STORIES

ել տրտմեցան. եւ ի վաղիւն էհարց զնոսա Յովսէփ. վասն տրտմութեանն:

68/ Եւ նոքա ասեն երազ տեսաք եւ ոչ ոք է որ մեկնէ մեզ: Ասէ Յովսէփ՝ ասացէք ինձ թէ զինչ տեսէք: Ասէ տակառապետն՝ թուէր առաջի իմ որթ մի խաղ<ող>ոյ. յորում էր Գ ուր կանաչ. եւ յամէն ուր Գ ողկոյզ:

69/ Եւ ես էի առաջի փարաւոնի. եւ բաժակն արքայի ի ձեռին իմում. եւ ես առնուի զողկոյզն. եւ ճմլէի ի բաժակն ոսկի. եւ ունէի առաջի փարաւոնի՝ եւ նա առեալ զայն ըմպէր: Ասէ Յովսէփ. Գ ուրն եւ Գ որդկոյզն. Գ աւուրք են. եւ հանգէ արքա զքեզ ի բանդ<էս>: եւ դիցէ յիշխանութեան քում: Եւ կացես առաջի փարաւոնի ի փառն քո: Բայց յիշեցես զիս՝ որ անպարտ կամ ի բանդիս:

70/ Իբրեւ ետես մատակարարն թէ բարիոք մեկնեաց զերազն տակառապետին. նայ եւ զիւրն ասաց. թէ ունէի Գ խան ի զլուխ իմ. եւ ի վեր ի խանն / fol. 185v / կայր յամենայնէ յորմէ ուտէր փարաւոն միս եփեալ: Եւ սեաւ հաւք գային առնուին զայն. եւ տանէին: Ասէ Յովսէփ. Գ խանն Գ աւուրք են. եւ հանեալ փարաւոն սպանանէ զքեզ եւ կախէ զփայտէ. եւ հաւք կերիցեն զմարմին քո:

71/ Եւ յետ Գ աւուր էհաս տաւն ծննդեանն փարաւոնի. եւ էհան զնոսա ի բանդէն. եւ այնպէս եղեւ երկուցն որպէս եւ Յովսէփի ասաց: Եւ տակառապետն մոռացաւ զՅովսէփի ամս Բ եւ այն վասն Բ պատճառի՝ Նախ զի Յովսէփ կարծացցի եղեւ՝ եւ ի մարդ յուսացաւ. վասն այնորիկ ասէ մարգարէն: Անիծեալ է որ դիցէ զյոյս իւր ի մարդ. զի բար<հ> է յուսալ ի Տէր քան յուսալ ի մարդիկք: Եւ Բ պատճառն այն է. որ այլ մեծագոյն[236] բանի պահեցաւ Յովսէփի. որ զերազն փարաւոնի մեկնէր:

72/ Յորժամ վաճառեցաւ Յովսէփի. էր ԺԷ ամաց. եւ Ժ ամ ի տուն Պետափրեայ եկաց. եւ Գ ամ ի բանդն արգելաւ. եւ Լ ամաց էր յորժամ զփարաւոնի երազն մեկնեաց. վասն որոյ եւ թագաւորեաց:

73/ Փարաւոն երազ[237] ետես է գէր եւ գեղեցիկ երինճք էլին ի գետոյն. <եւ արածին առ ափին գետոյն>: Եւ յետ այնորիկ էլին ի գետոյն. այլ եւս է երինչք. նիհարք եւ վտիտ: Եւ կլան է յետին վտիտքն. զէ գէրք առաջինքն:

74/ Եւ դարձեալ ետես ի մի բուռն աւրայ է. էլին է հա/ fol. 136r /

---

236. Perhaps corruption from բարէյոյս "having good hope."
237. There is a dittography of երազ in Ms A, marked with erasure signs.

PART FOUR 121

սկք ատոք. եւ լիահատք: Եւ յետ սակաւ միոյ պահու ելին ի նոյն բունն աւրայէ. այլ եւս է հասկք ազազունք. եւ խորշակահարք. Եւ կլան զէ ատոկ հասքն. յետինքն զառաջինսն: Զայս եւեւ փարաւուն արքայ. եւ զարհուրեցաւ՝ եւ ոչ ոք էր որ մեկներ նմա²³⁸ զգերազն իւր:

75/ Բայց Աստուածն Յակոբայ յայտնեաց Յովսեփայ <որ մեկնեաց> գերազն փարաւունի՝ եւ զէ երինջքն՝ կրկին. եւ զէ հասքն կրկին. վասն ստուգութեան բանին: Եւ փարաւուն յանձնեաց զիշխանութիւնն իւր ի Յովսեփի: Եւ արար զնա տէր. եւ հրամանատար²³⁹ թագաւորութեանն իւրոյ:

76/ Եւ յետ է ամբ լիութեանն ժողովեաց Յովսեփ. բազում գորեան եւ ամբարեաց՝ յանենայն տեղիս: Եւ փեսայեցաւ²⁴⁰ Յովսեփի Պետափիրեալ քմրին. եւ եղեն նմա Բ որդիք յԱսանեթայ. յառաջ քան զսովն յամս լիութեանն. Եբրեմ եւ Մանասէ: Եւ ապայ եղեւ սովն եւ ի Քանան նեղութիւն մեծ:

77/ Եւ լուաւ Յակոբ՝ թէ գոյ ցորեան յեգիպտոս. եւ առաքեաց զԺ որդիս իւր. հացագին: Եւ Յովսեփի ճանաչեաց զնոսա. եւ հացոյց զնոսա. թէ դուք լրտես էք՝ մինչեւ հարկեցան ասել թէ մեք առն արդարոյ եւ մարգարէի որդիք եմք. եղբայրք ԲԺ-անք: Եւ ասէ Յովսեփի թարգմանաւ. եւ ուր՞ են Բ եղբարքն որ ոչ են ընդ ձեզ:

78/ Եւ նոքա ասեն. կրսերն / fol. 186v /առ հայր մեր է՝ եւ միուսն չէ ի միջի: Եւ Յովսեփի եա ունել զՇմաւոն. եւ կապել առաջի եղբարցն եւ ասաց. Սա եւ կացցէ առ մեզ գրաւ մին<չ>եւ²⁴¹ դուք երդայք²⁴² առ հայրն ձեր. եւ բերջիք ընդ ձեզ զկրսեր եղբայրն ձեր: Եւ ապա գիտացից թէ արք արդարք եւ խաղաղութեամբ էք դուք: Եւ ասաց հազարապետին իւրոյ. առնուլ զին գորենոյն ի նոցանէ. եւ տալ նոցա գորեան:

79/ Եւ դարձեալ զիւրաքանչիւր զին հացին. յիւրում քրճին դնել ծածկաբար. զի մի գիտասցեն նոքա: Եւ այնպէս ուղարկեալ²⁴³զնոսա: Տալ նոցա եւ պաշար բաւական ճանապարհին ինքեանց եւ գրաստից իւրոց: Եւ գնացեալ հասին ի տունս իւրեանց. եւ տեսին զիւրաքանչիւր ծրարն ի քրճի իւրեանց: եւ զարմացան:

---

238. Above line p.m.
239. ւն above line p.m.
240. Observe the strange orthography.
241. չ omitted M.
242. Sic.
243. ա2° above line M.

80/ Եւ իբրեւ կերան զայն. եւ պակասեաց կերակուրն:Ստիպէր զնոսա Յակոբ՝ դարձեալ երթալ յԵգիպտոս: Եւ նոքա ասեն եթէ Բենիամին ընդ մեզ ոչ եկեսցէ՝ ոչ կարեմ<ք>[244] յանդիման լինել առն այնորիկ: Չի ինքն ասաց. թէ ձեր կրսեր եղբայրն՝ ընդ ձեզ ոչ լիցի. ոչ տեսանիցէք զերեսս իմ:

81/ Յայնժամ ելաց Յակոբ եւ ասաց. Յովսէփի ընդ այն կորեաւ. եւ Շմաւոն չէ ի միջի. եւ զԲենիամին եւս առնուք յինէն: Վայ ծերութեան իմ եւ բեկման սրտիս: Յայնժամ Յուդա առաջի կացեալ ասաց՝ հայր իմ յիս վստահացիր զԲենիամին. ահա՝ Բ որդիք իմ. սպան զնոսա. եթէ ոչ տեսցես զԲենիամին:

82/ Եւ հազիւ հաւանեալ Յակոբ. ետ ի Յուդայ զԲենիամին. եւ ասաց. տարէք ընդ ձեզ. ի պտղոյ երկրիս աղերս առն այնորիկ: Ռետինն որ է զազպէն. եւ բեւեկն. ընկոյզ. եւ խունկ: Եւ արծաթ որ կրկին առէք ընդ ձեզ. եւ զարծանքն որ դարձաւ ի քուրձս ձեր. տարէք ընդ ձեզ՝ եւ տուք ի նայ: Եւ Աստուածն[245] իմ. եւ հարց իմոց. առաջնորդեսցէ ձեզ ի բարի:

83/ Եւ յուղի անկեալ գնացին եւ հասին յԵգիպտոս. եւ յանդիման եղեն Յովսէփայ եդին առաջի զաղերսն Յակոբա եւ զարծաթն որ դարձաւ ի քուրցս[246] նոցա: Ետես զԲենիամին եւ ետ հանել զՇմաւոն ար եղբայրսն իւր եւ ասէ գնաաս. այդ է եղբայրն ձեր կրսեր. եւ նոքա ասեն. սայ է ծառայն քո: Եւ ասէ Յովսէփի զԲենիամին՝ աւրհնեսցէ զքեզ որդեակ Տէր Աստուած հարց քոց:

84/ Եւ դարձեալ[247] ասէ գնաաս. զիարդ կա ծերունի հայրն[248] ձեր: Եւ նոքա ասեն ողջ է ծառայ քո հայրն մեր ողորմութեամբ ձեր: Ասէ Յովսէփի. Տէր Աստուած ողորմեսցի նմա: Չայս ասաց[249] Յովսէփի. եւ զալարեալ խորովէր աղիք նորա. եւ մտեալ առ անձին ելաց եւ առեալ ջուր[250] լուաց զերեսս իւր. եւ ել արտաքս. Եւ ասաց մատակարարին իւրոյ՝ առնել զենմունս եւ հոգալ կերակուրն: Եւ ի հասարակէլ[251] աւուրն պատրաստեցաւ[252] կերակուրն:

---

244. ք omitted M.
245. Above line p.m. M.
246. Note the orthography in both manuscripts.
247. ալ above line p.m.
248. ն with erasure marks.
249. ալ above line p.m.
250. ջ above line p.m.
251. ար above line p.m.
252. ս above line p.m.

85/ Եւ եկեալ Յովսէփի բազմեցաւ. եւ ետ կոչել / fol. 187r /զնոսա ի ներքս։ Եւ իբրեւ եկին. ունէր Յովսէփ սկիհ մի առաջի իւր արծաթի. եւ միոյ միոյ հարկանէր մատամբն զսկիհն իբր թէ հմայելով։ Եւ այնու նստուցանէր զեղբարսն. ըստ աւագութեան կարգի։ գՌուբէն եւ զՇմաւոն. զրԴեփ. եւ զայլն ըստ կարգի՝ եւ տայր իւրաքանչիւր²⁵³ մասն։ Եւ յաւելաւ մասն Բենիամենի. հնգեպատիկ քան զայլոցն։
86/ Եւ յետ երից աւուրց ասաց Յովսէփի. հազարապետին իւրոյ տալ նոցա ցորեան. եւ դնել զիւրաքանչիւր²⁵⁴ զին ցորենոյն ի քրձի իւր անդ²⁵⁵՝ ծածկաբար. Ասաց դնել զսկ<ի>հն արծաթի ի բեռն Բենիամենի. եւ պաշարով ուղեւորել զնոսա։ Եւ իբրեւ զնացին աւուր միոյ ճանապարհի. զհետ հասին ծառայքն Յովսէփայ. մեղադրանաւք եւ ասեն։
87/ Այդ է տեառն մերոյ լաւութեանն փոխարէն զոր արարէք դուք. ոչ գիտէք դուք թէ մեծութիւն տեառն մերոյ սկիհն²⁵⁶ այն էր. որով հմայէր՝ եւ դուք գողացայք զայն։ Եւ նոքա վարանեալ տարակուսեցան։ Եւ ծառայքն Յովսէփայ՝ զբեռինս որոնեալ. գտին ի քուրձն Բենիամենի։ Յայնժամ սրտաբեկեալ²⁵⁷ նոքա ամենեքեան աբի բերան լեալ։
88/ Եւ բարձին ամենեք<եան> դառնալ յԵգիպտոս։ Եւ ծառայքն Յովսէփա ասեն՝ դուք երթալ զնացէք խաղաղութեամբ զճանապարհին ձեր. զի նա միայն է մեզ գող եւ պարտական. ուր զսկիհն գտաք։ Եւ նոքա ասեն՝ մեք առանց դորա՝ գերէսս հայր մերում տեսանել ոչ կարեմք։ Եւ դարձան <անդ>/ fol. 188r /րէն յԵգիպտոս ընդ Բենիամենի. եւ յանդիման եղեն Յովսէփայ։
89/ Եւ Յովսէփի ասէ ցնոսա. դուք զնացէք խաղաղութեամբ զճանապարհին ձեր. նայ միայն է մեզ գող առ որում զսկիհն գտաք։ Ասէ Յուդա՝ մեք ամենեքեան ի ծառայութիւն քեզ մտանեմք։ Չի ոչ գող հնար մեզ՝ տեսանել զերեսս հայր մերում առանց դորա։ Իբրեւ ետես Յովսէփի գթագնապ տառապանաց եղբարցն. խռովեալ այրէր սիրտ նորա. եւ զալարէին աղիք նորա։
90/ Եւ հրամայեաց Եգիպտացոցն ամենեցուն արտաքս ելանել. զի

---

253. իւ2° partly damaged.
254. ց above line p.m.
255. կ erased.
256. ի above line p.m.
257. սր above line p.m.

ծանաւթս տացէ Յովսէփի եղբարցիւրոց. Եւ իբրեւեղեւ[258] Յովսէփի
ինքն միայն. եւ եղբայրք իւր՝ սկսաւ զռռալ. եւ զիւրաքանչիւր
ոք յեղբարցն կոչէր առ ինքն յանուանել լայով եւ համբուրէր
զնոսա. ասելով: Ես եմ Յովսէփ եղբայրն ձեր՝ մի ինչ հոգայք.
եւ մի ամաչէք. զի Աստուած հայր մերում տնաւրինեաց զայս՝
զայ ինձ աստ յառաջագոյն. եւ լինէլ ձեզ ասպընջական:

91/ Եւ եղբարքն Յովսէփիա զառաջինն ի ծանաւթս տայն
ապշեցան եւ յիմարեցան զահի հարեալ՝ եւ իբրեւ տեսին զի
քաղցրութեամբ խաւսէր ընդ նոսա. ցնծացան եւ ուրախացան:
Եւ ասէ Յովսէփ. է ամ լիութիւն եղեւ ամենայն բարեաց. եւ
ես ժողովեալ ամբարեցի շատ ցորեան. եւ ըստ տեսլեանն
փարաւոնի է զեր երինջքն եւ է ատոք հասքն: Եւ կերակուրք
եղեն նիհարացն:

92/ Որ նշանակէր զէն ամք լիութեան եւ նոյն[259] <անդ>/ fol. 188r /
րէն զգուշվա եղեւ. եւ Բ ամք անցեալ է սովոյս. եւ Ե ամք դեռ եւս
զայոց են սդութեանն: Առէք ընդ ձեզ ճիա եւ չորիս. եւ սայլա.
եւ զնացեալ բարձէք՝ զկանայս եւ զտղայս՝ եւ զհայրն ձեր. եւ
եկայք յեզիպտոս. զի ապրեսջիք ի սովոյս: Եւ նորա զնացին
ամենայն պատրաստութեամբ ըստ հրամանացն Յովսէփիա:

93/ Եւ առին զՅակոբ. եւ զամենայն տուն նորա. եւ զրնդանիսն՝
ոգիս ՀԵ. եւ իջին յեզիպտոս: Եւ ել Յովսէփի ընդ առաջ
հաւր իւրո Յակոբայ. աւուր միոյ ճանապարհի՝ եւ տեսեալ
Յակոբայ զՅովսէփի,[260] պայծառացաւ լոյս աչաց նորա: Լուաւ
փ<ար>աւոն[261] զգալ եղբարցն Յովսէփիա. եւ ուրախացաւ. եւ
ասաց Յովսէփիա՝ բեր զհայր քո առ իս. զի տեսից զնա. եւ առից
զաւրինութիւն նորա:

94/ Եւ տարաւ Յովսէփի զՅակոբ առ փարաւոն՝ եւ փարաւոն ի
տեսեալ զԱկոբ՝ ուրախացաւ յոյժ. եւ հարցանէր զժամանակ
աւուրցն Յակոբայ: Եւ Յակոբ ասաց՝ թէ Ճ Լ ամ կենաց իմց: Եւ
էր Յակոբ յոյժ մեծաշուք. եւ փառահեղ. լայնամորուս է մեծակն
քաղցրատէ եւ վայելչազեղ ընդ որ հիացեալ փարաւոն եւ խառ
աւհնութիւն Յակոբայ. եւ շնորհակալեցաւ փարաւոն Յակոբայ.
վասն Յովսէփիա:

95/ Եւ ասաց՝ ահայ, երկիրդ ամենայն ձեռամբն Յովսէփիա առաջի
ձեր է. ուր եւ հաճոյ թուին ձեզ՝ բնակեսջիք անդ: Եւ բնակեցյց

---

258. Above line p.m.
259.] above line p.m.
260.] above line p.m.
261. ար omitted: line break.

PART FOUR

Յովսէփ գհայրն²⁶²՝ եւ գեղբայրսն²⁶³ իւր ի Գեսեմ. եւ եկաց անդ Յակոբ ամս ժէ: Եւ եղեն ամենայն / M fol. 193c / աւու<ր>ք կենացն Յակոբայ. ամք ՃԽԷ.

96/ Եւ յաւր վախճանին իւրոյ՝ նստաւ արտաքոյ²⁶⁴ մահճացն. եւ աւրհնեաց զորդիսն մարգարէաբար. եւ յայտնի արար գշարսն եւ գբարիսն: Եւ ասա եղեւ Յովսէփայ. թէ հայր քո մերձ է ի վախճան: Եւ առեալ Յովսէփ զԲ որդիսն իւր. զՄանասէ եւ զԵփրեմ: Եւ եկն առ Յակոբ հայրն իւր՝ առնուլ ի նմանէ աւրհնութիւն իւրն եւ տղայոցն:

97/ Եւ մինչդեռ նստեալ էր Յակոբ. եւ խաւսէր ընդ որդիսն իւր՝ ահա՝ եմուտ Յովսէփ. Եւ Յակոբ ջանաց ելանել ընդ յառաջ²⁶⁵ Յովսէփայ եւ ոչ կարաց: Այլ խոնարհեցոյց զգլուխն ի վերայ գաւազանին. եւ երկիր եպագ Յովսէփայ ի ծագ գաւագ<ան>ին իւրոյ : Եւ ասա կատարեցաւ երազն Յովսէփայ. որ արեգակն ժԱ աստեղաւք եւ լուսինն երկիր պագանէին նմա:

98/ Եւ վախճանեցաւ²⁶⁶ Յակոբ ի բարիոք ծերութեան. Եւ պակասեալ ասդի. աւելաւ առ հարս իւր: Եւ հրաման ետ Յովսէփ ծառայից իւրոց. դիազարդեաց.²⁶⁷ պատել գհայր իւր. Եւ լուացեալ պատեցին²⁶⁸ գՅակոբ. եւ առեալ տարան ի Քեփրոն. յայրին Սիկիմայ.²⁶⁹ ուր էին Աբրահամ եւ Իսահակ. Սառա եւ Լիա. անդ եղին եւ զՅակոբ:

99/ Եւ Յովսէփի ի մեռանելն իւրում պատուիրեաց եղբարց եւ որդոց իւրոց եւ ասաց: Յայցելութեանն յորում այց արասցէ ձեզ Աստուած. եւ հանցէ զձեզ յերկրէ աստի. հանէք / fol. 189v / <եւ> գոսկերս իմ ընդ ձեզ. եւ տարէք յերկիրն Իսրայէլի. եւ դիք առ հայրն իմ. եւ եղբայրսն յայրին Սիկիմայ:

100/ Եւ վախճանեցաւ Յովսէփի՝ Ճ ժ ամաց. Լ ամաց. յայտնեցաւ փարաւոնի. եւ Ձ ամ թագաւորեաց Եգիպտոսի. եւ որքան ինքն կենդանի էր. եւ եղբայրքն մեռան: Նա զամենեսեան ետ տան<էլ>²⁷⁰ առ հարսն ի Քեփրոն: Եւ իբրեւ ինքն վախճանեցաւ. եղին գնայ ի տապանի յԵգիպտոս:

---

262. ր above line p.m.
263. յ above line p.m.
264. ւն above line p.m.
265. նր written erroneously and with deletion marks.
266. վախճանեաւ p.m. erased.
267. g above line p.m.
268. հայր written erroneously and with deletion marks.
269. This geographical anomaly also occurs in Abraham texts.
270. տան emended.

101/ Եւ ‹ի յելանելն› Իսրայելի յեգիպտոսէ. Մովսէս գոսկերսն Յովսեփայ ունէր: որով ընդ ծովս անցին. եւ բերեալ ի Սիկիմ ‹ընդ› հարսն հանգուցին յայրին.²⁷¹

Variants

M=M1665; B=OXBod Arm c 3
49 խաշինս B եղբօր B Գ] Դ 50 թռուեցցի B երագ B] om M գոստկորիւ B լինել B կամին B կայցեն եւ] կազցեն B 52 յառաջ B ԴՃ] ԳՃ B : graphic գայր] + եւ կաղայր B գօրքն B 54 խոնջեալ B եղում B] բեղլահեմ M ծնունդ B այսորիկ B մագին] մագ B սեիր B եղում B բեթլահեմ B 62 ըսպանանեմք B զեղբայրն] զեղբարն B : corrupt Իսմայելացւոցս B ղան] ղան B եղբարցն] եղբարցց B իւրեանց B գծաղկեալ B] om M 63 Յովսեփայ B թաթաւեցցին B ձեռն B Յովսեփայ B զենին B կերան B յաղարկեցին B ազաւ B 64 յեգիպտոս B Պետափրեա] first letter unclear M Պետափրեայ B Յովսեփայ B ‹եւ ամենայն — Յովսեփա› B] om M : hmt 65 Պետափրեայ B ‹չար — Յովսեփայ›] B om M : hmt 66 չարախօսեաց B Պետափրէս B բանտին B բանտապետացն B Յովսեփայ B հաձելի M] ձելի B 67 խարարարին B էարկ B բանտ միում B տեսին B 68 ասեն] + թէ մեզ] + գայն B թռուեր B խաղ‹որդ›որ B] խաղոյ M 69 արքային B արքա զքեզ] զքեզ արքայ B բանտեւ] B բանտ Ա դիցխաղոյ է] դիցէ զքեզ B կացցես B տունս B բանդն B 70 եթէ B բարւոք B զերազ B նա B յորմէ] յորում B ունէ B ունէին] տանէին B Գ խասն] om B 71 տոն B ծննըդեանն M*] ծնըդեանն M° բանտէն B որպէս եւ] որպէս B կարճողի B է] om B անիծեալ է] անիծեալ B գյոյս իւր] om իւր B բար‹ի›] B բար M մարդիկք B այն է] այն B 72 տուն — Գ ամ] om B : hmt ի բանտ B 73 երինցք B զետուղն B : hypercorrection եւ2° — գետոյն2°] om M : hmt նիհարք B վտիտք B զերք առաջինքն] առաջին զերքն B 74 մի ոջ B ալրայն] որայն B : and thus henceforth հասակ B ատոր B հասկք] հասկուն B հասկքն] հասկուն B մեկնէ] մեկներ B 75 զերագն] որ մեկնեաց զերագն B հակուն B թագաւորութեան B 76 յետ] յէ B լութեան B վիսեաց] վիսաեցաւ B քըրի B եփրեմ B 77 որդիսն B ահացոյց B եղբայրք B 78 նորա ասեն] ասեն B հայր մեր] հօրն մերում B մեւսն] մեւսն B սա] սա եւ B մին‹չ›եւ] մինչ որ B երդայք] երթայք B եղբայր B խաղաղութեան B 79 դարձեալ] եւ դարձեալ B ուտարկել] ուղեւորեալ B եւ պաշար] պաշար B ծրար B արծարոյ] B արծի M 80

---

271. Both M and B have a colophon at this point.

դարձեալ երթալ] երթալ դարձեալ B բենիամին B կարեմք B] կարեմ M քէ] եթէ B ոչ3°] մի B 81 իմոյ B առ առաջի] յառաջ B տարայք B ահա] եւ ահա B 82 Յուդա B քուրձան B անկոչզ] ընկոչզ B տարայք B նայ] նա B Աստուածն B հարցն B 83 յեզիպտոս B Յակոբայ B կրսեր B սա է ծառայ B հարց քոց] հօր քո B 84 կայ B ասէ] ասսէ B հայր2°] հայր M· հայրն M° առանձինն B ձեր] քո over eras. B երեսս B° արտաքը] արտաքս B իւրն B կերակուրս B 85 եւ ի] եւ B առաջի իւր / արձարթի] ~ B զՌուբէն եւ] Ռուբէն B զՂեւի B մասն] իւր մասն B 86 ասաց Յովսէփի] ~ B զինա B քրձի իւր] քրձի B բեռն] բերն B մեղադրանօք B 87 փոխարէն] փոխան B զիտէք դուք] զիտէք B մեծութիւն] մեծութեան B Յովսեփու B էր] է B բերին B աքի] ափի B լեալ] եղեն B 88 ամենէք<եան>] B ամենէք M Յովսեփայ B զերեսս հօր B տեսանել / ոչ կարեմք] ~ B <անդ>րէն] անդրէմ B յեզիպտոս B 89 խաղաղութեամք] follows ձեր B նա B ի ծառայութիւն քեզ] քեզ ի ծառայութիւն B զտեսանել B 90 հրամաեաց] հրաման ետ B ծանօթս B եղբարքն B յանուանել B հօր B տնօրինաց B ասպընձական B 91 Յովսեփայ B ծանօթս B յիմարեցան] om B հարան B խօսէր B հասկքն B եւ կերակուրք] կերակուր B նիխարացն B 92 լիութեանն B չափովս B են] են սդութեան B Յովսեփայ B 93 զրնտանիսն B Հ եւ է B հօր զտփա] զտվոյս որ B հօր իւրոյ B 94 զակոբ B տեսեալ] տեսանելն B ամ] + է B լայնամօրուս B աւուր] աւուր B 95 ահա B Յովսեփայ B թրլի B իւր] om B եկաց B անդ] follows Յակոբ B ՃԽԻ B 96 յատուրս B <ազդ>] ասա M իւր B 97 խօսէր B յառաջ] առաջ M Յովսեփայ] follows իւրոյ B զաւաք<ան>ին B] զաւազին M աստեղօքն B 98 բարունք B յաւելաւ B դիազարդեաց] g above line M դիազարդաց B qՅակոբ] զհայր qՅակոբ with erasure of զհայր M qԱկոբ B Քեբրոն B յայրն B 99 պատուեր ետ B եղբարց իւրոց B <եւ> B] om M հարսն մեր B եղբարսն B 100 Խ եւ Ժ B եղբարքն B զնա B տան<էլ>] B տան M 101 ի յեչանելն] ի յելսն B Իսրայելի] om B Յովսեփիա B <ընդ> M] ըն B

Translation

49/ And when Jacob reached the ford of the Jordan, he tithed his sheep. And he took the tithes of 400 from all and he sent (them) to Esau his brother. And he made the remainder into two camps and brought them across the river. And he commanded (them) to say to all those who ask, "We are Jacob's, Esau's servant." 272 And

---

272. Genesis does not mention a tithe and it would be strange indeed for Jacob to give a tithe

on the next day he himself walked with a limp, and that for three reasons.

50/ First, lest his wrestling with the Lord God seem to him a dream.[273] And second, because those living will, wishing through piety towards God to live in Jesus Christ, be persecuted. Everyone who humbles himself will be raised on high.

51/ And third, so that Esau might see Jacob's limp and become merciful.[274]

52/ And when Jacob walked alone limping, and behold, Esau came to meet him with 400 mounted men.
When Esau saw Jacob coming, immediately Esau dismounted from (his) horse: and with him, all (his) force dismounted.[275]

53/ And the brothers embracing, they wept upon each other's neck.[276] And then, mounting horses, they went on. And Jacob brought (his) wives and sons to bow down to Esau, and he asked Esau to remain there, until these children (of his) are restored, for they were tired from the journey. And the lambing season for the sheep had arrived.[277] On account of this, they remained there. And Esau went to his home in Mount Seir that is Edom.[278] And after some days, Jacob set out and arrived close to Bethlehem.[279] There Rachel bore Benjamin and she died in childbirth.

54/ And Jacob called the boy's name Benjamin, which means "son of right hand."[280] And then, he reached Isaac his father in Mambrē, close by Hebron.[281] And the years of Isaac's life were 180. And Isaac died at good old age and Jacob and Esau, his sons, buried him in Hebron.[282]

---

to Esau. He did take some of his flocks and send them to Esau, see Gen 32:13-20.

273. Gen 32:24-25.

274. This third reason is not mentioned in Genesis.

275. Gen 33:1, 4. Genesis 33:4 says that Esau ran to Jacob; 33:1 mentions the four hundred men, but does not say that they were mounted. The Armenian tale, however, assumes that both the four hundred men, and also Esau himself were mounted on horses. Horses are first mentioned in Gen 47:17.

276. Gen 33:4.

277. Gen 33:5-14.

278. Gen 33:16.

279. The Bible talks about Shechem in this context. The Memorial of the Forefathers omits the incident of Shechem completely, as well as the death of Rebecca's nurse, Deborah (Gen 35:8) and Jacob's setting up an altar (Gen 35:7) and the consequent theophany (Gen 35:9-15). The place where Rachel died is called Ephrath identified as Bethlehem by Gen 35:6. Just how Luz = Bethel fitted in is not clear (Gen 35:6).

280. Gen 35:18.

281. Gen 35:27.

282. Gen 35:28. His burial in Machpelah is not mentioned in Genesis here. That detail is

And they placed (him) in the cave of Shechem where Abraham and Sarah were, in Hebron. And there they also put Leah, the mother of Jacob's sons.

55/ And Jacob loved Joseph more than (his) brothers, and he made him a flowered robe.[283] And one day, Joseph saw a dream. And he said to Jacob his father, "I and my brothers were binding sheaves in a field, and my sheaf stood up straight, and the sheaves of my brothers came and were bowing down to my sheaf."[284]

56/ When his brothers heard (this), they began to hate Joseph,[285] and Jacob loved him. And after some days, Joseph saw another dream, and he said to Jacob, "The sun and the moon and eleven stars came and were bowing down to me."[286] When his brothers heard (this), they hated him even more and said, "Will you become a king and shall we come to bow down to you?"[287]

57/ And it came to pass after some days, the brothers were at the lambing in Shechem. And Jacob sent Joseph to the vale of Hebron to (his) brothers to see about their wellbeing and to bring him a report. And Joseph came and he did not find his brothers in Shechem.

58/ And he went about there, he sought his brothers. And a man saw him wandering in the field and he asked, "What do you seek?" And he said, "My brothers." The man said, "Yesterday they went from here and I heard them saying, 'Let us go to Dothaim.'"[288]

59/ And Joseph went to Dothaim and he found them there. When the brothers saw Joseph coming, they said, "Come, let us kill him, and we shall see how his dreams are fulfilled."[289] And Reuben did not permit them to kill him, but said, "Let us cast him into a pit in the desert, and let us not sin against his blood."[290]

60/ Reuben said that so that he might free the youth and bring him to

---

drawn from Gen 49:31. There it also mentions Leah's burial in the same place. The strange statement that "the cave of Shechem" was in Hebron is discussed in Stone 2012, 57. It recurs here in §§98–101.

283. Gen 37:3.
284. Gen 37:6–7.
285. Gen 37:8. Here, the Armenian text adds bowing to the biblical tale, and this point is picked up later in the story.
286. Gen 37:9–11.
287. Gen 37:11.
288. Gen 37:12–17.
289. Gen 37:18.
290. Gen 37:21–22.

his father. And, taking (him), they cast him naked into an empty pit, because they took the flowered garment from his body.[291]

61/ And they themselves sat down and ate the bread that Joseph had brought to them. And Joseph remained in the deep pit for three days.[292] And behold, Midianites, trading men, came and passed by.[293]

62/ Judah said, "Why should we kill our brother? Come let us sell him to these Ishmaelites and let us not sin against his blood."[294] And Gad and Dan sold Joseph for thirty coins.[295] And they stole ten and showed the 20 to their brothers.[296]

63/ And they dipped Joseph's flowered shirt into the blood of a kid, which they slaughtered and ate. And they sent to their father that (shirt) soiled with blood saying, "A wicked beast ate your youth." And when Jacob saw that, he rent his garments and mourned greatly and wept inconsolably, "A wicked beast has eaten my boy."[297]

64/ And the Midianites proceeded and reached Egypt. And they sold Joseph to Pentap'rēs, Pharaoh's chief executioner.[298] And Joseph found grace before Pentap'rēs and he gave all his possessions into his hands (i.e., authority). <And all the chief executioner's affairs prospered in Joseph's hand> for the Lord was with him.[299]

65/ And it came to pass that Pentap'rēs's wife desired <with wicked desire to sin with Joseph.> And she attempted (i.e., to achieve that) with various potions and spells.[300] And she was unable to draw Joseph to sin. For this reason she maligned Joseph to her husband, Pentap'rēs. And they cast Joseph into Pharaoh's prison.[301]

---

291. Gen 37:22–24.
292. Three days are not mentioned in Genesis. Are they designed to suggest the three days between Christ's Crucifixion and Resurrection?
293. Gen 37:28.
294. Gen 37:26–27.
295. Reading դեցամ as դահեկան.
296. Here there is the resolution of a tension. Twenty pieces of silver are mentioned in Genesis. In the Third Story of Joseph (4.5 below), like here, thirty pieces of silver are Joseph's price in the present section, due to the view of Joseph as a type of Christ. See Matt 26:15; 27:3, 9. This difference is explained by the thievery of Gad and Dan. These two of the brothers are not mentioned in the sale of Joseph as delineated by Gen 37:28.
297. Gen 37:31–33.
298. Gen 37:36.
299. Gen 39:2–5.
300. Note the apocryphal tradition, cf. T. Jos. 6.
301. In contrast to the Third Story of Joseph, not much is made of his modesty in the incident of Potiphar's wife and no homiletics attend this recital. See Gen 39:7–20 where this incident is retailed.

66/ And the Lord gave him grace before the chief warden and all the prisoners, for the Lord was with Joseph. And he was pleasing in the eyes of all men.[302]

67/ And it came to pass that Pharaoh was wrath with his cook and his chief cupbearer and he cast them both into prison. And Joseph was at their service.[303] And on one night they both saw a dream and they were distressed. And on the morrow, Joseph asked them about their distress.[304]

68/ And they said, "We saw a dream and there is no one to interpret it to us." Joseph said, "Tell me what you saw." The chief cupbearer said, "A g<ra>pe vine appeared before me on which there were three green branches, and on each branch, three bunches of grapes.[305]

69/ "And I was before Pharaoh with the king's cup in my hand, and I was taking the bunch, I was squeezing (it) into a gold cup. And I held it before Pharaoh and he took it and drank." Joseph said, "Three branches and three bunches of grapes are three days. And the king will bring you forth from <this> prison and will set (you) in your office. And you will stand before Pharaoh in your glory.[306] However, mention me, who am in this prison blameless."[307]

70/ When the steward[308] saw that he had interpreted the chief cupbearer's dream favorably, then he told his as well. "I had three platters upon my head, and upon (each) platter was of all baked meat of which Pharaoh used to eat. And black birds came (and) were seizing it and taking it away." Joseph said, "The three platters are three days and Pharaoh bringing you forth, will kill you and hang (you) from a tree and birds will eat your body."[309]

71/ And after three days the festival of Pharaoh's birthday arrived and he brought them out of the prison. And it happened to the two of them just as Joseph had said.[310] And the chief cupbearer forgot Joseph for

---

302. Gen 39:21-23. The Armenian text adds the goodwill of all the prisoners to that of the keeper of the prison.
303. Gen 40:1-4.
304. Gen 40:6-7.
305. Gen 40:8-10. Observe that Joseph's pious coda, "Do not interpretations belong to God?" is omitted by the Armenian text.
306. Gen 40:12-13.
307. Gen 40:14-15. Commentators impute blame to Joseph for this request, opining that it shows a weakening of his faith in God. Here, that idea is present in §71.
308. I.e., the cook.
309. Gen 40:16-19.
310. A summary of Gen 40:20-22, followed by a moralistic expansion.

two years. And that was for two reasons. First, that Joseph was impatient and set his hope upon a human, concerning which the prophet says, "Cursed is he who sets his hope upon a man, for it is better to hope in the Lord than to hope in man."[311] And the second reason is that, that Joseph was reserved for a greater matter, (which was) that he would interpret Pharaoh's dream.

72/ When Joseph was sold he was 17 years old, and he was in the house of Pentap'rēs for ten years, and for three years he was shut up in prison. And he was 30 years old when he interpreted Pharaoh's dream, on account of which he also became king.[312]

73/ Pharaoh saw a dream. seven plump and beautiful heifers came forth from the river <and they were pasturing by the river bank>. And after that, another further seven heifers, thin and lean, came forth from the river and they swallowed the seven plump first ones.[313]

74/ And again he saw from one sheaf there came forth seven ears abundant and full. And after a short while, there came forth from the same sheaf yet seven more ears, lean and withered, and the latter swallowed up the former seven abundant and full ones.[314] Pharaoh the king saw this and he was at a loss and there was no one who could interpret his dream.[315]

75/ But the God of Jacob revealed the dream to Joseph <who interpreted (it)> to Pharaoh. And the seven heifers (were shown) twice and the seven ears twice, in order to make the matter precise. And Pharaoh transferred his authority to Joseph and he made him lord and commander of his kingdom.[316]

76/ And after the seven years of plenty Joseph gathered much wheat and stored it in every place.[317] And Joseph became the son-in-law of Pentap'rēs the priest, and he had two sons, Ephraim (Ebrem)[318] and Manasseh from Aseneth before the famine, in the years of plenty.[319] And then there was famine and great difficulty in Canaan.

---

311. Ps 118(117):9. The "prophet" is David, whom the Armenian tradition regards as such.

312. This chronological outline is not based on the biblical text, except for the age of thirty at which he entered Pharaoh's service: Gen 41:46. The age of thirty was considered especially favorable; see Stone 2012, 97.

313. Gen 41:1-4.

314. Gen 41:6-7.

315. Gen 41:8.

316. This section is a summary of Gen 41:14-45.

317. Gen 41:48-49.

318. An unusual orthography.

319. Gen 41:50-52. The Armenian text infers from the order of events in Genesis that the

77/ And Jacob heard that there was wheat in Egypt and he sent his ten sons to buy bread. And Joseph recognized them[320] and provided them with bread,[321] "You are spies!" until they were constrained to say, "We are 12 brothers, sons of a righteous man and prophet." And Joseph said through the dragoman,[322] "Where are your two brothers who are not with you?"

78/ And they said, "The youngest is with our father and the other is not present." And Joseph caused Simeon to be seized and bound before the brothers, and said, "This one shall remain with us as a surety until you go to your father and bring (back) your youngest brother with you. And then I shall know that you are righteous and peaceful men."[323] And he told his steward to take the price of the wheat from them and to give them wheat,

79/ and secretly to replace the price of each one's wheat into his sack, so that they should not know, and thus to send them off. (He commanded) to give them enough supplies for the way, for themselves and for their animals. And they went and reached their home, and they saw that each one's money (was) in their sacks, and they were amazed.[324]

80/ And when they had eaten that and food was short, Jacob urged them to go to Egypt again.[325] And they said, "If Benjamin does not come with us, <we> cannot stand before that man, for he said, 'If your younger brother is not with you, you will not see my face.'"[326]

81/ Then Jacob wept and said, "Joseph has perished with that, and Simeon is not present and would you take Benjamin from me as well? Alas, my old age and my heartbreak."[327] Then Judah came forward and said, "My father, entrust Benjamin to me. Behold, my two sons, kill them if you do not see Benjamin (again)."[328]

82/ And Jacob was persuaded with difficulty. He gave Benjamin to Judah

---

abundance of the first seven years was also the reason for Joseph's fruitfulness shown in the birth of his two sons.

320. Gen 42:7.
321. Or, with a slight emendation: drew them close. Gen 42:1–9 are summarized here.
322. The "interpreter" or "dragoman" is actually introduced at a later point in the biblical narrative, see Gen 42:23.
323. Gen 42:18–20.
324. Gen 42:25–27. In the Bible, they opened the sacks at their lodgings.
325. Gen 43:2.
326. Gen 43:3.
327. Gen 42:36.
328. Gen 43:8–9.

and he said, "Take with you of the fruit of this land as a gift[329] to that man, resin which is from the honeydew and juniper, nuts and incense and take with you the money which was returned to your sacks, and give (that) to him. And my God and (the God) of my fathers will lead you to the good."

83/ And taking,[330] they went. And they reached Egypt and stood before Joseph.[331] They set firstmost both Jacob's gifts[332] and the silver that was returned in their sacks.[333] He saw Benjamin and caused Simeon to be brought forth to his brothers[334] and said to them, "Is this your youngest brother?" And they said, "This is he, your servant." And Joseph said to Benjamin, "May the Lord God of your fathers bless you, son."[335]

84/ And again he said to them, "How is your aged father?" And they said, "Your servant, our father, is well through your mercy." Joseph said, "May the Lord God have mercy on him."[336] Joseph said this and his emotions were openly aroused.[337] And he went off[338] alone and taking water he washed his face, and he went out. And his said to his steward to slaughter (i.e., animals) and to take care of the food. And at midday the food was ready.

85/ And Joseph came and seated himself and had them summoned inside. And when they came, Joseph had a silver goblet in front of himself, and he struck the goblet with his fingers one after the other as if divining.[339] And he had the brothers seated according to the order of their ages: Reuben and Simeon, Levi and the others in order. And he gave each of them a portion and he made Benjamin's portion fivefold more than those of the others.[340]

86/ And after three days, Joseph said to his steward to give them wheat and secretly to place the price of each one's wheat in his sack. He said to put

---

329. Literally: supplication.
330. Probably either the loads or the goblet. Gen 43:11–14.
331. Gen 43:15.
332. See above, §82.
333. Gen 43:20–22.
334. Gen 43:23: in Genesis it is Joseph's steward who has Simeon brought.
335. Gen 43:29.
336. Gen 43:27–28.
337. Literally: his bowels (i.e., emotions) were … compassionated. Gen 43:30.
338. Literally: entered (i.e., another room). Similarly Gen 43:30–31.
339. This incident is embroidered, describing Joseph's divination by tapping the cup and deriving that idea from Gen 44:5. James Russell has suggested to me that the sound of the tapping may have an atropaic function (personal communication).
340. Gen 43:33–34.

the silver goblet in Benjamin's load and to despatch them with provisions.³⁴¹ And when they had gone one day's travel, Joseph's servants caught up and with accusation they said.³⁴²

87/ "Is that which you have done a recompense for our master's goodness? Do you not know that that goblet is our master's greatness, by which he divines, and you have stolen that?"³⁴³ And they, discomfited, were of two minds. And Joseph's servants searched in the loads; they found (it) in Benjamin's sack. Then they were all broken-hearted at its being at the mouth of the load.³⁴⁴

88/ And they all rose up to return to Egypt. And Joseph's servants said, "You go on your way in peace, for only he is ours (who is) the thief and the guilty one, where we have found the goblet." And they said, "We are unable to see our father's face without him." And they returned thence to Egypt with Benjamin. And they stood opposite Joseph.³⁴⁵

89/ And Joseph said to them, "Go on your way peacefully. Behold, for us only he with whom we found the goblet is a thief."³⁴⁶ Judah said, "We will all become slaves to you, for it is impossible for us to see our father's face without him." ³⁴⁷ When Joseph saw the grievous affliction of (his) brothers his heart was distressed and burned, and his mercies were aroused.

90/ And Joseph commanded all the Egyptians to go outside, so that Joseph might be known to his brothers.³⁴⁸ And when Joseph and his brothers were alone, he began to make a noise,³⁴⁹ and he summoned each of the brothers to him, naming (them) and weeping and he kissed them, saying, "I am Joseph your brother, have no care and be not ashamed, for the God of our father arranged this, my coming hither first and becoming a shelter for you."³⁵⁰

91/ And at first, Joseph's brothers were confounded when he made himself known and they were bewildered, smitten by fear. And when they

---

341. Gen 44:1–2.
342. Gen 44:4.
343. Gen 44:5–6.
344. Gen 44:12.
345. Gen 44:13–14.
346. Gen 44:17.
347. Gen 44:18–34. The section epitomises the dialogue between Judah and Joseph.
348. Gen 45:1–2.
349. I.e., lifted up his voice. Genesis 45:2 says, "And he wept so loudly that the Egyptians heard it, and the household of Pharaoh heard it."
350. Genesis 45:3–13 is much longer than this retelling of the events.

saw that he was speaking with them kindly, they rejoiced and were happy. And Joseph said, "For seven years there was a plenitude of all good things and I gathered and warehoused a great deal of corn. And according to Pharaoh's dream of seven fat heifers and seven full ears of corn, and they became food for the lean.

92/ "They symbolized the seven years of plenitude. And the famine was of the same measure (i.e., of years), and two years of this famine have passed and five years of difficulty are still to come.[351] Take horses and mules and carts with you and go and take you wives and sons and your father, and come to Egypt, so that you may be saved from the famine." And they went with all the preparations according to Joseph's commands.[352]

93/ And they took Jacob and all his house and his household, 75 souls,[353] and they went down to Egypt. And Joseph went forth to meet his father Jacob, one day's journey. And when Jacob saw Joseph, the light of his eyes was brilliant. Pharaoh heard of the coming of Joseph's brothers and he rejoiced and said to Joseph, "Bring your father to me that I may see him and receive his blessing."

94/ And Joseph took Jacob to Pharaoh, And Pharaoh, when he saw Jacob, rejoiced greatly. And he asked about Jacob's age.[354] And <J>acob said, "The years of my life are 130." And Jacob was very magnificent with glorious hair, wide-bearded and large-eyed, of kindly appearance and handsome. Pharaoh regarded him and received Jacob's blessing.[355] And Pharaoh was thankful to Jacob for Joseph's sake.

95/ And he said, "Behold all the land under Joseph's control[356] is before you. Settle wherever seems pleasant to you. And Joseph settled his father and his brothers in Goshen[357] and Jacob remained there for 17 years. And all the days of the life of Jacob were 147 years.[358]

---

351. Only this last sentence is close to Genesis (45:6). The preceding is all added to the biblical story.
352. In fact, in Genesis, Pharaoh gives the instructions: see Gen 45:17–21. Joseph's gifts (Gen 45:21–23) are not mentioned.
353. Gen 46:26–27, and Exod 1:5 both speak of seventy souls. Genesis 46:27 also reckons Joseph and his two sons among the Israelites, making 73. The source of 75 souls going down to Egypt with Jacob is unclear.
354. Literally: the time of the days of Jacob. The incident is related in Gen 47:8–9.
355. Gen 47:10.
356. Literally: hands.
357. Gen 47:11–12.
358. Gen 47:28.

96/ And on the day of his death, he sat up out of the bed and blessed his sons prophetically, and made evident[359] the evil things and the good ones.[360] And Joseph was <notified>, "Your father is close to (his) death." And Joseph took his two sons, Manasseh and Ephraim, and he came to Jacob his father, to receive his own blessing and his sons' from him.[361]

97/ And while Jacob was sitting up[362] and speaking with his sons, behold, Joseph entered. And Jacob strove to go forth to meet Joseph and he was unable. However, he inclined his head downwards upon his staff, and he bowed down to the lowest point on his staff to Joseph.[363] And here the dream of Joseph was fulfilled that the sun, with 11 stars and the moon were bowing down to him.

98/ And Jacob died in good old age, and he was removed from this world and put together with his ancestors.[364] And Joseph commanded his servants the embalmers to wrap his father in winding cloths. And they washed and wound <J>acob and they took him and brought him to Hebron, to the cave of Shechem,[365] where Abraham and Isaac, Sarah and Leah were; there they put Jacob as well.[366]

99/ And Joseph on his own death gave a command to his brothers and his sons and said "In the visitation in which God will visit you and bring you forth from this land, also bring forth my bones with you and bring (them) to the land of Israel and set (them) by my father and brothers in the cave of Shechem."[367]

100/ And Joseph died at 110 years. At 30 years he was made known to Pharaoh and at 80 years he became ruler of Egypt. And while he was alive, whoever of his brothers died, he had them taken to the fathers in Hebron. And when he himself died, they put him in a coffin in Egypt.[368]

101/ And at the <going forth> of Israel from Egypt, Moses had the bones

---

359. Or: revealed.
360. The Blessing of Jacob in Gen 49:1–27 was given various eschatological interpretations. This is what the present text also indicates. Jacob's prophetic status is also stressed in §77.
361. Gen 48:1.
362. Gen 48:2. The narrative line is simplified here.
363. See Gen 47:31, Heb 11:21.
364. Gen 49:33.
365. On this confusion, see Stone 2012, 57. The incident is described in Gen 50:7–13.
366. Gen 49:31.
367. Gen 50:24–25.
368. Gen 50:26. The first two sentences add details to the biblical account of Joseph's death; see Gen 50:22–23.

of Joseph, by which they crossed the Red Sea.[369] And having brought him, they laid him to rest <with> his fathers in the cave in Shechem.[370]

4.4. Years and Names of the Forefathers in Order

This document is a list of national leaders, that is, patriarchs, judges, and kings down to the birth of Christ. We have edited the text as far as the beginning of material leading into the genealogy in Matthew. The section we are publishing ends with a chronological summary, like those in *Biblical Paraphrases*[371] and *Dates*,[372] which makes it reasonable to break at that point. More chronological summaries are published in the present volume.

For each personage mentioned a life span is given, and starting from King David, some further brief remarks are added. The lifespans and dates in the present text follow the Septuagint and the Classical Armenian Bible, with some variants that are signalled in the notes. There is very little information in this document that is not already in the books of the Pentateuch, Joshua, Judges, Samuel, Kings, and Chronicles. It is of interest for the way it expands lists of patriarchs, prophets, and kings, using texts drawn from the Bible and sometimes weaving them together and harmonizing them.

In addition to M512, other texts exist with similar titles and content. On M451, fol. 1v is a text that is very like §§1-2 and the beginning of §3 of the text being published here. It is titled *Years of the Lives of the Forefathers*. After the entry for Jacob, it jumps to Moses, Aaron, and Joshua b. Nun. Then it gives some totals of years elapsed and, on the last line of the folio reads, "The name of Moses' father (was) Amram and his mother (was) Jochebed[373] and Moses's wife was Zippora." Another text with a title similar to M512, that is, Անուանք Նախահարցն, "Names of the Forefathers" is preserved in J1171, p. 104 (1406).[374]

The manuscript, M512, is written in *notrgir* and was proofread and corrected by the original scribe. It was copied in 1701 by the priest Tʻomas and has 275 fols. The text being published here is found on fols. 86r–90v. Following this text, on fol. 90v, the *Lives of the Prophets* ensues.

---

369. The bones are, it seems, wonderworking, perhaps a reflection of Christian attitudes to relics.
370. An undated scribe's colophon occurs here.
371. See Stone 1982, 82–83.
372. Stone 1996a, 84–89 and 98–100.
373. The form of this name is corrupted in Armenian.
374. See Bogharian 1960, 4:268–70.

Text

1/ / fol. 86r / Ադամ.   ՁԼ:
    Սէթ.   ՋՃԲ:
    Ենովս.   ՋԵ:
    Կայնան.   ՋՃ:
    Մաղաղիէ<լ>.   ՊՂԵ:[375]
    Յարեդ.   ՋԿԲ:
    Ենովք.   ՅԿԵ:
    Մաթուսաղայ.   ՋԿԹ:[376]
    Ղամէք.   ՋՁԳ:
2/ Նոյ.   ՋՌ:
    Սէմ.   Ճ:
    Արփաքսաթ.   ՅԼ:
    Կայնան.   ՃԻ:
    Սաղա.   ՅԼ:
    Եբեր.   ՄՀ:
    Փաղեկ.   ՄԹ:
    Ռագաւ.   ՄԷ:
    Սերուք.   Մ:
    Նաքովր.   ՃԻԲ:
    Թարայ   ՄԵ:
3/ Աբրահամ.   ՃՀԵ:
    Սահակ.   ՃՁ:
    Յակոբ.   ՃԽԷ:
    Փարես. ՃԹ ամաց ծնանի զեզրոն:
    Եզրոն. ՃԼ ամաց ծնանի զԱրամ:
4/ Արամ ԽԵ ծնանի զԱմինադաբ:
    Ամինատաբ ԽԵ ծնանի զՆայասօն: Սա էր իշխան յելս Եգիպտոսէ:
    Նայասօն ԽԴ ծնանի զՍաղմօն: Նայասօն իշխան յանապատին. եւ քոյր սորա եղեւ կին Ահարոնի:
    Սաղմօն. ԼԵ ծնաւ զԲոյոս: Սաղմօն իշխան էր յորժամ անցին ընդ Յորդանան. եւ սա էառ զՌահաբ կին իւր:
5/ Բոյոս ՃԲ ծնանի զՈվբէք ի Հռութայ. զի Բոյոս էառ կին զՀռութ:
    Ովբէք ՃԲ ծնանի զՅեսսէ:

---

375. Doubtless a final լ has fallen from this name.
376. Կ above line p.m.

Յեսսէ ՃԼ ծնաւ զԴաւիթ:
Այսուհետեւ կարգ թագաւորացն է. որոց առաջինն Սաւուղ. յազգէն Բենիամենի. թագաւորեալ ամս Խ յերրորդ ամին կոտորեաց զԱմադեկ. եւ ի Ժ ամին ծնաւ Դաւիթ. եւ ի ԺԵ ամին սպան Դաւիթ զԳողիաթ. Եւ յԼ ամին Դաւթի մեռաւ Սամուէլ: Եւ յետ է ամի մահուանն Սամուէլի սպանին Սաւուղ եւ Յովսափան:

6/ Դաւիթ թագաւորեաց ի Քեբրոն է ամ. սա էառ զերուսաղէմ. եւ շինեաց զՍիոն եւ թագաւորեաց անտ ամս ԼԳ. եւ ի Ժ ամի թագաւորութեան իւրոյ. էհան զտապանակն ի տանէ Աբիաթարայ. եւ քահանայապետ էր Աբիաթար. եւ մարգարէք Գադ. Նաթան. եւ Ասափ. եւ թագաւորեաց ամս Խ եւ մեռաւ:

7/ Սողոմոն որդի նորա ԲԺ ամաց³⁷⁷ թագաւորեաց եւ ի Դ ամի թագաւորութեան³⁷⁸ իւրոյ. սկսաւ շինել զտաճարն. եւ յԷ ամս. կատարեաց:

8/ Ի Մոսիսէ յելիցն Եգիպտոսէ. մինչ ի շինուած տաճարին. են ամք ՆՁ: յԱդամայ ՏՃԿԹ: Սա քակեաց³⁷⁹ զԱնդիոք. եւ շինեաց է քաղաքս. մերձ Հեմսայ. յաւուրս սորա՝ Աքաց մարգարէ տանէ: զի լուծք երինջոցն կոխէին զերուսաղէմ. եւ զտաճարն եւ զքահանայսն: եւ ասաց Սողոմոնի թէ կանայք այլազգիք հե/ fol. 86v /նացուցեն զքեզ յԱստուծոյ:

9/ առ սա եկն դշխոյն հարաւային. սայ եւ գովեաց զկազմուած տաճարին. եւ զապասատուրս նորա. որ ըստ ամնոյ պաշտէին առաջի Տեառն. ԲԺ դասք. ԻԴ. Ռ ի դաս մի. Յ դատաւորք. եւ Տ դռնապանք. զոր Դաւիթ հայր³⁸⁰ նորա կարգեալ էր:

10/ Եւ չափ տաճարին Կ կանգուն երկայն. եւ Ի լայն. եւ Ի բարձր: Եւ Ժ սեղան ոսկի. եւ Ժ աշտանակ ոսկի. եւ Բ սին արտաքոյ: Եւ սուրբն սրբոց. Ի կանգուն երկայն եւ Ի լայն. Եւ ետ նմա տիկինն ՃԻ տաղանդ ոսկոյ. եւ խունկս անոյշ. Եւ թագաւորեաց ամս Խ եւ ամենայն ամք կենաց նորա ՅԲ եւ յոյժ շռջացեալ մեռաւ: Եւ թաղեցաւ.

11/ Եւ թագաւորեաց Ռոբովամ որդի նորա ԺԷ ամ: Եւ բաժանեցան Ժ գեղքն. եւ եղին իւրեանց զերոբովամ³⁸¹ որդի Նաբուտայ. ի գեղէն Եբրեմի. եւ թագաւորք կոչեցան Իսրայելի

---

377. ԲԺ ամաց in marg. p.m.
378. թագաւորութեանց with g erased.
379. քա above line p.m.
380. հայր above line, smaller, p.m.
381. Ե omitted] above line p.m.

եւ Եփրեմի ի Սամարիայ. որք եւ կանգնեցին զԲ ոսկի երինջսն ի Դան եւ ի Բեթէլ. եւ անկան ի կռապաշտութիւն. Եւ Յովդայ եւ Բենիամին եղեն ընդ որդոյ Սողոմոնի յերուսաղէմ. եւ կոչեցան թագաւորք Յուդայ եւ Երուսղեմի. զի գերուսաղէմ նստէին:

12/ Եւ յաւուրս ուցա մարգարէք. Սադովկ եւ Աքիա Սիլոնացի. եւ Սամեա: եւ իմաստասէր Հոմերոս եւ Իխտորոս. Եւ ԺԷ ամին Ռոբովամայ. ել Սոսակիմ արքայ Եգիպտոսի յերուսաղէմ. եւ կողոպտեաց զտաճար Տեառն եւ գնաց:

13/ Եւ թագաւորեաց Աբիու որդի նորա. յամի Շ ու Ժ ամի թագաւորութեանն Ռոբով<ա>մայ որդոյն Նաբոտայ. Գ ամ թագաւորեաց. եւ արար ուղղութիւն եւ մեռաւ.

14/ Եւ թագաւորեաց Ասայ որդի նորա ամս ԽԱ յամի Ի-երրորդի Րոբովամայ որդոյ Նաբոտայ որ թագաւորեաց ի վերայ Իսրայելի ամս ԻԲ. եւ Ասայ արար ուղղութիւն / fol. 87ա / եւ եհան զմայր իւր ի տիկնութենէ վասն Սամարիայ կռոցն զոր պաշտէր:

15/ Եւ թագաւորեաց Իսրայելի Նապոտ որդի Րոբավայ ամս Բ. եւ յետ նորա Բայաս. ամս ԻԴ եւ պատերազմ էր ի մէջ Ասայ եւ Բայասու. եւ մարգարէք Աքիա. Սամեա. եւ Յովէլ. Ազարիա. որ եւ Սադովկ: Եւ Յովաս որ յանդիմանեաց զՐոբովամ:

16/ Իսկ Բայաս սպան զՆաբոտ որդի Րոբովամ. յԲ կամ ի Դ ամին Ասայի արքային Յուդայ: Եւ ինքն թագաւորեաց ամս ԻԴ. եւ չնչեր գտունն Րոբովմու արքայի Իսրայելի. եւ ոչ եթող եւ ոչ մի. ըստ բանին Տեառն զոր խօսեցաւ ի ձեռն Աքիայ:[382] Եւ Բայաս արար չար առաջի Տեառն. եւ սմա ետւ բարկացաւ Տէր հնազօյն Րոբովամ ի ձեռն յԵսուայ մարգարէի. որդոյ Անանիա. եւ մեռաւ Բայաս:

17/ Եւ թագաւորեաց Եղայ որդի նորա յամի ԻՁ-երրորդի Ասայի արքայի Յուդայ ամս ԻԲ եւ կատարեցաւ ասացեալն ի Տեառնէ. զի յարոյց զՁամբրի ծառայ իւր. որ սպան զէլայ. եւ էհար գտունն Բայասու. եւ ոչ եթող եւ ոչ մի:
Եւ թագաւորեաց Ձամբրի է օր. եւ նեղացեալ ի զօրաց. որք պաշարեալ էին զնա. եւ անկեալ ի սենեկին արքայական. եւ այրեաց զտունն եւ մեռաւ ի նմին:

18/ Եւ թագաւորեաց Ամրի յԼԱ ամի Ասայի արքայի Յուդայ: Սա գնեաց զլեառն Սամիրոն ի Սամարիայ. եւ շինեաց զայն քաղաք. եւ կոչեաց Սամարիայ. յանունն լերինն. եւ կոչեցաւ

---

382. Erasure in text, Աքիայ in margin p.m.

Սեբաստիայ. եւ այժմ Նաբլուս. եւ թագաւորեաց Ամրի ամս ԺԲ վեռաւ եւ թաղեցաւ:³⁸³

19/ Եւ թագաւորեաց Աքայաբ որդի նորա յամի ԼԸ-երորդի Ասայի Յուդայ. եւ թագաւորեաց ամս ԻԲ եւ արար չար առաջի Տեառն, առաւել³⁸⁴ քան զամենայն թագաւորս Իսրայելի:

20/ Եւ յալուրս սորա շինեաց Աքիէլ Բեթելացի զԵրիքով Աբիրոնաւ անդրանկաւ էսրի. զհիմունս. եւ զերծելաւ կտաւ³⁸⁵ կանգնեաց զդրունս նորա. ըստ բանին Յեսուայ. Եւ թագաւորեաց Աքայաբ ամս ԻԲ Եղիայ մարգարէ ի նոյն աւուրս.

21/ Եւ թագաւորեաց Յովասափայ որդի Ասայ յերուսաղէմ յամի չորրորդի Աքայաբու, ի ոցա ժամանակս էր Եղիայ մարգարէ. եւ Միքիայ եւ զնաց Աքայաբ յՌամովթ ի Քղայաթ ի պատերազմս / fol. 87v / Յովասափաղ հանդերձ. եւ խոցեցին նետիւ զԱքայաբ մեծ վիրօք. եւ եղին ի կառս եւ բերին ի Սամարիայ. եւ մեռաւ:

22/ Եւ ի հոսմանէ բազում արեանն ներկեցան³⁸⁶ կառքն. եւ լուացին յաւազանն Սամարիայ. եւ լեզուին խոզքն եւ շունք զարիւն. եւ լուացան բոզք յարեանն.

23/ Եւ թագաւորեաց Օքոզիայ. որդի Աքայաբու ամս Բ ի ԺԷ ամին Յովասափաղ. Եւ թագաւորեաց Յովասափատ յերուսաղէմ ամս ԻԵ եւ մեռաւ ի քաղաքի իւրում:

24/ Եւ Իսրայելի թագաւորէ Յովրամ. եղբայր Օքոզիայ. ԺԲ ամ. ի ԺԸ-երորդ ամին Յովասափատու արքային Յուդայ. ի սորա Ե ամին թագաւորեաց Յովրամ արքայ Յուդայ. որ եղեւ չար. եւ սպան զԵ եղբարսն իւր. եւ առաքեաց Եղիա առ նա եւ ասէ. վասն զի ոչ գնայէր զճանապարհս Յովասափատու հօր քո. եւ սպաներ զեղբարս քո. վասն այսորիկ ստակեցէ Տէր. եւ հեղցի փոր քո. եւ եղեւ այսպէս զի կոտորեցին այլազգիքն եւ Արաբացիքն զքեզ³⁸⁷ զամենայն տուն նորա. եւ զորդիսն. եւ մնաց միայն պատանի մի Օքոզիայ անուն:

25/ Եւ թագաւորեաց Օքոզիա որդի Յովրամայ արքայի Յուդայ յերուսաղէմ Ա ամ. վասն զի գնաց ի պատերազմի ընդ Յովրամայ արքայի Իսրաելի: ի վերայ Ազայելի արքայի Ասորւոց յՌամաթ եւ հրամանաւ Յովրամ. եւ էջ յԵզրայել

---

383. եւ թաղեցաւ in margin.
384. Abbreviation mark omitted,
385. In margin, meaning unclear. Perhaps corrupt for կրսեր "younger."
386. կ omitted, in margin p.m.
387. Above line.

բժշկիլ. եւ Որոգիա ցնաց տեսանել զնա. եւ յորժամ սպան Յէու
զՅովրամ որդի Աքայաբու. եւտես զնա անտ եւ զնա եւս սպան:

26/ Եւ թագաւորեաց Յէու ամս ԻԸ ի Սամարիա: Եւ յառաջին
ամի սորա թագաւորեաց ի վերայ Երուսաղեմի Գողողիայ. որ
մայր էր Որոգիայ թագաւորին Յուդայ. եւ քոյր էր Աքայաբու
թագաւորին Իսրայելի. ամս Է. որ եւ սպան զամենայն զաւակ
թագաւորութեան տանն Յուդայի. եւ մնաց միայն որդի մի
Որոգիայ թագաւորին Յուդայ Յովաս անուն. զոր փախեայց
Յովսաբէէ դուստրն Յովրամայ արքայի Յուդայ եւ քոյր
Որոգիայ: եւ էր կին Յովիդեա քահանայի.

27/ Սա պահեաց զտղայն Յովաս ամս Զ գաղտ ի Գողողիայէ. մինչ
քահանայն Յովիդեայ ժողովեաց զամենայն Ղեւտացիս եւ
զՅուդայ / fol. 88r / եւ տարան զմանուկն Յովաս ի տան Տեառն.
եւ օծին թագաւոր ի վերայ Յուդայ եւ զԳողողիայ սպանին. որ
թագաւորեաց ամս Է.

28/ Եւ թագաւորեաց Յովաս յԵրուսաղեմ ամս Խ. յէ ամի
թագաւորութեանն Յէուայ. եւ արար ուղղութիւն առաջի
Տեառն ի ձեռն Յովիդեայ քահանայի. ի սորա ԻԲ ամին
թագաւորեաց Իսրայելի Յովաքազ որդոյ Յէուայ ամս ԺԷ. եւ
արար չար առաջի Տեառն. եւ ետ զնա Տէր ի ձեռս Ազայիելի
արքայի Ասորւոց:

29/ Եւ թագաւորեաց որդի նորա Յովաս ի վերայ Իսրայելի յամի
Լէերորդի Յովասու արքայի Յուդայ. ամս ԺԲ եւ արար չար
առաջի Տեառն. եւ շատ նեղութիւն անցոյց ընդ Յուդայ. պակեաց
զպարիսպն Երուսաղեմի. Յ. կանգուն:

30/ Եւ թագաւորեաց Ամասիայ որդի Յովասու արքայի Յուդայ
յԵրուսաղեմ. յերրորդ ամին Յովասու արքային Իսրայելի[388]
ամս ԻԹ. եւ պարտեցաւ ի Յովասէ արքայէն Իսրայելի: որ
կալաւ զնա ողջ. եւ տարան ի քաղաքն իւր Երուսաղեմ. եւ
պակեաց զպարիսպն Երուսաղեմի. Յ կանգուն եւ զամենայն
զանձ տան թագաւորին. եւ տան Տեառն. եբեր ի Սամարիա:
եւ ոչ սպան զԱմասիայ: այլ մնաց յետ մահուանն Յովասու
արքայի Իսրայելի ամս ԺԷ. եւ ժողովեցան ի վերայ նորա զօրքն
իւր. եւ փախեաւ ի Լաքիս. եւ անտ սպանին զնա. եւ բարձին ի
ձի եւ բերեալ յԵրուսաղեմ թաղեցին:

31/ Յամի ԵԺ-աներորդի Ամասիայ թագաւորին Յութայ
թագաւորեաց Րերովամ որդի Յովասու ի վերայ Իսրայելի.

---

388. ամս ԻԹ. — Իսրայելի in margin p.m.

ամս Խ. եւ արար չար առաջի Տեառն. ըստ մեղացն առաջնոց եւ մեռաւ:

32/ եւ թագաւորեաց յերուսաղէմ Ազարիա. որ եւ Ոզիա. ամս վԲ յամի ԻԷ-երորդի Յերոբովմա թագաւորի Իսրայելի. եւ արար բարի առաջի Տեառն. զոր արար հայր իւր Ամասիայ. եւ համարձակել մտանել ի տաճար Տեառն եւ խնկարկել. եւ բորոտեցաւ զամենայն աւուրս իւր:

33/ Յամի ԼԷ-երորդի Ոզիայ թագաւորեաց Իսրայելի. Զաքարիայ որդի Յերեբովամայ. Զ ամիս եւ արար չար առաջի Տեառն. եւ սպանին զնա գորք իւր. ըստ բանին Տեառն ատ Յէու. թէ քեզ որդիք. չորորդք նստցին յաթոռն Իսրայելի. եւ եղեւ այնպէս:

34/ Եւ թագաւորեաց Իսրայելի Սելլում. որդի Յաբեսսեայ ամ մի. Եւ թագաւորեաց Մանայեմ յԼԹերորդի ամին. Ոզիայ Ժ ամ: / fol. 88v / եւ Յալուրս սորա ել Փուայ արքայ ասորեստանացոց ի վերայ Իսրայելի. եւ Մանայեմ ետ նմա Ռ. տաղանդ արծաթոյ. եւ էարկ զարծաթն զօրու զօրութեանց տալ արքայի Ծ սկեղ արծաթոյ առ այր մի. եւ ննջեաց Մանայեմ որ եկաց թագաւոր Ժ ամ. թագաւորեաց որդի նորա Փակէէ Ժ ամ:

Եւ ապա Փակէէ որդին Ռոմելյայ. Ի ամ ի վԲ ամին Ոզիայ. եւ արար չար առաջի Տեառն: Յալուրս սորա եկ Թակլաթ Փաղասար արքայ Ասորեստանեայց. եւ գերեաց զԶ ազգն եւ զնեփթադիմ:

35/ Եւ թագաւորեաց Յովրամ որդի Ոզիայ յերուսաղէմ. ամս. ԺԶ. յերկրորդ ամի թագաւորութեանն Փակէէ արքային Իսրայելի:

36/ Եւ Աքազ թագաւորեաց յամի ԺԷ-երորդի Փակէէ թագաւորին Իսրայելի. եւ թագաւորեաց ԺԶ ամ. եւ արար չար առաջի Տեառն. եւ եկ Հռասիմ արքայն Ասորուց. եւ Փակէէ որդին Ռոմելյայ արքայն Իսրայելի յերուսաղէմ. եւ էառ Հռասն զմեծ մասն Յուդայ. եւ էհան զբնակիչսն. Իսկ Աքազ առեալ զամենայն ոսկի եւ զարծաթ զգտեալս ի տան Տեառն. եւ առաքեաց զԹակլաթ Փաղասարայ. ասելով ծառայ քո եմ. եւ ել նա ի վերայ Հռասունի. եւ սպան զնա. եւ զմեծ մասն Իսրայելի:

37/ Եւ Ովսէէ որդին Ելայ գումարեաց գունդ. ի վերայ Փակէի. եւ սպան զնա. եւ ինքն թագաւորեաց Իսրայելի յամի ԲԺ-երորդի ամացն Աքազու ամս Թ: ի սորա ել Սաղմանասար արքայն Ասորեստանեայց. եւ Գ ամ պաշարեալ էառ զՍամարիայ եւ բովանդակ զամենեսեան գերի տարաւ յԱսորեստան: Եւ անտի առաքեաց բնակիչս ի նոսա. յերկրէն իւրմէ. եւ այնք Սամարացիք կոչեցան. այսինքն պահապանք. յինն ամին Յովսէի որդւոյ Ելայ. եւ բարձան թագաւորք Իսրայելի:

PART FOUR 145

38/ / fol. 89r / Եւ թագաւրեաց Երուսաղեմի Եզեկիա. որդի Աքազու յերրորդ ամին Յովսէի թագաւորին Իսրայելի: Եւ ի Ձ ամին Եզեկիոյ Սաղմանասար եկն ի վերայ Յովսէի թագաւորի Իսրայելի ի Սամարիայ. Եւ երբարձ զթագաւրութիւնն Իսրայելի. որք տեսեցին ամս ՄԾ յերոբովամէ մինչեւ Յովսէէ. որ զերի վարեցաւ ինքն եւ ամենայն ժողովուրդն յԱսորեստան եւ մնացին թագաւորքն Յուդայ: Եւ աստ Եզեկիա:

39/ Եւ այս են թագաւորք Իսրայելի. որք թագաւորեցին ի Սամարիայ.
Առաջինն Րոբովամ որդին Նաբոտայ. ԻԲ ամ: Նաբոտ որդի նորա. Բ. ամ: Բայաս ԻԴ: Ելայ. Բ ամ: Զամբրի. է օր: Ամրի հայրն Աքաբու. ԺԲ ամ: Աքայաք. ԻԲ ամ: Ոքոզիա որդի նորա. Բ ամ: Յովրամ եղբայրն Ոքոզիա. ԺԲ ամ: Յէու. ԻԸ ամ: Յովաքազ որդի նորա. ԺԵ ամ: Յովաս որդի նորա. ԺԲ ամ: Րեբովամ որդի նորա. ամս Խ. Զաքարիայ որդի նորա. Զ ամիս: Սեղում որ չէր յազգէն. եւ սպան զնա. թագաւորեաց ամիս մի. կամ ամ մի: Մանայեմ որ սպան զՍեղում. Ժ ամ: Փակէէ որդի նորա. Ժ ամ: Եւ յետ Փակէէ որդին Ռոմելայ. Ի: Ովսէէ որ սպան զՓակէէ եւ թագաւորեաց Թ ամ: Եւ բարձան թագաւորք Իսրայելի. որ լինի միահամուռ ՄԾ ամ: Բայց ըստ թուոյն. Ե ամ պակաս քաջ ՄԽԵ:

40/ Եւ մնացին թագաւորք Յուդայ. եւ յամին չորեքտասներորդի Եզեկիա. ել Սենեքերիմ արքայն Ասորեստանեայց. ի վերայ ամուր քաղաքացն Յուդայ. եւ էառ զնոսա. եւ խրոխտաբար առաքեաց զՌափակ առ Եզեկիա. եւ պատուհասեալ եղեւ ի Տեառնէ ի ձեռն կոտորող հրեշտակին որ էհար ՃՁԵ Ռ ոգի ի միում գիշերի. յաւուրսն այնոսիկ հիւանդացաւ Եզեկիա եւ Աստուած կեանս շնորհեաց նմա ԺԵ ամ. վասն սրբութեան սրտին իւրոյ. եւ թագաւորեաց ամս ԺԹ. եւ ընչեաց զի յոյժ բարի էր: / fol. 89v /

41/ Եւ թագաւորեաց Մանասէ որդի նորա. ամս ԾԵ եւ արար չար առաջի Տեառն յոյժ. եւ Տէր մատնեաց ի ձեռս արքային Ասորեստանեայց. եւ տարան կապանօք ի Բաբելոն. եւ յետոյ յոյժ լալով զղջեցաւ. եւ Տէր դարձոյց զնա յերուսաղեմ վերստին ի թագաւորութիւնն իւր եւ յետոյ յոյժ ուղղութիւն արար առաջի Տեառն. եւ երբարձ զամենայն զարշալիսն ի տանէ Տեառն եւ յերկրէն եւ ընչեաց խաղաղութեամբ:
Եւ թագաւորեաց Ամովս որդի նորա ԺԲ ամ. եւ արար չար առաջի Տեառն եւ հարին զնա ի տան իւրոյ եւ մեռաւ:

42/ Եւ թագաւորեաց Յովսիա որդի նորա. Լ ամաց էր ի թագաւորելն

իւրում. եւ ԼԱ ամ թագաւորեաց. եւ արար ուղղութիւն առաջի Տեառն. եւ գնաց ի ճանապարհս Դաւթի հօր իւրոյ եւ Քեղկի պահանայ եգիտ զգիր երկրորդ օրինացն ի տան Տեառն ընդ արձագօցն. եւ մատոյց սա Յովսիաս. եւ նա պատառեաց զպատմուճանն իւր. եւ ուխտեաց ուխտ առաջի Տեառն. պահել զամենայն գրեյսն ի նմա։
Եւ արար զզատիկն ի չորեքտասանն Նիսան ամսոյ. որպէս պատուիրեաց Մօսէս։

43/ Եւ էլ Նեբաւով արքայն Եգիպտոսի եւ երթայր ի վերայ արքային Ասորեստանեայց. առ գետովն Եփրատու. եւ գնաց արքայն Յովսիա ընդդէմ նորա. վասն որոյ առաքեաց Նեբաւով առ նա եւ ասէ։ Զի՞ կա իմ եւ քո. երթ յինէն խաղաղութեամբ. եւ ոչ լուաւ նմա։ Եւ հարին աղեղնաւորքն զարքայ Յովսիաս. եւ յոյժ վտանգեցաւ եւ եկն յԵրուսաղէմ եւ մեռաւ։

44/ Եւ թագաւորեաց Յովաքազ որդի նորա. Գ ամիս. եւ կապեաց զնա Նեբաւով փարաւօն. եւ տարաւ Եգիպտոս. եւ անդ մեռաւ։

45/ Եւ թագաւորեցոյց փարաւօն զԵղիակիմ որդի Յովսիայ զեղբայրն Յովաքազայ զոր տարաւ Եգիպտոս. եւ թագաւորեցոյց Եղիակիմ որ փոխեաց զանունն ի Յովակիմ։ ամս ԺԱ եւ արար չար առաջի Տեառն։ / fol. 90r / Յայսուր սորա էլ Նաբուգոտոնոսոր արքայ Բաբիլօնի յԵրուսաղէմ. եւ ծառայեցին նմա Գ ամ. եւ յետոյ ապստամբեցին ի նմանէ. եւ դարձեալ էլ Նաբուգոդոնոսոր ի վերայ Երուսաղէմի յաւուրս Յեքոնիայ՝ որդւոյ Եղիակիմայ. որ եւ Յովակիմ. որ ննջեալ էր առ հարս իւր։

46/ Եւ թագաւորեալ էր Յովակիմ որ եւ Յեքոնիա ամիսս երիս. եւ ի գալ թագաւորին Նաբուգոդոնոսորայ յԵրուսաղէմ. եւ Յեքոնիայ եւ ամենայն արք իւր. երեւելի արամբք ընդ առաջ. եւ նա ամենայնիւ գերի վարեաց զնա ի Բաբիլօն։ Զի յառաջին գնայն իւր յաւուրս Եղիակիմայ. զոսկի եւ զարծաթ. եւ զամենայն պատուական սպասք տաճարին. եւ Ժ. բիւր այր. եւ զԴանիէլ. եւ զԳ մանկունքն. հանդերձ ամենայն պատուական աղխիւն տարաւ ի Բաբիլօն.
Եւ յերկրորդ գայս. տարաւ զՅեքոնիա եւ զմայրն. եւ զկանայսն. եւ {Սենեքերիմ}[389] եւ զամենայն երեւելի այր. ի Բաբիլօն։

47/ Եւ թագաւորեցոյց զՍեդեկիա մասցեալ ժողովրդեանն. որ

---

389. The text reads incomprehensibly Սենեքերիմ "Sennacherib," but this is a corruption of ներքինիս "eunuchs," a graphic error.

եկաց թազաւոր ամս ԺԱ յետոյ եւ սա եւս³⁹⁰ ապստամբեցաւ։
Եւ յինն ամի թազաւորութեանն Սետեկիայ. երրորդ անգամ էլ
Նաբուգոդոնոսորը ի վերայ Երուսաղէմի. եւ Գ ամ պաշարեաց.
եւ էառ զնա եւ զանհնարին աղետն ո՛ կարէ ընդ գրով արկանել.
քանզի կալաւ զՍեդեկիա եւ փորեաց զԲ ակն նորա. եւ առ
հասարակ զերեաց. եւ յետ Ե ամսոց. եկն Նաբուգոդոնոսորը
դահճապետն եւ հրձիգ արար զտաճարն. եւ զպարիսպն
կործանեաց. եւ զսիւնսն պղնձի եւ արծաթի տարաւ ի Բաբիլոն։
48/ Տեւեաց տաճարն ՆԽԲ ամ։
Եւ յելիցն Եգիպտոսէ՛ մինչեւ ի Սողոմոն են ամք. ՆՁ.
Եւ յառաջին շինուածն տաճարին մինչեւ յերկրորդն. ՇԺԲ.
Ի նորոգմանէ տաճարին մինչ ի ծնունդն Քրիստոսի Աստուծոյ.
մերոյ ամք ՇԺՂ.
ՅԱդամայ ի չրհեղեղն ՍՄԽԲ.
Եւ ի չրհեղեղէն յԱբրահամ ՋԽԲ.
Եւ ի ծնընդենէն Աբրահամու / fol. 90v / մինչեւ յելսն ամք ՇԵ.
Միանգամայն յԱդամայ մինչեւ ի ծնունդն Քրիստոսի ՐՃՂՂ։

The continuation of the text takes this chronicle down to the genealogy in Matthew. On fol. 90v, *Vitae Prophetarum* ensues.

Translation

1/	Adam	930[391]
	Seth	912
	Enosh	905
	Kenan (Kaynan)	910
	Mahalalel	895
	Jared	962
	Enoch	365
	Methusaleh	969
	Lamech	753[392]

---

390. Above the line p.m.
391. This is Adam's age at death as given in the genealogical list Gen 5. Genesis 5 is also the source of the figures given in this text down to Shem. From Shem on, the figures are drawn from Gen 11. When the numbers in this text do not match the age of death as given in Gen 5 and Gen 11, it will be noted.
392. This number does not match Lamech's age of death in Gen 5:31 which is 777. Yet it agrees with the age of death given in the LXX.

BIBLICAL STORIES

2/	Noah	950[393]
	Shem	500[394]
	Arpachshad	330[395]
	Kenan (Kaynan)	120[396]
	Sela	330[397]
	Eber	270[398]
	Peleg	209[399]
	Reu	207[400]
	Serug	200[401]
	Nahor	122[402]
	Terah	205
3/	Abraham	175[403]
	Isaac	180[404]
	Jacob	147[405]

Perez at the age of 59 years begot Hezron.[406]

---

393. Gen 9:29.

394. This number does not match Gen 11:10–11 which says that Shem died at the age of 600. The difference between the numbers could possibly be a mistake, for 500 is the number of years that Shem lived after the birth of Arpachshad.

395. Arpachshad's age at death in Gen 11 is 565 in LXX and 438 in MT. The source of 330 is a misreading of Arm Bible Gen 11:13, and 330 is the number of years he lived after the birth of his son. This error is repeated in the preceding lines and recurs below several times.

396. The appearance here of Kenan (Kaynan), son of Arpachshad indicates that this list is based on LXX because according to MT (Gen 11, 1 Chr 1) Arpachshad does not have a son named Kenan (Kaynan). In LXX, however, Kenan (Kaynan) is the son of Arpachshad and the father of Sela, yet his age at death according to LXX is 460.

397. Sela's age at his death was 460 according to LXX Gen 11:14–15 and 433 according to the Hebrew. The origin of 330 is not biblical but perhaps contamination from Arpachshad.

398. Eber's age at his death was 504 according to LXX Gen 11:16–17 and 464 according to the Hebrew.

399. Peleg's age at his death was 339 according to LXX Gen 11:18–19 and 239 according to the Hebrew. Peleg lived 209 years after the birth of Reu.

400. Reu's age at his death was 339 according to LXX Gen 11:20–21 and 239 according to the Hebrew text Reu lived 207 years after the birth of Serug.

401. Serug's age at his death was 330 according to LXX Gen 11:22–23 and 230 according to the Hebrew. Serug lived 200 years after the birth of Nahor.

402. Nahor's age at his death according to Gen 11:24–25 is 208, and 148 according to the Hebrew. Nahor lived 119 years after the birth of Terah and died at the age of 148.

403. Gen 25:7.

404. Gen 35:28.

405. Gen 47:28.

406. From here on the list is based on several sources: Ruth 4:18–22; Gen 46:12; Num 26:21; 1 Chr 2; Luke 3:23–38 etc. Yet none of these sources contain the ages of Perez and his sons,

PART FOUR 149

    Hezron at the age of 58 years begot Aram[407]
4/   Aram at the age of 45 begot Aminadab[408]
    Aminadab at the age of 45 begot Nahshon.[409] He was a prince[410] at the exodus from Egypt. Nahshon at the age of 44 begot Salmon.[411] Nahshon was prince in the desert and his sister was Aaron's wife.[412] Salmon at the age of 35 begot Boaz. Salmon was prince when they crossed the Jordan, and he took Rahab as his wife.[413]
5/   Boaz at the age of 108 begot Obed from Ruth, for Boaz took Ruth as wife.[414]
    Obed at 102 begot Jesse.
    Jesse[415] at the age of 30 begot David.
    Henceforth is the order of the kings, the first of whom was Saul of the tribe of Benjamin.[416] He ruled[417] for 40 years.[418] In the third year he cut down Amalek.[419] And in the tenth year David was born and in the 28th year David killed Goliath.[420] And Samuel died[421] in David's 30th year.[422] And seven years after Samuel's death, Saul and Jonathan were killed.[423]
6/   David ruled in Hebron for seven years.[424] He took Jerusalem[425] and

---

only their names. Also, the listing of Perez as the son of Jacob, not of Judah, if that is what the sequence implies, does not agree with any of these sources.
    407. Probably Ram of the Hebrew: see Ruth 4:19. The Arm Bible reads Aram.
    408. Nahshon was son of Aminadab, see Ruth 4:20.
    409. Ruth 4:20.
    410. See 1 Chr 2:10.
    411. See Ruth 4:20 where Salmon is mentioned.
    412. Exod 6:23. Note that the coordination of disparate verses is implied here.
    413. Salmon marrying Rahab is taken from Matt 1:5. Our text contradicts rabbinic traditions about Rahab marrying Joshua: see Jewish Encyclopedia s.v. Rahab II.
    414. Ruth 4:21, 1 Chr 2:12. Neither in the case of Obed nor in that of Jesse is there any biblical basis for the life spans.
    415. Ruth 4:22, 1 Chr 2:12.
    416. 1 Sam 10:20–21.
    417. Literally: "having ruled," a participle.
    418. According to 1 Sam 13:1 Saul only ruled for two years, yet Josephus mentions that he ruled for forty years. The NRSV translators assume a lacuna here. See Ginzberg 1909–1938, 6:239.
    419. 1 Sam 15:3–9.
    420. 1 Sam 17.
    421. 1 Sam 25:1, 28:3.
    422. 2 Sam 5:4.
    423. 1 Sam 31:1–6.
    424. 2 Sam 2:11, 5:5, 1 Kgs 2:11.
    425. 1 Chr 11:4–6.

built Zion[426] and ruled there for 33 years.[427] And in the tenth year of his rule, he brought forth the Ark[428] from Abiathar's house. And Abiathar was High Priest, and the prophets were Gad, Nathan and Asaph.[429] And he ruled for 40 years and he died.

7/ Solomon, his son[430] ruled for 20[431] years and in the fourth year of his rule he began to build the temple[432] and in the seventh year he finished.[433]

8/ From Moses, from the exodus from Egypt up to the building of the temple was 480 years[434]; from Adam (it was) 4,169 (years).[435] He destroyed Antioch[436] and built seven cities close to Xēms.[437] In his days, Ahaz was the prophet of the Lord. Four yokes of heifers trampled Jerusalem and the temple and the priests.[438] And Solomon said that foreign wives distance one from God.[439]

9/ The Queen from the South came to him and she praised[440] the built temple and its servants, that 12 courses (i.e., of priests) served God by

---

426. In 1 Chr 11:5 we are not told that David built the fortress of Zion but that he captured it. It was called the city of David according to 1 Chr 11:7.

427. 2 Sam 5:5, 1 Chr 29:27.

428. Compare with 2 Sam 6:2–12, 1 Chr 13:6–14, 15:3–16:1. The event is mentioned but not the tenth year.

429. 1 Chr 25:1–2, 29:29. See the Story of the Prophet Asaph (text 4.11) here.

430. 1 Kgs 1: 33–35, 1 Chr 23:1.

431. 1 Kgs 11:42 and 2 Chr 9:30 both state that Solomon ruled for forty years.

432. 1 Kgs 6:1.

433. According to 1 Kgs 6:38 the building took seven years and was completed in Solomon's eleventh year. The Armenian could be read as referring to the seventh year of building, though in context that seems less likely.

434. 1 Kgs 6:1.

435. According to *Biblical Paraphrases*, it was 4,171 years from Adam to the building of the temple; Stone 1982, 120. However, in *History of Adam and His Grandsons* §23 the figure is 4,169 like here; see Stone 1996a, 98–99. In *Dates*, 100–101 it is 4,175.

436. This sentence refers to the city Antioch, which was built around 300 BCE and it is anachronistic. In fact, it is also very unlikely that Solomon's kingdom spread so far north. In other texts in this volume, we have observed ahistorical "updating" of geographical names. See, for example, 4.13 §5.

437. This might be the city of Homs in present-day Syria. It was named Emesa in antiquity.

438. The reference of the "yokes of heifers" remains obscure.

439. See 1 Kgs 11:1–6, Prov 2:16. This prohibition is put into God's mouth in 1 Kgs 11:2, and is contrary to Solomon's own practice. Compare the apocryphal works on the penitence of Solomon discussed in Stone 1978, 1–19.

440. 1 Kgs 10:1–10.

PART FOUR 151

the month 24,000 in one course, 6,000 judges and 4,000 doorkeepers whom David, his father, had arranged.[441]

10/ And the dimension(s) of the temple (were) 60 cubits length, 20 cubits width, and 20 cubits height;[442] and (there were) ten golden altar(s)[443] and ten gold candelabra[444] and two pillars outside.[445] And the Holy of Holies was 20 cubits long and 20 wide.[446] And the lady gave him 120 talents of gold and sweet incense.[447] And he ruled for 40 years[448] and all the years of his life were 52 and having repented exceedingly, he died and he was buried.[449]

11/ And Rehoboam, his son, ruled for 17 years.[450] And these ten tribes separated themselves and set up for themselves Jereboam the son of Naboth from the tribe of Ephraim.[451] And they were called Kings of Israel and Ephraim in Samaria,[452] who set up the two gold calves in Dan and in Bethel.[453] And they fell into idol-worship.[454] And Judah and Benjamin were with Solomon's son in Jerusalem[455] and they were called kings of Judah and Jerusalem, because their seat was Jerusalem.

12/ And in their days were the prophets Zadok and Ahijah of Shiloh and Samea. And the philosophers were Homer and Isidoros.[456] And in the 17th year of Rehoboam, Shishak (Sosakim) king of Egypt went forth to Jerusalem and he plundered the temple of the Lord and went (away).[457]

13/ Abijam (Abihu) his son became king in the 18th year of the rule of

---

441. 1 Chr 9:1–32.
442. 1 Kgs 6:2. The height there is 30 cubits.
443. 1 Kgs 7:48 only mentions one altar.
444. 1 Kgs 7:49.
445. 1 Kgs 7:15–22.
446. 1 Kgs 6:20.
447. 1 Kgs 10:10.
448. 1 Kgs 11:42.
449. 1 Kgs 11:42–43. On Solomon's repentance, see note 439.
450. 1 Kgs 14:21.
451. See 1 Kgs 12:16, 20; compare 1 Kgs 11:13, 29–36.
452. The kings of Israel are sometimes titled "King of Samaria," see 1 Kgs 21:1, 2 Kgs 1:3. Likewise, the kingdom of Israel is sometimes called "Ephraim," see, for example, Isa 7:17, Hos 5:3.
453. 1 Kgs 12:28–29.
454. 1 Kgs 12:30–33.
455. 1 Kgs 1:17, 20, 21, 29–36, 11:13.
456. Isidoros is unidentified, but according to the online Athenian Onomasticon, the name does not appear before the first century BCE. So, here it remains a puzzle.
457. 1 Kgs 14:25–26. According to 1 Kgs 14:25 this was in the fifth, not the seventeenth, year of Rehoboam's kingdom. The name of the Egyptian king was Shoshak (*ketib*) or Shishak

Rehoboam, son of Naboth.[458] He ruled for three years[459] and acted uprightly[460] and he died.[461]

14/ And Asa his son ruled for 41 years.[462] In the 20th year of Rehoboam the son of Nabot[463] who ruled over Israel for 22 years, Asa also acted uprightly[464] and he expelled his mother from (the position of) Queen Mother on account of the idols of Astarte which she worshipped.[465]

15/ And Nabot[466] son of Rehoboam[467] ruled Israel for two years,[468] and after him[469] Baasha for 24 years.[470] And there was war between Asa and Baasha.[471] And the prophets were Ahijah,[472] Samea, and Joel, Azaria who is also Zadok, and Joad,[473] who opposed Rehoboam.

16/ Then Baasha killed Nabot (i.e., Nadab) in the second or the fourth year[474] of Asa, king of Judah. And he himself ruled for 24 years[475] and he annihilated the house of Rehoboam[476] king of Israel and he did not leave a single one, according to the word of the Lord which he spoke through Ahijah. And Baasha did evil before the Lord[477] and the Lord was even more angry with him than with the ancient Rehoboam

---

(*qerê*). The mistake might stem from contamination from 1 Kgs 14:21. Arm sets it in the year of Rehoboam's accession.

458. 1 Kgs 14:31 and 15:1. 1 Kgs 15:1 says that this was in the eighteenth year of Jereboam, not Rehoboam. According to 1 Kgs 14:25 Shishak's invasion happened during the fifth year of Rehoboam's reign.

459. 1 Kgs 15:2.

460. 1 Kgs 15:3; 1 Kings says the exact opposite of the text, that Abijam worshipped other gods.

461. 1 Kgs 15:8.

462. 1 Kgs 15:10.

463. 1 Kgs 15:9. Rehoboam, as happens sometimes in this text, is confused with Jereboam.

464. 1 Kgs 15:11–12.

465. 1 Kgs 15:13.

466. Nadab in MT and Nabat in Arm (1 Kgs 15:25).

467. Sic.

468. 1 Kgs 15:25.

469. 1 Kgs 15:28.

470. 1 Kgs 15:33.

471. 1 Kgs 15:16–21, 32.

472. Ahijah is mentioned in 1 Kgs 14:4–5; Samea remains unidentified; Joel is mentioned in Joel 1:1; Azaria was actually son of Zadok according to 1 Kgs 4:2.

473. Compare *Life of Joad* in *Vitae Prophetarum*.

474. The scribe was uncertain. 1 Kgs 15:25 sets his rule at two years, and 1 Kgs 15:28, 33 speaks of his third year.

475. 1 Kgs 15:33.

476. This should be Jereboam: cf. 1 Kgs 15:29.

477. 1 Kgs 15:34.

through Jehu (Esu) the prophet, son of Anania (Hanani),[478] and Baasha died.[479]

17/ And Elah his son ruled in the 26th year of Asa, king of Judah for 22 years.[480] And that thing said by the Lord was carried out for he raised up Zimri (Zambri) his servant who killed Elah. And he smote the house of Baasha and he did not leave even one.[481] And Zimri ruled for seven days[482] and, being afflicted by forces which had besieged him, he fell in the royal chamber and burnt the house and died.[483]

18/ And Omri became king in the 31st year of Asa, king of Judah.[484] He bought the mountain of Shemer (Samiron) in Samaria and he built that city and he called (it) Samaria after the name of the mountain, and it was (also) called Sebastia,[485] and (it is) now Nablus. And Omri ruled for 12 years[486] (and) he died and was buried.[487]

19/ And Ahiab (Ahab) his son became king in the 38th year of Asa of Judah. And he ruled for 22 years.[488] And he did evil before the Lord, more than all the kings of Israel.[489]

20/ And in his days Hiel (Ahiel) of Bethel built Jericho (at the price of) Abiron his firstborn of Êsr. He founded it and he set up its gates at the price of his younger (son) according to the word of Joshua.[490] And Ahab ruled for 22 years.[491] Elijah the prophet (was) in those days.[492]

21/ And Jehosaphat son of Asa became king in Jerusalem in the fourth

---

478. 1 Kgs 16:1–4, 7.
479. 1 Kgs 16:6.
480. 1 Kgs 16:8. The biblical text including Arm says that Elah ruled for two years, not twenty-two years. The text here is probably an error.
481. 1 Kgs 16:9–13.
482. 1 Kgs 16:15.
483. 1 Kgs 16:17–18.
484. 1 Kgs 16:23.
485. 1 Kgs 16:24. Note that according to the MT the mountain's name was Shomron (Arm has Unupnù Somron). "Sebastia" is an example of the text's geographical anachronisms or updatings. Omri bought it from Shemer (Arm Uɯɯɾp Samer).
486. 1 Kgs 16:23.
487. 1 Kgs 16:28.
488. 1 Kgs 16:29.
489. 1 Kgs 16:30.
490. 1 Kgs 16:34; Hebrew Bible says he built the gate at the price of his youngest, Segub, and according to God's order transmitted by Joshua bin Nun.
491. 1 Kgs 16:29.
492. 1 Kgs 17:1.

year of Ahab.[493] In their times Elijah was a prophet[494] and Michiah.[495] And Ahab went to Ramoth Gilead in a war with Jehosaphat. And they wounded Ahab with an arrow, a grave wound and they put (him) in a chariot and brought (him) to Samaria, and he died.

22/ And from the flowing of the blood the chariot was reddened and they washed (it) in the pool of Samaria, and the pigs and dogs were licking (his) blood and the whores bathed in (his) blood.[496]

23/ And Ahaziah (Okʻozia) son of Ahab ruled for two years in the 17th year of Jehoshaphat.[497] And Jehoshaphat ruled in Jerusalem for 25 years[498] and he died in his city.[499]

24/ And in Israel, Jehoram brother of Ahaziah became king for 12 years in the 18th year of Jehoshaphat king of Judah.[500] In his fifth year, Jehoram became king of Judah,[501] who was evil[502] and killed his own five brothers.[503] And Elijah sent to him[504] and said, "Because you did not go in the paths of Jehosaphat your father, and you killed your brothers, because of this the Lord will cut (you) down and will pour out your entrails." And it happened thus that gentiles and Arabs cut (him) down (and) all his house and his sons. And only one youth remained, by the name of Okʻozia.[505]

25/ And Ahaziah son of Jehoram ruled as king of Judah in Jerusalem for one year.[506] Because he went to war with Jehoram king of Israel against Hazael (Azayēl),[507] king of the Arameans (Syrians)[508] in Ramot

---

493. 1 Kgs 22:41.
494. This repeats the last sentence of §19.
495. 2 Kings 1 is the start of the Elijah cycle, and compare 2 Chr 21:12-15. Michiah was a prophet; see 1 Kgs 22:15-22. Elijah prophesied to the son of Jehoshaphat.
496. 1 Kgs 22:34-38.
497. 1 Kgs 22:51.
498. 1 Kgs 22:42.
499. 1 Kgs 22:51; i.e., in Jerusalem. 1 Kings 22:50 says "in the city of his father David."
500. See 2 Kgs 1:17 and 3:1. Asa ruled for twelve years.
501. 2 Kgs 8:16.
502. 2 Chr 21:6 on his character.
503. 2 Chr 21:4.
504. Sent a letter; 2 Chr 21:12. The message in the text here differs from that given in 2 Chr 21:12.
505. 2 Chr 21:12-15; the attack of the Arabs is described in the following verses but not in Elijah's prophecy.
506. 2 Kgs 8:25-26. Here the date "in the twelfth year" found in the biblical text is omitted.
507. That is, "the Aramaean."
508. Throughout, the Arm Bible translates Aram as Asoṙi, etc., the usual Armenian word

PART FOUR 155

<Gilead>,[509] and at Jehoram's command he went down to Jezreel to be healed and King Ahaziah came to see him.[510] And when Jehu killed Jehoram son of Ahab,[511] he saw him there and he killed him too.[512]

26/ And Jehu ruled for 28 years in Samaria.[513] And in his first year, Athaliah (Godolia) who was mother of Ahaziah king of Judah[514] and sister of Ahab king of Israel ruled in Jerusalem for seven years.[515] She also killed all the royal seed of the house of Judah[516] and only one son of Ahaziah king of Judah remained, Joash by name, him Jehosheba (Yovsabēē), daughter of Jehoram king of Israel had made flee.[517] And she was wife of Jehoida the priest.[518]

27/ She kept the boy Joash secretly for six years from Athaliah,[519] until the priest Jehoida assembled all the Levites and Judah and they brought the boy Joash to the house of the Lord and they anointed (him) king over Judah and killed Athaliah, who ruled for seven years.[520]

28/ And Joash became king in Jerusalem for 40 years in the seventh year of the rule of Jehu.[521] And he acted uprightly before the Lord through Jehoiada the priest.[522] In his 22nd year, Jehoahaz son of Jehu became king of Israel for 17 years.[523] And he did evil before the Lord.[524] And the Lord gave him into the power of Hazael king of the Arameans.[525]

29/ And his son Joash became king over Israel in the 37th year of Joash

---

for Syriac speakers, Syriac language, etc. We have translated this as Aram, Aramaean in this document.
509. 2 Kgs 8:28; Ramat is corrupt for Ramoth Gilead.
510. 2 Kgs 8:29.
511. 2 Kgs 9:24.
512. 2 Kgs 9:27.
513. 2 Kgs 10:36.
514. 2 Kgs 11:1. Both Athaliah and Ahab were descendants of Omri; see 1 Kgs 16:28; 2 Kgs 8:26.
515. 2 Kgs 11:3-4.
516. 2 Kgs 11:1.
517. 2 Kgs 11:2.
518. So 2 Chr 22:11.
519. 2 Kgs 11:2.
520. 2 Kgs 11:4-16 and 20.
521. 2 Kgs 12:1-2.
522. 2 Kgs 12:2.
523. 2 Kgs 13:1. MT says this was in the twenty-third, not the twenty-second, year of Joash, but Arm has twenty-second.
524. 2 Kgs 13:2.
525. 2 Kgs 13:3.

king of Judah for 12 years[526] and he did evil before the Lord[527] and he brought much distress upon Judah. He razed the walls of Jerusalem for 300 cubits.[528]

30/ And Amaziah the son of Joash became king in Jerusalem of Judah in the third year of Joash king of Israel[529] for 29 years.[530] And he was defeated by Joash king of Israel, who captured him complete[531] and he was brought to his own city, Jerusalem. And he (i.e., Joash) razed the walls of Jerusalem for 300 cubits.[532] And all the treasure of the royal palace and the temple he brought to Samaria,[533] and he did not kill Amazia. He remained for 17 years after the death of Joash, king of Israel.[534] And his own army assembled against him, and he fled to Lachish and there they killed him.[535] And they raised him up onto a horse and brought him to Jerusalem and buried him.[536]

31/ In the 15th year of Amaziah king of Judah, Rehoboam[537] son of Joash became king over Israel for 40 years[538] and he did evil before the Lord, according to the former sins[539] and he died.[540]

32/ And Azaria, who was also Uzziah, became king over Jerusalem for 52 years, in the 27th year of Jeroboam son of Joash king of Israel.[541] And he did good before the Lord, which his father Amazia had done (as

---

526. 2 Kgs 13:10; MT says Joash ruled for sixteen years, not for twelve as does the Armenian version.
527. 2 Kgs 13:11.
528. This phrase is unique to Arm It is a contamination from §30.
529. 2 Kgs 14:1. According to MT it should be the second year but Arm has the third year.
530. 2 Kgs 14:2.
531. I.e., unwounded.
532. 2 Kgs. 14:11–13; the Bible says Joash razed 400, not 300 cubits of wall.
533. 2 Kgs 14:14.
534. 2 Kgs 14:17; the Bible says he ruled for another fifteen years, not seventeen years. This may be an error generated by the similarity of Armenian notation of 5 and 7.
535. 2 Kgs 14:19.
536. 2 Kgs 14:20.
537. Read as: Jeroboam, see §32.
538. 2 Kgs 14:23. The Bible, including Arm, says that Jeroboam ruled forty years. Here it is Rehoboam and he ruled for forty years.
539. 2 Kgs 14:24; the Bible writes specifically that he followed Jeroboam son of Nabat, not just "according to the former sins."
540. 2 Kgs 14:29.
541. 2 Kgs 15:1–2.

PART FOUR 157

well).[542] And he dared to enter the Lord's temple and to cense[543] and he became leprous all his days.[544]

33/ In the 35th year of Uzziah, Zechariah son of Jeroboam became king of Israel for six months[545] and he did evil before the Lord.[546] And his army killed him,[547] according to the word of the Lord to Jehu, "Your sons up to the fourth (generation) will sit on the throne of Israel."[548] And thus it happened.

34/ And Shallum (Sellum) son of Jabesh was king of Israel for one year.[549] And Menahem (Manayēm) became king in the 39th year of Uzziah[550] for ten years.[551] And in his days Pua[552] king of the Assyrians went forth against Israel and Menahem gave him 1,000 talents of silver.[553] And he put (i.e., a tribute) of silver upon the powerful to give the king 50 shekels of silver per man.[554] And Menahem slept,[555] who had been king for ten years.[556] His son Pekah(iah) (Pʻakēē) ruled for ten years[557] and then Pekah son of Remaliah for 20 years[558] up to the 52nd year of Uzziah,[559] and he did evil before the Lord. In his days,[560] Tiglath Pileser King of Assyria sallied forth and he took captive the six families (or: clans) and Naphtali.[561]

---

542. 2 Kgs 15:3.
543. This is an exegesis based on 2 Kgs 15:4c where the people are said to have burned incense on high places. This is interpreted to mean that the king dared burn incense in the temple and the leprosy was a punishment for that. There is just the possibility of a corruption in Greek from ἐθυσίαζεν to ἐθυμίαζεν, which produced յամձայեաց "dared."
544. 2 Kgs 15:5.
545. 2 Kgs 15:8 says this was in Azariah's (not Uzziah's) thirty-eighth (not thirty-fifth) year.
546. 2 Kgs 15:9.
547. 2 Kgs 15:10. There it says that Shallum son of Jabesh conspired against him.
548. 2 Kgs 15:12, here dependent on 10:30.
549. 2 Kgs 15:13; the Bible says he ruled one month, not one year. This is an inner-Armenian confusion of ամիս "month" with ամ "year."
550. The Bible has Azariah. This is written in 2 Kgs 15:17; it is inferred from 2 Kgs 15:13 and 14.
551. 2 Kgs 15:17.
552. So Arm Bible. The other versions have Pul.
553. 2 Kgs 15:19.
554. 2 Kgs 15:20.
555. I.e., died, cf.1 Kgs 15:22.
556. 2 Kgs 15:17 and 22.
557. 2 Kgs 15:23. The Biblical text says he ruled for two years, not ten.
558. 2 Kgs 15:25 and 27.
559. 2 Kgs 15:27. This is when Pekah's rule started, not finished.
560. 2 Kgs 15:28.
561. 2 Kgs 15:29. The Biblical text says he took seven cities, not six and "Naphtali" means "the tribe of Naphtali."

35/ And Jehoram[562] son of Uzziah became king in Jerusalem for 16 years, in the second year of the rule of Pekah, king of Israel.[563]

36/ And Ahaz became king in the seventeenth year of Pekah, king of Israel.[564] And he ruled for 16 years and he did evil before the Lord.[565] And Rezin (Hrasim),[566] king of the Arameans and Pekah son of Remaliah king of Israel went forth against Jerusalem.[567] And Rezin took the greater part of Judah, and he expelled the inhabitants.[568]

Then Ahaz took all the gold and silver that was found in the Lord's house and sent it to Tiglath Pileser saying, "I am your servant."[569] And he went forth against Rezin and he killed him[570] and the greater part of Israel.

37/ And Hosea the son of Elah[571] gathered a host against Pekah, and he killed him. And he himself became king of Israel in the twelfth year of the years of Ahaz for nine years,[572] Shalmaneser king of Assyria went forth, and having besieged Samaria for three years, he took it and he brought all of them together as captives to Assyria,[573] And thence he sent inhabitants to them from his land and those ones were called Samaritans. that is "guardians."[574] In the ninth year of Hoshea son of Elah, the kings of Israel were ended.[575]

38/ And Hezekiah son of Ahaz became king in Jerusalem in the third year of Hosea king of Israel.[576] And in the sixth year of Hezekiah, Shalmaneser came against Hoshea king of Israel in Samaria and he removed the kingdom of Israel[577] which lasted 250 years from Jeroboam up to

---

562. Corrupt for Jotham, see 2 Kgs 15:32–33.
563. 2 Kgs 15:32–33.
564. 2 Kgs 16:1; the Bible has the seventeenth year.
565. 2 Kgs 16:2.
566. 2 Kgs 16:5.
567. 2 Kgs 16:5; 2 Chr 2:5–6.
568. 2 Kgs 16:6; the Bible does not write about "the greater part of Judah."
569. 2 Kgs 16:7–8.
570. 2 Kgs 16:9; him, i.e., Rezin.
571. 2 Kgs 18:1.
572. 2 Kgs 17:1.
573. 2 Kgs 17:3–6.
574. This onomastic gloss resembles those already noted. It is based on the root $š.m.r$.
575. 2 Kgs 17:6, 23, 18:10–11; these sources describe the whole of the kingdom of Israel or the whole nation, not just the kings.
576. 2 Kgs 18:1.
577. 2 Kgs 17:6, 23, 18:10–11.

PART FOUR 159

Hosea,[578] who was himself exiled and all the people to Assyria,[579] and the kings of Judah remained and there was Hezekiah.[580]

39/ And these are the kings of Israel who ruled in Samaria.

The first was Rehoboam son of Naboth,[581]	22 years;
Naboth his son,	2 years.[582]
Baasha	24 years.[583]
Elah	2 years.[584]
Zimri	7 days.[585]
Omri, father of Ahab	12 years.[586]
Ahab	28 years.[587]
Ahaziah, his son	2 years.[588]
Jehoram, brother of Ahaziah	12 years.[589]
Jehu	28 years.[590]
Jehoahaz, his son	15 years.[591]
Joash, his son	12 years.[592]
Rehoboam, his son	40 years.[593]
Zechariah, his son	6 months.

---

578. The figures in the Bible add up to 219, seven months and one week; the figures in the text add up to 254 years, one month and one week. Differences in spans of years have already been noted.
579. 2 Kgs 17:6, 23, 18:10–11.
580. 2 Kgs 18:13–19:36.
581. 1 Kgs 12: 20; 11:13, 29–36. This should be Jeroboam.
582. 1 Kgs 15:25; the Bible says Nadab son of Jereboam, not Nabot son of Rehoboam.
583. 1 Kgs 15:28, 33.
584. 1 Kgs 16:8.
585. 1 Kgs 16:15.
586. 1 Kgs 16:23.
587. According to 1 Kgs 16: it should be twenty-two years, which is also the number given in §18 above.
588. 1 Kgs 22:51.
589. 2 Kgs 3:1. 2 Kings does write explicitly that he is the brother of the former king, and that he ruled for twelve years.
590. 2 Kgs 10:36.
591. 2 Kgs 13:1; the biblical text says he ruled for seventeen years, not for fifteen. This difference of two is often a graphic variant of the Armenian notations for five and seven, which are very similar.
592. 2 Kgs 13:10; MT and LXX say that Joash ruled for seventeen years. Arm Bible has twelve years.
593. 2 Kgs 14:23; 2 Kings says that he ruled for forty-one years. The name should be Jeroboam.

Shallum, who was not of the family (clan) and killed him, ruled for one month or one year.[594]

Menahem, who killed Shallum	10 years.[595]
Pekah, his son	10 years.[596]
And after him, Pekah son of Remaliah	20.[597]
Hoseah, who killed Pekah and ruled	9 years.[598]

And the kings of Israel were removed. They are altogether 250 years but by number five years lack, which yields 245.[599]

40/ And the kings of Judah remained.[600] And in the 14th year of Hezekiah, Sennacherib king of Assyria went forth against the fortified cities of Judah.[601] And he took them[602] and haughtily he sent Rab-Shakeh (Rapak') to Hezekiah[603] and he was punished by the Lord by the hand of the slaughtering angel who smote 185,000 people in one night.[604] In those days, Hezekiah fell ill[605] and God granted him 15 years because of the purity of his heart.[606] He ruled for 19 years and he fell asleep[607] for he was very good.[608]

41/ And Manasseh his son ruled for 55 years.[609] And he did evil before the Lord exceedingly[610] and the Lord gave him over into the hands of the king of Assyria.[611] And they brought him in shackles to Babylon.[612] And afterwards with great weeping, he repented and the Lord returned

---

594. 2 Kgs 1:10, 13.
595. 2 Kgs 15:14, 17.
596. 2 Kgs 15:23: twenty years in MT and LXX, but ten years in Arm. The name is Pekahiah in the Bible.
597. 2 Kgs 15:25, 27.
598. 2 Kgs 17:1.
599. Totals of the biblical figures differ from those in our text. The numbers do not add up to 245 either.
600. 2 Kgs 17:6, 23, 18:10-11: these sources all describe exile of Israel, not Judah: see 2 Kgs 19:32-34.
601. 2 Kgs 18:13.
602. 2 Kgs 18:13.
603. 2 Kgs 18:17.
604. 2 Kgs 19:35.
605. 2 Kgs 20:1.
606. 2 Kgs 20:6.
607. I.e., died.
608. 2 Chr 31:20.
609. 2 Kgs 21:21.
610. 2 Kgs 21:11.
611. 2 Kgs 21:13-15.
612. Chronicles has the story of Manasseh's repentance; see 2 Chr 33:16.

him to Jerusalem again to his kingdom and subsequently he acted with great uprightness before the Lord. And he removed all the abominations from the house of the Lord and from the land, and he fell asleep peacefully.[613]

42/ And Josiah, his son, became king.[614] He was eight years old when he was made king and he ruled for 31 years,[615] and he acted with uprightness before the Lord and he went in the ways of David his ancestor.[616] And Helkiah the priest found the second book of the Law (perhaps: the book of Deuteronomy) in the house of the Lord with the silver (coins) and delivered it to Josiah.[617] And he (Josiah) rent his garment[618] and swore an oath before the Lord to observe all the things written in it.[619] And he celebrated Passover on the fourteenth of the month of Nisan,[620] as Moses commanded.[621]

43/ And Neco, king of Egypt issued forth and went against the king of Assyria by the Euphrates River. And king Josiah went against him.[622] On account of this Neco sent to him and said, "What do we have between us?[623] Go from me peacefully." And he did not listen to him.[624] And the archers struck king Josiah[625] and he was most gravely wounded and he came to Jerusalem and he died.[626]

44/ And Jehoahaz his son reigned for three months. And Pharaoh Neco bound him and brought him to Egypt. And there he died.[627]

45/ And Pharaoh made Eliakim, son of Josiah, brother of Jehoahaz whom he had taken to Egypt, king,[628] And he made Eliakim, who changed

---

613. 2 Chr 33:20, cf. 2 Kgs 21:18.
614. 2 Kgs 21:24: According to the Bible he was Manasseh's grandson, and between them Ammon was the king.
615. 2 Kgs 22:1.
616. 2 Kgs 22:2.
617. 2 Kgs 22:3, 4, 8.
618. 2 Chr 34:19.
619. 2 Kgs 23:3.
620. 2 Chr 35:1. Note the month name "Nisan," which occurs only twice in the Hebrew Bible, both in post-Exilic texts. Here the Bible reads "first month." The Armenians knew the Jewish month names. See, for example, Stone 1988, 5–12.
621. 2 Kgs 23:21–22; 2 Chr 35:17–18.
622. 2 Kgs 23:29.
623. Literally: what is mine and yours?
624. This sentence is not in the biblical text.
625. 2 Chr 35:23.
626. 2 Kgs 23:30, 2 Chr 35:20–24.
627. 2 Kgs 23:31, 34.
628. 2 Kgs 23:34.

his name to Jehoiakim,[629] king for 11 years[630] and he did evil before the Lord.[631] In his days Nebuchadnezzar king of Babylon went forth against Jerusalem.[632] And they served him for three years and afterwards they revolted against him.[633] And Nebuchadnezzar went forth once more against Jerusalem in the days of Jechoniah,[634] son of Eliakim,[635] who was also (called) Jechoniah, who slept[636] with his fathers.

46/ And Jehoiakim, who was also called Jechoniah, was king for three months,[637] and when King Nebuchadnezzar came to Jerusalem, both Jechoniah and all his men, with distinguished men in the van, all he brought captive to Babylon.[638] For on his first coming, in the days of Eliakim, he took gold and silver to Babylon and all the precious vessels of the temple[639] and 100,000 men and Daniel and the three Young Men with all the precious goods.[640] On his second coming he led off Jechoniah and his mother and his wives and his <eunuchs> and all prominent men to Babylon.[641]

47/ And he made Zedekiah king of the remainder of the people.[642] And he was king for 11 years.[643] Afterwards, he too rebelled.[644] And in the ninth year of Zedekiah's rule, Nebuchadnezzar went forth for a third time against Jerusalem and he besieged it for three years,[645] and he took it. And who can commit to writing the insupportable tragedy! For he took Zedekiah and put out his two eyes and exiled him in com-

---

629. 2 Kgs 23:34; Yovakim.
630. 2 Kgs 23:36.
631. 2 Kgs 23:37.
632. 2 Kgs 24:1, 2 Chr 36:5–6.
633. 2 Kgs 24:1.
634. 2 Kgs 24:12.
635. 2 Kgs 24:1, 6.
636. Literally: had fallen asleep.
637. 2 Kgs 24:8.
638. 2 Kgs 24:12–16.
639. 2 Chr 36:7; and see Dan 5:2–4.
640. This is an addition to the narrative from the book of Daniel; see Dan 1:2, 6.
641. 2 Kgs 24:12–15.
642. 2 Kgs 24:17.
643. 2 Kgs 24:18.
644. 2 Kgs 24:20.
645. 2 Kgs 25:1–2.

mon.[646] And after five months,[647] Nebuchadnezzar[648] came, the chief executioner, and set fire to the temple and destroyed the wall and took the pillars of bronze and silver to Babylon.[649]

48/ The temple lasted for 442 years.[650]
And from the exodus from Egypt up to Solomon were 480 years.[651]
And from the first building of the temple up to the second were 512 years.[652]
From the rebuilding of the temple up to the birth of Christ our God (were) 518 years.
From Adam to the flood were 2242 years.[653]
And from the flood to Abraham were 942 years.[654]
And from Abraham's birth up to the exodus (were) 505 years.
The total from Adam up to the birth of Christ (were) 5,138 years.[655]

The continuation of the text takes this chronicle down to the genealogy in Matthew. On fol. 90v, *Vitae Prophetarum* ensues.

4.5. Short History of the Holy Forefathers

This text is to be found in M2111, *Miscellany*, copied in 1652–1679, fols. 230r–231r.[656] It is followed by a text concerning Christ's tunic (fols. 231r–232v). Cross-references are given in the notes where appropriate. The manuscript is written in a cramped *notrgir* script, and raises some challenges in decipherment.

The first part of this text is a somewhat different version of the retelling of the early Genesis stories than those occurring in *History of Adam and His Grandsons* (Stone 1996a, 80–100). However, as becomes evident from the

---

646. 2 Kgs 25:6–7.
647. The figure is taken from 2 Kgs 25:8.
648. This name should be Nebuzaradan, see 2 Kgs 25:8.
649. 2 Kgs. 2:9, 10, 13, 17. According to the Bible the pillars were made from bronze only, not silver, which is added by our text.
650. This is the figure according to the Acts of Paul: see Stone 1982, 83. For the use in *Dates*, see Stone 1996a, 99–100.
651. 1 Kgs 6:1.
652. 2 Chr 36:21–23. The figure is 511 in *Biblical Paraphrases*; Stone 1982, 83.
653. So also *Biblical Paraphrases* (Stone 1982, 83).
654. So also *Biblical Paraphrases*.
655. This total varies in different sources.
656. On this manuscript, see Tēr-Vardanean 2012, 7:52–62, esp. 55.

notes on the translation, this work is closely related, often verbatim, to *History of the Forefathers, Adam and His Sons and Grandsons* (Stone 1996a, 180–200). Indeed the word "short" seems to indicate that it is an abbreviation of that work, but, I may add, an abbreviation that has been reworked. From §28 on it shares the story, but not much language, with *Concerning the Good Tidings of Seth* §§12–35 (see Lipscomb 1990, 175–81 [Armenian] and 192–97 [(translation)]).

The question of the interrelation of the Armenian narratives of the expulsion of the Protoplasts from the Garden and the *Urgeschichte* down to the flood, demands a full, separate investigation. Here our aim is to publish the text with a translation and to add such notes as facilitate reading of it.

Text

0/ / fol. 228r / Պատմութիւն համառօտ՝ նախահարցն սրբոց:
1/ Եւ յորժամ ել մարդն Ադամ ի դրախտէն. մնաց Լ ամ ի սգի: Եւ ապա ծնաւ զԿային հրամանաւ Աստուծոյ, եւ պատգամաւ հրեշտակի. եւ զԱբրուսաք քոյր նորա ընդ նմայ: Եւ ապա յետ Լ ամաց ծնաւ զՀաբէլ. եւ զՍամա քոյր նորա ընդ նմա:
2/ Եւ Հաբէլ լեալ Լ ամաց՝ սպանաւ ի Կայենէ՝ զոր սգացին Ադամ եւ Եւայ զամս Խ: Եւ ապա յետ ՄԼ ամաց եղանելոյն Ադամայ ի դրախտէն՝ ծնաւ զՍէթ ըստ կերպարանաց իւրոց. զի ծանիցէ զզօրութիւն Արարչին իւրոյ, որ ի խաւարչտին տեղւոջ ի մէջ աղեացն յօրինեաց զՍէթ ի նմանութիւն Ադամայ, անպակաս ի կազմածոյ մասանցն, եւ ի գեղոյ երեսացն:
3/ Եւ եկաց Ադամ յետ ծնանելոյն զՍէթ, այլ եւս ամս Չ, մինչեւ ի ՃԼԵ ամն Մադաղիէլի, եւ ծնաւ ուստերս եւ դուստրս. Լ փոր Կ տղայ: Որով զուգէր զառաջին քոյրն յետին եղբօրն. եւ զյետին քոյրն առաջին եղբօրն:
4/ Եւ լեալ Ադամայ. ՋԼ ամաց, եւ մեռաւ ի ժամ երեկոյին աւուրն. յառաջին Ռ-ին, Ձ եւ Լ ամին, որ յայս Տեառն իբրեւ զմի օր է:
5/ Եւ տարակոյս է թէ Ադամ յառաջ մեռաւ՝ թէ Եւայ. ոմանք ասեն զԵւա յառաջ մեռանել. զի նախ նա մեղաւ՝ եւ ապա Ադամ, զի թէ մահն վասն մեղացն էր՝ պարտ էր Եւայի յառաջ մեռանել. զի նախ նա[657] մեղաւ՝ եւ ապա Ադամ:
6/ Եւ այլք ասեն թէ Ադամ նախ մեռաւ. զի առաջ նա ստեղծէր՝

---

657. Straight line follows նա.

պարտ էր նմա յառաջ մեռանել. եւ ապա Եւայի։ Ադամն կաւ ասի. եւ Եւայն ոձ։

7/ Եւ Սէթ լեալ Ճ եւ Ե ամաց՝ ծնանի զՀենվսա՝ յԱզովրայ կնոջէն իւրմէ։ Եւ եկաց այլ եւս ԷՃ եւ Է ամ. մինչեւ ի Ի ամս Ենովքայ. եւ ծնաւ ուստերս եւ դստերս եւ մեռաւ. Թ եւ ԺԲ ամաց։

8/ Եւ Ենվս յուսացաւ կոչել զանուն Տեառն Աստուծոյ. զի մինչ ի նա՝ ոչ ոք իշխեր տալ զանուն Աստուծոյ։

9/ Ենվս ի Քաղդերէնն մարդ ասի, որ անդրադարձի եւ լինի դրամ. տեղի անուանն Աստուծոյ՝ որ է թագաւոր ամենայնի։ Եւ արդ՝ գիտելի է՝ զի բազում կերպիւ ցուցաւ նորոգումն ապականեալ պատկերիս մարդոյ ի յԵնվս։ Նախ՝ անուամբն՝ զի Ենվս մարդ ասի. ի նմանութիւն սկզբնատպին Աստուծոյ։

10/ Երկրորդ զի յԱդամայ մինչ ի սա. ոչ ոք էած զմտաւ զյոյս հանդերձեալ կենացն։

11/ Երրորդ զի ուղղութիւն եւ պարկեշտութիւն ստացաւ՝ յուսելով թէ գոյ հատուցումն յԱստուծոյ, եւ ոչ լինի մոռացեալ որպէս Ադամ եւ Եւայ. եւ Կայեն. որ յուսահատեալ եղեն. իբր թողեալք ի ձեռաց Աստուծոյ։

12/ Չորրորդ՝ զի յուսացաւ կոչել զանուն Տեառն Աստուծոյ՝ թէ Աստուած է մեր, եւ ոչ թէ վասն կորստեան էած զմեզ աստ. այլ ի կեցուցանել։ եւ անտի ընկալան մարդիկք կոչել զանուն Աստուծոյ յօգնութիւն յամենայն գործս իւրեանց[658] ասելով թէ օգնեա Աստուած. եւ թէ անունն Աստուծոյ։

13/ Հինգերորդ՝ զի յուսացաւ կոչել զանուն Տեառն Աստուծոյ. թէ Տէր է եւ ոչ քարշի ի ծառայիցս։

14/ Վեցերորդ՝ Զի երկու արձան հաստատեաց՝ հակառակ որդւոցն Կայենի, այս է գլյուսն եւ զգործան բարի. զոր նոքա ոչ ունէին։

15/ Եօթներորդ՝ Զի արար զիր. եւ գրեաց ի վերայ թրծեալ աղիւսոյ եւ պղնձոյ սեան. եւ մարգարէացաւ անցանելն երկրի ջրով եւ հրով վասն մեղաց մարդկան։ Եւ ընկեց զթրծեալ աղիւսն ի ջուր եւ զպղինձն ի հուր. փորձելով, թէ յառաջ հուրն գայցէ՝ պղինձն հալեցից. եթէ նախ ջուրն գայցէ՝ աղիւսն ապականի։

16/ Եւ այնու գիտաց որ նախ ջուրն էր գալոյ՝ եւ ապա հուրն։ Եւ այս / fol. 230v / յուսոյ է գործ։ Եւ գրեալն յերկուս սիւնսն՝ զամենայն իրաց անուանն էր գրեալ. զի գիտաց որ ի լեզուստ եւ ի թլատ. ի զնչոտ եւ ի կակզոտ մարդկանէ ապականելոց

---

658. Editorial sign follows this word and ասելով is in the margin.

էր լեզուն, եւ խանգարէին անուանք իրաց եղելոցս՝ զոր Ադամ
կոչեալ էր եւ եղեալ։ Վասն որոյ գրեաց յերկուս սիւնսն եւ եթող։
17/ թէ չուրն գայր յառաջ՝ եւ գհողերէն արձանն թրջեալ
ապականէր՝ պղնձի գիրն եւ անուանք իրացն մնայր. որ յետ
հեղեղին եւ ժամանակաց անցելոց ի բան գայր։
18/ Նոյնպէս եւ թէ հրեղէն հեղեղն գայր եւ զպղինձն հալեալ
զգիրն ապականէր՝ խեցերէն առաւել թղձեալ մնայր։ Եւ այս
ճշմարիտ գործ յուսոյ է։
19/ Ութերորդ՝ Չի ենովս քարշեաց որդւոց իւրոց. վարս
պարկեշտս եւ անբիծ ստանալ՝ վասն արդար հատուցմանն
Աստուծոյ։ Որք ուսեալք ի նմանէ ոգիք Մ. յիշեցին զկեանս
դրախտին. եւ ինքեանց ուխտ եդին կեալ սրբութեամբ, եւ
կոչեցան որդիք Աստուծոյ. վասն յուսոյ եւ պարապման
երկնաւոր փափագմանն։
20/ Իսկ Սէթ վախճանեցաւ յետ Չ եւ Խ ամաց. նոյնպէս եւ որդին
իւր ենովս. նոյն թվով ապրեցաւ։ Հարիւր եւ Դ ամաց էր
ենովս, եւ ծնաւ զԿայնան. եւ Կայնան զՄաղաղիէլ ծնաւ. եւ
Մաղաղիէլ զՅարեդ ծնաւ. գհայրն ենովքայ։ Իսկ յորժամ ծնաւ
ենովք ի Յարեղայ, եւ եղեալ ի չափ հասակի. ծնաւ նմա որդի
Մաթուսաղա։ Ապա հարցանէր ենովք զԱդամ եւ ասէր. զի՞նչ
եղեւ պատճառ յաքսորանացն քոց ի դրախտէն փափկութեան։
21/ Ասէ Ադամ. վասն հնազնդելոյ զբանն Տեառն. եւ պտղաճաշակ
պատուիրազանցութեւէն. ի պատճառս աստուածանալոյ։ Ասէ
ենովք՝ եթէ վասն այդր բանի բարկացաւ Արարիչն. կենդանի է
անուն նորա եթէ կերայց միս. եւ կամ զինչ ելանէ ի մոյ, եւ կամ
ճաշակեցայց ի պտղոյ երկրի, զամենայն աւուրս կենաց իմոց։
Եւ այնուհետեւ արար սկիզբն ապաշխարութեան, եւ չափ եդ
ի գլուխն իւր. վասն արժանի չհամարելոյ զինքն տեսանել
զերկինս՝ որ է աթոռ Աստուծոյ։
22/ Եւ տնկեաց դրախտ մեծ եւ վայելուչ. յամենայն պտղոց որ են
յերկրի, եւ ամենեւին ինքն ոչ պտխեցաւ ի պտղոյ դրախտին, այլ
ի պէտս այլոց վաստակեցաւ։ Եւ փոխեաց զնա Տէր Աստուած
յերկրէ վասն բազում պատճառի։
23/ Նախ՝[659] զի թոռն Կայենի Ղամեք՝ որ սպան զԿայէն եւ զորդին.
վասն բառնալոյ զնախատինս յազգէն իւրեանց. նա յորժամ
ետես զենովք՝ այնպէս հանդիսացեալ առաքինութեամբ՝

---

659. Armenian numerals in left margin mark this list.

որ կամեր հաճոյանալ Աստուծոյ, նա խանձեցաւ եւ կամեր սպանանել⁶⁶⁰ զնա՝ որպէս Կայէն զՀաբէլ:

24/ Երկրորդ՝ զի յերկրաւոր ժառանգութենէս որոշեաց զինքն. փոխեաց զնա Աստուած ժառանգել զերկիրն կենդանեաց: Եւ մեզ ամենեցուն յոյս հաստատութեան տուաւ վարքն եւ փոխիլն նորա:

25/ Երրորդ՝ զի յորժամ ի սէր ադինական դրախտին ինքն դրախտ տնկեաց եւ անվայել ՝մայր, փոխեաց զնա Տէր ի դրախտն աստուածատունկ:

26/ Չորրորդ, փոխանակ զի ոչ ճաշակեաց զայս զզալի եւ զապականացու պտուղս, Ճաշակեցէ հանապազ զանապական եւ զանձորելի պտուղսն:⁶⁶¹

27/ Վեցերորդ՝ Զի ոչ համարեցաւ զինքն արժանի հայել յերկինս որ է աթոռ Աստուծոյ, վասն այսորիկ մարմնով վերացաւ ի նմա ի հանդիպումն Աստուծոյ, եւ ի տեսութիւն լուսեղէն Սերովբէիցն եւ Քերովբէիցն, որ են աթոռք անեղին Աստուծոյ:

28/ Եօթներորդ՝ Զի իմացուք թէ ոչ միայն Եղիա, որ կուսութեամբ եկաց եւ յանապատին ճգնեցաւ փոխեցաւ յերկինս. Այլ ածցուք օրինակ զԵնովք, որ օրինաւոր ամուսնութամբ ճգնեցաւ / fol. 231r / յերկրի. պաշօք եւ աղօթիւք. եւ եղեւ ժառանգորդ լուսեղէն դրախտին եւ անմահական կենացն: Սա մարգարէացաւ վասն կատարածի աշխարհիս. եւ արդար դատաստանին. եւ հատուցմանն ըստ իւրաքանչիւր գործոց՝ արդարոց եւ մեղաւորաց:

29/ Եւ յետ փոխելոյ սորա, երկերիւր անձինք յազգէն Սէթայ՝ ուխտեցին եւ ելին ի լեառն Ահերմոն. ճգնել վասն անմահութեան. եւ Նոյ ընդ նոսա, եւ անուանեցան որդիք Աստուծոյ: Վասն այսորիկ նախանձեալ ընդ նոսա ազգն Կայենի. եւ հնարս իմացեալ զարդարեցին զկանայս իւրեանց անգուրով եւ ծարուրով:

30/ Եւ առեալ բազում կերակուրս եւ ըմպելիս. եւ երգեցիկ զուսանս, որ նոր սահմանեցաւ ի ժամանակին յայնմիկ. ի հնարիցն սատանայի: Եւ եկեալ բնակեցան ընդդէմ լերինն այնմիկ. կերան եւ արբին. հարին զփողսն, եւ պարեցին զուսական երգով, եւ կաքաւեցին առաջի նոցա: Զոր տեսեալ ճգնաւրացն

---

660. Over սպանանէր p.m.
661. The fifth reason is omitted.

եւ իշին մի մի առ նոսա. կերան եւ արբին. եւ խառնակեցան ընդ նոսա, եւ որդիքն Աստուծոյ՝ եղեն որդիք կորստեան:

30/ Իսկ Նոյ միայն գտաւ կեալ յուխտին Տեառն, եւ ապրեալ եղեւ ի փորձութեանցն. եւ ընկալաւ զանուն յորդեգրութեանն Աստուծոյ: Նոյ որդի էր Ղամեքայ. ո՞չ թոռինն Կայենի որ սպան զԿայէն, այլ Ղամեքայ՝ որդւոյն Մաթուսաղայի, որդւոյն Ենովքայ:

31/ Սա եկաց կուսութեամբ ի տղայութենէ զամս Շ. մինչեւ ընկալաւ հրաման յԱստուծոյ, առնուլ կին, են ծնանիլ որդիս, եւ շինել տապանս վասն հանդերձեալ ջրհեղեղին որ գալոց էր. վասն չար գործոց ժամանակին:

32/ զի ապականեաց ամենայն մարմին զճանապարհս իւր ի զանազան չարիս: Վասն որոյ արար Նոյ՝ զոր հրամայեաց նմա Աստուած, եւ շինեաց զտապանն ի փրկութիւն տանն իւրոյ: որով եւ զմեզ փրկեսցէ Տէր Աստուած աղօթիւք նորա, ի հրեղէն հեղեղէ ամէն:

Translation

0/   Short Story of the Holy Forefathers

1/ And when the man, Adam, went forth from the Garden, he remained in mourning for 30 years.[662] And then he begot Cain at God's command and the angel's instruction, and Abusakʻ his sister with him. And then after 30 years he begot Abel and Sama his sister with him.[663]

2/ And when Abel was 30 years old, he was killed by Cain. Adam and Eve mourned him for 40 years.[664] And then, 230 years after Adam went forth from the Garden, he begot Seth according to his image, so that he might recognize the power of his Maker, who in a dark place, in the midst of the inward parts formed Seth in Adam's likeness, faultless in formation of (his) members and in the beauty of his face.[665]

---

662. This is close to *Adam and His Grandsons* §1 and *History of the Forefathers*, both works published in Stone 1996. This span of time is attested in numerous sources; see Stone 1996a, 92. The names of the sisters are mentioned in *History of the Forefathers* §27 and they are discussed in the notes to that section.

663. The opening is a short form very similar to *History of the Forefathers*; Stone 1996a, 193–94 §27. The names of the sisters of Cain and Abel occur in that text, as does the age of 30 years. On the names of the sisters, see Stone, 1996, 118.

664. *History of the Forefathers* has 140 years. This section is almost verbatim identical with *History of the Forefathers* §27; Stone 1996a, 193–94.

665. This is very close, except for the "230 years" to the latter part of *History of the Forefathers*

PART FOUR   169

3/   And after begetting Seth, Adam remained for another 700 years, up to the 135th year of Mahalalel, and he begot sons and daughters, 30 pregnancies (and) 60 children. He paired the first sister with her later brother, and the latest sister with her first brother.[666]
4/   And when Adam was 930 years old, he died in the evening of the day, in the first 1,000, (aged) 900, and 30 years, which is like one day in God's eyes.[667]
5/   And it is doubtful whether Adam died first or Eve. Some say that Eve died first, since she sinned first, and then Adam. For, if death was on account of sins, Eve should have died first, because she sinned first, and then Adam.
6/   And others say that Adam died first, for he was created first, he should have died first, and then Eve. Adam means "clay"[668] and Eve, "serpent."[669]
7/   And Seth at 205 years begot Enosh from Azovra his wife.[670] And he lived another 707 years, until the 20th year of Enoch, and he begot sons and daughters and he died at 902 years.
8/   And Enosh hoped to call the name of the Lord God, for up to him no one could give the name of God.[671]
9/   In Chaldean (Aramaic) Enosh means "man" which backwards is dram (money), place[672] of the name of God, who is King of everything.[673] And now, it is to be known that the renewal of the corrupted image was

---

§28; Stone 1996a, 194.

666. *History of the Forefathers* §29; Stone 1996a, 195. See commentary there on the thirty pregnancies and the marriage patterns.

667. *History of the Forefathers* §30; Stone, 1996a, 195. The biblical allusion is to Ps 90(89):4: "For a thousand years in thy sight are but as yesterday."

668. Compare Stone 2013, 13, 42, 293. Again the section is virtually identical with *History of the Forefathers* §§31–32.

669. Observe the use of onomastic elements to serve the author's purpose. I remarked on this usage and given chief bibliographical indications above in part 3, note 19.

670. In Gen 5:6 we read 105 in the MT and 205 in the LXX. In *History of the Forefathers* §33 the very similar text gives for his lifespan 105 + 507 years = 612. In Adam and His Grandsons §§7 we find 205 +707 = 912; which is like the present text. Depending on the notation used, the confusion 5/7 may have affected this because of the graphic confusion of ƀ/ƫ; see part 2, note 97 above.

671. *History of the Forefathers*, Sons §34; based on LXX of Gen 4:26. The life span of Enosh is 912 in both the MT and LXX of Gen 5:8.

672. The meaning is unclear.

673. *History of the Forefathers*, Sons §§35–41 contains many of these traditions. The wording is similar, but the text here is abbreviated.

demonstrated in Enosh in many forms.[674] First, by name, that Enosh means "man," in the likeness of God's prototype.[675]

10/ Second that from Adam to him no one considered the hope of the future life:[676]

11/ Third, since he acquired uprightness and modesty through hoping that there is reward from God, and he had not forgotten like Adam and Eve and Cain who despaired, as having been abandoned by God.[677]

12/ Fourth, that he hoped to call on the name of the Lord God, that he is our God and that he did not bring us[678] here for the sake of destruction, but to make us live. And then humans took it on themselves to call on God for help in all their actions, saying, "Help, God," and (this was done) in the name of God.[679]

13/ Fifth, because he hoped to call on the name of the Lord God, that He is the Lord and does draw away from his servants.

14/ Sixth, because he established two stelae against the sons of Cain. They are hope and good works, which they did not have.[680]

15/ Seventh, because he made[681] writing and wrote upon stelae of baked brick and of copper, and he prophesied that the earth will pass away through water and fire because of the sins of men. And he cast the baked brick into the water and the copper one into fire, testing (whether) if the fire will come first, the copper will melt, if the water will come first, the brick will be spoiled.

16/ And by this[682] he knew that the water will come first and then the fire. And this is an action of hope. And the writing on the two pillars had written the names of all things, for he knew that by men (who were) stammerers and lispers and stutterers and sputterers[683] the language would be corrupted. And they would confuse the name of the these

---

674. Or: forms.
675. *History of the Forefathers* §35b. Now there ensues a number of interpretation of the Septuagint translation of Gen 4:26 where "began" is read "hoped," taking the Hebrew consonantal text to derive from a different root.
676. Fraade (1984, index s.v. "hope") discusses this theme throughout his work.
677. *History of the Forefathers* §37.
678. The phrase "bring us here" reflects the common Armenian etymology of Աստուած "God." See NBHL s.v.
679. *History of the Forefathers* §39, where this is the text of the fifth reason, and the text of the fourth reason in *History of the Forefathers* §38 is the fifth reason here.
680. *History of the Forefathers* §40.
681. Perhaps, "invented." The theme is widespread: see already Josephus, *A.J.*, 1.70–71.
682. Apparently, through the prophecy mentioned in §13.
683. Reading the Armenian as կակղտուն, which is its form in both texts.

PART FOUR 171

things that had come into being, which Adam had named and fixed. For this reason, he wrote (them) on two pillars and left them.[684]

17/ If the water came first and destroyed the baked earthen monument, the writing and the names of things on bronze would remain, so that after the flood and some time passed, it (they) would come into use.

18/ Similarly, if the fiery flood would come and the copper melted and spoiled the writing, the baked pottery would remain more. And this is a true action of hope.

19/ Eighth, because Enosh brought his sons to accept modest and blameless conduct, on account of God's just recompense. 200 souls who learned from him remembered the life of the Garden and they made a covenant among themselves to live with holiness and they were called children of God, on account of hope and occupation with heavenly delight.[685]

20/ Then Seth died after 900 and 40 years, likewise also his son, Enosh, lived the same length of time.[686] Enosh was 100 and 90 years old and he begot Kenan,[687] and Kenan[688] begot Mahalelel, and Mahalelel begot Jared, Enoch's father. Then, when Enoch was begotten by Jared and reached adulthood, Methuselah was born to him. Then Enoch asked Adam and said, "What was the reason of your exile from the Garden of Delight?"[689]

21/ Adam said, "Because we derided the Lord's word and tasted (i.e., the fruit) disobediently, in order to become divine."[690] Enoch said, "If God was wrath at that thing, as his name lives if I will[691] eat meat or what issues from meat, or I will taste the fruit of the earth all the days of my life." And thenceforth he made a beginning of repentance and he put a

---

684. *History of the Forefathers* §§41–43.
685. *History of the Forefathers* §45. The rest of this document is not found in *History of the Forefathers*. This Euhemeristic explanation of Gen 6:1 is widespread. See note 704 below.
686. Gen 5:8 gives Seth's life as 912 years while Gen 5:11 gives Enosh's lifespan as 905 years. Neither agrees with §21.
687. Gen 5:9 in MT gives ninety years and in LXX, 190. The two versions agree that Enosh lived 905 years.
688. Kenan is not included in some genealogical lists: see notes 107 and 186.
689. The textual material henceforth is not in *History of the Forefathers*, which concludes with material parallel to §18. Instead, it shares the story, but not much language, with *Concerning the Good Tidings of Seth* §§12–35, see Lipscomb 1990, 175–81 (Armenian) and 192–97 (translation).
690. The three finite verbs in this English translation are actually verbal nouns in Armenian.
691. I.e., "I will not."

measuring vessel on his head, because he did not think himself worthy of seeing the heavens, which are the throne of God.[692]

22/ And he planted a great and delightful garden with all the fruit which was on the earth and he did not give himself up to the fruit of the garden, but he labored for the needs of others.[693] And the Lord God transferred him from the earth for many reasons.

23/ First, because of Cain's grandson, Lamech, who killed Cain and his son for the sake of removing jealousy from their generation. When he[694] saw Enoch, he was so conflicted by virtue, so that he wished to please God, he was inflamed and wished to kill him, as Cain (had killed) Abel.[695]

24/ Second, because he separated himself from this earthly heritage, God transferred him to inherit the land of the living, and his conduct and transferral gave us all hope of the firmament.[696]

25/ Third, because when for love of the Edenic Garden, he himself planted a garden and did not enjoy (it),[697] the Lord transferred him to the divinely planted Garden.

26/ Fourth, in exchange for his not eating this perceptible and corruptible fruit, he will always eat the incorruptible and unrotting fruit.

27/ Sixth,[698] because he did not reckon himself worthy of looking at the heavens, which are God's throne, on account of this he was taken up in the body to encounter God in them, and to the vision of the luminous Seraphs and Cherubs who are the thrones of the increate God.[699]

28/ Seventh, so that we might understand that not only Elijah, who remained virginal and lived the ascetic life in the desert, was trans-

---

692. These two acts are found in various Armenian sources: Enoch did something related to gardens and fruit (planted a garden, refrained from fruit, etc.) and he did not look at the heavens, and in some texts as here put a sort of metal helmet on his head. They are discussed by Lipscomb 1990, 99–101 and Stone 2010 and are typical in Armenian.

693. Thus completing a statement about an ascetic life: he refrains from fruit, meat and meat products, and gives food to the need. See §28 below.

694. I.e., Lamech.

695. See the discussion of this tradition here pp. 92–93. There is confusion of the Cainite Enoch and the Sethite Enoch behind this statement. See the variant tradition in *History of the Forefathers* §16 and *Question* §5.3.

696. "Firmament" is odd here. Perhaps some form of հատուցումն "recompense, reward" has been confused with հաստատութիւն, "firmament."

697. Literally: remained without enjoyment of.

698. The fifth item in this list is lacking.

699. God sits on or between the Cherubs: Exod 25:22, Num 7:89, 2 Sam 6:2; 22:11, etc. The Seraphs in the Bible are not a throne for the Almighty.

ferred to the heavens, but let us take Enoch as an example who, being lawfully married, lived the ascetic life on the earth through fasts and prayers, and he inherited the luminous Garden and the immortal life. He prophesied about the end of this world and the just judgement and the recompense of the deeds of each of the righteous and of the wicked.[700]

29/ And after his transfer, two hundred persons of the race of Seth swore (an oath) and climbed mount Hermon, to live ascetically for the sake of immortality.[701] And Noah was with them and they were called "Sons of God." For this reason, the race of Cain envied them and they learned wiles, they adorned their wives with rouge[702] and antimony.[703]

30/ And they took much food and drink and songful minstrels who were newly defined also in that time by the wiles of Satan. And they came and dwelt opposite that mountain. They ate and drank, blew trumpets and danced to the song of the minstrels and they pranced before them. When the ascetics saw that, one by one they climbed down to them. They ate and drank and had intercourse with them, and the sons of God became sons of perdition.

30/ But Noah alone was found steadfast in the oath to God and he lived through the trials and received the title of adoption by God.[704] Noah was Lamech's son, not (Lamech) the grandson of Cain who killed Cain, but Lamech, son of Methusaleh, son of Enoch.

26/ He lived in virginity from his boyhood for 500 years, until he received a commandment from God to take a wife and to beget sons and to build this Ark because of the future flood which was coming on account of the evil deeds of the time.[705]

27 For all flesh corrupted their ways in various evils. On account of this Noah did what God had commanded him and built the Ark for the

---

700. This sentence does not seem anchored to a biblical text, but to a tradition connecting Enoch with learning. See Stone 2010, 517–30, esp. 522, 527. See also Reed 2014, 149–87.

701. Observe that in 1 En. 6 two hundred angels swore an oath and descended on Mt. Hermon to lie with human women. Scholars connect "oath" with "Hermon" via the Hebrew root ḥ.r.m.

702. ակզուր; see Stone 1996a, 177.

703. Reading ծաղուր as ծաղիր. This is the Euhemeristic reading of Gen 6:1–2 on which see the introductory remarks to 3.3 above. The text is close to *Concerning the Good Tidings of Seth*, but shorter, as it tells the stories of the Sethites and the Cainites.

704. Presumably an exegesis of Gen 6:9 "and Noah walked with God." Arm Gen 6:9 reads, "And Noah was pleasing (huanj) to God."

705. The theme of Noah's long virginity is widespread. See in this book text 3.8 §17.

4.6. Joseph and Jacob: An Allegory

This text is found in M2111, fol. 229v. There is no indication of authorship and date beyond the date of the manuscript, a *Miscellany*, copied in 1652–1679. On the whole the text is a clear allegory, but there are on or two obscure readings, which are signalled in the notes.

Text

1/ Գրեալ է յԱրարածրն, թէ Յովսէփի տարաւ զորդիսն իւր առ Յակոբ նահապետն՝ զի օրհնեցէ զնոսա։ Եւ եղեալ զՄանասէ յաջկոյսն Յակոբայ, եւ զԵփրեմ ի ձախմէ։

2/ Իսկ Յակոբ փոխեաց զաջ իւր ի գլուխն Եփրեմի. եւ զձախն ի Մանասէի։ Եւ ասէ Յովսէփ՝ ոչ այնպէս հայր. այլ զաջ քո դիր ի վերայ Մանասէի. զի նա է աւագն. այլ Յակոբ զխտեր զինչ առներ։

3/ Յակոբ ցուցանէ զԱստուած. եւ Յովսէփի ...[706] եւ Բ որդիքն զմեծատունս եւ զաղքատս։

4/ Մանասէ կոչի զմոռացումն՝ որ ցուցանէ զչար մեծատունն. որք մոռացան զերախտին Աստուծոյ։

5/ Իսկ Եփրեմ ասի՝ պտղաբեր եւ լայնացեալ. որ նշանակէ զաղքատս հոգեւոր. որ բազում զոհութիւնս պտղաբերէ Աստուծոյ։ Եւ թէպէտ աստ ի նեղութեան է, այլ լայնացեալ արձակի ի հանդերձեալն։

6/ Եւ զի մեծատունն է ի կեանս յայս աշկոյս. զի յաջողի նմա ամեն ինչ մարմնական։[707] եթէ տեսի զամբարիշտն վերացեալ բարձ<ր> անցի եւ ահա ոչ էր։

7/ Այլ աղքատն է ի ձախ կոյս. որպէս ասէ աղքատացեալն վասն մեր Քրիստոս. երանի աղքատացդ հոգւով. զի ձեր է արքայութիւն երկնից։ Եւ եթէ որ սիրէ զանձն արձակէ զնա. եւ

---

706. Illegible in the image: perhaps զայս, i.e., զԱստուծոյս, but if that is the reading, the meaning remains puzzling. The section commences the allegory.
707. Erasure of four words.

որ ատեա‹ց› զանձն իւր յաշխարհս յայսմիկ ի կեա(abbrev).⁷⁰⁸ զի աղքատն ի տառապանս եւ ի հալածանս կայ միշտ:
8/ Այլ յորժամ հայր մեր երկնաւոր Քրիստոս գայ ի դատաստանն, կացուցանէ զհոգեւոր աղքատս ընդ աջմէ իւրմէ ասելով. եկայք օրհնեցէք հօր իմոյ ժա." Եւ չար մեծատունսն ի ձախմէ՝ ասելով. եթայք յին"
9/ Չի յայնմ աււր զաջն ի ձախ. եւ զձախն յաջ փոխելոց է: որպէս յայտ է յաւետարանին որ ասէ՝ այր մի էր մեծատունն եւ ազազանէր բեհեզ.
10/ Դարձեալ մինչեւ ի Քրիստոս աջ էին հրեայք. եւ ձախ հեթանոսք. Իսկ զալստեամբ որդւոյն Աստուծոյ աջ եղեն հաւատովք ի Քրիստոս, որք կոչեցան նոր Իսրայէլ: Եւ ձախ հրեայք անհաւատութեամբ՝ եւ աստուածապանութեամբ.

Translation

1/ It is written in Genesis that Joseph brought his sons to the patriarch Jacob, so that he might bless them.⁷⁰⁹ And he put Manasseh at Jacob's right side and Ephraim at (his) left.⁷¹⁰

2/ Then Jacob transferred his right hand to Ephraim's head, and his left hand to Manasseh. And Joseph said, "Not thus, father, but place your right hand on Manasseh for he is the older."⁷¹¹ But Jacob knew what he was doing.⁷¹²

3/ Jacob indicates God and Joseph the {   }⁷¹³ and the two sons, the rich and the poor.

4/ He called Manasseh the forgetting,⁷¹⁴ which indicates the evil grandees who forgot God's beneficences.

5/ But Ephraim means, "Fruitful and broadened," which signifies the

---

708. This and several other places uses an apocopation of a word, followed by an abbreviation mark in the form of a double quotation mark. Here it is կեա, which I have interpreted as from կեանք "life."
709. Gen 48:1.
710. Gen 48:13–14, 17.
711. Gen 48:18.
712. Gen 48:19.
713. Illegible.
714. This is the usual meaning of Manasseh found in Gen 41:51 and in Armenian onomastic lists, see Wutz 1915, 914–15; Stone 1981, 140–41.

spiritual poor one, who is fruitful with many praises to God.[715] And, despite the fact that here[716] he is straitened, yet the future (world) having become broadened, he will be freed.

6/ And because the wealthy is on this right hand side in this life, for every bodily thing succeeds for him. If I saw the impious being elevated, and passing on high, behold he was not.[717]

7/ But the poor man is on the left hand side, just as Christ the one who became impoverished on our account, said, "Blessed (be) the poor in spirit, for yours is the kingdom of heaven."[718] And if he who loves his soul releases it, and he who hates his soul in this world, (is destined) for life,[719] since the poor always suffers and is always persecuted.

8/ But when our heavenly Father, Christ comes to the judgement he sets the spiritual poor man at his right hand, saying, "Come, let us bless my Father's inheritance [720] And the evil wealthy ones are on his left, saying, "Go to …"

9/ For on that day the right will be exchanged for the left, and the left for the right, just as is revealed in the Gospel, which says, "There was a rich man, who was clothed …"[721]

10/ Again, up to Christ, the Jews were on the right and the gentiles on the left, but through the coming of the Son of God, the believers in Christ became the right, who are called New Israel, and the left (is) the Jews through unbelief and through deicide.[722]

4.7. Third Story of Joseph

This homiletic narrative contains two different types of material. First, it retells in considerable detail the story of Joseph, his captivity, and his authority in Egypt, up to his commandment to his children and brothers to take his

---

715. This is the meaning Gen 41:52 gives for "Ephraim." See also Wutz 1915, 886–87; Stone 1981, 134–35.
716. Perhaps, "in this world."
717. The second half of this section, following the erasure, is somewhat obscure.
718. Matt 5:3.
719. Cf. John 12:25.
720. Here is another of these apocopations: ձա can be taken ձառանգութիւն, "inheritance" reflecting Mat 25:34. The source of "right hand" is the preceding verse of Matthew and in fact the parable of the sheep and the goats in Matt 25:32 may lie behind the entire section.
721. Luke 16:19.
722. No biblical source could be discovered for this supersessionist passage.

bones out of Egypt (§§1–94: cf. Gen 37:2–50:25, and Exod 13:19). This narrative is close to the Genesis story, but does differ in a number of details as will be observed in the notes below. The one substantial section which is added to the biblical is Joseph's homiletic disquisition on his mother's grave as he left the Land of Israel in the hands of the merchants (§§26–37).

In addition to this passage, elsewhere the document contains a strong homiletic element, with hortatory remarks interwoven with the narrative and also a long section following the conclusion of the narrative (§§94–102). In §103 there is a pious prayer and invocation.

Textually, the document depends on the Armenian Bible or the LXX. Since Arm was translated from LXX, it is not always possible to distinguish between them.[723] The text occurs in M2242, a seventeenth-century *Miscellany* on fols. 330r–349v. Another copy is found in M2245, 148v–158r, but was not available to me at the time of writing.

Text

1/ [724] / fol. 330r / Երրորդ պատմութիւն Յովսեփի գե[ղ]եցկին է եւ ողջախոհին:
Այս Յակոբ ԲԺ-ան որդիս ունէր որոց անուանքն այս են. Ռուբէն. Շմաւոն. Ղեւի. Յուդա: Սաքար. Զաբողոն. Դան. Նեփթաղիմ. Գադ. Ասեր. Յովսեփի. Բենիամին: ի մէկ մօրէ ի Հռաքելայ. եւ սիրէր Յակոբ զՅովսեփ եւ զԲենիամին, առաւել քան զայլս. զի կրսեր էին քան զայլ որդիս.

2/ Եւ մայրն նոցա Հռաքել ի ծնանել զԲենիամին, մեռաւ ի ծնունդն. եւ Յակոբ առանց մայր[725] սնոյց զԲենիամին:

3/ Եւ էին այլ որդիքն Յակոբայ խաշնարածք ի դաշտին: Եւ Յովսեփի եւ Բենիամին ի տան բնակէին առ հայրն իւրեանց Յակոբայ:

4/ Եւ յաւուր միում ի գիշերի տեսիլ տեսէս Յովսեփի, եւ պատմեաց եղբարցն իւրոց. եւ ասէ, տեսի յայսմ գիշերի. զի արտ հնձէաք ես եւ երկոտասան եղբայրքս իմ. եւ տեսի, զի օրեայքն եղբարց իմոց զային եւ երկրպագէին օրային իմոյ:

---

723. A. S. Zeyt'unyan's edition of Arm Genesis does not help in this task, see Zeyt'unyan 1985, and on this edition see Cox 1988, 87–125; Zeyt'unyan 1993, 306–12; and Cox 1993, 313–15.

724. Marked խը in intercolumnar space.

725. A genitive would be expected.

5/ Եւ լուեալ եղբարցն նորա ասէին⁷²⁶{գ}ընդ⁷²⁷ միմեանս՝ միթէ այսպէս լինիցի սա. զի մեք մետասան եղբարքս նմա երկիր պագանեմք. եւ նա թագաւորէ ի վերայ մեր. եւ այսպիսի ոչ կամաց գծշմարիտօն ասելով մեկնէին զերազն յինքեանք. եւ այնու չարէին ընդ տեսիլն Յովսեփայ:

6/ Եւ Յովսէփի դարձեալ կրկին եւտես երազ. եւ պատմեաց հօր եւ եղբարցն. եւ ասէ յայսմ գիշերիս տեսի զի արեգակն եւ լուսինն հանդերձ մետասան աստեղօք՝ զայլին եւ ինձ երկիր պագէին:

7/ Եւ լուեալ եղբարցն / fol. 330v / գշարացեալ եւ ոչ կամաց մեկ<ն>էին⁷²⁸ զերազն. եւ ասէին՝ զի միթէ թագաւորել կամի սայ՝ եւ մեք եւ հայրն մեր զամք յերկրպագութիւն սորա. եւ յայսմ օրէ ընդ ակամբ հայէին եղբարքն ընդ Յովսէփ. եւ ոչ կարէին տեսանել զնա:

8/ Տես գշար նախանձուն. զի որ զեղբարքն ի յատելութիւն դարձոյց. զի հանապազ չարէին զնա. եւ խորհուրդ արարեալ զի սպանցեն զնա. եւ դիպող ժամու ստիպէին. ո վ այս չար խորհուրդա եմուտ ի նոսա: Եւ ապա յետ այսորիկ հեռագոյն էին գնացեալ եղբարքն Յովսեփու զհետ խաշանցն ի դաշտին:

9/ Եւ յայնժամ ասէ Յակոբ ցՅովսէփ որդին իւր՝ ա՛ռ որդեակ հաց եւ տար եղբարց քոց ի դաշտին. եւ ունէր Յովսէփ պատմուճան ծաղկեաւ: Եւ յարեաւ առեալ զհացն եւ տանէր եղբարցն իւրոց՝ եւ մոլորեցաւ ի ճանապարհին: զի յիշէր գշարութիւն եղբարցն.

10/ Եւ ապա ի միտս իւր եկեալ՝ գայ գտանէ զեղբարսն իւր ի դաշտին. եւ իբրեւ տեսին եղբարքն գՅովսէփ՝ ասեն ընդ միմեանս այսպէս՝ աha գայ երազատեսն. եւ արարին խորհուրդ սպանութեան եւ նենգութեան վասն Յովսէփու թէ որպէս կորուսցեն զնա:

11/ Ո՛վ չար նենգութիւն եւ նախանձու անօրէնութիւն, որ զերախտաւորն եւ զբարեգործ սպանանել կամէին. Յովսէփ նոցա հաց ի կերակուր տանէր. եւ նոքա սպանանել խորհէին:

12/ Ո՛վ չար նենգութիւն եղբարցն, զի ոչ է պարտ եղբայրս⁷²⁹ կոչել զնոսա. այլ մանաւանդ գազանս. զի ոչ զեղբօրս բանս գործեցին, այլ գշար գազանի եւ չար թշնամւոյն:

13/ Ո՛վ անզգնութիւն⁷³⁰ / fol. 331r / եղբարցն. զի Յովսէփի

---

726. նորա ասէին *inter lineas*.
727. The preposition g is corrupt. There is a correction here in the text.
728. Corrupt, omit ն.
729. յ over g p.m. See Stone and Hillel, "Index," no. 49.
730. The word as written is not in NBHL. However, it might be a variant orthography of

անմեղութեամբ եւ աշխատութեամբ կերակուր տաներ նոցա. եւ սոքա ի չար խորհուրդն սպանութեան մատնէին գՅովսեփ ի ճանապարհին. նոքա մոլորեալ ի չարն ընթացան. ով սքանչելեաց. զի թվեր թէ զայն յայտներ մոլորելն Յովսեփայ ի ճա‹նա›պարհին զնենգութիւն եղբարցն գուշակեաց՝ եւ ցուցանէր նմա Աստուած գհամբերութիւն, զի մի՛ փորձեցի. նեղ սրտութեամբ վասն չարութեան եղբարցն. զի գիտասցէ եւ Աստուած ապաւինեցի, այն որ գՃանապարհին ուղեց. նա կարող է որ գչար նենգութիւն եղբարցն ի բարի դարձուցանէ։

14/ Տեսէք եղբարք՝ եւ զգուշացարուք ի չար նախանձուէ եւ ատելութենէ աճի չարութիւն. եւ ի չարութենէ, բուսանի նախանձ. եւ ի նախանձէ, ծնանի ատելութիւն. եւ ատելութենէ, կատարի եղբայրասպանութիւն։

15/ Տեսէք եղբայրք. զի նախանձ չարութեանն եւ ատելութեանն՝ արար զԿային՝ եղբայրրսպան. եւ նոյն չար նախանձն արար գորդիսն Յակոբայ՝ եղբայրատեաց եւ սպանող. զնոյն եւ առաքեալն ասէ Յակոբ. թէ որ ատէ զեղբայր իւր մարդասպան է կատարեալ. զի չար նախանձով վաճեալ եղբարքն Յովսեփիու կամէին սպանանել զնա. Նոյնպես նախանձն որ առ Հրէայսն էր որ չարացոյց զնոսա՝ մինչեւ զՏէրն մեր սպանին.

16/ զի Յովսեփի յաչս եղբարցն սպանած էր՝ բայց յաչս Աստուծոյ թագաւորելոյ սկիզբն արարեալ՝ նոյնպես եւ Տէրն յաչս հրէից նախանձորդաց մեռեալ թվեր, բայց աստուածութեամբ կենդա / fol. 331v /նի էր. այլ որպէս գՅովսեփ{ի}ն⁷³¹ մերկացուցին եւ եղին ի գբին. նոյնպէս եւ զՏէրն մերկացուցին եւ ի խաչ հանին՝ եւ եղին ի գերեզմանի. զի նոյն ազգն էր որ զնոյն գործեցին՝ նոցա որդիքն էին՝ որ զայն կատարեցին. եւ որպէս նոքա գՅովսեփի վաճառեցին յեզիպտոս Լ արծաթյն. նոյնպէս եւ որդիք նոցա հրէայքն գՏէրն վաճառեցին ի խաչ հանել ընդ Լ արծաթոյ։ եւ այս է նոցա չարութիւն զոր հարքն առին ի զինս Յովսեփայ. եւ որդիք նոցա եւուն ի զինս Քրիստոսի. եւ որպէս եմուտ Յովսեփի ի գուբն բանդին. եւ եմուտ Տէրն մեր ի տապան գերեզմանին. եւ որպէս ելաւ⁷³² Յովսեփի ի բանդէն եւ ի ծառայութենէն՝ թագաւորեաց ի վերայ երկրի.

17/ եւ որպէս եղբարքն որ վաճառեցին գՅովսեփի. տեսին զնա թագաւորեալ եւ անկան կործանեցան եւ զամօթի հարան վասն

տրնութիւն "watchfulness" with the privative ան-.
731. Corrupt case ending. An accusative would be expected.
732. Postclassical form.

չար գործող իւրեանց զոր գործեցին՝ առ Յովսեփի։ Նոյնպէս յետ յարութեանն տեսեալ Հրէիցն զՏէրն յամօթ լինէին։ Պարտ է մեզ վերստին դառնալ ի պատմութիւնն. իսկ եղբարքն Յովսեփայ մինչդեռ էին ի չար խորհրդի. յայնժամ գայ Յովսէփի բերելով զկերակուր նոցա. եւ տուեալ ողջոյն. խանդաղամիտ սրտիւ. եւ եդ առաջի նոցա զհացն զոր եբեր։

18/ Իսկ եղբարքն չարութեամբ վառեալ էին. ոչ կամէին ուտել զկերակուրն՝ զոր Յովսէփի եբեր. այլ զչար խորհուրդս իւրեանց կամեցան ի գլուխ հանել. յայնժամ բուռն հարին Յովսեփայ եւ մերկացուցին. եւ ընկեցին զնա ի զուր մի ցամաք։ Եւ ապա ինքեանք նստեալ ուտէին զբերեալ կերակուրն Յովսեփու ան / fol. 332r / հոգութեամբ. իբրեւ յաղթութեան իմս համարէին։

19/ Այսպէս եւ Հրեայքն առ Տէրն արարին, զպարգեւս Աստուծոյ առեալ եւ զպարգեւատուն. այսն առնէին զՏէրն ի գերեզմանի դնելով յաղթութեան իմս համարեցան. եւ անհոգաբար զատիկն ուտէին։

20/ Եւ յայնժամ առեալ այծ մի զենեցին եւ զպատմուճանն Յովսեփու առեալ յարիւնն թաթխեցին. եւ ուղարկեցին առ հայրն իւրեանց եւ ասեն զայս գտաք ի դաշտին. տես թէ որդոյ քում Յովսեփայ է պատմուճանդ՝ քանզի գազանաբեկ եղեալ է։

21/ Ո՜ վանմտութիւն եղբարցն զհանդերձն Յովսեփայ մերկացուցին եւ հօրն պատմեցին՝ զնա գազանաբեկ լեալ. յայտնի է որ զինքեանս արարին գազանս. եւ այնպէս գազանաբեկ ասաց զի ինքեանք եղեն գազանք չար խորհրդով վարժեալ խորհէին թէ զինչ արասցեն զնա. կէսքն ասին եկայք սպանցուք զնա. կէսքն ոչ կամելով ասին մի լիցուք արեան պարտական։ Իսկ ումանքն ի նոցանէ ասին թողցուք զնա յանդրէն ի զբին զի անդ մեռցի։

22/ Եւ ապա մինչդեռ յանխորհուրդն էին. պատրաստեաց Տէրն որ կամէր զնա կեցուցանել. եւ յայնժամ քաւրան եկեալ. եւ վաճառականք բազում ընդ անցանելով բարձեալ ղտին եւ գնային յեզիպտոս. տեսեալ զայն եղբարցն Յովսեփու ասին ընդ միմեանս. եկայք վաճառեցուք զՅովսէփի զի երթիցէ յօտարութիւն՝ եւ ի գերութիւն աշխարհի հեռի. զի ոչ կատարեցի երազն նորա։ Եւ այն որ թազաւորել / fol. 332v / կամեր երթիցէ ի գերութիւն եւ խափանեցից երազ նորա. եւ որպէս սուտ համարել. եւ յայնժամ առեալ հանին զՅովսէփի ի զբոյ անտի եւ վաճառեցին զնա եւ առին զգինն Յովսեփայ. Լ դեկան. եւ Յովսէփի համբերեալ նոցա չարեացն, եւ ոչ ստեր վաճառականացն թէ ի զուր վաճառեն զիս՝ զի կրսեր եղբայր եմ ես սոցա, զի վաճառեն զիս. ոչ ասաց այաց բանիցս Յովսէփ՝ եւ ոչ մի. եւ այլ ոչ յանդիմանեաց զչարութիւն եղբարցն:

23/ զայսոսիկ եւ Տէրն արար. զի ոչ յանդիմանեաց զհրէայսն. որ կատաղեալ էին չարեօքն ի վերայ Քրիստոսին մերոյ. որպէս Եսայեաս մարգարէն ասէ. զհամբերութիւնն Քրիստոսի առ չարչարանսն, ոչ խստանամ. եւ ոչ ի դէմ դառնամ. զթիկունս իմ ետու ի հարուածս, եւ ծնօտ իմ յապտակս. եւ դարձեալ ասէ իբրեւ գոչխար ի սպանդ վարեցաւ. եւ իբրեւ գոռոչ առաջի կտրչի անմռունչ կայ. այնպէս ոչ բանայ զբերան իւր. զայս կատարեաց Յովսէփի. զօրինակ Տեառն իւրոյ. զի ոչ հակառակեցաւ՝ վասն չարութեան եղբարցն:

24/ Ջնջյն արար եւ Շուշան առաջի չար եւ դառն ծերոցն. զի նոքա վկայէին սուտ զբանս չարութեան ի վերայ նորա. եւ նա լուր ետեթ կայր. եւ ոչ յանդիմաներ զատութիւն նոցա. մինչեւ Աստուած ի յերկնից նայեցեալ ետես. զանիրաւ պատուհասն՝ եւ յայտներ զղատասստանն եւ զարդարն ապրեցուցանէր. եւ չար սուտ վկայսն տանջեր պատուհասիւ: / fol. 333r /

25/ Այսպէս եւ մեզ պարտ է համբերել յորժամ զայցէ մեզ զուր բանք, եւ փորձութիւնք. եւ յայնժամ տեսանէ Աստուած զհամբերութիւնն մեր. եւ փրկէ զմեզ ի փորձութենէ. եւ զչարախօսն մեր ամօթ առնէ. եւ յանդիմանէ զի ամենայն առաքինութեան գլուխն համբերութիւնն է, որպէս զհամբերութիւն Յովսեփու. զի Յովսէփի համբերութիւն թարգմանի.

26/ եւ զի չար նենգութիւն եղբարցն որ վաճառեցին զնա. իսկ Աստուած զչարութիւն նոցա ի բարին փոխարկեաց Յովսեփու. այնպէս առնէ Աստուած ամենայն մարդոյ որ համբերէ փորձութեանց. զչարութիւն չարեցացն ի գլուխ նոցա դարձուցանէ. եւ զհամբերօղն փրկէ ի փորձութեանց:

27/ Եւ յայնժամ վաճառականքն հանին զՅովսէփ ի վերայ ուղտոյ եւ գնացին զճանապարհին իւրեանց. եւ եկին ի տեղին յորում մայրն Յովսեփու Հռաքել թաղեալ կայր.

28/ իբրեւ ետես Յովսէփի զգերեզման մօրն իւրոյ. ի վայր անկաւ յուղտոյն՝ եւ ընթացեալ անկանէր ի վերայ գերեզմանին մօրն եւ լայր դառնապէս. աղիողորմ արտասուսն փախփախ թափեր յաչաց նորա. մինչեւ ամենայն վաճառականքն ընդ նմա լացին.

29/ եւ ճայն բարձեալ ողբական՝ եւ խանդաղատական գթովք առ մայրն ասեր այս. ո՞ւր ես մայր իմ սիրելի. արի՛ տես զքո սիրելի որդիս զՅովսէփ. զիարդ վաճառական ուր եմ ի գերութիւն.

արի մայր իմ տես գորդեակս քո՝ զի զնամ օտար աշխարհ. ո՛վ մայր իմ ուտն կաց եւ / fol. 333v / տես գորդիս քո գՅովսեփի, զոր դու ազատ ծնար, այժմ ի ծառայութիւն վարիմ՝ ի ձեռաց եղբարց իմոց. զի զոր[733] դու ազատածնար արարեր նռքա ի ծառայութիւն եոուն. տես մա՛յր իմ՝ զի գորդիս քո անոգնական զնամ ի գերութիւն, եւ ոչ ունիմ զոք՝ զի ընդանաբար հոգասցէ զլինեն:

30/ Ո՛վ մայր իմ՝ բաց զայս քո. եւ տես զվիշտս եւ զնեղութիւնս որդւոյ քո Յովսեփու. զի դու ի գերեզմանիդ անհոգ[734] ննջես՝ եւ մայրական զուք քո առ որդիս քո՝ լռեալ է. ոչ տեսանեք[735] զորդիս ձեր ի չար եղբարցն. իբրեւ զգառն ի մէջ գայլոցն վարատեալ. եւ ի ձնողաց վարատեալ եւ հեռացեալ. այլ ոչ գիտեմ թէ զինչ լինելոց եմ.

31/ Ո՛վ մայր իմ տես գորդի քո զի զնամ յոտար երկիր՝ եւ այլ ոչ տեսանեմ զգերեզմանս քո. տե՛ս մայր իմ Հռաքէլ գորդիս քո՝ զի երթամ ի գերութիւն վաճառել, եւ ոչ ունիմ զոք որ գերեդարձ առնէ զիս:

32/ Ո՛վ մայր իմ Յովսեփու՝ բաց զայս քո եւ տես զգերութիւն իմ. զի թեպետ դու հայրենիքն[736] քո գողացար, ոչ զի պաշտպիր զկուռսն՝ այլ զի խափան լիցիս այլոց կռապաշտիցն։ Իսկ այժմ զորդիս քո սիրելի գողացեալ է եղբարցն վաճառեցին. եւ հորն իմոյ գազանաբեկ ասացին լինել զիս:

33/ Ո՛վ գերութիւնս Յովսեփու որդւոյ քո սիրելոյ. մայր իմ սիրելի հայեաց եւ տես գտառապանս որդւոյ քո՝ զի անպատճառ զնամ ի գերութիւն եւ ոչ գոր / fol. 334r / ունիմ օգնական. ի քէն վաղ գրկեցայ մայր իմ Հռաքէլ. եւ ի հօրէ եւ սիրելի եղբօրէս Բենիամենէ. այսօր հեռանամ. եւ ոչ ունիմ ակն թէ տեսանեմ զձեզ. ո՛վ մայր իմ ի քէն մահուամբ հեռացայ՝ եւ ի հօրէ եւ յեղբօրէս ծառայութեամբ հեռանամ:

34/ Տեսանեք ո՛վ այրք եւ վաճառանք եւ օգնեցէք յաղխտիս իմոյ՝ եւ լացէք զիս զայսպիսի թշուառական մանուկս. եւ թոյլ տուք ինձ[737] սակաւիկ մի. զի լացից զմահ մօր իմոյ՝ եւ զգերութիւն անձին իմոյ:

35/ Ո՛վ մայր իմ Հռաքէլ՝ հայեաց եւ տես գչար նախանձ եղբարցն.

զի որպէս չարացան սպանանել զիս եւ կորուսանել. բաց զայս քո՝ եւ զարթիր ի գերեզմանեդ մայր իմ, զի այսօր որդի քո ոտարանամ ի քէն՝ եւ այլ ոչ եւս տեսանեմ. զայս չարութիւն եղբարց իմոց որ նախանձու որկեցին[738] զիս՝ ի սիրելի եղբօրէն եւ ի ծնօղաց իմոց. անյոյս արարին զիս. եւ զի անշունչ ես մայր իմ, եւ անմռունչ լեալ:

36/ Եւ ապա վաճառականքն միթարեցին գՅովսէփ. թափել զարտասույացացն. եւ զուգնի մտացն. եւ առեալ գնա հանին ի վերայ ըղտոյն. եւ այսպէս ասէ Յովսէփ ատ դիմաց գերեզմանին մօր իւրոյ. ողջ մա՛ մայրիկ իմ՝ զի գնամ ոտարութիւն, եւ այլ ոչ եւս տեսանեմ զգերեզմանս քո մայր իմ. եւ ո՛վ պատմեսցէ զայս հօր իմոյ. զի գերութիւն գնամ եւ ոչ եմ լեալ կերակուր գազանի. / fol. 334v / եւ զայս ասէր՝ ողջ մա՛այ մայր իմ, եւ ողջ մա՛այ հայր իմ, եւ ողջ մա՛այ եղախտաւոր եղբայր իմ Բենիամենի՝[739] զի դուք ոչ գիտէք, զի ես ի գերութիւն վաճառեցայ. եւ ոչ եմ լեալ գազանաբեկ:

37/ Ողջ մա՛այ երկիր գերեզմանաց իմոց ծնօղաց զի այլ ոչ տեսանեմ<ք>[740] զձեզ աչօք իմովք: Բայց թէ ոսկերք իմ հան{ց} իցեն[741] ի ձեզ: Ողջ մա՛ացէք գերեզմանք նախահարց իմոց. Աբրահամու եւ Սահակայ եւ մօր իմոյ Հռաքէլի. այլ զի ակն ոչ ունիմ տեսանել կենդանի աչօք իմովք. այլ մեռեալ ոսկերօք հանդիպիմ բնակիլ ատ ձեզ:

38/ Ո՛վ աղետիս եւ թշուառական ժամուս զի որդի ազատոց, եւ ազատ ծնօղաց հետացեալ յոտարութիւն եւ ի գերութիւն վարիմ եւ ոչ ոք պատմեսցէ զայս հօրն իմում Յակոբայ. զի որդին քո սիրելի Յովսէփի՝ ոչ է յափշտակեալ գազանաց, այլ ի չար նախանձու եղբարց վաճառեցին:

39/ Եւ յայնժամ ասէ Յովսէփ. հայր իմ եւ մայր իմ. թողին զիս՝ եւ դու Տէր Աստուած իմ մի թողուր զիս. ոտար էի ես եղբարց իմոց. եւ անձանօթ յայս որդլոց հօր իմոյ. բայց դու Տէր Աստուած՝ որ եղեր ընդ հօր իմոյ Յակոբայ, մինչդեռ երթայր փախստական յեղբօրէ իւրմէ Յեսուայ. նոյնպէս Տէր Աստուած մեր լեր ընդ իս. եւ մի թողուր զիս՝ եւ լեր ինձ պահապան եւ օգնական ամենայն տեղիս՝ ուր եւ երթիցեմ. զի ես ոչ գիտեմ թէ ուր զիս տանիցեն. զի դու Տէրդ որ կարօղ ես օգնեա ինձ ամենայն ժամ.

---

738. Postclassical form.
739. No reason for the oblique (genitive or dative) case of "Benjamin" is evident.
740. The plural should be emended to singular. It was created by dittography.
741. The first g was written by error and is surmounted by a dot as an erasure mark.

40/ Եւ իբրեւ զամենայն կատարեաց Յովսէփի ի վերայ գերեզմանի մօրն / fol. 335r / իւրոյ. եւ յայնժամ առեալ զնացին զնա վաճառականքն՝ եւ իջուցին զնա յԵգիպտոս. եւ վաճառեցին զնա Պետաբփրեայ իշխանին Եգիպտացւոց. եւ կացեալ Յովսէփի ի ծառայութիւն առ Պետափրայ ամս է. եւ էր նմա հնազանդ. եւ Տէր Աստուած էր ընդ Յովսէփեայ. ետ Աստուած շնորհս Յովսէփեայ առաջի{ն}⁷⁴² իշխանին։ եւ կացոյց Պետափրա զՅովսէփ ի վերայ ամենայն տանն իւրոյ՝ իշխան եւ հրամանատար ամենայն ծառայիցն նորա. եւ էր Յովսէփի <յ>իշխանութիւն.⁷⁴³ եւ ոչ ի ծառայութիւն ի տանն Պետափրայ.

41/ յայնժամ ետես սատանայ որ ոչ կամի զբարի մարդոյ. այլ չարութեամբ նախանձու վարի ընդ ազգս մարդկան առ ի կորուսանել զմարդիկք։ Յայժնամ սատանայ եմուտ ի կինն Պետափրայ. որպէս ի ձեռն կնոջն զԱդամ եհան ի դրախտէն. եւ ամենայն տեղի կնոջով խաբէ զմարդիկք զամենեսեան եւ կորուսանէ. ջանայ սատանայ եւ այժմ ընդ Յովսէփի ի ձեռն կնոջն Պետափրայ, հանել զնա ազատական ի բնութենէն.

42/ զի Յովսէփի թեպէտ մարմնով ծառայէր. բայց հոգւովս եւ մտօքն ազատ էր. նոյնպէս եւ ամենայն մարդ հոգւով եւ մտօքն ազատ է. թեպէտ եւ բիւր մարդկան ընդ իշխանութեամբ է ոչ է ծառայ. զի ծառայն այն է որ հոգին եւ միտքն սհիւ իւիք կապած է. զի հոգի որ մեղօք իւիք ընմբռնեալ է նմին եւ ծառայ կոչի. զի ծառայ ոչ այն կոչի որ մարմնով մարդկան ծառայէ. այլ ծառայ այն կոչի որ հոգւովս է ծառայ. կամ ազահութեամբ. / fol. 335v / կամ մեղաց. կամ ընչից. կամ ցանկութիւն.⁷⁴⁴ կամ այլ ինչ եւ իցէ, ամենայն չարիք ի վերայ երկրի՝ զոր գործեն մարդիք, նոցին եւ ծառայ կոչին. զի որ ազահ է թեպէտ եւ թագաւոր է՝ ծառայ է ազահութեանն. նոյնպէս եւ չարիք եւ թէ ընչասէր է, ծառայ է ընչիցն եւ ոչ է ազատ. թէ շնացող է՝ նոյն շնութեանն է ծառայ, եւ ոչ է ազատ:

43/ Եթէ բարկացող է, սրտին է ծառայ. եթէ արբեցող է, գինոյն է ծառայ եւ ոչ է ազատ. եթէ դիսակալ է՝ սատանայի է ծառայ, զի սատանայ հանապազ զդիս ունի, եւ չարական զմեր բարին, եւ դիսայ ընդ մեր առաքինութիւնն:

44/ Եւ դիսակալ է եւ չարակն. եւ մախացող. եւ նենգածուտ. ստախոս երբեմն ուրացող. եւ սուտ երդումն. հպարտ ամբարտաւան

---

742. Here առաջի would be expected.
743. The preposition ի (յ-) is called for, just as it occurs with the next noun.
744. An oblique case ending would be expected.

փառասէր շռզմող. հայհոյիչ. թշնամանողս. բամբասող.⁷⁴⁵ գող. այսռքիկ եւ որոց⁷⁴⁶ ոսցին նման են՝ սռքա սատանայի կոչին ծառայքն եւ որդիք. զի ասէ Տէրն յաւետարանին որ առ Հրէայսն չար նախանձն. թէ դուք ի հօրէ սատանայի էք, եւ զցանկութիւն հօրն ձերոյ կամիք կատարել՝ զի նա մարդասպան էր ի սկզբանէ. եւ որ սուտ խօսի՝ իւրոց անտի խօսի. զի ստութեան հայրն նորա սատանայ է. եւ որք սուտ են՝ ստուգապէս ասեմք թէ որդի է սատանայի. այլ նոյն ինքն բոլորովին սատանայ է. մարդ որ քսմոս է եւ բանսարկու ի մէջ մարդկան եւ զխաղաղութիւնն ի խռովութիւն շարժէ. զի թէպէտ խաղաղարարն որդի Աստուծոյ է:

45/ ապա ստոյգ խռովարարն որդի է սատանայի. եւ որ կերօղն է եւ / fol. 336r / ըմբօղն եւ արբեցօղն. նա որռվայնի է ծառայ. որպէս ասէ Պօղոս. լայով ասեմ զթշնամեաց խաչին Քրիստոսի, որոց կատարածն կորուստ է, որոց աստուածն որռվայնքն իւրեանց է, եւ փառքն՝ ամօթն իւրեանց. զնոյն տէրն ասէ ի յաւետարանին թէ գործէ զմեղս, ծառայ է մեղացն. զինչ եւ իցէ. եւ արդ ահա այս ամենայն են որ ծառայեցուցանեն զմարդիք, որք ընդ նոցա իշխանութեամբն իցեն. ի յայսմ ամենայնէ ազատ էր Յովսէփի. թէպէտ եւ մարմնովս էր յիշխանութեամբ Պետափրայ. բայց ոչ էր ծառայ մեղաց եւ ցանկութեանն եւ չարութեանն. զի եղբարքն որ վաճառեցին զնա. նորա ծառայք էին չար նախանձօյն. եւ Յովսէփի որ վաճառեցաւն ի նոցանէ ազատ էր ի յամենայն չարեաց:

46/ Իսկ կինն Պետափրայ. որ տիկինն էր Յովսէփայ՝ կամեցաւ ցանկութեամբ պատրել զՅովսէփի եւ խաբել. զի ընդ նմա մեղս գործիցէ. բայց զի Յովսէփի աստուածային շնորհքն էր զարդարեալ. եւ էր գեղեցիկ տեսլեամբն ոչ խաբեցաւ ի կնոջէն այնմանէ, այլ գտիկան հայրենի՝ հաստատուն պահեր ողջախոհութեամբ զանձն զարդարեալ էր եւ կայր ի տանն իշխանին իւրոյ. ազատաբար մտօք իբրեւ զվէմ հաստատուն:

47/ Իսկ կինն իշխանին այնչափ բռբռքեալ էր ի սիրոյն Յովսէփայ. եւ ամենեւին ոչ կարաց զՅովսէփի հաւանեցուցանել իւր ցանկութեանն. եւ դիտացեալ էր⁷⁴⁷ ընդ Յովսէփու՝ զի ոչ կատարէր զկամս ցակութեանն տիկնօջն. եւ եղեւ յաւ / fol.

---

745. Above line p.m.
746. The oblique case of the relative pronoun is formed by attraction from the following word.
747. Above line p.m.

336v / ուր միում են երկոքեան միայն էին ի տանն. եւ յայնժամ բուռն եհար կինն զհանդերձէն Յովսեփու. եւ կամէր զնա ինքն մերձեցուցանել։ Իսկ Յովսէփ աստուածային զօրութեամբն՝ թոյլ ետ զհանդերձն ի կինն եւ փախեաւ՝ եւ ել ի ձեռաց նորա։

48/ Իբրեւ տեսեալ կնոջն. թէ փախեաւ Յովսէփ ի նմանէ՝ երկեաւ⁷⁴⁸ ի միտս իւր եւ ասէ, մի գուցէ եւ յանդիմանեցէ զիս ի հրապարակս առաջին տեառն իմոյ։

49/ Ապա ինքն առաջեց. եւ յորժամ եկն Պետափրա ի տուն, եւ պատմեաց կինն առն իւրում. եւ ասէ՝ ի գուր վասն Յովսեփու ընդէ՞ր ածեր զօտար ծառայս ի տունս մեր՝ խաղք եւ ծաղր կամէր առնել զմեզ. եւ հանեալ էցուց նմա զհանդերձս Յովսեփու՝ եւ ասէ, տե՛ս թէ զոր կամէր գործել ընդ իս՝ եւ զայդ խլել եմ ի ձեռաց նորա. եւ այսպէս զրպարտեաց զՅովսէփ. կինն չարութեան՝ խօսելով զչարն ի վերայ նորա. եւ յայնժամ բարկացեալ իշխանն ի վերայ Յովսեփու. եւ առաքեաց զօրականս՝ եւ եդ զՅովսէփ ի բանտին. ի գնտան թագաւորին. եւ այս՝ երկրորդ ծառայութիւն Յովսեփու։

50/ Բայց զի Աստուած ընդ նմայ էր ոչ եթող զՅովսէփ ի ձեռաց, այլ ընդ նմա եւ բանդ զնդանին մտանէր Աստուած. եւ տուեալ⁷⁴⁹ Աստուած շնորհս Յովսեփու. եւ ետ բանտապետն՝ զիշխանութիւն բանտին ի ձեռս Յովսեփու. եւ էր ազատ Յովսէփ՝ եւ ոչ ի ծառայութիւն բանդին։ կացեալ Յովսէփ ամս Գ. եւ յայնժամ եղեւ բարկութիւն⁷⁵⁰ թագաւորին ի վերայ ծառայից իւրոց եւ երկոցունց՝ / fol. 337r / մատռուակին՝ եւ հացարարին, եւ առաքեաց զնոսա եդ ի բանդին՝ {որ}⁷⁵¹ էր Յովսէփի, եւ կացին անդ ի բանդին ծառայքն թագաւորին։

51/ Եւ եղեւ յաղուր միում ի գիշերին. զի երազ տեսին երկոքեան ծառայքն՝ եւ տրտմեալ էին յոյժ. եւ եմուտ Յովսէփի առ նոսա եւ ասէ՝ եղբայրք ընդէ՞ր տրտմեալ էք այսոր, եւ ոչ էք ուրախ իբրեւ զերեկն եւ զերանդն. ասեն ծառայքն ընդ Յովսէփի. երազ տեսաք այսմ գիշերի՝ եւ երկուցեալ եմք՝ եւ ոչ գիտեմք թէ զի՞նչ ինելոց եմք, կամ զինչ բերէ մեզ երազն մեր։ ասէ ցնոսա

---

748. + ի նմանէ with erasure dots, correction.
749. Notice the post-classical orthography.
750. This word is written above the line, in a similar, but perhaps not identical hand as the text.
751. This should be ուր "where." See Stone and Hillel, "Index," no. 407, but this should be added as a separate entry.

Յովսէփ. ասացէք ինձ զերազն ձեր, եւ ես պատմեմ ձեզ թէ զի՞նչ լինելոց է ձեզ եւ պատահելոց:

52/ մին ասաց որ հացարար էր՝ տեսի զի այսմ գիշերի սեղան մի լի հացիւ՝ եւ այլ կերակրոք զի բարձեալ էի <ի>⁷⁵² վերայ գլխոյ իմոյ՝ եւ զայլն բազում թռչունք երկնից եւ ուտէին զհացն եւ զկերակուրն. յայնժամ ասէ Յովսէփ. ասաց Գ աւուր հանէ զքեզ ի բանդէս, եւ կախեսցեն ընդ ծառով. թռչունք երկնից զան եւ ուտեն զմարմին քո. եւ յետ երից աւուրցն զոր ասաց Յովսէփ՝ այնպէս եղեւ. հանեալ զմուտպային՝ կախեցին ընդ ծառով մի եւ կատարեցաւ երազն ի վերայ նորա:

53/ Իսկ մատռուական պատմեաց Յովսէփու զերազն իւր եւ ասէ՝ թէ եւ ես տեսի՝ յայսմ գիշերիս. զի ունէի գոսկի բաժակն ի ձեռին իմում լի գինով. եւ կայի առաջի թագաւորին. յայնժամ ասէ ցնա Յովսէփ ի վաղիւն հանեն զքեզ ի բան/fol. 337v /դէս եւ տանին առ թագաւորն՝ եւ հաստատեն զքեզ ի յառաջին գործ քո՝ որ զրմպելին մատուցանէիր առաջի թագաւորին:

54/ Եւ նոյնպէս եղեւ պատմութիւնն Յովսէփու՝ զոր ասաց վասն նորա. եւ ասէ Յովսէփ ցմատռուականն՝ թէ եւ զիս յիշեա առաջի թագաւորին: եւ եղեւ ի հանել նորա տարան առ թագաւորն՝ եւ կարգեցին զնա ի գործս իւր առաջին. եւ մոռացաւ մատռուական զպատուէրն Յովսէփու. եւ ոչ յիշեաց զնա՝ մինչեւ անցին ի վերայ երեք ամք:

55/ Եւ յայնժամ ետես թագաւորն փարաւոն երազս զարհուրելի՝ եւ կոչեաց առ ինքն զամենայն գիտնականքն եւ զիմաստունսն իւր՝ զի պատմեսցեն զերազն. եւ ամենեքեան ոչ կարացին մեկնել զերազն թագաւորին. եւ յոյժ բարկացաւ թագաւոր ի վերայ նոցա, եւ տրտում կայր, զի ոչ ոք էր որ մեկնէր զերազն նորա. յայնժամ ի միտս եկեալ մատռուականն՝ եւ յիշեաց զբանն Յովսէփու: եւ եմուտ առաջի թագաւորին. եւ ասէ ո՜վ թագաւոր մահապարտ եմ ծառայս քո. իբրեւ եհարց թագաւորն զբանն. եւ ասէ մատռուականն՝ յորժամ բարկացար դու մեզ, ո՜վ թագաւոր եւ եդեր զմեզ ի բանդի. եւ մեք երկոքեանս երազ տեսաք՝ եւ տրտմեալ էաք վասն երազոյն: Եւ յայնժամ եկն Յովսէփ եւ մեկնեաց մեզ զերազն մեր՝ եւ զոր պատմեաց մեզ՝ այնպէս եղեւ. եւ որպէս ասաց նա մեզ:

56/ Յայնժամ հրամայեաց թագաւորն եւ ասէ՝ երթ կոչեա զայրն՝ զի թերեւս զերազս մեր պատմեսցէ. եւ իբրեւ կոչեցաւ Յով/ fol.

---

752. ի lost by haplography.

338r /սեփ ի թագաւորէն. եւ ելաւ[753] ի բանդէն եւ եկն առաջի թագաւորին. ասէ թագաւորն ցՅովսէփ կարիցես հանել զերազն իմ զոր տեսի։ եւ ասէ Յովսէփ՝ ո՛ չ թագաւոր ոչ է կարողութիւն մարդոյ այդպիսի՝ այլ շնորհիքն Աստուծոյ է որ տայ մարդկան զիտենալ զերազն եւ պատմել. ասասցէ թագաւորն զերազն, եւ յայտնէ մեզ Աստուած զմեկնութիւն նորա։

57/ Եւ իբրեւ զիտաց թագաւորն եթէ կարող է Յովսէփի մեկնել զերազն։ Ասէ թագաւորն տեսի ես ի գիշերի միում երազ՝ եւ ահա է երինձք զերք եւ պարարտք ելանէին եւ արածէին առ ափն գետոյն.[754] եւ յետ այսորիկ տեսի եւ ահա այլ է երինձք նուազք եւ նիհարք, եւ չորացեալք ելանէին եւ ուտէին զզեր եւ զպարարտ երինձսն՝ եւ ոչ երեւէր ի փորի նոցա. եւ յայնժամ զարթեայ՝ եւ դարձեալ ննջեցի. եւ տեսի է փունջ հասկ ելեալք յափն գետոյն ստուարք եւ ատոք. եւ չորեն զէր ի մէջ հասկին. եւ զեղեցիկ տեսանելով։ Եւ յետոյ տեսի. ահա եւ այլ է հասկ չորենդյ ելանէին, վտիտք եւ նուազք որ ոչ կայր հատ չորենդյ ի մէջ նոցա. եւ կլանէին զհասկերն.[755] որ չորենալիցն էին, որպէս նուազք երինձքն. զզէր երինձքն կերան. եւ ոչ երեւէր ի փորի նոցա. այս է երազն իմ։

58/ Յայնժամ ասէ Յովսէփ. Աստուած մեծ իրս ցոյց արքայիդ. զոր ինչ լինելոց է, ապայ ժամանակ աշխարհիս այսմիկ. եօթն երինձքն առաջինքն / fol. 338v / զերքն եւ պարարտք է տարի լիութիւն գայ. եւ առատ ամենայն ինչ որ ոչ եղեալ այնպիսի լիութիւն ի վերայ երկրի. եւ է երինձքն նուազքն է տարի սով գայ՝ որ ոչ զտանի հաց ի վերայ երկրի։

59/ Եւ արդ թագաւոր տես թէ որպէս հոգասցես աշխարհս քո. զի մի կորիցեն ի սովոյ. ընտրեսցես քեզ այր իմաստուն զոր կացուցես ի վերայ աշխարհիս, որ մարթասցէ հոգալ եւ ժողովեցէ չորեան որով կերակրէ աշխարհս քո ի յաւուրց սովու։

60/ Յայնժամ ասէ փարաւոն թագաւորն Եզիպտացւոց ցՅովսէփ. ստուգապէս հոգի Աստուծոյ գոյ ի քեզ. եւ ոչ ոք կարէ այդպէս ի մարդկանէ մեկնել զերազն որպէս դու մեկնեցեր եւ ոչ ոք կարասցէ հոգալ զաշխարհս իմ զի մի կորիցէ ի սովու։ Բայց միայն քեզ պարզեւեաց մեզ Աստուած կերակրիչ, եւ պաշխիչ եւ դարմանող աշխարհիս իմոյ։ Եւ ասէ թագաւորն ցՅովսէփ դու

---

753. Nonclassical form.
754. Plural. A singular is demanded by the story; perhaps graphic յ/գ.
755. Note medieval Armenian plural ending.

լիցիս՝ թագաւոր եւ իշխան ի վերայ ամենայն երկրի մերոյ. եւ
ես միայն թագիւս ի վեր քան զքեզ. այլ դու հաւասար զլիսոյ իմոյ
լիցիս. եւ ոչ ոք դիմադարձ լիցի քեզ. զի ունիցիս իշխանութիւն
սպանանել եւ կեցուցանել զոր եւ կամիս. եւ հրաման ետուր քեզ
տէր լինել ի վերայ աշխարհիս Եգիպտացւոց.

61/ Եւ ետ թագաւորն զմատանին իւր զիշխանական ի ձեռս
Յովսեփու. որով զիշխանութիւն ընդ նմին ետ։ Եւ էառ Յովսեփի
զիշխանութիւն եւ թագաւորեաց ի վերայ յԵգիպտոսի. որպէս
ասէ մարգարէն Դաւիթ.⁷⁵⁶ զամենայն յանցս չար/ fol. 339r /
չարանացն՝ որ էյանց ընդ Յովսեփ. խոնարհ արարին ի
կապանս զոտս նորա, եւ էանց ընդ երկաթ անձն նորա։
մինչեւ եկեսցէ բանն Աստուծոյ՝ որ ուխտեաց, Աբրահամու,
բազմանալ զաւակի նորա օտար երկիր. եւ բանդն փորձեաց
զՅովսեփի զհամբերութիւն նորա եւ զողջախոհութիւն Յովսեփու
յայտնի կամեցաւ առնել, եւ երեւի Աստուած. եւ ապա ասէ
թագաւորելոյն:

62/ Եւ յայնժամ առաքեաց թագաւորն եւ ելոյծ զնա. եւ իշխան
ժողովրդեան եթող զնա. ի վերայ ամենայն զանձուցն
Եգիպտացւոց: խրատել զիշխանս նոցա Յովսեփի որպէս
զինքն. եւ զծերս նոցա իմաստունս արասցէ. այս ամենայն
կատարեցան ի վերայ Յովսեփու.

63/ Եւ էառ Յովսեփի զթագաւորութիւնն եւ նստաւ ի վերայ
Եգիպտոսի. յայնժամ Յովսեփի Լ. ամաց էր. եւ Զ. ամ
թագաւորեաց Յովսեփի յԵգիպտոս։ Եւ սկսաւ զալ տարիքն ի
լիութիւն ամենայն բարեաց աշխարհին. եւ Յովսեփի շինեաց
ամբարայնոց մեծամեծս որ⁷⁵⁷ զգործեան երկրին ժողովեր եւ
ամբարէց զքազմութիւն գործենյն ամենայն աշխարհին. զի
այլ ոչ ինչ առնոյր զհարկ աշխարհին՝ ոչ ոսկի եւ ոչ արծաթ.
բայց միայն ցորեն. եւ ժողովեաց զայն է տարին՝ եւ էարկ
ամբարայնոցն:

64/ Եւ ապա յետոյ է տարոյն լիութեանն, սկսաւ զալ. եւ էօթն
տարի սով. եւ Յովսեփի գեօքն տարու ցորեն սկսաւ բաշխել
աշխարհին. եւ զոր յառաջն ոչ առնոյր ի հարկն ոսկի եւ /
fol. 339v / արծաթ բայց միայն ցորեն. այժմ առնոյր զոսկի եւ
զարծաթն. եւ տար erasure ca. 7 letters եւ ժողովեաց Յովսեփի
զանձս բազումս. եւ եղեւ սով մեծ ընդ ամենայն աշխարհն

---

756. Ps 105(104):17–22.
757. Reading որ as ուր.

Եզիպտացոց՝ եւ Յովսեփի բաւական եղեւ ժողովեալ հացին զերկիրն ամենայն կերակրել.

65/ Եւ եկն սովս երկիրն Քանանացոց. յորում Յովսեփիայ հայրն եւ եղբարքն բնակեալ էին. Եւ լուաւ Յակոբ թէ գտանի կերակուր Եզիպտոս. եւ առաքեաց զորդիսն իւր զեղբարքն Յովսեփու, եւ եղբարքն Յովսեփու ոչ էին լուեալ զթագաւորելն Յովսեփու յեզիպտոս. զի մոռացեալ էին զՅովսեփ զի Իէ ամ անցեալ էր ի վերայ վաճառելոյն. եւ նոքա ոչ զիտացին զշնորհսն Աստուծոյ, զոր տուեալ էր Յովսեփու՝ եւ ոչ ակն ունէին թագաւորութեանն նորա:

66/ Իսկ առեալ եղբարցն Յովսեփու զզրաստ իւրեանց եւ արծաթ բազում եկին Եզիպտոս առ Յովսեփի զնել հաց. եւ Յովսեփի նստեալ իշխանութեան թագաւորութեանն. իբրեւ եկին եղբարքն նորա երկիր պագին նմա Յովսեփու. եւ ոչ ծանեան զնա զի եւ ոչ իսկ կասկած կայր նոցա, այնպիսի թագաւորելոյն[758] Յովսեփու. եւ Յովսեփ ծանեաւ զեղբարքն իւր ոչ ետ իւր եղբարցն ծանօթութիւն. այլ իբրեւ անծանօթ եղեալ՝ ի ծածուկ սրտին լայր. եւ յիշէր զ vacat 2 letters զուլ եղբայրութեանն. յայնժամ ասէ Յովսեփ ընդ եղբայրս իւր ուստի՞ էք, կամ ո՞ր <յ>աշխարհէ / fol. 340r / կամ թէ ոչ էք հացագին, այլ լրտեսէք՝ եկեալ լրտեսել զաշխարհս. իսկ նոցա անկեալ առ ոտս Յովսեփու՝ ադաչէին զի մի բարկացի տիրութիւն նորա ի վերայ նոցա եւ ասեն՝ ծառայք քո եմք: եղբայրք ԲԺ-ան էաք. միոյ հօր որդիք. գմինն զազանն յափշտակեաց ի դաշտին՝ եւ միւսն փոքրիկ է կայ ի տանն առ հօր մերում. եւ հայր մեր ծերացեալ է, եւ ծառայքս քո հովիւ եմք՝ եւ ոչ պատերազմօղք:

67/ Ո՛վ անմտութեան եղբարցն՝ զի թէպէտ զհայրն խաբեցին վասն Յովսեփու՝ թէ զազանն եկեր զնա. աստ առաջի եղբօրն զհա՞րդ կամեր ստել զի ոչ ոք էր, որ վրէժխնդիր լինէր Յովսեփու թէ ընդէ՞ր վաճառեցիք զնա. եւ նոքա սուտ խօսէին եւ ոչ զիտէին թէ նա էր Յովսեփին զոր նոքա սուտ խօսէին եւ զազանակեր ասէին զնա՝ որ թագաւոր կայր ի վերայ նոցա. եւ զի այսպէս կայր էր[759] նախանձ չարութեանն որ տայ իմանալ զինչ գործէ կամ զինչ խօսի:

68/ բայց դու տես զիմաստութիւնն Յովսեփու. եւ զանխսակալութիւն նորա զի ոչ յիշեաց զչարութիւնն նոցա

---

758. Abbreviation mark omitted.
759. էր *inter lineas*. One verb is superfluous, apparently կայր.

եւ ոչ գառնելիքն եղբարցն չար գործցն այլ վածառեցին զնա.
եւ նա ոչ յանդիմանեաց զնոսա. որ ասացին զնա գազանաբեկ
լեալ. եւ ոչ ասաց նոցա, թէ ոչ ահաւասիկ ես եմ Յովսէփ. զոր
դուք գազանաբեկ ասէք. ես այժմիկ թագաւոր եմ, զի ա″րդ /
fol. 340v / ստէք առաջի իմ. մի թէ եւ զիս կամիք խաբել, որպէս
զհայրն իմ խաբեցէք՝ եւ զիս գազանաբեկ ասացիք նմա.
բայց զի ամենայն աստուածային շնորհօքն էր զարդարեալ
Յովսէփ. հեզէր եւ խոնարհի անիսակալ եւ անյիշաչար. ոչ
ասաց եւ ոչ յանդիմանեաց զնոսա՝ այլ իմաստութեամբն
զմարդասիրութիւնն էցոյց նոցա.

69/ եւ եղ առաջի նոցա սեղան՝ եւ կերակրեաց զնոսա։ եւ ասէ
գնոսա՝ թէ այդպէս է զոր ասացերդ թէ հայր մեր ծերացեալ է,
եւ մի եղբայրն փոքրիկ առ հօրն՝ այլ զմինդ ի ձէնջ ոչ թողից
եւ պահեցից առ իս մինչեւ զմիւս եղբայրն առ իս բերիցէք, եւ
ապա արձակեցից զձեզ. եւ նոքա հաւանեալ թողին զՇմաւոն
եղբայրն իւրեանց՝ գրաւական Յովսեփու՝ որ թագաւորն էր։

70/ Եւ հրամայեաց զի բարձին զզրաստս իւրեանց հաց՝ եւ եդեալ
զարծաթն ի բեռինս նոցա. եւ գնացին առ հայրն իւրեանց
Յակոբ՝ եւ սկսեալ պատմեցին զվիշտսն եւ զրումբնանքն
Յակոբու՝ զոր արգիլեցոյց Յովսէփ զեղբայրն760 զՇմաւոն. այլ
պատիւն եւ զմեծարանսն761՝ զոր Յովսէփի արար նոցա. իսկ
հայրն հարցանէր վասն որդւոյ իւրոյ Շմաւոնի. եւ նոքա ասեն
Եզիպտացւոց տէրն գօրենոյն՝ որ վածառեր, նա գրպարտեց
զմեզ եւ ասէ լրտես էք. եւ ասեմք ոչ եմք այլ ծառայք քո որդիք
եմք հօր մերում. եւ մի եղբայր փոքրիկ առ հօր մերում կայ.
եւ նա ասէ մեզ՝ եթէ ոչ էք լրտես որպէս ասէքդ՝ թողէք զմին
եղբայրս առ իս գրաւական մինչեւ զփոքր եղբայրն ձեր / fol.
341r / բերիցէք առ իս, եւ ապա հաւատամ ձեզ թէ ոչ էք լրտես
եւ ոչ նենգաւորք.

71/ եւ արդ հայր մեր՝ հրամայեա գործիդ քո Բեն<ի>ամենի՝762 զի
տարցուք եւ թափեցուք զՇմաւոն. եւ այլ հաց զնեցուք եւ
բերիցուք բաւական մեզ. եւ յայնժամ տրտմեցաւ Յակոբ հայրն
նորա՝ եւ ասէ վա՛յ ինձ որդեակք իմ, զի մանկակոտոր եւ
որդեկորուստ արարիք զիս. զՅովսէփ գազանակեր ասացիք
լինել, ու763 զՇմաւոն թէ Եզիպտոս մնաց. եւ զԲենիամենի այլ

---

760. զեղբայրն in margin.
761. մեծարանքն would be expected.
762. The manuscript has Բենիամենի, which is corrupt.
763. Postclassical form.

կամիք հանել յինէն. յայնժամ յառաջ եկաց աւագ որդին եւ ասէ ըռուբէն ցհայր իւր. հայր՝ մի՛ ⁷⁶⁴ բարկանար մեզ. Յովսեփի ի զագանէն յափշտակեցաւ. իսկ Շմաւոն՝ ի թագաւորէն Եգիպտացւոց ընբռնեցաւ։ զի կամեր զամենեսեան զմեզ սպանանել. արդ ողորմեցաւ մեզ միայն զրաւական առեալ զՇմաւոն. մինչեւ տարցուք զԲենիամի<ն>, որով թափեցուք զՇմաւոն. եւ ապա զերկուսեանն հանցուք։ եւ ես Ռուբեն երեշխաւոր որդւոց քոց, զի տեսցես զնոսա՝ եւ ուրախասցիս:

72/ եւ այնպէս հաւանեցեալ զՅակոբ հայրն իւրեանց. զի թողուցու զԲանիամենի:⁷⁶⁵ եւ առեալ նոցա զԲենիամենի զկրսեր եղբայրքն⁷⁶⁶ իւրեանց եւ իջին յԵգիպտոս՝ զի զնեսցեն հաց ի կերակուր, որպէս զառաջինն, եւ իբրեւ զնացին առաջի Յովսեփու, եւ երկիր պագին նմա. եւ յորժամ ետես Յովսեփ զԲենիամենի. եւ շարժեալ աղեւն՝ եմուտ ի սենեակն, եւ ելաց սաստիկ / fol. 341v / դառնապէս՝ զի յիշեաց զզուրթ եղբայրութեանն. զի նոքա միայն էին եղբայր համամայրք եւ միահայրք. եւ իբրեւ ելաց Յովսեփի՝ քանզի շարժեցան աղիքն եւ գութն ի վերայ Բենիամենի. եւ յայնժամ առեալ Յովսեփի չուր՝ եւ լուացաւ. եւ հրաման եդ սեղան կազմել. եւ եղեալ առաջի եղբայրն. եւ նստոյց զեղբարսն ըստ կարգի, որպէս եւ ծնեալ էին. նոյնպէս նստոյց եւ զԲենիամենի ի մօտ առ ինքն ի սեղանի. եւ եդ զմասն եւ զբաժինն Բենիամենի մեծ քան զայլ եղբարցն. եւ յորժամ կերակրեցան չափեաց նոցա զգործեանն եւ երբարձ զզբրաստա նոցա:

73/ Իսկ զաղտնաբար գրսկի բաժակն՝ որով Յովսեփ զգինին ըմբեր. եաո ի բեռին զԲենիամենի, որ ոչ ոք իմացաւ. եւ իբրեւ ելան ի ճանապարհիս իւրեանց, եւ Բենիամենի զհետ նոցա. յայնժամ առաքեաց շրութակս զհետ եղբարցն՝ եւ ասէ, գրսկի բաժակն իմ տարան գողութեամբ. յայնժամ հասեալ գորակնացն՝ եւ ընբրնեցին զամենայն քարանն,⁷⁶⁷ եւ ասեն՝ ո՛վ էառ գրսկի բաժակն թագաւորին. ընդէ՛ր գործեցիք՝ զմահաբեր գողութիւնդ՝ քանզի թագաւորն մեր բարկացեալ է, արդ տեսէք նօ՛ նք ի ձենջ զմասա գործեալ է:

74/ Իբրեւ լուան զբանն զայն՝ եւ տրտմեցան ամենեքեան եւ ասեն

---

764. Thus the manuscript. A *šešt* would be expected.
765. Observe that quite often this name has a suffixed -ի when, as here, it is not in an oblique case.
766. Observe the anomalous plural ending.
767. A variant orthography or a corruption of քավրան, which appears in §20.

ոչ գիտեմք զիրդ զոր ասէք։ Եւ յայնժամ իջուցեալ զթերինսն ի գրաստէն ի վայր, եւ բացեալ զամենեցուն զիակ քրձիցն. եւ զտեալն⁷⁶⁸ / fol. 342r / զրաժակն ի քուրձն Բենիամենի. իբրեւ տեսին զայն եղբարցն՝ դարձան ի վերայ Բենիամենի. եւ բազում բանիւք արհամարհեցին զնա՝ եւ այնպէս ասէին. գիտեմք զքնական գշարաբարութիւնդ ձեր, քո եւ եղբօր քում. վասն այսորիկ եւ նա գազանաբեկ լեալ, զի ամբարտաւանութեամբ թագաւորել կամէր, եւ ետես Աստուած զիպարտաբարս նորա, եւ մատնեաց զնա ի ձեռս գազանի՝ որ ոչ է եւ դու այնպէս կամեցար. գողութիւն. եւ զբարկութիւն թագաւորին աձել ի վերայ մեր. եւ վասն քո չար բարուցն որ ցանկացար ոսկի բաժակիդ՝ եւ արդ զամենեսեան կամի սպանումա աձել. յայնժամ դարձեալ ասեն ընդ սպասաւրսն թագաւորին՝ ահաւասիկ ճառայ թագաւորութեան եղիցի որ զգողութիւնդ արար։

75/ Իսկ նորա կալեալ զԲենիամենի, եւ զեղբարսն իւր։ եւ յայնժամ սկսաւ սաստիւ խօսել ընդ նոսա Յովսէփ՝ այդ է փոխանակ սիրոյն զոր ես ցուցի ձեզ. եւ արարի եւ կերակրեցի զայդ արարիք, որ գողութեամբ յափշտակեցիք զոսկի բաժակն իմ. եւ թէ ես զձեր խելացդ առնեմ՝ եւ զձեր առնելեացդ՝ ապա զամենեսեանդ զձեզ սպանանէի, զի այտպէս իսկ զրանէ չարք էք եւ չարանխանձք։

76/ Իսկ եղբարքն ամենեքեան անկեալ առաջի նորա լային դառնապէս եւ ասէին. մի բարկանար դու մեզ ո՛վ թագաւոր զի անպարտ եմք մեք ի փասաող յայդմանէ՝ այլ միայն փոքրաւոր տղայդ՝ այդ է / fol. 342v / պարտական մեղացդ զի տխմար է. այդպէս է բնութիւն դղցա՝ զի եղբայր դորա Յովսէփի այդպիսի էր, զի ինքն ինքենէն թագաւորել կամէր՝ եւ նստեալ մեզ երազ պատմեր նշանակ թագաւորութեանն. վասն այն ետես Աստուած զանմտութիւնն նորա՝ եւ կերակուր ետ գազանի՝ եւ ոչ եհաս թագաւորութեանն. նոյնպէս եւ տղայդ այդ ոչ իրաց զմեզ ոչ եհարց, որ ով գողացաւ զոսկի բաժակդ՝ եւ արդ մեք անպարտ եմք ի փասաող ճառայսա քո։

Յայնժամ ասէ Յովսէփի եթէ այդպէս է զոր ասէք՝ թէ դուք անպարտ էք՝ ես զնա, որ պարտական է ինձ ի ճառայութիւն կացուցից. եւ դուք երթիցուք զճանապարհս ձեր։

77/ Յայնժամ որ երեց եղբայրն է նոցա Ռուբէն յառաջ եկաց եւ

---

768. An erasure mark surmounts եւ:.

երկիր պազ թագաւորին Յովսէփայ եւ ասէ. ո՛վ թագաւոր՝ նախ զիս սպան եւ ապա արցես զԲենիամին769 քեզ ծառայ՝ զի ես երաշխաւոր եմ առեալ զդա՝ եթէ ոչ տանիմք զդա առ հայր մեր՝ ոչ կարեմք տեսանել զերեսն հօր մերում. զի ամենեքեան մեք ամօթով եմք՝ զի դայ է հօրն փոխանակ Յովսէփայ, զոր եկեր գազան. եւ թէ զդայ ոչ տեսանէ հայրն մեռանի ի տրտմութենէն. զի կուրացեալ է ի լալոյն վասն Յովսէփայ. եւ այլ չունի զոք մխիթար. եւ այժմ ո՛վ թագաւոր պարտ է քեզ քաղցրանալ եւ առնուլ գօհնութիւնս հօր մերոյ Յակոբայ. քանզի եւ նա իսկ աստուածատես է՝ եւ զոր նա օհնէ, օհնեալ լիցի, եւ զոր անիծէ / fol. 343r / անիծեալ լիցի. եւ այժմ մի աՆեր զանէսու հօրն ի վերայ մեր եւ ի վերայ քո. այլ արդ լու՛ր աղաչանաց մերոց ո՛վ թագաւոր՝ եւ թող զպատանեակդ Բենիամին. եւ կամ սպան զմեզ զամենեսուն՝ զի ոչ կարեմք զնա տրտում տեսանել. կամ զծերութիւն նորա ցաւօք եւ տրտմութեամբ իջուցանել ի դժոխս. զի լաւ է թէ զամենեսեան ոչ տեսանէ հայրն մեր՝ քան զպատանեակդ զայդ:

78/ Իբրեւ զայս ամենայն կատարեաց Ռուբէն, եւ այլ եղբարքն լալով առաջի Յովսէփայ, եւ յայնժամ շարժեցաւ զուլթ եղբայրութեան, եւ հօրն յիշատակ որ ծերացեալ էր վասն սիրոյ Յովսէփայ՝ յայնժամ ոչ կարաց համբերել. այլ յայտնեաց զինքն Յովսէփ եղբարցն իւրոց. եւ արտասուօք ասէ, ո՛վ եղբայրք յիմարք եւ ծառայք շար նախանձու եւ ատելութեան զձեզ770 ոչ կարացիք ճանաչել զիս քանզի ես եմ եղբայրն ձեր այն զոր դուք վաճառեցիք, եւ զհայրն մեր խաբեցիք թէ զգազանն է յափշտակեալ զիս, ես եմ Յովսէփին, զոր դուք թագաւորել ոչ կամէիք ի վերայ ձեր. ես եմ եղբայրն ձեր՝ զոր դուք յօտարութիւն վաճառեցիք. ես եմ Յովսէփին՝ զոր դուք սպանանել կամեցայք եւ եսուք ի գերութիւն վաճառեցիք:

79/ Բայց <Աստուած>771 հարց իմոց ոչ եթող զիս, եւ ոչ ընդ վայր եհար զիս. դուք զիս ի ծառայութիւն վաճառեցիք՝ եւ իմ զնայովա մեծանալ կամէիք՝ բայց Աստուած թագաւոր արար զիս որպէս տեսանէքս. դուք ոչ կամեցայք զերազն թագաւորութեան իմոյ ի գլուխ ելանել: բայց / fol. 343v / Աստուած ո<չ>772 արար ի ձեր սրտիցդ: այլ կատարեցաւ երազն իմ, եւ արար զիս թագաւոր

---

769. ի2° over և p.m.
770. It is difficult to construe this accusative.
771. Editor's emendation; omitted from the manuscript.
772. Editor's emendation of the relative pronoun որ.

PART FOUR 195

80/ որպէս եւ այժմ տեսանէքդ. եւ ահա կատարեցաւ երազն իմ. եւ դուք եկէք այս քանի անգամ երկիր պազանէք (sic!) ինձ:
իբրեւ լուան զայն երկիր պազին, եւ զամօթի հարան եւ անկաւ ահ ի վերայ նոցա. եւ մռացան ցկեանս իւրեանց, եւ անկաւ խաւար ի վերայ աչաց նոցա. ի յառաւել ամօթոյն եւ յերկիւղէն մուքն կալալ զամենեսեան՝ եւ ամենեցին ի վեր ոչ կարէին հայել կամ տեսանել զերես Յովսեփայ. այլ ամօթով ընդ զետինն հայէին՝ եւ ոչ զիտէին տալ պատասխանի Յովսեփայ. զի այլազունեցան երեսք նոցա՝ եւ սպառեցան բանք ի մտաց նոցա. եւ կապեցան լեզուք ի քիմս նոցա. եւ եղեն դէմք նոցա իբրեւ մահապարտից. եւ ահա նման էր օրն այն մահապարտից թազաւորի.

81/ եւ յայնժամ իմացեալ թազաւորն կոչեաց զնոսա եւ հարցանէր զպատճառս չարութեան նոցա՝ եւ ոչ նոքա կարէին տալ պատասխանի նորա.⁷⁷³ այսպէս եղեն եղբարքն Յովսեփու իբրեւ զանբանս կային բերակապք առաջի { }⁷⁷⁴ եւ ոչ կարէին խօսել զի զիտէին զառնելիքն չարութեան իւրեանց. եւ ինքեանք իւրեանց դատաստանս առնէին եւ ասէին ի վերայ իւրեանց վա՜յ ի վերայ անձանց մերոց զի արժանի եղաք դառն մահու եւ դատապարտութեանն:

82/ Յորժամ եւտես Յովսէփի զամօթի՝ եւ զերկիւղի նոցա որ ինքեանք զինքէ/ fol. 344r /անս դատապարտին. ապա քաղրազոյն երեւեցաւ նոցա Յովսէփ զի հոգի առնուցուն՝ եւ մի մեռանիցին՝ յահէն եւ յերկիւղէն. յայնժամ Յովսէփի խօսեցաւ ընդ նոսա եւ ասէ.

83/ Ո՛վ եղբայրք իմ եւ որդիք հօր իմոյ Յակոբայ՝ մի երկնչիք, զի ոչ եմ նենզածոտ իբրեւ զձեզ. զի ահա մատնեաց Աստուած զձեզ այսօր {եւ այլ}. եւ այլ յառաջագոյն ի ձեռս իմ. եւ թէ կամեցեալ էի զձեզ սպանանել՝ կամ այլ նեղութիւն չարչարեալ էի որպէս եւ դուք զիտէք զձեզ արժանի տանջանաց վասն չար զործող ձերոց, զոր դուք առ իս արարիք՝ կարօղեմ եւ ես փոխարէն առնել ձեզ որպէս կամիմ ըստ ձեր արժանեցացդ որ ոչ այրէիք ի ձեռաց իմոց. բայց տեսէք եւ զիտացիք զառաջին մարդասիրութիւնն՝ զոր ես առ ձեզ արարի. եւ այժմ մի երկնչիք զի որ զչարութիւնն ձեր Աստուած ի բարին դարձոյց. ապա եւ ես ոչ յիշեմ զչարութիւնն ձեր եւ ոչ պահեմ ոխս վասն

---

773. նորա is genitive; a dative would be expected.
774. A word has fallen out.

շար գործոց ձերոց զոր գործեցիք դուք՝ այլ թողեալ եմ զմեղս ձեր զոր մեղաք դուք առ իս, եւ մի երկնչիք դուք յինէն, զի ոչ եմ եբրայրսպան. այլ մարդասէր՝ եւ ոչ եբրայրատեցդ՝ այլ եբրայրասէր. եւ ոչ հատուցանեմ շար փոխանակ շարի. այլ հատուցից ընդ ձեր շարունեանն՝ ձեզ բարի՝ որ դուք սվամահ ի գբին կամեցաք առնել զիս. եւ զձեզ կերակ/ fol. 344v /րեցի ի սովոյ յայսմանէ:

84/ դուք զիս երեսուն դահեկան վաճառեցիք: Ես զարծաթն ձեր զգին ցորենին ի ձեզ դարձուցի. դուք զիս հօրս գազանաբեկ ասացիք: Ես ձեզ հաց կերակուր բաշխեցի. դուք ինձ ի գազան եդէք. եւ ձեզ դարմանիչ եղէ, եւ զի Աստուած հարց իմզ՝ կատարեաց զուխտն իւր ընդ նոսա, եւ ոչ անտես արար զիս. վասն այնորիկ՝ եւ ես ոչ յիշեցից զչարութիւնս ձեր. այլ հատուցից ձեզ բարի փոխանակ շարեցան. զի Աստուած այնպէս հրամայեաց թէ մի հատուցանէր շար փոխանակ շարի:
85/ Եւ քայս արար երանելին Յովսէփի ըստ հրամանին Պօղոսի՝ որ ասէ՝ թէ քաղցեալ է թշնամին քո հաց տուր նմա՝ կամ ծարաւի՝ ջուր տուր նմա. քայս արարեալ կայծակունս հրոյ կու տեցաս ի գլուխ նորա. մի յաղթիր ի շարէն, այլ յաղթեայ բարեօքն շարին. քայս ամենայն կատարեաց Յովսէփի յառաջ քան զիրամայելայլն. եւ յորժամ քայս ամենայն եւ որ սոցին նման էր խօսեցաւ սուրբն Յովսէփի առ եբրայրսն իւր՝ եւ յանդիմանեաց զնոսա. եւ ապա յառաջ կոչեաց զմի եղբարցն իւրոց. եւ համբուրէր արտասուօք. եւ զիրկս արկեալ եւ լայր ի վերայ նոցա զջթով, եւ եբրայրական սիրով:

86/ Իսկ նոքա յորժամ տեսին զքաղցրութիւն Յովսէփիայ՝ յայնժամ երես անկեալ երկիր պագանէին լալով եւ ասէին. Տէր եբրայր մեր եւ թագաւոր՝ մի յաւիտեան բար/ fol. 345r /կանար մեզ. եւ մի յաւիտեան պահեր ոիս. եւ մի յիշեր զչարիս մեր առաջի քո. եւ մի հատուցաներ՝ զոր մեք գործեցաք. քանզի Աստուած ետուես զհամբերութիւն քո եւ ետ քեզ պատիժ թագաւորութիւն. արդ աղաչեմք զքեզ՝ որովհետեւ յայտնեաց Աստուած ի կորրստենէն՝ որ մեք անցաք եւ կամեցաք կորուսանել զքեզ:
87/ Բայց Աստուած բարձրացոյց զքեզ՝ այժմ ուրախացո՛ զմեզ՝ ո՛վ եբրայր մեր թագաւոր եւ զուարճացո՛ զծերացեալ հայրն մեր եւ քո. զի մի անյուսահատութենէն ընկղմեալ կորիցէ վասն քո, եւ վասն մեր յամելոյն: եւ քայս իբրեւ ասացին եբրարքն⁷⁷⁵

---

775. ք over յ p.m. The scribe varies եբրայրք and the classical form եբրարք.

Յովսեփու, առ նա դիմեցին ամենեքեան եւ զիրկս արկեալ արտասուօք համբուրեցին զնա՝ եւ ադադակ բարձեալ առ հասարակ լացին՝ մինչեւ ամենայն քաղաքն լուեալ գճայն լալոյն՝ եւ եկին ի տես համբաւոյն. եւ իբրեւ գիտացին թէ եղբայրքն Յովսեփու են ուրախացան յոյժ:

88/ Եւ եհաս բանն առ թագաւորն. յայտնի եղեւ թագաւորին թէ եղբարքն Յովսեփու եկեալ են: Առաքեաց թագաւորն եւ կոչեաց զՅովսեփի եւ ասէ՝ զի՞ նչ է բանդ զոր լսեմ թէ եղբայր<ք>[776] քո կան եւ եկեալ են. եւ ասէ Յովսեփի՝ այո՛ թագաւոր եկեալ են ի հեռաստանէ աշխարհէ. եւ ասէ թագաւոր ընդէ՞ր թողեալ ես զնոսա յայնդր. առաքեա եւ կոչեա զնոսա զի երկիրս ամենայն առաջի քո է. / fol. 345b / եւ յուր հաճոյ թուի քեզ բնակեցո՛ զնոսա.

89/ Եւ դարձեալ Յովսեփի առ եղբարսն իւր եւ ուրախացոյց զնոսա. եղ առաջի նոցա սեղան ուրախութեամբ՝ եւ բաժակ մատուցանէր նոցա՝ եւ ելից զզրաստն նոցա հացիւ. եւ առաքեաց զնոսա առ հայրն իւր եւ ասէ՝ աւետիս քեզ այս ի Յովսեփայ. այլ եւ թագաւորելոյս իմոյ քեզ կրկին ուրախութիւն, եւ այժմ հայր իմ յարիցես եւ եկեցես առ որդիս քո եւ տեսցես զքո սիրելի որդիս քո զոր կորուսեր: Ջոր գազանքեր բերանով եղբարց իմոց, զոր օտար աշխարհի ծառայ վաճառեցին եղբարք իմ: Բայց Աստուած հարց քոց՝ Աբրահամու եւ Սահակայ աղօթիւք նոցա փրկեաց զիս ի ծառայութենէ եւ թագաւոր արար. եւ արդ հայր իմ սիրելի՝ մի արգելուր զզալն քո եւ յամեր. այլ եկեցես փութով՝ զի աշխարհիս ընդ իմով իշխանութեամբս է, ուր բարի ոք թուեցի քեզ՝ անդ բնակեցես:

90/ Այլ երեսաց սովուս ապրեալ լիցիս դու եւ որդի<ք>դ քո. զի դեռ աւուրս բազումա զալոց է սով ի վերայ երկրի. եւ առաքեաց սայլ բազում զի բերցեն զՅակոբ հայրն ամենայն տամբ իւրով:

91/ Եւ յայնժամ էջ Յակոբ յԵգիպտոս ամենայն տամբ իւրով հոգիս Հ եւ Ե. Եւ իբրեւ ետես Յակոբ զՅովսեփի խնդաց. եւ ի խնդութենէն արտասուեաց եւ բացան աչքն Յակոբայ, այն որ կուրացեալ էր ի լալոյն / fol. 346r / վասն Յովսեփու. եւ բերկրեցան ամենեքեան ի տեսանել զմիմեանս:

92/ Եւ Յակոբ ուրախութեամբ լցեալ եւ գոհանայր զՏէառնէ Աստուծոյ իւրմէ եւ ասէ: Օրհնեալ է Տէր Աստուած հարց իմոց, Աբրահամու եւ Սահակայ. զի ոչ եթող զիս՝ եւ ոչ ընդ վայր եհար

---
776. Corruption by haplography.

qիu. զի շնորհեաց ինձ տեսանել զորդեակս իմ զկորուսեալ. եւ այսպէս ուրախացեալ Յակոբ՝ կրկին ուրախութեամբ. զի որպէս ի վերայ մահուանն որդոյն տրտմեալ էր՝ եւ լայր անմխիթար. մի թէ մեռած ասացին զՅովսէփ: Երկրորդ զի զազանաց կերեալ համարէր: Իսկ Յակոբ ի տեսանել զորդին կրկին ուրախացաւ, քանզի կենդանի է եւ չէ մեռեալ:

93/ Երրորդ. զի թագաւորն է ամենայն Եգիպտացւոցն՝ եւ եղեւ կերակրիչ ամենայն եղբարցն. եւ կատարեցաւ երկրորդ երազն Յովսեփու այն որ արեգակն եւ լուսին նմա երկիր պագանէին հանդերձ մետասան աստեղօքն՝ այս են հայրն եւ մայրն՝ եւ մետասան եղբարքն777 նորա:

94/ Եւ Յովսէփի էր ամուսնացեալ եւ առեալ էր զԱսանէթ զդուստր Պետ{բ}ափրեա778 իշխանին. այս այն Պետափրայ է որ յառաջն զՅովսէփի ի ծառայութիւն զնեաց. եւ Յովսէփի ծնեալ էր երկուս որդիս՝ զԵփրեմ եւ զՄանասէ:

95/ Եւ էին վատնեալ ա<ղ>քն Յակոբայ: Եւ կոչեցեալ առ ինքն զորդիսն իւր, եւ օրհնեաց զնոսա մի ըստ միոջէ՝ սկսեալ ի / fol. 346v / յառաջնէն եւ եկեալ ի չո<ր>րորդ Յուդայ. եւ ասէ ընդ Յուդայ. զքեզ օրհնեսցեն եղբայրք քո. եւ ձեռն քո ի վերայ թիկանց թշնամեաց քոց. ի շառաւիղէ որդեակ եւ որ օրհնէ զքեզ՝ օրհնեալ եղիցի. եւ որ անիծէ՝ անիծեալ եղիցի. եւ այլ բազում օրհնութեամբ՝ օրհնեաց Յակոբ զՅուդայ զորդի իւր. եւ այս մարգարէութիւն էր, որ զայր կատարէր ի վերայ փրկչին մերոյ յայտն vacat 5 lett. մերոյ Յիսուսի Քրիստոս. քանզի եւ զաւակ է. եւ ի գեղէ Յուդայի զալղց էր Քրիստոս եւ ծնանելոց էր ըստ մարմնոյ եւ զթագաւորութիւն Յակոբ՝ Յուդայի ետ. որպէս ասէ օրհնութիւն մի պակասեսցէ. իշխանութիւն Յուդայէ մինչեւ եկեսցէ այն որ իւր թագաւորութիւն, որ է ինքն փրկիչն Քրիստոս. եւ նա է ակնկալութիւն հեթանոսաց. եւ եկեալ առ Յովսէփի՝ զովեաց զնա եւ ասէ օրհնութեանց արժանի Յովսէփի. եւ օրհնեալ ես ի Տեառնէ Աստուծոյ. որդեակ զի դու ես ինձ հանգիստ հօր քո եւ եղբարց քոց եւ կերակրիչ անձանց մերոց՝ եւ դու ես ընդունիչ հօր քո՝ եւ դարմանիչ եղբարց քոց. եւ օրհնեալ լիցիս դու ի Տեառնէ եւ զաւակ քո թագաւորութեան հասցեն եւ քեզ եղիցի բաժին ի տեղւոջն ուր զՍուգեմացին կոտորեցին. զոր եւ մարգարէն Դաւիթ ասէ եւ վկայէ ի դիմաց

---

777. ր written over յ.
778. Corruption.

Յակոբայ, գնծացայց բարձր եղեց բաժանեցայց զՈւզեմա և հովիտան յարկաց շափեցից։

96/ Իմ է Գայլայաթ և իմ Մանասէ Եփրեմ / fol. 347r / հզորիչ զլխոյ իմոյ։ այս է թագաւորութիւն Յուդայ թէ Յուդայ թագաւոր իմ Մովաբ աւագան յուսոյ իմոյ։ և մատոյց Յովսէփ գրդղիսն իւր առ հայրն իւր Յակոբ. զի օրհնեսցէ զնոսա գեփրեմ և զՄանասէ. և զի վատեալ⁷⁷⁹ էին աչքն Յակոբայ. մատոյց Յովսէփի զանդրանիկն՝ յահեակն Յակոբայ. և կրսերն ընդ աջմէ Յակոբայ և տես զքանչելիսն Աստուծոյ. զի Յակոբ գձեռն իւր խաչանման տարածեաց. և եդ ի վերայ յորդոցն Յովսէփայ՝ և օրհնեաց զնոսա. և յայնժամ հանգեաւ ընդ հայրասն⁷⁸⁰ իւր. որպէս ասէ Պօղոս՝ հաւատոք Յակոբ ի մեռանելն իւրում զիւրաքանչիւր ոք յորդոց Յովսեփու օրհնեաց. և երկիր եպագ ի ծագ զաւազանի իւրոյ. և հրաման ետ Յովսէփի դիազարդիցն դիապատել զԻսրայէլ հայրն իւր <և հանեալ Յովսէփի զհայրն իւր>⁷⁸¹ Յակոբ ի յաշխարհէն Եգիպտացւոց. և յուղարկեց ի յերկիրն Քանանու. և թաղեցին զնա ի գերեզմանն հարց իւրոց Աբրահամու և Սահակայ. և լացին զնա Լ օր։

97/ Իսկ Յովսէփի կացեալ անդ Եգիպտոս⁷⁸² թագաւոր բազում տարիք. ամս ութսուն։ և ի մեռանելն իւրում կոչեաց զեղբարսն իւր, և զորդիսն օրհնեաց զնոսա. և ասէ՝ եղբայրք իմ և որդիք օրհնեալ եղիցիք ի յԱստուծոյ հարց իմոց Աբրահամու Սահակայ Յակոբայ. բայց տեսէք եղբայրք իմ և որդիք։ Յորժամ այց արասցէ ձեզ Տէր Աստուած հարց իմոց. և / fol. 374v / բարի արասցէ ձեզ. և հանգէ գձեզ յերկրէս յայսմանէ. և տարցէ գձեզ ի յերկիրն զոր խոստացաւ մեզ ժառանգութիւն և բնակութիւն. արդ զզուշ լերուք յելանելն ձեր յերկրէս յայսմանէ հանջիք և զիմ ոսկերս ընդ ձեզ. և այսպես կացեալ Յովսէփի բարիոք իշխանութեամբ և առաքինութեամբ ամս բազումս՝ մեռաւ խաղաղութեամբ, և թաղցաւ յԵգիպտոս. և եթող մեզ օրինակ բարեաց հեզութեամբ և խոնարհութեամբ, ողջախոհութեամբ և պարկեշտութեամբ. անխակալութեամբ և համբերութեամբ. ի վերայ այն ամենայնի հաւատով և յուսով և սիրով Աստուծոյ լցեալ էր, և զօրացեալ. այս ամենայն բարութիւնս ամբարեալ կայր առ Յովսէփի. և եհաս

---

779. Erasure of ն after տ.
780. ս above line, s.m.?
781. In margin, p.m.
782. A genitive case would be expected.

թագաւորութիւնն՝ եւ ոչ հպարտեցաւ ի միտս իւր. եւ ոչ սնափառեաց՝ եւ ոչ ռիսս պահեաց ընդ չարութեանն եղբարցն. եւ ոչ հատոյց չար փոխանակ ընդ չարին. այլ ամենայնի նմանեալ էր Աստուծոյ մարդասիրութեանն. որպէս ասէ Տէրն՝ յաւետարանին. Եղերուք գթածք։ եւ եղերուք կատարեալք, որպէս եւ հայրն ձեր երկնաւոր գթած է եւ կատարեալ։

98/ Եւ արդ[783] եղբարք հայրք եւ որդիք իմ սիրելիք լուարուք զպատմութիւնս Յովսեփու առաջինոյ եւ ողջախոհի հեզի եւ պարկեշտի. եւ առէք զվարս սորա յանձինս ձեր. եւ ընկալարուք զսէր հոգեւոր առաքինութիւնն, եւ զանխսակալութիւնն. զի այսպիսի {բա}[784] / fol. 347v / բարութեամբս մարդն հաճոյ լինի Աստուծոյ. Եւ Աստուած բարձրացուցանէ զնա, որ հեզ լինի ի խոնարհի. եւ որ սրտիւն ողորմած լինի, նա առնու զերանին Աստուծոյ։

99/ որ ասէ յաւետարանին երանի է ողորմածաց. զի նոքա ողորմութիւն գտցեն. եւ որ եղբայրասէր լինի. այս է պատուէրն Աստուծոյ՝ սիրեցես զընկեր քո՝ իբրեւ զանձն քո. եւ որ ողջախոհի լինի՝ առնու զերանին եւ զԱստուած տեսանէ՝ որ ասէ. երանի այնոցիկ որ սուրբ են սրտիւք զի նոքա զԱստուած տեսցեն. եւ ի վերայ այս ամենայնի համբերող լինի։

100/ Յորժամ ի փորձութիւն անկանի զի այն է կատարեալ առաքինութիւն, որ ի նեղութեան ժամանակին համբերէ. եւ զի Տէրն զայն արժանի արար կենաց ասելով թէ որ համբերէ սպառ նա կեցցէ յաւիտեան. զնոյն արար Յովսէփի եւ համբերեաց. վասն որոյ Աստուած բարձրացոյց եւ թագաւորութեանն հասոյց զնա՝ այսպէս առնէ Աստուած ամենայն մարդոյ որ համբերէ։

101/ Մարդ որ համբերող լինի. նա Աստուած փրկէ զնա ի փորձութենէ. եւ ազատէ ի հանդերձեալ տանջանաց որպէս ասէ Տէրն յաւետարանին. թէ յորժամ հալածեսցեն զձեզ եւ նեղեն եւ չարչարեն՝ ցնծացէք եւ ուրախ լերուք զի վարձք ձեր բազում են յերկինս։

102/ Դարձեալ ասէ՝ թէ համբերութեամբ ձերով ստասջիք զոգիս ձեր։[785] ահա տեսէք զհամբերութիւն Յովսեփու. զի անուն Յովսէ/ fol. 348v /փայ զհամբերութիւն թարգմանէ[786] զի նա

---

783. Over արք.
784. Surmounted by deletion marks.
785. Luke 21:19.
786. This onomastic element is discussed in part 3, note 19.

յառաջ հեզ էր, եւ հօրն հնազանդ. վասն այնորիկ հայրն սիրէր զնա առաւել քան զայլ որդիսն. այնպէս մեք հեզ լինիմք առ միմեանս հնազանդ լինիմք Աստուծոյ որ հայրն է հասարակաց. եւ զկամս Աստուծոյ անխափան կատարեմք. եւ լինիմք հնազանդ ծնողաց մերոց, որպէս եւ գրեալ է յօրէնս Տեառն. թէ պատուեա զհայր քո եւ զմայր. եւ որ բամբասէ զհայր իւր կամ զմայր՝ մահու վախճանեցի.⁷⁸⁷ եւ յորժամ զմեր հնազանդութիւնս տեսանէ Աստուած՝ յայնժամ եւ նա սիրէ զմեզ առաւել քան զայլ երբայրսն. եւ քան զամենայն ազգս որ ի վերայ երկրիս. եւ որպէս Յովսէփի ունէր պատմուճան ծաղկեայ, այսինքն հանդերձ աստեղազործ փայլեալ՝ այնպէս եւ մեզ զգեցոյց Տէրն մեր հանդերձ փառաց եւ պատմուճան ուրախութեանն, եւ հաւատս <Ճշմարիտ քրիստոնէութեան. որ փայլէ՝>⁷⁸⁸ ոչ որպէս զաստեղս, այլ իբրեւ զարեգակն այս կեանքս. եւ առաւել ի հանդերձեալն:

103/ Եւ որպէս եղբայրքն Յովսեփու՝ չարութեամբ էին ընդ նմա. եւ նա նոցա բարերար եւ կերակրիչ քանզի ամենայն ազզ⁷⁸⁹ ատեն զմեզ վասն մեր սերտ հաւատոցս, եւ ամենեքեան չարութեամբ են ընդ մեզ. եւ զմեր աշխատանքն եւ զքրտինքն. եւ զամենայն բարիսն առեալ յափշտակեն եւ ունեն. եւ մեզ մահու սպառնայցեն. նոյնպէս եւ եղբայրքն / fol. 349r / Յովսեփու հեռացեալ ի հօրէն եւ ի դաշտին զխաշինս արածէին, այնպէս եւ մարմնասէր այլազզիքն հեռացեալ են ի պատուիրանէն եւ ի հօրէն աշխարհիս եւ ի դաշտիս զանքանութիւն անասնական բնութեամբ դարմանէն՝ այս է որ զմարմինս՝ հեշտութեամբ սնուցանեն. ուտելով եւ ըմպելով. եւ անառակ⁷⁹⁰ վարիւք՝ եւ որպէս եղբայրքն Յովսեփու:

104/ Յորժամ Յովսեփին կերակուր տանէր նոցա ի դաշտին. յայնժամ տեսին զնա՝ եւ սպանութեամբ մտաբերեցին. նոյնպէս եւ սուրբ զմեր աշխատեալ կերակուրս՝ յափշտակեալ ունեն. եւ մեզ մահու խորհին. բայց մեզ պարտ է. Ո վ երանելի եղբարք զօրինակ Յովսեփու ի մեջ բերեալ՝ յանձն առնուլ զամենայն նեղութիւնս, զոր զան ի վերայ մեր՝ թէ եղբարց մերոց՝ եւ թէ օտարաց. զի զՅովսեփի այլ ինչ ոչ բարձրացոյց՝ բայց

---

787. This orthography is found in manuscripts. See Stone and Hillel, "Index," 317.
788. *inter lineas.*
789. The pluralizing ք is often lost on words ending with a palatal; see Stone and Hillel, "Index," nos. 333, 334.
790. Erasure of two letters.

համբերութիւն եւ ողջախոհութիւնն՝ եւ այն որ ոչ հատոյց չար
փոխանակ չարին. նոյնպէս մեզ պարտ է համբերել եւ զվարս
մեր պարկեշտ անցուցանել ի յայսմ աշխարհիս. եւ ոչ տալ զմեզ
խաբել այս կենացս, եւ ընկենուլ զմեզ երեսացն Աստուծոյ։
105/ Այլ պարտ է մեզ զամենայն նեղութիւնս յանձն առնուլ՝ եւ
միայն Աստուծոյ պատուիրանացն ոչ հեռանալ եւ օտարանալ
մեզ պարտ է ի ծնողաց եւ ի յերբարց եւ ի աշխարհէ. յաշխարհս
երթալ եւ զերութիւն եւ ի / fol. 349v / ծառայութիւն չար
մարդկանց՝ Աստուծոյ ծառայութենէն մի ելցուք. յաշխարհէ,
յաշխարհի վտարեցցուք եւ յերկնից յարքայութենէն մի
զրկեցցուք՝ ի բանդ եւ ի կապանս մտցուք վասն սիրոյն
Քրիստոսի Աստուծոյ մերոյ՝ եւ վասն հաւատոյ մերոց՝ որ ի
Քրիստոսու Յիսուս ի Տէր մեր. զի սակաւիկ մի այս տանջանօքս՝
ի յատենատանջանացն փրկեցցուք.
106/ Որով զմեզ եւ զձեզ փրկեցէ Քրիստոս Աստուած՝ ի
յամենայն փորձութենէ, եւ ի դիւական ի խռովութենէ. ամբողջ
պահեցէ զհոգի եւ զմարմին մեր մինչեւ ի կատարումն
ժամանակաց մերոց. եւ նմա փառք եւ պատիւ զոհութիւն եւ
երկրպագութիւն անբաժանելի սուրբ երրորդութեանն այժմ
եւ միշտ եւ յաւիտեանս ամէն։

Translation

1/   Third Story of Joseph, he is beautiful and also modest.[791]
This Jacob had 12 sons, whose names these are: Reuben, Simeon, Levi, Judah, Issachar, Zebulun, Dan, Naphtali, Gad, Asher, Joseph, Benjamin.[792] Joseph and Benjamin were from one mother Rachel, and Jacob loved (them) more than the others, for they were younger than (his) other sons.[793]

2/ And Rachel their mother died in the course of bearing Benjamin, in childbirth.[794] And Jacob nurtured Benjamin without a mother.

---

791. Joseph's beauty is clearly stated in the Bible (Gen 39:6). The statement about him being modest apparently refers to the story about Potiphar's wife.
792. Gen 35:22.
793. Gen 37:3 and compare 44:30.
794. Gen 35:19.

PART FOUR 203

3/ And Jacob's other sons were shepherds in the field,[795] and Joseph and Benjamin lived in a house[796] with their father Jacob.

4/ And one day,[797] in the night, Joseph saw a dream and he told his brothers and he said, "I saw in this night that we were reaping a field, I and my 12[798] brothers, and I saw that my brothers' sheaves came and bowed down to my sheaf."[799]

5/ And his brothers, having heard (this) said to one another, "Will it be thus,[800] that we 11 brothers will bow down to him and will he rule over us?"[801] And he did not wish, (that) thus by (his) telling the truth they would interpret the dream to one another, and through this (i.e., interpretation) they resented Joseph's dream.

6/ And Joseph again saw a second dream and he told it to (his) father and brothers, and he said, "In this night I saw that the sun and the moon with eleven stars were coming and were bowing down to me."[802]

7/ And when the brothers heard, they were angered and unwillingly they interpreted the dream, and they said, "Is it that this one wishes to rule and we and our father come for prostration before him?"[803] And from that day the brothers looked at Joseph jealously and were unable to see him.[804]

8/ See the evil of envy that it turned the brothers to hatred, for they always resented him and made a plan to kill him, and they were forced to an apposite time.[805] Alas, this evil thought (plan) entered them! And then, after this,[806] Joseph's brothers went far off after the sheep in the field.[807]

9/ And then Jacob said to his son Joseph, "Child, take bread and bring it

---

795. Gen 37:12.
796. Or: at home
797. From this point on the text retells the tale of Joseph as it is related in Genesis. I note points at which the text's narrative differs significantly from that of Genesis.
798. An error, for Jacob had twelve sons in all, counting Joseph, and later on (§5) the text correctly refers to Joseph's eleven brothers.
799. Gen 37:6–8.
800. Or: will this one be thus.
801. Gen 37:8.
802. Gen 37:9.
803. Gen 37:9. In Genesis Jacob administers the rebuke.
804. I.e., unable to bear seeing him. See Gen 37:11.
805. This is a homiletic aside, of which there are a number in the text.
806. Genesis does not say the brothers plot against Joseph before they "go far off after the sheep" and we are only told about a plan to harm Joseph when he meets up with them in Dothan.
807. Gen 37:12. It was in Shechem, according to the biblical narrative.

to your brothers in the field.⁸⁰⁸ And Joseph had a floral cloak.⁸⁰⁹ And he rose up, took⁸¹⁰ the bread and was bringing it to his brothers, and he got lost on the way, for he remembered his brothers' resentment.

10/ And then, coming (back) to his intention,⁸¹¹ he came (and) found his brothers in the field. And when Joseph's brothers saw (him) they spoke to one another thus, "Behold, the seer of dreams is coming." And they made a plan of murder and deceit concerning Joseph, and how they might destroy him.

11/ Oh, evil deceit and lawlessness of envy, that they wished to kill (their) beneficent one and the benefactor. Joseph was bringing them bread to eat and they were planning to kill (him).⁸¹²

12/ Oh, evil deceit of (his) brothers, for one should not call them brothers, but rather beasts. For they did not do fraternal acts, but those of an evil beast and an evil enemy.

13/ Oh, the unwatchfulness of the brothers! For Joseph innocently and laboriously brought food to them, and they for the evil plan of murder, betrayed Joseph on the way. They having wandered, ran to evil. Oh, for the wonder. For apparently getting lost on the way revealed that, it foretold the brothers' deceit to Joseph, and God showed patience to him so that he should not be tried by distressful anger on account of the brothers' wickedness, so that he should apprehend and trust God, Him who made the way straight. He is powerful, he transforms the brothers' evil deceit into good.

14/ See, brothers and beware of evil jealousy and from hatred wickedness increases, and from wickedness envy grows, and envy begets hatred and from hatred fratricide eventuates.

---

808. According to Gen 37:14 Jacob sent Joseph not to bring bread to his brothers, but to check on their wellbeing.

809. For ծաղկեայ Bedrossian gives "flowered; party-coloured; figured, embroidered." The story in Gen 37:3 has כתנת פסים, which literally means "striped coat" and traditionally interpreted as "coat of many colours" (King James version), probably under the influence of the LXX translation ποικίλον. Targum Pseudo-Jonathan has פרגוד מצויר which can be translated as "a decorated clothing item." RSV and NRSV translate the Hebrew as "a long robe with sleeves."

810. Literally: taking.

811. Unusual. It may be understood as follows. The end of §8 is the apparent *non sequitur* "and be got lost on the way, for he remembered his brothers' resentment." If he lost the way because he was thinking of his brothers' evil, the start of §9 means that he returned to his former intention and set out once more to find them.

812. Again apparently the author of this text adds homiletic comments to the Joseph story. They highlight the teaching function of the document that was perhaps the primary motive for its composition.

PART FOUR 205

15/ See brothers that wicked and hateful envy made Cain a brother-killer and the same evil hatred made the sons of Jacob hateful of brothers, and killers.[813] James the apostle says the same thing, that he who hates his brother is a complete murderer.[814] For Joseph's brothers, inflamed by wicked envy wished to kill him. In the same way, envy which was rife among the Jews made them so evil that they killed our Lord.[815]

16/ For in (his) brothers' eyes Joseph was killed, but in God's eyes he made a beginning of becoming a king. In the same way also the Lord appeared dead to the eyes of the envious Jews, but he was alive through (His) divinity. Moreover, just as they stripped Joseph naked and put him in the pit, in the same way they stripped the Lord naked and brought (him) forth to the cross and put him in a tomb. For it was the same people that did that same (thing); those who carried that out were their sons. And just as they sold Joseph to Egypt for 30[816] pieces of silver, in the same way their sons, the Jews, sold the Lord to be crucified in exchange for 30 pieces of silver. And this is their wickedness, that which the fathers received as Joseph's price, their children also gave as the price of Christ. And just as Joseph entered the pit of the prison, our Lord also entered the tomb's coffin. And just as Joseph came out of the prison and of slavery, He ruled over the earth.

17/ And just as the brothers who sold Joseph saw him ruling and they fell,[817] perished, and were smitten with shame on account of their evil deeds which they did to Joseph,[818] in the same fashion after the resurrection the Jews, having seen the Lord, became ashamed. It is obligatory for us to turn again to this story. Then while Joseph's brothers had this evil plan, then Joseph came bringing them food and greeted them with a tender heart and he placed the bread which he brought before them.[819]

18/ Then, the brothers were inflamed with evil. They did not wish to eat

---

813. Cain killed his brother, Abel: Gen 4:8. The brothers resolve to kill Joseph: Gen 37:18.

814. James 1:15. This long passage sets forth the well-known idea of Joseph as a type of Christ, showing how various elements of the Joseph story presaged the events of the Passion. The most striking instance is found in the next note, where Genesis's 20 pieces of silver become 30.

815. The idea that Joseph corresponded typologically to Christ permeates this work and is a very common typological exegesis in early Christian sources.

816. "Twenty" in Hebrew and Greek Gen 37:28. The number thirty derives from Matt 26:15 and 27:3, under the influence of the typological exegesis. See the same in Memorial of the Forefathers §61 and notes there.

817. I.e., on their faces.

818. Here the idea of Joseph as a type of Christ is developed.

819. Gen 37:14 and 23 do not refer to Joseph bringing food.

the food which Joseph brought, but they wished to carry out their evil plan. At that time they seized Joseph and stripped (him) naked and cast him into a dry pit.[820] And then they themselves sat down and ate heedlessly the food which Joseph had brought, and reckoned (it) some sort of victory.

19/ Thus the Jews also did to the Lord—having receiving God's gift, they mocked the Lord, giver of gifts by putting Him in a tomb. They reckoned it as some sort of victory and heedlessly ate the Passover (meal / lamb).[821]

20/ And then, taking a goat they slaughtered it and wet Joseph's cloak with the blood and sent it to their father and said, "We found this in the field. See whether this cloak is your son Joseph's, because he has become a wild beast's prey."[822]

21/ Oh, the brothers' mindlessness! They stripped off Joseph's garment and told (their) father that he had become a wild beast's prey. It is evident that they made themselves into wild beasts, and thus it (Scripture) said "wild beast's prey" for they themselves became wild beasts. Having been directed by a wicked plan they consulted as to what they would do to him. Some said, "Come, let us kill him." Some, unwilling to (do this), said, "Let us not be guilty of blood." Then certain of them said, "Let us leave him here in a pit, so that he might die there."

22/ And then, while they had no plan, the Lord, who wished to keep him (Joseph) alive made preparations. And then a caravan came and numerous merchants, passing through bringing resin, were going to Egypt.[823] Seeing this, Joseph's brothers said to one another, "Come, let us sell Joseph, so that he goes to foreign parts and in captivity to a distant land, so that his dream will not be fulfilled. And he who wished to be king shall go into captivity and (his) dream will be foiled."[824] And what a false reckoning! And then, having seized (him), they drew Joseph out of the pit and sold him and received as Joseph's price 30 coins.[825] And Joseph remained patient with their evils and did not lie to the merchants (saying), "They are selling me vainly, for I am their

---

820. Gen 37:23. The preceding part of this section is an expansion.
821. See Exod 12:3–4.
822. Gen 37:31–33.
823. Gen 37:25.
824. According to Gen 37:27 Joseph's brothers decided to sell him, rather than kill him, because he was their brother, their own flesh and blood.
825. See note 611 above.

younger brother," for he did not say, "They are selling me." Of these words Joseph (did not speak), not even one. Neither did he reproach the brothers' evil.[826]

23/ The Lord also did these things, for he did not rebuke the Jews, who were crazed with evil against our Christ, as the prophet Isaiah says (Isa 50:6), "I do not (have) the patience of Christ. I do not regard the sufferings severely and I do not oppose (them). I gave my shoulders (back) to blows and my cheek to slapping." And again he says (Isa 53:7), "I was led like a sheep to slaughter, and like a lamb before the shearer he is silent." In this way he does not open his mouth. This was fulfilled for Joseph, just as for his Lord, because he did resist[827] on account of the wickedness of (his) brothers.

24/ Susanna too did the same before the evil and bitter old men, for falsely they testified evil words against her. And she only remained quiet and did not oppose their falsity until God looked from heaven and saw the unjust happening and made the judgement and the just (innocent) known and punished the evil false witnesses with punishment.[828]

25/ Thus we too are obliged to be patient when vain things[829] and trials come upon us, and then God sees our patience and saves us from (the) trial and shames him who speaks evil against us and rebukes (him), for patience is the chief of all virtues. Just like Joseph's patience, for Joseph is translated "patience."[830]

26/ And as for the evil falsity of the brothers who sold him, indeed God changed their wickedness to good for Joseph.[831] Thus God does for every human who is patient in trials, he turns the wickedness of the evil ones back onto their own heads and saves the patient one from trials.

---

826. The lack of Joseph's reaction to being sold in Genesis is probably the driving force of this remark and that in the next section.

827. Or: oppose.

828. This story is related in the composition called "Susanna," which is included in the Greek translation of Daniel. There are two known Greek versions of the story of Susanna: Old Greek (OG) and Theodotion (Th). In general, in the Book of Daniel, Arm Bible is closer to Th. According to Th, and in contrast to the Joseph story, Susanna does cry out to the Lord, see Sus (Th) 1:42–43. This part of the text is absent from Sus (OG). On Armenian Daniel, see Cowe 1992.

829. Or: words.

830. This etymology of Joseph is difficult to explain. Gen 30:24 gives the meaning of the name as: "May the LORD add to me another son!" In the onomastic literature, OnaV reads, "Lord's increase"; see Stone 1981, 146–47. Moreover, the sentence is unclear.

831. Or: through Joseph.

27/ And then the merchants brought Joseph forth upon a camel and went on their way.[832] And they came to the place where Rachel, Joseph's mother was buried.[833]

28/ When Joseph saw his mother's tomb, he fell down[834] from the camel and running, he fell upon (his) mother's tomb and wept bitterly. Doleful tears dripped from his eyes, until[835] all the merchants were weeping with him.

29/ And raising up a voice of lamentation and with moving compassion he said this to (his) mother, "Where are you, my beloved mother? Come, see me your beloved son Joseph, where I am in captivity like merchandise. Arise, my mother, see me your son, for I am going to a foreign land. Oh, my mother, stand up and see me your son Joseph whom you bore free, now I am led into slavery at the hands of my brothers. For him whom you made freeborn, they gave into slavery. See, my mother, that I, your son, go helpless into captivity and I have no one who will care in a family fashion about me.

30/ "Oh, my mother, open your eyes and see the sufferings and the difficulties of your son Joseph. For you sleep uncaring in your grave and your maternal pity for me your son is silenced. Do you not see me your son among[836] (his) evil brothers, wandering[837] like a lamb among the wolves, and wandering from (his) parents and made distant. I no longer know what will happen to me.

31/ "Oh my mother, see your son, that I am going to a foreign land, and I will no more see this grave of yours. See, my mother Rachel, me your son, for I am going to be sold into captivity and I have no one who will redeem me.

---

832. The camel is an addition to the biblical story.
833. There is no mention in the biblical Joseph story of the merchants making a stop at Rachel's grave, at Ephrath near Bethlehem (Gen 35:19), yet a tradition of Joseph's lament on Rachel's grave is cited by Ginzberg 1909–1938, 2:20–21which he drew from the later mediaeval composition *Sefer HaYashar*. The date of this work is debated, some setting it as late as the fifteenth century. On it, see Dan 1986 (in Hebrew). It was very popular, also in English translation and the material interesting us occurs on, pp. 103–31 of the translation of 1840. The incident is greatly developed in the present text in §§26–37 and may well come, ultimately, from a Greek or Latin source. See the introductory remarks, above.
834. Note that in Gen 24:64, describing Rebecca's speedy descent from a camel, Hebrew uses the verb *wattippol*, "and she fell." The English "alighted" may ultimately reflect the LXX κατεπήδησεν, while Arm Bible has էջ, "descended" from the same Greek.
835. Or: so that.
836. Literally this is an oblique case, presumably an ablative.
837. Literally: dispersed. Twice in this section.

32/ "Oh, my, Joseph's mother, open your eyes and see my captivity, for although you were stolen from your fatherland, (it was) not so that you would serve idols, but so that you might become an obstacle for other idol-worshippers.[838] But now, the brothers have stolen me, your beloved son. They sold (me), and they said to my father that wild beasts tore me.[839]

33/ "Oh, this[840] captivity of Joseph, your beloved son. My beloved mother, look and see the sufferings of your son, for without cause I am going to captivity and I have no one as helper. I was deprived of you earlier, my mother Rachel, and today I am made distant from (my) father and my beloved brother Benjamin, and I have no hope of seeing you.[841] Oh, my mother, I was made distant from you by death, and I am made distant from my father and brothers by captivity.

34/ "You see, O men and merchants, and help (me) in my misfortunes, and bewail me, this youth who am in such misery, and permit me for a short time to bewail the death of my mother and my own captivity.

35/ "Oh my mother Rachel, look and see (my) brothers' evil envy, how they were wrathful to kill and destroy me. Open your eyes and awake from your tomb, my mother, for today I, your son, am made alien from you and I will not see this wickedness of my brothers again, who through envy sent me away from (my) beloved brother and from my parents. They made me lose hope and you, my mother, are without breath and have become speechless."

36/ And then the merchants took pity on Joseph, as the tears dripped from (his) eyes, and mourning from (his) mind. And taking him they mounted[842] him upon the camel. And Joseph opposite his mother's tomb said thus, "Be well, my mother, for I am going to a foreign (land) and I will not see this tomb of yours again, my mother.[843] Who will tell my father this? That I am going into captivity and I have not become food for a wild beast."[844] And he said this, "Farewell my mother and

---

838. Intriguingly, Joseph points out the parallels between his and Rachel's abandonment of their birthplaces and argues that Rachel's removal from her birthplace had a positive purpose.
839. According to the biblical narrative line, Joseph could not have known what his brothers told Jacob.
840. Or: my captivity, Joseph's.
841. "You" is plural, referring to those enumerated.
842. Literally: brought him forth.
843. Literally: "and who."
844. Here, again, the narrative confusion mentioned above in note 839 above. This continues below.

210　　　　　　　　　　　　BIBLICAL STORIES

farewell my father, and farewell my kind brother Benjamin, for you do not know that I have been sold into captivity and I did not fall prey to a wild beast.

37/ "Farewell the land of the graves of my parents, for I will not see you again with my eyes, except if they will bring forth my bones to you.[845] Farewell the graves of my forefathers, of Abraham and Isaac, and of my mother Rachel. I have no hope of seeing (them) again with my eyes (while I am) alive, except if after my death I will happen to dwell with you as dead bones."

38/ "Oh, my calamity and my misfortune, for (being) a son of free men and of free parents I am going afar to a foreign land and I am led into captivity and no one will tell my father Jacob this, that 'Your beloved son Joseph has not been seized by wild animals, but through the evil envy of (his) brothers, did they sell him.'"

39/ And then Joseph said, "My father and my mother abandoned me, and you, Lord my God, do not abandon me.[846] I was a stranger to my brothers and unknown[847] in the eyes of my father's sons. But you, Lord God, who were with my father Jacob while he fled from his brother Esau,[848] in the same way Lord our God, be with me and do not abandon me, and be a guardian for me and a helper everywhere[849] I go, for I do not know where they will bring me. Since you, O Lord, are powerful, help me always."

40/ And when Joseph had finished all this[850] upon his mother's tomb, then the merchants took him, went[851] and brought him down to Egypt. And they sold him to Potiphar,[852] the prince of the Egyptians.[853] And Joseph remained in slavery in Potiphar's house for seven years,[854] and

---

845. A clear reference to the ongoing tradition about Joseph's bones, which is first mentioned in Gen 50:25 when Joseph asks for his bones to be brought into the Land of Israel, a request that is later fulfilled in Exod 13:19 and Josh 24:32.

846. Ps 27(26):10.

847. Or: unrecognized.

848. Gen 27–33.

849. Literally "all places," and a preposition seems to lack. The addition or omission of initial յ is extremely common.

850. I.e., "saying all this."

851. The word order in the Armenian text seems confused.

852. Gen 39:1. Here Armenian has Petabp'reay, the usual spelling of Petap'ra in this text.

853. In Gen 37:36 and 39:1 Potiphar is called סריס פרעה and שר הטבחים, which literally mean "Pharaoh's eunuch" and "chief butcher." The word "prince" should not be taken literally as "son of a monarch" but designates a high officer in the service of government.

854. The Bible does not mention how long Joseph stayed in Potiphar's house.

obeyed him. And the Lord God was with Joseph. God gave Joseph grace before the prince,[855] and Potiphar appointed Joseph over his entire house, as prince and commander to all his slaves.[856] And Joseph was <in> authority in Potiphar's house and not in servitude.

41/ Then Satan saw (this); he does not wish for the good of humans, but conducts himself with wicked envy[857] against the race of humans in order to destroy mankind. Then Satan entered into Potiphar's wife.[858] Just as he brought Adam out of the Garden through the woman, (thus) also everywhere he deceives all men through women and destroys them. Now also Satan strove with Joseph through Potiphar's wife, to bring him forth from (his) free nature.[859]

42/ For Joseph, although he was a slave in the body, still was free in his soul and mind. In the same way also every human is free in soul and mind, even if he is under the authority of ten thousand men he is not a slave. For that person is called a slave whose spirit and mind are bound by some fear or other. For the spirit that has been seized by any sin is indeed[860] called a slave. For that one who serves men with his body is not called a slave, but that one is called a slave who by (his) spirit is a slave, through gluttony, or sin, or possessions, or desire, or whatever it be (of) all the evils upon the earth that humans do, they are called slaves to them. For one who is gluttonous although he be a king is a slave to gluttony, similarly evil people,[861] and if one loves possessions he is a slave to possessions and is not free. If one is an adulterer, the same is a slave to adultery and is not free.

43/ If he is an angry person, he is slave to (his) heart. If he is a drunkard, he is a slave to wine and he is not free. If he is vengeful, he is a slave

---

855. I.e., caused the prince to like him.
856. Gen 39:2–4.
857. Literally: the wickedness of envy.
858. Perhaps meaning "possessed"; compare *Adam, Eve and the Incarnation* §2.
859. The Bible does not mention Satan in the Joseph story nor in that of Adam and Eve, yet his introduction into these two incidents here clearly reflects a widespread tradition. The motif of women as temptresses is present in both stories and it has prominent presence in their Jewish and Christian retellings. For further reading see Kvam, Schearing, and Ziegler 1999. The phrase "bring him forth from his free nature" is introduced to heighten the parallel with the story of the Expulsion from Eden. Here both in the case of Potiphar's wife and that of Eve, demonic possession by Satan is described. This is often said to be the relationship between Satan and the serpent. See Stone 2000, 141–86.
860. ɨɫ is translated "indeed" here.
861. The syntax here is problematic.

44/ And he is vengeful and begrudging, and jealous and false, sometimes a lying apostate and false swearing, a proud, vain, glory-loving slanderer, this blasphemous enemy, a slanderer, a robber. These and those who are like them, are called the slaves and sons of Satan. For the Lord says in the Gospel that among the Jews is evil envy, "You are from the father Satan and you wish to carry out your father's desire, for he was a murderer from the beginning." [862] And he who speaks a lie, speaks of his own, since Satan is the father of falsity. And a person who is false, we may accurately say that he[863] is a son of Satan. Moreover, the very same is Satan. A man who is a slanderer and an intriguer among men, shifts peace into tumult, although the peacemaker is a son of God.

45/ Then precisely the maker of tumult is son of Satan. And he who is eater and drinker and potator, he is a slave to (his) belly, as Paul says, "Weeping I say concerning the enemies of Christ's cross, whose end is destruction, whose god is their belly, and glory (is) their shame."[864] The Lord says the same in the Gospel that "He (who) does sin is a slave of sin,"[865] whatever it be. And now, behold these all are those who enslave men who are under their authority. From all this Joseph was free although he was in body under the authority of Potiphar, yet he was not a slave of sin and desire and wickedness. For the brothers who sold him were slaves of evil envy and Joseph who was sold by them was free of every evil.

46/ Then Potiphar's wife, who was Joseph's mistress, wished to overcome Joseph by desire and to deceive (him), so that he might sin with her.[866] But, since Joseph was adorned with divine grace and was beautiful in appearance, he was not deceived by that woman, but he kept his father's example firmly, adorning himself with modesty. And he remained in his ruler's house, as firm as a rock by means his free mind.

47/ Then the wife of his ruler was so impassioned by the love of Joseph and was completely unable to persuade Joseph to her desire, that she bore a grudge against Joseph, for he did not carry out the desire of his mistress's will. And it came to pass one day that the two of them were

---

862. John 8:44; cf. Rom 1:28–29.
863. Confusion of number.
864. Phil 3:18–19.
865. John 8:34.
866. Gen 39:7.

alone in the house, and then the woman seized Joseph's garment in her hand and wished to draw him close to herself. Then Joseph with divine power, left his garment with the woman and fled, and got out of her hands.[867]

48/ When the woman saw that Joseph had fled from her, she was afraid[868] and said, "Lest he reproach me in the courtyard before my lord."

49/ Then she went forward[869] and when Potiphar came home the woman told her husband and said vainly concerning Joseph, "Why did you bring this foreign slave to our house? He wished to make us a game and a mockery." And bringing out Joseph's garment, she showed (it) to him and said, "See what he wished to do to me; and I wrested this from his hands."[870] And thus the wicked woman[871] overcame Joseph, by speaking evil against him. And then the prince became angry with Joseph and sent soldiers and imprisoned Joseph in the king's dungeon. And this (is) Joseph's second servitude.

50/ But because God was with him, He did not let Joseph go from his hands,[872] but God entered with him into the prison of the dungeon. And God, having given grace to Joseph, the head of the prison gave authority over the prison into Joseph's hands, and Joseph was free and not in the prison's servitude.[873] And Joseph remained (there) for three years.[874] And then the king became angry with his two servants,[875] the cupbearer and the baker. And he sent them, put (them) in the prison <where> Joseph was and the king's servants were in the prison there.[876]

51/ And one day it came to pass in the night that the two slaves saw a dream and they were very sad. And Joseph came in to them and said, "Brothers, why are you sad today, and you are not happy like yesterday and the day before?" The servants said to Joseph, "We saw a dream last[877] night and we are afraid and we do not know what will happen to

---

867. Gen 39:12.
868. Literally: afraid in her mind.
869. This means, she took action to anticipate such a rebuke.
870. Gen 39:17–18.
871. Literally: woman of wickedness.
872. Or: power.
873. Compare Gen 39:21–23 where this is described.
874. Genesis has no explicit time reference, compare Gen 40:1.
875. Or: "slaves."
876. Gen 40:2–3.
877. Literally: "this."

us or what our dream brings[878] us." Joseph said to them, "Tell me your dream and I will tell you what is going to take place for you and going to happen."[879]

52/ One, who was the baker, said, "I saw this night a table full of bread and other victuals, which I was carrying on my head. And many birds of the heavens came and were eating the bread and the victuals."[880] Then Joseph said, "In three days from now they will bring you forth from this prison and hang (you) on a tree.[881] The birds of the heavens will come and eat your body." And after three days, that which Joseph said took place. Having brought the cook[882] forth, they hanged him on a tree and the dream about him was fulfilled.[883]

53/ Then the cupbearer told Joseph his dream[884] and said, "I too saw this night, that I held the golden goblet in my hand, full of wine. And I stood before the king." Then Joseph said to him, "Tomorrow they will bring you forth from this prison and lead (you) to the king. And they will fix you in your former work, that you were serving drinks before the king." [885]

54/ And in the same fashion that which Joseph related took place, which he had said concerning him. And Joseph said to the cupbearer, "Remember me before the king." And it happened that when they brought him forth, they led him to the king, and established him in his former work. And the cupbearer forgot Joseph's command and did not remember him until three years had passed.[886]

55/ And then the king, Pharaoh saw frightening dreams and he summoned him all his knowledgeable and his wise ones, so that they might relate the dream. And they all were unable to interpret the king's dream. And the king was very angry with them and was sad, for there was no one who (could) interpret his dream. Then the cupbearer recalled and remembered Joseph's word. And he went in before the king, and he said, "Oh, king, I, your servant, am worthy of death." When the king

---

878. Or: portends.
879. Gen 40:6–8. Note that in Genesis Joseph piously says "Do not interpretations belong to God?"
880. Compare Gen 40:16–19.
881. Literally: "the tree."
882. Word not found in the standard Armenian dictionaries.
883. I.e., "came true."
884. In Gen 40:16–19 the baker is the first to tell his dream to Joseph.
885. Compare Gen 40:9–13.
886. Two years according to Gen 41:1.

enquired about the matter, the cupbearer said, "When you were angry with us, O king, and you put us in prison, and we both saw a dream, and we were sad on account of the dream. And then Joseph came and interpreted our dream to us, and what he related to us, thus it happened and just as he said to us."

56/ Then the king commanded and said, "Go, call the man, for perhaps he can relate (interpret) our dreams." And when Joseph was called by the king, he went forth from the prison and came before the king. The king said to Joseph, "Can you bring forth (i.e., the meaning of) my dream which I saw?" And Joseph said, "Oh king, human capability is not of this sort, but it is a gift of God which causes men to know the dream and relate (it). Let the king say the dream and God (will) reveal its interpretation to us."

57/ And when the king discerned that Joseph was able to interpret the dream, the king said, "I saw a dream in one night, and behold, seven fat and plump heifers were coming forth and were grazing on the bank of the rivers. And after this, I saw and behold, another seven heifers lean and thin and dried up were coming forth and were eating the fat and plump heifers. And it[887] was not visible in their stomachs. And then I awoke. And I fell asleep again, and I saw seven clusters of ears of wheat having come forth to the river bank, heavy and full of corn, and fat grain was in the ears, beautiful in appearance. And afterwards I saw, behold seven other ears of corn were coming forth, lean and thin, in which there was no grain, and they swallowed the ears which were full of corn, just as the lean heifers ate the fat heifers and nothing was seen in their belly. This is my dream."[888]

58/ Then Joseph said, "God showed this great matter to you, O king, what is going to come to pass in the future time in this world. The seven first heifers, fat and plump—during seven years fullness is coming. First (there will be) seven fat and plump years and everything will be copious such as there has not been such fullness upon the earth. And the seven lean heifers—seven years famine is coming, during which there will be no bread upon the earth.

59/ "And now, <O> king, see how you will care for your country so that they do not perish from the famine. You shall choose for yourself a wise man whom you will appoint over this country, who will be able to

---

887. I.e., the ingestion of the fat heifers.
888. The incident of Pharaoh's dreams is related in Gen 41:1–24. There each dream is reported twice.

care, and he will collect corn with which he will feed this land of yours in the days of famine."[889]

60/ Then Pharaoh, king of the Egyptians, said to Joseph, "Verily, the spirit of God is in you, and no one of men can thus interpret the dream in such a way as you have interpreted and no one will be able to care for this land of mine that it should not perish in the famine. God has bestowed you alone upon us as a nurturer and a provider and a feeder of this land of mine." And the king said to Joseph, "You will be king and ruler over all our land, and I by the crown alone am above you. But you will be equal to my head, and no one will be opposed to you, for you shall have the power to kill and to keep alive whomever you wish. And I have commanded you to be lord over this land of Egypt."[890]

61/ And the king gave his ring of authority into Joseph's hands, by which he gave authority to him.[891] And Joseph received the authority and ruled over Egypt as the prophet David says, all the sins of tortures, which passed over Joseph, were made low to the fetters of his feet and his soul passed through fire with iron, until the word of God will come who swore to Abraham to multiply his seed in a foreign land, and the prison tested Joseph (with respect to) his patience.[892] He wanted to make Joseph's modesty known and God appears. And then he said to the king.

62/ And then the king sent and released him. And he permitted Joseph (to be) prince of the people, over all the treasures of the Egyptians, to counsel their princes like himself. And he will make their elders wise. All this was carried out upon Joseph.

63/ And Joseph received the kingdom, and he sat over Egypt. Then Joseph was 30 years old and Joseph ruled Egypt for 80 years. And the years began to come for fullness of all good things of the land. And Joseph built a very large granaries where he collected the corn of the whole land, for he took no other taxation of the land, not gold and not silver, but only corn. And he gathered that for seven years and set (it) in the granary.[893]

64/ And then after the seventh year of fullness, the famine for seven years began to come, and Joseph began to distribute to the land the corn

---

889. Compare with Gen 41:33–39.
890. Literally, "Egyptians." See Gen 41:39–41.
891. Gen 41:42.
892. The passage Ps 105(104):18–19 seems to be in the background of this statement.
893. Gen 41:48.

PART FOUR 217

of the seven years. And that gold or silver that previously he did not take in tax, now he received the gold and silver. And {erasure ca. 7 letters} and Joseph collected many treasures. And there was a great famine throughout all the land of the Egyptians and Joseph had gathered enough to feed the land with bread.[894]

65/ And the famine reached the land of the Canaanites, in which Joseph's father and brothers lived. And Jacob heard that there was food <in> Egypt and he sent his sons, Joseph's brothers.[895] And Joseph's brothers had not heard that Joseph was ruling in Egypt. For they had forgotten Joseph, since 27 years had passed since[896] the sale. And they did not know God's grace which he had given Joseph. And they did not expect his kingdom.[897]

66/ And Joseph's brothers took their beasts (of burden) and much silver and they came to Egypt to Joseph to buy bread. And Joseph was seated (in) authority over the kingdom. When his brothers came, they bowed down to him, to Joseph, and they did not recognize him for they also did not suspect that Joseph thus ruled.[898] And Joseph recognized his brothers and did not give recognition to his brothers, but he being as if unknown, he wept secretly in his heart and he recalled brotherly concern.[899] Then Joseph spoke with his brothers, "Where are you from and from which land? And you are not buyers of bread but spies, come to spy out the land." Then they fell at Joseph's feet, begging that his lordship not be angry against them, and they said, "We are your slaves; we were 12 brothers, sons of one father. A wild beast seized one in the field, and the other is small and remains in our father's house. And our father has become old, and we your servants are shepherds and not warriors."[900]

67/ Oh, the brothers' foolishness, that although they deceived their father concerning Joseph, (saying) that a wild beast had eaten him, here before (their) brother, he[901] wanted to lie, for there was no one who would revenge Joseph. Why did you sell him? And they lied and did not know that it was Joseph to whom they were lying and they said that

---

894. Gen 41:57.
895. Gen 42:1–3.
896. Literally: over.
897. I.e., that he was king.
898. Gen 42:6, 8.
899. I.e., did not exhibit brotherly love.
900. Gen 42:7.
901. "he," i.e., the brother who was speaking.

he was prey to a wild beast, he who was king over them. And thus there was the evil envy which caused (him) to discern what he did and what he said.⁹⁰²

68/ But you, regard the wisdom of Joseph and his not being vengeful.⁹⁰³ For he did not keep alive the memory of their wickedness and nor his brothers' doing evil deeds. But they sold him and he did not reproach them, who said that he was a wild beast's prey and he did not say to them, "No, behold I am Joseph whom you said to have fallen prey to a wild beast. I am now a king, how do you lie before me? Do you not wish to deceive me, just as you deceived my father and said to him that I fell prey to a wild beast."⁹⁰⁴ But since Joseph was adorned with every godly grace, he was mild and humble and not vengeful and did not remember evils, he did not say (this) and did not reproach them, but with wisdom showed them kindness.

69/ And he set a table before them and fed them. And he said to them, "Is it thus which you said, 'Our father has grown old and there is one small brother with (our) father,' but one of you I will not permit (to leave) and I will keep (him) with me until you bring your other brother to me and then I will send you away." And they, assenting, left Simeon their brother, as a guarantee for Joseph, who was king.⁹⁰⁵

70/ And he commanded that they (his servants) should load their beasts with bread and put the money in their baggage.⁹⁰⁶ And they went to their father Jacob, and they started to tell Jacob the hardships and their seizure, that Joseph held back (their) brother Simeon. Also the honor and the greatness which Joseph did them. Then (their) father asked concerning his son Simeon and they said, "The Egyptians have⁹⁰⁷ a lord of the corn who sells (it). He falsely accused us and said, 'You are spies.' And we said, 'We are not but your servants are sons to our father, and one small brother is with our father.' And he said to us, 'If you are not spies as you say, leave this one brother with me as a guarantee until you bring your small brother to me, and then I will believe you that you are neither spies nor treacherous.'⁹⁰⁸

---

902. One would expect "not to discern."
903. My translation is periphrastic. The Armenian word is literally "not-vengefulness."
904. Observe that here the narrative anomaly, that Joseph knew what the brothers said to their father, persists.
905. The biblical narrative is concentrated here, see Gen 42:13–20, 24.
906. See Gen 42:35. The order of the incidents is changed here.
907. Thus interpreting the dative case of "Egyptians."
908. Gen 42:30–34.

71/ "And now, our father, command your son Benjamin so that we may bring (him) and release Simeon and buy more bread and bring enough for us." And then Jacob their father was saddened and said, "Woe is me, my sons, for you have made me a child-murderer and destroyer of sons. You said that Joseph fell prey to a wild beast and that Simeon remained in Egypt, and also concerning Benjamin, you wish to take (him) away from me."[909] Then the oldest son stepped forward and Reuben said to his father, "Father, do not be angry with us. Joseph was seized by the wild beast, while Simeon was arrested by the king of the Egyptians, for he wished to kill us all. Now he had pity on us and only took a guarantee, Simeon, until we bring Benjamin, by which we will release Simeon. And then we will bring both of them out. And I, Reuben, am a guarantor of your sons, that you will see them and will rejoice."[910]

72/ And thus having persuaded Jacob their father, so that he permitted Benjamin,[911] they took Benjamin, their youngest brother and went down to Egypt to buy bread to eat as formerly. And when they went before Joseph, they bowed down to him. And then Joseph saw Benjamin and his distress was aroused, he went into the room and wept very bitterly. For he remembered (his) brotherly concern, for they (i.e., Joseph and Benjamin) alone were brothers sharing father and mother. And when Joseph wept, because his feelings and concern were aroused towards Benjamin, then Joseph took water and washed and commanded to prepare a feast.[912] And he placed it before his brother, and he seated (his) brothers according to the order of their birth. Likewise he also seated Benjamin close to him at the table.[913] And he made[914] Benjamin's part and portion greater than the other brothers'.[915] And when they had eaten, he measured out the corn for them and loaded their beasts of burden.

73/ Then secretly he put the golden goblet, with which Joseph would drink wine, into Benjamin's baggage, so that no one knew.[916] And when they

---

909. Gen 42:36.
910. Reuben's giving his two sons as a guarantee for Benjamin is omitted; see Gen 42:37, 43:8–9.
911. I.e., to go.
912. Literally" "a table," Gen 43:16. He weeps apart from his brothers according to Gen 43:30.
913. The special seating of Benjamin is an addition to the text of Genesis. See Gen 43:32.
914. Literally: "put, set."
915. Gen 43:34.
916. Gen 44:2.

set forth on their way, and Benjamin was with them, then he sent <his steward>⁹¹⁷ after (his) brothers and said, "They took my golden goblet by theft." Then the soldiers reached (them) and seized all the caravan and said, "Who took the king's golden goblet? Why did you do this mortal theft, because our king became angry? Now, see which of you did this hurt."⁹¹⁸

74/ When they heard this speech, they were all grieved and said, "We do not know this matter which you say." And then, having taken down the luggage from the beast of burden, they opened everyone's sackcloth bag. And they found that the cup was in Benjamin's sackcloth (bag).⁹¹⁹ When the brothers saw that, they turned against Benjamin and put him to shame with many words. And they said thus, "We know your naturally evil ways, yours and your brother's. For this reason he became prey to a wild beast, for proudly he wished to rule and God saw his vanity, and delivered him into the power of a wild beast, he who is not. And you too thus desired the theft and brought the king's anger upon us. And because of your evil conduct that you desired this golden goblet, now he wishes to bring death upon us all." Then they spoke again with the king's servant, "Now behold, let him who carried out this theft be a servant of the kingdom."

75/ Then they seized Benjamin and his brothers. And then Joseph began to rebuke them, "Did you do this in exchange for the love which I showed you and I also acted and nurtured you, that by theft you seized my golden goblet? And if I acted according your thought and your actions, then I would kill you all, for you are thus evil and envious in relation to this matter."⁹²⁰

76/ Then all the brothers falling down before him, wept bitterly and said, "Do not be angry with us, O king, for we are blameless in this matter, but only this small boy, he is guilty of this sin, for he is stupid. This is their nature, for his brother Joseph was such a one, for he wished to rule alone, and we sat and he told us a dream, a symbol of rule. Because of this God saw his mindlessness and gave him as food to a wild beast, and he did not achieve the kingship. In the same way this boy did not

---

917. The word շնուրական was not found in dictionaries. We surmise the meaning on the basis of Genesis. See Gen 44:4.
918. Gen 44:4–6.
919. Gen 44:12.
920. This expansion presents the brothers as unrepentant of selling Joseph.

ask us about the matter, he who stole this golden goblet, and now we your servants are blameless in the matter of this damage."
Then Joseph said, "If it is thus, as you have spoken, that you are blameless, I will put him who is guilty to me in slavery, and you go on your way."[921]

77/ Then Reuben, who was their oldest brother, went forward and bowed down to Joseph, the king, and said, "O king, kill me first and then take Benjamin as a slave to you.[922] For I, as guarantor, took him. If we do not bring him to our father, we will be unable to see our father's face, for we are all ashamed, for he is for (our) father in place of Joseph, whom the wild beast devoured. And if (our) father does not see him, he will die from grief. For he has become blind from weeping on behalf of Joseph and he has no other comforter (i.e., than Benjamin). And now, O king, you must be gentle and receive our father Jacob's blessings, because he is indeed a seer of God,[923] and the one whom he blesses will be blessed and the one whom he curses will be cursed.[924] And now, do not bring (our) father's curse upon us and upon you, but now hearken to our supplication, O king, and forgive this lad Benjamin, or kill us all for we cannot see him mournful, or his old age going down to Hades from pains and grief. For it is better that (our) father does not see (us) all, than (that he does not see) this lad." [925]

78/ When Reuben finished all of this and the other brothers were weeping before Joseph, then too (his) brotherly concern was aroused and then he was unable to bear the memory of (his) father who had aged because of love of Joseph. Joseph[926] made himself known to his brothers and tearfully he said, "O brothers, fools and slaves of evil envy and hatred, could you not recognize me, since I am that brother of yours whom you sold, and you deceived our father (saying) that it was the wild beast that seized me? I am Joseph whom you did not wish to reign over you. I am your brother whom you sold to a foreign land. I am the Joseph whom you wished to kill and you gave into captivity (and) sold.

---

921. Gen 44:17.
922. At this point in the biblical narrative, in Gen 44:16, it is Judah who speaks, not Reuben.
923. This is one of the meanings of "Israel," who is Jacob, in the *Onomastica Sacra*; compare also Gen 32:28.
924. Gen 47:10.
925. The text both shortens and expands the Reuben's words in comparison with those that Gen 44:18–34 attributes to Judah. The theme of Jacob's prophetic blessing is added. Joseph's speech is much expanded: see Gen 45:3–13.
926. The word ոլլ at the start of the sentence carries a contrastive meaning.

79/ "But <the God> of my fathers did not abandon me, and he did not smite me to the ground. You sold me into captivity, and wished to become great by my departure, but God made me king, as you see me. You did not wish that my dream of reign be fulfilled. But God did <not> do what was in your hearts, but carried out my dream and made me king, as you see now. And behold, my dream was fulfilled and you came (and) bowed down to me these several times."

80/ When they heard that they bowed down and were ashamed, and fear fell upon them and they forgot their lives, and darkness fell upon their eyes. And gloom seized all of them from the increase of (their) shame and fear. And they could not look up at all or see Joseph's face, but for shame they looked at the ground and did not know how to answer Joseph. For their faces changed color and words were exhausted in their minds, and their tongues were bound to their palate,[927] and their countenances were like those condemned to death, and behold, that day was like a king's condemnation to death.[928]

81/ And then the king having learned (of this) he summoned them and asked after the reason of their evil,[929] and they were unable to answer him. Thus Joseph's brothers became like dumb ones, they stood tongue-tied before[930] <the king> and they could not speak for they knew what evil things they had done. And they themselves judged themselves and said against themselves, "Woe! upon ourselves, for we were worthy of bitter death and condemnation."

82/ When Joseph saw concerning their shame and fear, that they condemned themselves, then Joseph showed himself most gracious unto them, so that they might receive their lives and not die from fear and from terror. Then Joseph spoke to them and said,

83/ "O my brothers and sons of my father Jacob, fear not, for I am not deceitful like you, for behold God has given you over this day and for the future into my hands.[931] And had I wished to kill you or to make you suffer any other difficulties, inasmuch as you know that you are worthy of punishment on account of your evil deeds which you did to me, I can also recompense you just as I wish, according to your deserts, so that you would not have been saved from my hands. But, you saw

---

927. Compare the turn of phrase with Ps 22:15(21:16) and 137(136):6.
928. The brothers' response is not mentioned in the Bible.
929. I.e., evil deeds.
930. Apparently a word has fallen out, likely թագաւորին "the king."
931. Or: power.

and you apprehended the former humane actions which I did to you, and now, fear not, for God has turned your evil into good. Then I also do not recall your evil and do not bear a grudge on account of your evil deeds which you did, but I have forgiven your sins which you did against me. And do not be afraid of me for I am not a fratricide but humane, and not brother hater but brother lover. And I do not repay evil with evil, but I shall recompense good to you for your evil, that you wished me to die of hunger in the pit and I fed you from this famine.

84/ "You sold me for 30 coins; I returned your silver to you, the price of the corn. You said to my father that I fell prey to a wild beast; I dispensed to you bread as food. You were to me as beasts; and I was gentle to you. And since the God of my fathers carried out his oath to them, and did not make me unobserved, on account of that I also did not recall your evil, but repaid you good for evil, for God commanded thus, not to recompense evil with evil."[932]

85/ And this the blessed Joseph did, according to Paul's command, which is, "If your enemy is hungry—give him bread, or thirsty—give him water. Doing this you will see coals of fire on his head. Be not vanquished by evil, but vanquish evil with good.[933] Joseph did all this before the commands were issued,[934] and when Joseph had spoken all this and the like, the holy Joseph spoke to his brothers and rebuked them and then he summoned forward one of his brothers and kissed him tearfully and embraced (him) and wept over them pityingly and with brotherly love.[935]

86/ Then they, when they saw Joseph's tenderness, then falling on their faces they prostrated themselves weeping and said, "Lord, our brother and king, be not eternally wrath with us, and bear not a grudge forever, and recall not our evil before you, and do not recompense that which we did, because God saw your forbearing[936] and gave you royal honor. Now we beseech you, since God has revealed the destruction which we underwent and wished to destroy you.

87/ But God elevated you, now make us happy, O our brother, king and make our and your aged father glad, lest being submerged by hopelessness, he perishes on your account and on account of our delaying."

---

932. A phrase common in the New Testament Epistles: see Rom 12:17, 1 Thess 5:15, 1 Pet 3:9.
933. Rom 12:20–21.
934. Here the author handles the anachronism.
935. See Gen 45:15.
936. Or: patience.

And when Joseph's brothers said this, they all turned to him and tearfully embraced and kissed him. And crying out, they wept together, until all the city heard the sound of the weeping and came to see the (source of the) noise, and when they learned that they were Joseph's brothers, they rejoiced greatly.

88/ And the word reached the king; it was made known to the king that Joseph's brothers had come. The king sent and summoned Joseph and said, "What is this thing that I hear, that you brother<s> are here and have come?" And Joseph said, "Yea, king, they have come from a distant land." And the king said, "Why did you leave them there? Send and summon them, for all this land is before you, and settle them wherever it pleases you."[937]

89/ And Joseph returned to his brothers and made them happy. Joyously he set a feast before them, and offered them a goblet and filled their beast of burden with corn. And he sent them to his father and said, "This good news to you (is) from Joseph, and moreover through my being king, (there is) a redoubled joy to you. And now, my father, rise up and come to me your son and you will see me, your beloved son whom you lost, who (fell) prey to the wild animals according to my brothers' mouth, whom my brothers sold to a foreign land. But the God of your fathers, of Abraham and of Isaac, through their prayers redeemed me from slavery and made (me) a king. And now, my beloved father, do not delay your coming, and (do not) tarry, but come quickly, for this land is under my authority, wherever it will seem good to you, there shall you dwell.

90/ "Moreover, you will be saved from before this famine, you and your son<s>, because still for many days famine will come upon the land." And he sent many wagons so that they might bring (his) father Jacob with all his household.[938]

91/ And then Jacob went down to Egypt with all his household, 75 souls.[939] And when Jacob saw Joseph he rejoiced and wept for joy. And Jacob's eyes were opened, he who had become blind from weeping on Joseph's account. And all rejoiced at seeing one another.[940]

92/ And Jacob, weeping for joy, praised concerning the Lord his God[941]

---

937. Gen 45:16-20.
938. The gifts that Joseph gave them are omitted, compare Gen 45:22-23.
939. The number is given as sixty-six in Gen 46:26; in Exod 1:5 it is seventy.
940. Gen 46:29. The Armenian text adds the theme of blindness at this point.
941. Literally: "concerning the Lord etc."

and said, "Blessed is the Lord God of my fathers Abraham and Isaac, who did not abandon me and did not smite me to the ground. For he has granted me the grace to see my lost son." And thus Jacob rejoiced with redoubled joy. For, just as he was sad over the death of his son and wept inconsolably, first that they said that Joseph was dead, and secondly that he was considered consumed by wild animals, then Jacob rejoiced doubly on seeing (his) son, that he was alive and not dead.

93/ Third, that he is king of all the Egyptians, and he became nurturer of all (his) brothers. And Joseph's second dream was fulfilled, that one that the sun and moon bowed down to him with the eleven stars, that is (his) father and mother and his eleven brothers.[942]

94/ And Joseph was married and he had taken Asenath the daughter of prince Potiphar, this is that Potiphar who previously bought Joseph into slavery. And Joseph begot two sons, Ephraim and Manasseh.[943]

95/ And Jacob's eyes were poor and he summoned his sons to himself and blessed them one by one. He began from the first and reached Judah, the fourth. And he said to Judah, "Your brothers will bless you and your hand (shall be) upon your enemies' backs by a shoot,[944] son. And he who blesses you will be blessed and he who curses (you) will be cursed." and Jacob blessed Judah his son with many other blessing(s).[945] And this prophecy came to be fulfilled concerning our Saviour, know vacat of us, Jesus Christ, because he is (his) descendant. And Christ was to come from the tribe of Judah and was to be born according the body. And Jacob gave the kingdom to Judah, as the blessing says, "Let rule not cease from Judah until the man whose kingdom it is,"[946] who is the Savior himself, Christ. And he is the hope of the gentiles.[947] And when he reached Joseph he praised him and said, "Joseph worthy of blessings. And you will be blessed by the Lord God, son, because you

---

942. All this and the preceding section are not part of the biblical narrative. Moreover the genealogy of Jacob's descendants in Gen 46:8–26 is omitted by the Armenian text.

943. Compare Gen 41:45, 50, 46:20.

944. The first part of the sentence is taken from Gen 49:8, "Judah, your brothers shall praise you; your hand shall be on the neck of your enemies." In Arm Gen 49:9 we read ի շառաւիղէ "from, by a shoot," translating the similar Greek ἐκ βλαστοῦ. The Hebrew is מטרף, translated in NRSV "from the prey." The Greek translator reads of טרף as טָרָף which means "fresh (twig)" Gen 8.11, "fresh shoot" Ezek 17.9. The word only occurs in these two places in the Hebrew Bible. So it appears that the LXX translator has a distinctive rendering of a homograph (Claude Cox).

945. The blessing of Judah in Gen 49:8–12 is quite elaborate. Here part of it is interpreted as explicitly Christian. It is commonly taken as a prophecy of Christ.

946. Gen 49:10.

947. Cf. Rom 15:12.

are a respite for me your father and for your brothers and feeder of our selves. And you are receiver of your father and nurturer of your brothers, and may you be blessed by the Lord and your offspring will achieve kingdom and you will have a portion in the place where they cut down the Shechemite, which the prophet David also says and witnesses before Jacob's face, 'I will rejoice, I will be high, I will divide Shechem and I will apportion the valley for dwellings.'"[948]

96/ "Mine is Gilead[949] and mine (is) Manasseh. Ephraim is strengthener of my head; this is (the) kingship of Judah, and Judah is my king, Moab the font of my hope."[950] And Joseph brought his sons near to his father Jacob, so that he might bless them, Ephraim and Manasseh. And because Jacob's eyes were weak,[951] Joseph brought the firstborn near, on Jacob's left, and the younger on Jacob's right. And see God's wonder! for Jacob held out his hands like a cross and placed (them) upon the sons of Joseph and he blessed them.[952] And then he rested with (his) fathers, as Paul says, "By faith, Jacob when he was dying blessed each of the sons of Joseph."[953] And he bowed down to the end of his staff[954] and Joseph commanded the embalmers to wind[955] his father Israel.[956] <And Joseph took forth his father> Jacob from the land of the Egyptians and sent (him) to the land of Canaan. And they buried him in the grave of his fathers Abraham and Isaac. And they bewailed him for 30 days.[957]

97/ Then Joseph remained there as king of Egypt for many years, for eighty years. And when he was dying, he summoned his brothers and sons. He blessed them and said, "My brothers and sons, you will be blessed by the God of my fathers, of Abraham, of Isaac, of Jacob. Nonetheless see, my brothers and sons, when the Lord God of my fathers will visit you and benefit you and bring you forth from this land and lead you

---

948. Ps 60:6(59:8), 108:7(107:8). This section does not reflect the language of the blessings of Joseph in Gen 48:15–16 and 49:22–26.
949. See Num 26:29. Gilead is a descendant of Manasseh.
950. This reference is obscure, unless it is to Ruth the Moabite, the ancestor of Jesus's genealogy.
951. Perhaps inferred from Gen 48:2 and, of course, 48:10.
952. Gen 48:13–14.
953. Heb 11:20.
954. Heb 11:21.
955. I.e., "in winding cloths."
956. Gen 50:2.
957. Gen 50:3 talks of forty days' embalming followed by thirty days' mourning. On Jacob's burial in Canaan, see Gen 50:5–10, 12–13.

to the land that he promised us as an inheritance and a dwelling: now be careful when you go forth from this land, also take forth my bones with you."[958] And Joseph remained thus, with good rule and virtue for many years. He died peacefully and was buried in Egypt. And he left us an example of the good, with tenderness and modesty, with humility and forbearing, not bearing grudges and patient. Above all that he was filled and strengthened by faith and hope and love of God. And these goodnesses were gathered to Joseph and he achieved kingship, and he was not proud in his mind and he did not seek glory and did not bear a grudge for (his) brothers' evil. And he did not pay back evil with evil, but in all he resembled God's love of man, as the Lord says in the Gospel, "Be merciful, and be perfect as your heavenly Father is merciful and perfect."[959]

98/ And now, brothers, fathers, and my beloved sons, hearken to this story of Joseph of the virtuous and modest, of a gentle and pious one, and take his customs into yourselves and receive spiritual love, virtue, and ungrudgingness. For through this sort of goodness, man becomes pleasing to God, and God will elevate him, for he is gentle to the modest. And he who is merciful in his heart, receives God's blessing.

99/ As is says in the Gospel, "Blessed is the merciful, for they will find mercy,"[960] and as for him who is lover of his brother, this is God's commandment, "You shall love your fellow as your self."[961] And he who is modest received the blessing and sees God, as it says, "Blessed are those who are pure in heart, for they will see God."[962] And he will be longsuffering above all this.

100/ When he falls into trials—for that is perfect virtue that he is forbearing in time of difficulty and that the Lord made that one worthy of life, by saying, "He who is completely forbearing will live forever."[963] That very thing Joseph did and he was forbearing, on account of which God elevated (him) and caused him to achieve kingship. Thus God does to every man who is forbearing.

101/ A man who is patient, behold God will save him from trial and frees him from future punishment, as the Lord says in the Gospel, "When

---

958. Joseph gives this command in Gen 50:25.
959. Luke 6:36.
960. Matt 5:7.
961. Matt 19:19, Mark 12:31, etc.
962. Matt 5:8.
963. Matt 10:22, 24:13, Mark 13:13.

102/ they will persecute you, oppress you and do you evil, rejoice and be happy for your reward in heaven is great."⁹⁶⁴

102/ Again it says that through your forbearing you will receive your souls. Behold, you see Joseph's forbearing, for the name "Joseph" translates "forbearing."⁹⁶⁵ For he was first, gentle and obedient to his father. For that reason (his) father loved him more than (his) other sons. Thus we are gentle to one another; we are obedient to God who is the father of all, and we carry out God's will without restraint. And we are obedient to our parents, as is written in the Lord's law, "Honor your father and mother."⁹⁶⁶ And he who maligns his father or his mother, will surely die. And when God sees this our obedience, then he loves us more than (our) other brothers and than all the peoples upon this earth. And just as Joseph had a flowery robe, that is a garment made of shining stars, in that way the Lord garbed us with a garment of glory and a robe of joy. And the true faith of Christianity, which shines, not like the stars but like the sun during this life and more in the future one.

103/ And just as Joseph's brothers were wicked to him, and he (was) their benefactor and nourisher, because⁹⁶⁷ all nations hate us on account of this firm faith of ours, and they all act evilly to us and they take, seize and eat our labors and sweat and all good things and threaten us with death. In that fashion also Joseph's brothers, were far from (their) father and in the field shepherding the sheep. Thus also the body-loving others are distant from the commandment and from the Father of this world, and in the fields of the dumb animals and they eat with a beastly nature. This is those who nourished (their) bodies with luxury, by eating and drinking, and by a debauched way of life, just like Joseph's brothers.

104/ When Joseph brought food to them in the field; then they saw him and considered (him) murderously. In the same fashion they, having seized our food for which we labored, eat it and plan our death, but it is our due desert. O blessed brothers, bringing to us after the fashion of Joseph, to take to themselves every difficulty which came upon us, either our brothers' or strangers'. For nothing else elevated Joseph but forbearing and humility, and that he did not repay evil with evil. In the

---

964. Matt 5:11–12.
965. This is not the meaning of the Hebrew, and a name midrash is given in Gen 30:4. This meaning also has no place in published Armenian onomastic texts.
966. Exod 20:12, Deut 5:16.
967. The exact import of պալղը is unclear here.

same way, we are obliged to be forbearing and to pass our life piously in this world, and not allow ourselves to be deceived in this life, and to fall from God's face.

105/ But were are obliged to accept all difficulties, and only not to become distant from God's commandments and we are obliged to alienate ourselves from parents and from brothers and from the world; to go in this world into captivity and servitude to evil men. Let us not go out of the servitude to God, from[968] the world. Let us put away the world[969] and let us not be separated from the kingdom of heaven, let us enter prison and shackles for the sake of the love of Christ our God and of our faith which is in Christ Jesus, our Lord, so that by this small punishment we may be redeemed for eternity.

106/ By which may Christ God save and you from every trial and from demonic disturbance. Let him completely guard our souls and bodies until the completion of our times. And to him, glory and honor, praise, and prostration, the indivisible holy Trinity. Now and always and forever. Amen.

4.8. The Israelites in Egypt

This narrative text, found in M6340, a *čaṛĕntir* (*A Collection of Homilies*) copied in the seventeenth century[970] on fols. 36r–50r carries the story of the Israelites from Joseph's death to Moses's. The story follows and expands upon the biblical text from the beginning of Exodus up to the giving of the Law. Following that point, it is more episodic in its coverage, dealing with Israel's murmuring and complaints about Moses and against God, the sin of the Golden Calf (though in this text it is not golden), Korah, Baal Peor, and the like. It concludes with a brief summary concerning the Ark and Moses' death.

The text does not have any particular ideological or theological tendency that can be discerned. As a Christian document, it introduces various touches, such as Moses making the sign of the Cross at the splitting of the Red Sea. Moreover, it sometimes draws on New Testament formulations of Old Testament traditions, such as the urn of manna being golden (see Heb 9:4) or Moses's angelic burial. The text is followed by some pages of homiletic teaching. After that, the story of Jonah ensues.

---

968. Or: through.
969. The initial յ is not translated. The addition/omission of this prefix is common.
970. See Eganyan et al. 1970, 2:298–99.

Text

1/ / fol. 36r / ԻՍԿ ՅԵՏ ....[.....⁹⁷¹ Յովս]եփայ բազմացան ազգն Իսրայէլացոց:

2/ Եւ յարեաւ այլ թագաւոր. եւ ոչ սիրեաց զազգն Իսրայէլի. եւ ոչ ընդունէր մինչեւ Կ տարի: Եւ յետ նորա փոխեցաւ այլ թագաւոր. այլ չարագոյն նեղեր զնոսա ՅԵ տարի. Եւ փոխեցաւ այլ թագաւոր այլ աւելի նեղեր զնոսա. մինչեւ ԿԲ տարի: Եւ փոխեցաւ այլ թագաւոր չար քան զառաջինն. այլ աւելի տանջէր զնոսա ԿԵ տարի:

3/ Փոխեցաւ այլ թագաւոր տանջէր զնոսա քան զառաջինն. ՕԲ տարի:
Դարձեալ փոխեցաւ այլ չարագոյն փարաւոն աւելի չարութեամբ քան զամենայն: Հրամայեաց / fol. 36r / իսրայէլացոցն Գ քաղաք շինել վասն փարաւոնի. ադիւս թրծեալ եւ քարբից այրեալ:

4/ Յաւուր միում ելաւ⁹⁷² փարաւոն ժողովեաց զամենայն ազգն Իսրայէլի. եւ տեսաւ զբազմութիւն նոցա. զարմացաւ եւ ասաց իշխանացն:
Քանզի յոյժ բազմացան ազգն Իսրայէլի. զուգէ եւ այլ բազմասցին պատերազմեցեն ընդ մեզ. եւ չարդեն զազգն մեր. եւ խլեցեն զքաղաքս ի ձեռաց մերոց. հնարս իմացեալ եմ որ այլ ոչ թողում զնոսա աճել: Եւ ասացին իշխանքն բարեոք հրամայես արքայ:

5/ Եւ կոչեաց փարաւոն զամենայն մանկաբարձսն՝ եւ ասաց խեղդել զամենայն արու մանուկ նոցա զաղտն ի ծնաւդացս յորժամ նոր ծնցի մանուկն: Իսկ մանկաբարձքն երկեան Աստուծոյ եւ ոչ արարին այնպէս: Եւ կոչեաց զնոսա թագաւորն եւ ասաց. ընդէր ոչ խեղդէք զմանկունս իսրայէլացոցն:

6/ Եւ նոքա ասացին թէ՝ իսրայէլացիքն ոչ են իբրեւ զմեր ազգն:⁹⁷³ զի արք նոցա ի ժամ ծնընդեանն գան եւ ի վերայ կանգնեն. եւ ոչ թողուն փասել զմանկունս նոցա. վասն այն ոչ կարեմք խեղդել: Իսկ փարաւոն հրամայեաց յայտնի խլել զմանկունս նոցա եւ ի գետն խեղդել: Մինչ ի ԻԴ տարի այսպէս արարին:

7/ Ապա՝ ծնաւ Մովսէս կայտառ եւ յոյժ գեղեցիկ. / fol. 37r / Մինչեւ Գ ամիս ծածուկ պահեցին: Իբրեւ տեսին ծնաւղքն նորա որ այլ ոչ կարեն պահել. եղին ի մէջ սնդուկի, կարեցին եւ տուին քույրն

---

971. The colored words of the title are not visible on the photograph.
972. Postclassical form.
973. One word erased.

Մովսեսի. եւ նա տարեալ արկ ի ծովն. եւ ինքն հեռաստանէ հայէր տեսանել թէ զինչ լինիցի մանուկն:

8/ Եւ նոյնժամայն դու<ս>տրն փարաւոնի եկն ի ծովափն խաղալ ընդ կանանց եւ աղջկանց: Եւ վարձեալ ձնկորս⁹⁷⁴ մի որ ինչ որսացէ իւրն լինիցի: Եւ ի հորսելն⁹⁷⁵ նորա. ալիք ծովուն հանին զսնդուկն ի յեզր ծովուն:

9/ Եւ բացեալ տեսին մանուկն ի նմա կայտառ եւ գեղեցիկ: Ուրախացաւ դու<ս>տրն փարաւոնի եւ ասաց. չու<լ>նիմ⁹⁷⁶ որդի զմանուկս սնուցանեմ եւ ինձ որդեգիր առնեմ զի որդի լիցի ինձ:

10/ Եւտես անդ զքոյրն Մովսեսի որ հեռաստանէ հայէր. գոչեաց առ ինքն եւ ասէ: Գնա տես թէ ով կա ծծմայր կին գայ զի վարձ տամ նմա սնուցանէ զմանուկս վասն իմ:⁹⁷⁷ Իսկ նա՝ գնացեալ գոչեաց զմայրն Մովսեսի. եկեալ առ դուստրն փարաւոնի եւ ասաց. տուր ինձ վարձ սնուցանեմ զմանուկդ: Ասէ դուստրն փարաւոնի. լօ պահեայ. ամիսն Բ կարմիր վարձ տամ քեզ: Եւ մայրն տարեալ սնուց զօղէն.⁹⁷⁸ մինչեւ Գ տարի⁹⁷⁹ եւ կտրեալ ի ստենէ զՄովսէս. եւ ետ ի դուստրն փարաւոնի:

11/ Եւ հաձր թռվեցաւ մանուկն ի աշ/ fol. 37v /քն փարաւոնի: Առեալ ի գիրկն զի համբուրեցէ: Իսկ Մովսէս Բ ձեռաւքն ձանկեաց գերսեսն եւ զմաւրուսն փարաւոնի: Եւ փարաւն կամէր սպանանել զմանուկն: Իսկ իշխանքն եւ մեծամեծքն բարեխաւս կացին եւ ասցին. անզիտութեամբ արար:

12/ Իսկ թագաւորն փորձեաց. եւ ետ բերել մէկ սկտեղք ոսկի մէկ սկտեղք⁹⁸⁰ կրակ եւ ետ առաջի Մովսէսի: Իսկ Մովսէս փութացեալ էառ զկրակն արկ ի բերանն այրեաց զմատունքն եւ զլեզուն. վասն այն թլալեզու էր Մովսէս:

Իբրեւ ի լաց ընկաւ Մովսէս եւ նուաղեցաւ. ապա հաւատաց փայրաւն որ անմեղութեամբ արար զայն: Ողորմեցաւ եւ ոչ սպանեց զՄովսէս:

Իբրեւ զարգացաւ Մովսէս շրջէր հանապազ ընդ իսրայէլացոց ազգին եւ սիրէր զնոսա:

---

974. One short word erased following.
975. This should be յորսելն. The alternation of h/յ is not listed in Stone and Hillel 2012, "Index."
976. Emended.
977. Two words erased; underwriting is a dittography of զի վարձ.
978. Note the strange orthography.
979. տարի is a correction p.m. above the line.
980. One word, արձաք erased.

13/ Ի միում աւուր եւեւ եզիպտացի մի հարկաներ զիսրայէլացի։ Իսկ Մովսէս սպան զեգիպտացին. եւ թաղեալ ի մէջ աւազոյ եւ կորոյս գտեղին եւ գնաց։ Իսկ աւուր միում գնաց ի մէջ իսրայէլացոցն եւ շրջէր։ Եւ եւեւ Բ մարդ իսրայէլացի կռուէին ընդ իրար։ Ասէ Մովսէս ընդեր կովիք եղբարք։ Իսկ մինն ասաց ո՞ վ կացոյց զքեզ դատաւոր եւ իշխան ի վերայ մեր. միթէ կամիս սպանանել զիս. որպէս սպանեցեր յերեկ զիսրայէլացին։

14/ Իբրեւ եւեւ Մովսէս որ յայտ/fol.38r/նի եղեւ մարդասպանութիւն իւր. փախեաւ յե{տ}իպտոսէ՝ [981] եւ հեռացաւ. եւ գնացեալ ի տեղ մի. եւ հանդիպեցաւ ի ջրհոր մի. եւ հովիւքն ջուր հանէին ջրել գոչխարան։ Երկու աղջիկ անտ ջուր հան{է}էլ [982] կամէին վասն անասոնց իւրեանց. եւ հովիւքն ջուր ոչ տային նոցա։

15/ Իսկ Մովսէս ջուր խլեաց ի հուուացն [983] եւ արբուց ոչխարաց աղջկանցն։ Եւ նոքա գնացեալ տունն իւրեանց պատմեցին հաւրն թէ այր մի օտարական ջրեաց գոչխարան մեր. եւ զանասունսն մեր։

16/ Ասէ հայրն, գնացէք եւ բերէք զայրն զի հաց կերիցէ։ Մեծարեցին գՄովսէս եւ սեղան եդին։ Երբ լիացաւ եհարց գնա Յոթորը՝ թէ ով ունիս։ Ասէ Մովսէս ոչ որ ունիմ. ոչ ազգ եւ ոչ ընդանի։ Ասէ Յոթորը. երբ ոչ որ չունիս. իմ Բ ոչ է դուստր ունիմ բագում ինչք եւ ոչխարք. առ ի դստերաց իմոց զորն որ կամիս. ես քեզ հայր դու իմ որդի։

17/ Հաւանեցաւ գՄովսէս. եւ էառ զմեծ դուստրն եւ արար իւրն կին։ Եւ ծնաւ Բ որդիս։ Եւ յաւուր միում մինչ արածէր գոչխարան ի լերինն. եւ յանկարձակի հուր վառեցաւ ի մէջ մորենոյ՝ վառէր եւ բոցն ելանէր երկնական [984] եւ ոչ այրէր մորենին։

18/ Իբրեւ կամեցաւ ի մաւտ երթալ տեսանել թէ զինչ իցէ, ձայն եղեւ ի հրոյն որ ասէր. Մովսէս Մովսէս՝ հանէ / fol. 38v / գկօշիկտ. զի տեղիտ որում դու կաս սուրբ է։ Ասէ Մովսէս դու ո՞ ես Տէր [985]։ Ասէ Տէր. ես եմ Տէր Աստուած հարց քոց. Աստուած Աբրահամու. Աստուած [986] Սահակայ եւ Աստուած Յակոբայ։ Այցելով այց արարի ժողովրդոյդ իմոյ. եւ կամիմ փրկել գԻսրայէլ ի ձեռաց նեղչաց իւրեանց։

---
981. Corrupt, ւո for զ.
982. Correction, partial.
983. Note the odd spelling.
984. Represented by the ideogram for "heaven" followed by ն.
985. Erasure follows.
986. Erasure follows.

19/ Եւ դու գնացեալ ասասցես առաջի փարօնի. զի այսպէս ասէ Տէր Աստուած հարցն մերոց. Աստուած Աբրահամու, Աստուած Յակոբայ, եւ Աստուած Սահակա: Մի՛ նեղացուցաներ զժողովուրդս իմ. եւ եթէ ոչ լուիցէ քեզ պատուհասիւ խրատեմ զնա:
20/ Ասէ Մովսէս: Տէր զի՞ ես թլալէզու եմ որպէս կարեմ խաւսել առաջի նորա: Ասէ Տէր. զի ես տամ քեզ լէզու եւ իմաստութիւն խաւսել առաջի փարաւոնի: Առ՛ ընդ քեզ Ահարոն. նայ եղիցի քեզ բերան. եւ խաւսեցէ վասն քոյ:
Ասէ Մովսէս. եւ թէ ասիցէ փարաւոն թէ զի՞նչ նշան ունիս Աստուծոյ քումէ. զինչ ասացից: Ասէ Տէր. զինչ կա ի ձեռինդ: Ասէ Մովսէս գաւազան: Ասէ Տէր. արկ զգաւազանդ: Իբրեւ արկ Մովսէս զգաւազանն եւ եղեւ վիշապ: Եւ ասէ Տէր ցՄովսէս. հար ձեռաւրդ բունէ[987] զմրտանէն: Իբրեւ բունեց Մովսէս զվիշն վիշապին եւ եղեւ գաւազան:
Դարձեալ ասէ Տէր. զի՞նչ տեսանես առաջի քոյ: Եւ ասէ Մովսէս ջուր տեսանեմ: Ասէ Տէր առ կից մի: Եւ իբրեւ խառ եղեւ արիւն: Եւ ասաց Տէր. /fol. 39r/ արկանել ջուրն գետեղին: Եւ իբրեւ արկ ջուրն ի տեղին. դարձեալ եղեւ ջուր:
21/ Դարձեալ ասէ Տէր ցՄովսէսի արկ զձեռն քո ի ծոց քո եւ հան: Իբրեւ Մովսէս արկ զձեռն ի ծոց իւր եւ եհան եւ տեսաւ բորոտեալ եւ սպիտակեալ: Դարձեալ ասէ Տէր ցՄովսէսի. արկ զձեռն քո ի ծոց քո եւ հան. Եւ իբրեւ Մովսէս նոյնպէս արար. դարձեալ ձեռն եղեւ մարմազոյն իբրեւ զառաջինն:
22/ Ասէ Տէր. զայդ Գ նշանդ արա՛ առաջի փարաւունի. թէ ոչ լուիցէ քեզ ապայ պատուհասիւ խրատեմ զնայ: Եւ գնաց Մովսէս ի մէջ ժողովրդեանն Իսրայէլի. եւ աւետիս ետ նոցա վասն փրկութեանն նոցա:
23/ Եւ Ահարոն առեալ ընդ իւր գնացին առ փարաւոն. եւ խաւսեցան առաջի նորա: Եւ արար Գ սքանչէլիս: Իսկ փարօն ասաց. ոչ ճանաչեմ զԱստուած քոյ եւ ոչ արձակեմ զԻսրայէլ: Եւ ասաց Մովսէս. թէ ոչ արձակես զԻսրայէլ. բազում փասա եւ պատուհաստեսանեւապագատուտեսԻբրեւելինՄ<ն>վսէս[988] եւ Ահարոն ըսկիսբն արար Աստուած պատուհասիւ խրատել փարաւոն եւ Եգիպտոս: Առաջին պատուհասն շանաձանձ

---

987. Omitted from text and written in left-hand margin p.m.
988. Omitted ւ.

ետ նոցա որ ոչ կարէին բանալ զաչս եւ զերեսս իւրեանց. խոցոտէին եւ ուռչէին:

24/ Երկրորդ պատուհասն. գործիւ ապականեաց գտունս եւ զքնակութիւնս նոցա: Երրորդ պատուհասն ետ ժանկոյ զվաստակս նոցա: Չորրորդ. մճացեալ վաստակն / fol. 39v / մարախոյ եւ խառնիչ ետ: Հինգերորդ պատուհասն. եհար կարկտիւ զայգիս եւ զքզենիս նոցա հրոյ ետ: Վեցերորդ պատուհասն. եղեմամբ չորացոյց զմսացեալ տունկս նոցա: Եօթներորդ՝ պատուհասն. դարձոյց զանձրեւս նոցա արիւն. զչուրս եւ զզետս նոցա արիւն փոխեցաւ. որ ոչ կարէին ըմպել: Չի մի գետ խմէին իսրայէլացիքն եւ եգիպտացիքն: իսրայէլացիքն խմէին չուր էր. եւ եգիպտացիքն խմէին արիւն դառնայր: Պատուհասն ամէն ի մէջ նոցա երեւէր. եւ պատուհաս մի ոչ մերձենային ազգն Իսրայէլի:

25/ Իբրեւ ոչ դարձաւ ի չարութենէն փարաւոն. դարձեալ երեւեցաւ Տէր Մովսէսի եւ ասաց. երթ խրատեա զժողովուրդ քո զի այս չաքաթս պադարճ կերիցեն խմորոյն հաց մի կերիցեն: Գառնազէն արասցեն. եւ զարիւն զատին թացցեն զչորս կողմ սեմոց դրանցն խաչանման:

26/ Չի այսմ գիչերի առաքեմ զսատակիչ հրեչտակ իմ ի մէջ յԵգիպտոսի. զի որ սեմոց դրանցն նչան տեսանէ. անտ ոչ մերձենայ սատակիչ հրեչտակն: Եւ այնպէս սատկեցաւ մահն ի վերայ Եգիպտոսի՝ մինչ ի մէում գիչեր ի միաւրական տղայէն մինչեւ է տարեկանն այլ մին կենդանի չէ մնաց. ոչ արու եւ ոչ էգ:

27/ Չի որպէս հրամայէ[աց] Տէր Մովսէսի զպադարծն եւ զզառնազենն. այնպէս արար Մովսէս: Եւ մարդ մի ոչ / fol. 40r / պակասեաց իսրայէլացոց ազգին: Եւ ահ մեծ անկաւ ի վերայ փարաւոնի եւ եգիպտացոցն: Այս եղեւ ութ<երորդ> պատուհասն:

28/ Դարձեալ երեւեցաւ Տէր Մովսէսի եւ ասաց. գնա առ փարաւոն եւ ասա. ազատեա զժողովուրդ իմ. մինչեւ Գ աւր տանն կատարեն զատիկ արասցեն. դարձեալ եկեցեն եւ ծառայեցեն քեզ: Եւ եթէ ոչ լուիցես. դարձեալ պատուհաս գա ի վերա ձեզ. եւ նա թողու զձեզ: Չի ամենայն մարդ ի տիրոչէն ածեն զարդարանքն: Եւ կանայքն ի տիկնաց իւրեանց խնդրեսցեն զարդարանք. քանզի այլ ոչ տեսանէք զնոսա:

29/ Եւ եկեալ Մովսէս խաւսեցաւ ընդ փարաւոնի եւ ասաց: Այսպէս ասէ Տէր Աստուած հարցն մերոց: Արձակեա զժողովուրդ իմ

PART FOUR 235

մինչեւ Գ աւր: Քանզի ահ պատեալ էր զնոսա եւ արձակեաց զժողովուրդն. համարով եւ գրով ետ ի ձեռս նորա եւ ասաց: Յետ Գ աւուրն բերել զնոսա եւ տալ ի ձեռն փարօնի. զի էին թուով ՋՀՀԲ.[989]

30/ Իբրեւ էլ Մովսէս ի քաղաքէն. եւ ամենայն ժողովուրդն ընդ իւր. եւ գնացին ի եզր Կարմիր ծովուն: Եւ անդէն աղիհեին զԱստուած եւ ուրախանային: Եւ Մովսէս քարոզէր ի մէջ նոցա եւ ասէր: Այլ ո՛չ մտանէք յԵգիպտոս եւ ոչ ծառայէք փարաւոնի: Իսկ փարաւոն[990] ոմն մի լրտես ծածուկ առաքեալ էր ընդ նոսա. զի գիտասցէ թէ՝ զի՞նչ կամին առնել Մովսէս եւ ժողովուրդն Իսրայէլի:

31/ Իբրեւ լուաւ զայս խալ<ս>քս[991] ի բերանոյն Մովսէսի թէ այլ ոչ / fol. 40v / ծառայէք փարաւոնի: Փութով գնացեալ պատմեաց փարաւոնի: Եւ բարկացեալ փարաւոն հրամայեաց փութով ժողովեաց զամենայն հեծելն. եւ գնաց ի վերայ ժողովրդեանն Իսրայէլի եւ ասաց իւր հեծելին. կոտորեցէք զարուսն.[992] եւ գերեցէք զկանայսն եւ զաղջկունս նոցա:

32/ Իբրեւ մօտահաս եղեն հեծելն. հայեցաւ ի հեռաստանէ Մովսէս. եւ տեսաւ[993] զի զային հեծելն. հրամայեաց Մովսէս եւ ամենայն ժողովուրդեանն աղաչել զԱստուած առնուլ զինչս իւրեանց մտանել ի ծով: Եւ առեալ ինքն զմարմինն Ովսեփայ ի շալակն. առեալ զզաւազանն ի ձեռն խաչակնքեաց ի վերայ ծովուն ասելով:

33/ Տէր Ահիայ[994] Աշրահիայ Աղովսիայ Տէր: Ա[ ]է Տէր աւդեա ապրեցոյց փրկեա զմեզ: Եւ առ ժամայն բացաւ ճանապարհ. եւ ամենայն ժողովուրդն Իսրայէլի մտան ընդ ճանապարհ ծովուն: Իբրեւ իսրայէլացիքն անցին զկէս ծովուն. եկին փարաւոն եւ ամենայն հեծելն մտան ի մէջ ծովուն. զի գերեսցեն զազգն Իսրայէլի:

34/ Իբրեւ ժողովեաց փարաւոն զզօրսն իւր եւ ամենայն եգիպտացիք ի մէջ ծովուն. եւ առ ժամայն չուր ծովուն ծածկեաց զնոսա. ընկղմեցան եւ [խե]ղդեցան ի չուրս ծովուն,

---

989. I.e., 672.
990. Erase one letter.
991. Note that խալք is treated as a singular noun ending in -ք. Also, one letter has been omitted.
992. ս above line p.m.
993. Postclassical form.
994. Erased letter, either յ or գ, following հ.

փարատուն եւ ամենայն գօրն իւր. եւ մի ի նոցանէ ոչ ապրեցաւ։
Եւ անփասս[995] անցին ժողովուրդն Իսրայելի ընդ ծովն։

35/ Եւ բնակեցան Ադեմ. ան/ fol. 41r /դ ՀԲ արմաւենիք կային։ Եւ վեմ մի կայր. ի նմանէ ԺԲ աղբիւր ելանէր։ Զոր ինչ մարդ սիրտն ուզէր զայն համովս ճաշակեր աղբեր [ ] թէ եղ եւ թէ մեղր. թէ ձէթ եւ թէ չոր. եւ թէ գինի։ Հաց երկնից իջոյց առ նոսա. թռչունք թեւաւորք եւ սիրամարգ[996] իբրեւ զաւագ ծովու։ Դարձեալ ոսկեղէն սափորիւ մանանայ ետ նոցա կերակուր։ Մինչեւ ԽԳ տարի այսպէս կացին։ Ան ոչ վարէին եւ ոչ վաստակէին ոչ զն{ա}էին եւ ոչ վաճառէին։

36/ Այնպէս անվաստակ ուտէին եւ ըմբէին. ո՛չ քաղցեան եւ ոչ ծարաւեցան։ Չի յորժամ լուսինն հնանայր հանդերձքն հնանայր։ Երբ լուսինն նորոգէր. դարձեալ հանդերձքն նորոգէր եւ պա<յ>ծառանայր իբրեւ զառաջինն։ Յերեկն ամբ հովանի էր նոցա. եւ գիշերն հրոյ լոյս տայր նոցա։ Չի ոչ ամառն յարեւ նեղէին. եւ ոչ ձմերն գրտոյ։

37/ Չի հանապազ Մովսէս խաւսէր ընդ Աստուծոյ վասն իսրայելաց ազգին. եւ խնդրէր վասն ժողովրդեանն զինչ եւ կամէր. եւ գիր օրինաց երեր{եր} վասն նոցա գրեալ ի վերայ քարեղէն տախտակին գրեալ Ե պատգամաց։ Իսկ չարացն ընդ չար խ[ ] ղ[997] եւ ոչ ընդունեցին զպատգ<ա>մն։

Իսկ Մովսէս բարկացեալ խորտակեաց զտախտակն [ ][998] վասն չարութեան ժողովրդեանն {ժողովուրդնն}։[999]

38/ Չի ասէին ժողովուրդքն. ընդեր միայն երբաս եւ խաւսիս ընդ / fol. 41v / Աստուծոյ. եւ ոչ տանես զմեզ ընդ քեզ։ Մեղադրէին զՄովսէսի եւ ասէին. ընդե՞ր հաներ զմեզ յԵգիպտոսէ. ծածուկ կուռք շինեցին. եւ պաշտէին։

39/ Եւ ի միում գիշերի օձ թօթափեաց եւ խայծատեցին զժողովուրդն։ Իսկ Մովսէս ասճ պղնծի արար. եւ կախեալ ի ճաղդի. եւ ամենայն խայթալն ի յաւձիցն հայէին ի յաւձն պղնձի. զի որք հաւատացեալ էին կռօցն թէ չաստուած է սատակէին։ Եւ այնոքիք[1000] որք զԱստուած պաշտէին. թէպետ

---

995. Erasure of two letters follows.
996. Initial two letters uncertain. The reading should be լորամարգ "quail," but what looks like the upright of an հ can be read.
997. Middle two letters erased.
998. չփայարութեան p.m.
999. Probably a dittography.
1000. Note այնոքիք for այնոքիկ: confusion of ք and կ.

յօձն խայծատեալ էր զնոսա. երբ հայէին ի յօձն պղնձի առ ժամայն բժշկէին:

40/ Դարձեալ գնաց Մովսէս խնդրել նոր պատգամ. իբրեւ գնաց Մովսէս Խ օր մնաց: Ժողովեցան ժողովուրդքն. գոչեցին զԱհարոն եւ ասացին: Չի Մովսէս հանեաց զմեզ յերկրէն եգիպտացոց. եւ բերեալ զմեզ աւտար երկիր եւ ինքն փախեաւ: Ահա Խ աւր է գնացեալ է. խօսել ընդ Աստուծոյ. ընդէ՞ր ոչ տանէ զմեզ ընդ իւրն. մեք ոչ պաշտեմք զԱստուած նորա. շինեայ կուռք զի պաշտեսցուք չաստուած:¹⁰⁰¹

41/ Ասէ Ահարոն. ե՞րբ կուռք պաշտէք բարկանայ ձեզ Աստուած եւ ցամաքի աղբիւրս: Եւ նոքա ոչ լուան խրատուն Ահարոնի. եւ ցամաքեցաւ ԺԲ աղբիւրն:

42/ Բերին զԱհարոն եւ ասացին. զի դուք բերիք զ[մեզ] ի տեղիս այս. եւ չորացուցէ[ր] զաղբիւրս: Եւ թէ ոչ բղխեցուցանէք զաղբիւրսն. / fol. 42r / քարկոծ առնեմք զձեզ: Իսկ Ահարոն աղաչեաց զԱստուած. եւ բղխեցին աղբիւրքն: Դարձեալ բերին Ահարոն ի մէ{ն}ջ. եւ խնդրեցին ի նմանէ շինել կուռք զի պաշտեցեն: Իսկ Ահարոն ափուշ մաց եւ ասաց թէ ոսկի եւ արծաթ եւ ակունք բերէք զի շինեցից ձեզ կուռք:

43/ Վասն այն ասաց. զի թերեւս ոչ տացեն: Եւ ի միում ժամու այնչափի ոսկի եւ արծաթ վայր աձին որքան զմարդաչափի բարձրացաւ: Իբրեւ ետես Ահարոն որ այլ ճար ոչ գիտէ [ ]էլ:¹⁰⁰² Եւ բերեալ զոսկին եւ զարծաթն եւ ակունքն. վառեաց հուր ի վերայ մանր քարի զնկլի եւ ալագու. եւ արկ ի մէջ հրոյն զոսկին եւ զարծաթն. եւ ակունքն. հալեցան ոչընչացան եւ կորեան ի մէջ ընկլիկին եւ ալագին:

44/ Իսկ սատանայն եղեւ իբրեւ յորթ մի ի մէջ կրակին. եւ ել արտաքս: Իբրեւ տեսին ժողովուրդքն երկիր պագեցին {որդոյն}¹⁰⁰³ խոտակերի: Եւ չաստուած¹⁰⁰⁴ պաշտեցին գնայ մինչ ի գալն Մովսէսի:

45/ Եւ ետ Աստուած քարեղէն տախտակ գրեալ ի նմա Ժ պատգամ: Նախ. սիրեսցես զՏէր Աստուած քո յամենայն սրտէ քումմէ. եւ յամենայն անձնէ քումմէ. եւ ամենայն մտաց քոց. եւ ամենայն զաւրութենէ քումմէ:
Պատուեա զհայր քոյ եւ զմայր քոյ եւ սիրեսցես զնկեր քո իբրեւ

1001. ա of abbreviation upside down with infralinear dot.
1002. Illegible.
1003. Apparently corrupt for յորթոյն.
1004. Abbreviated as above.

զանձդ քո: Մի շնար. մի գողանար. մի սպանաներ. մի սուտ երդնուր. մի սուտ վկայեր:
Իբրեւ ետ տախտակն քարեղէն ի ձեռն Մովսէսի. տեսիլ նորա ոչ էր / fol. 42v / [1.8 lines]] լար [.4 line] լ կարէր մարդ [.3 line] երեսն նորա. եւ քաւլ [ ]^{1005}կար ներ երեսին ապայ թէ մարդ կարէր խաւսել ընդ նմա:

46/ Իբրեւ եկն ի մէջ բանակին. ահ մեծ անկաւ ի վերայ ժողովրդեանն: Եւ հրամայեաց Մովսէս. եւ ետ բերել գյորթն եւ աւազան մի. եւ սատկացոյց գյորթն. եւ որոշեաց զմիսն. եւ զմորթն. եւ այրեաց:
Եւ զմոխիրն էած ի մէջ աւազանին. եւ զոսկերն յորթյուն մանրեաց եւ փոշի արար երկաթի քերչաւք. եւ ելից ի մէջ աւազանին. եւ բազմացոյց զջուրն. եւ արբոյց ամենայն ժողովուրդեանն:

47/ Իսկ որք գյորթն աստուած պաշտեալ էին. ամենեքեան ուրան ճաքրուցեան եւ պատարեցան եւ սատկեցան: Իսկ որք^{1006} զԱստուածն Մովսէս[ի]^{1007} պաշտէին. ոչ ինչ փասեցան: Եւ ջուրն խա[ ]յով պահեցին մինչ ի գալուստն Քրիստոսի. զի այն էր [ ]դում նոցա որ փորձութ[եան] ջուր ասէին: Իսկ որ [ան]մեղ լինէր ոչ ինչ փաս[է]. Դարձեալ չարացան ժողովուրդն մոռացան զերախտիսն [Մով]սէսի եւ ասէին. ընդէր հ[ա]ներ զմեզ յԵգիպտոսէ. [տա]քրիր այս աւտար աշխարհի[ ] Ուտիցէնք եւ ըմբէինք շի[ր]ինք^{1008} ի մէջ Եգիպտոսէ:^{1009}

48/ Իսկ Մովսէս խնդրեաց եւ եկն լորամարգ երկնի[ց] եւ տեղաց ի նոսա միս. որպէս [ա] / fol. 43r / լագ. եւ հաց երկնից իջոյց առ նոսա եւ մանանիլ կերակրեաց զնոսա: Իբրեւ կերան եւ լիացան. բարկացաւ Տէր ի վերայ նոցա. պատարեցաւ երկիր եւ եկուլ զԿորախի եւ զԴատան եւ ծածկեաց զբանականն զԱբիրոնի:
Եւ հուր վառեաց ի ժողովուրդա նոցա. եւ բոց մաշեաց զնոսա: Եւ բազում ընդիր ընդիրսն Իսրայէլի սատակեաց:
Եւ Բենեհէս այր արդար միջնորդ եղեւ եւ աղաչեաց զՄովսէս եւ հաշտեցոյց ընդ ժողովրդեանն: Իսկ Մովսէս եւ Փենեհէս աղաչէին զԱստուած եւ արզելաւ մահ:^{1010}

49/ Դարձեալ Մովսէս առ Տէր: Իսկ Մովդատ եւ Եղդատ ՀԲ հոգի

1005. Text illegible.
1006. ր above line p.m.
1007. The coming lines of text are illegible in photograph due to overly tight binding.
1008. Late borrowing into Armenian.
1009. Case is strange.
1010. The Bible does not relate any incident of Moses and Phineas together beseeching God.

ընդ իւրեանս եւ գնացին ընդ {իւրեանս} Մովսէ<սի>: Չի տեսցեն թէ որպէս խալսի Տէր ընդ Մովսէսի: Իբրեւ հասին ի Քորեբ որոտաց եւ թնդաց. եւ փայլատակեաց հուր Աստուածութեան. եւ ամենեքեան անկան ի վերայ երեսաց եւ կիսամեռ եղեն: Երբ զարթեան տեսին զլերինն մեծ եւ մառախալդ. այլ ոչ տեսին Մովսէս. եւ զաշակերտն: Եւ անդ մնացին զալուրս խ: Եւ յետ խ ալուրն. էլ Մովսէս լուսափայլ երեսալք եւ ամենեքեան անկեալ երկիր պագանէին Մովսէսի:
Եւ ուրախութեամբ գնացեալ ի բանակն:

50/ Տեառն հրամանալ սինն ամպոյ եւ լուս կանգնեցալ ի վերայ բանակին մինչ երկինս: Եւ աստուածախալսութիւն լինէր ի նմանէ: Եւ յետոյ վրան սահմանեաց եւ աստուածախալսութիւն / fol. 43v / ի նմանէ լինէր: Դարձեալ հրամանան Աստուծոյ շինեաց տապան անփոյթ փայտէ. եւ ոսկով պատեաց զնա. եւ ետ ի մէջ նորա զքարեղէն տախտակն. եւ ոսկեղէն սափորն լի մանանիւ: Եւ բուրվառն Ահարոնի որ պղնձի էր ոսկի փոխեցալ: Եւ աստուածախալսութիւն լինէր ի նմանէ: Եւ այլ բազում սքանչելիս արար Մովսէս զոր ոչ կատարելապէս գրեցալք զպատմութիւն իւր: Եւ ոչ ոք գիտէ զգերեզմանն Մովսէսի. հրեշտակք ամփոփեցին զնա:

At this point, in col. 1 of fol. 43v a new text starts, which is a typological commentary on the preceding.

Translation

1/ Then after ... [... of Jos]eph,[1011] the people of Israelites multiplied.
2/ And another king arose and he did not like the people of Israel, and he did not accept (them) for 60 years. And afterwards he was replaced by another king; he oppressed them even more wickedly for 55 years. And he was replaced by another king. He oppressed them even more for 62 years. Again another Pharaoh replaced him, more wicked than the former.[1012] He tortured them even more for 67 years.

1011. This could be the end of a sentence similar to Exod 1:6 which reports Joseph's death, since the next phrase here reports the multiplication of Israelites, does Exod 1:7.
1012. According to this passage, there were four Pharaohs (and at least 179 years) between the time of Joseph and the generation of the exodus. The usual exegesis of biblical text reads the verse Exod 1:7 as if the new Pharaoh arose directly after Joseph's death, but that is not the only possible reading. Pharaoh's death is related in Exod 2:23.

3/ He was replaced by another king. He tortured them more than the preceding for 62 years. Again he was replaced by a yet more evil Pharaoh, more wicked than all. He commanded the Israelites to build three cities for the sake of Pharaoh, firing bricks and burnt....[1013]

4/ One day Pharaoh went forth. He assembled all the people of Israel and saw the multitude of them. He was astounded and said to (his) princes,[1014] "Since the people of Israel has multiplied exceedingly, perhaps they will multiply even more (and) do battle with us and slaughter our people and wrest the cities from our hands. I have conceived a method so that I no longer let them multiply." And the princes said, "You command well, O king."[1015]

5/ And Pharaoh summoned all the midwives and said (to them) to strangle all their male infants of theirs in secret from their parents, when the infant is newly born.[1016] But the midwives feared God and did not act thus.[1017] And the king summoned them and said, "Why do you not strangle the infants of the Israelites?"[1018]

6/ And they said, "The Israelites are not like our people, for their men come at the hour of birth and protect and do not let (anybody) hurt their infants. For that reason, we are able to strangle (them)."[1019] Then Pharaoh commanded to seize their infants[1020] openly and to drown them in the river. They did this for 24 years.[1021]

7/ Then Moses was born, lively and very beautiful.[1022] For three months[1023] they kept (him) secretly. When his parents saw that they could no longer keep him (thus), they placed (him) in a chest, they tarred (it)[1024]

1013. The word ṗuṗṗẖẕ is problematic. In context it should mean "straw." The word ṗuṗṗ denotes a poisonous snake.
1014. Exod 1:9 has, "to his people."
1015. This differs from Exod 1:9, in which Pharaoh fears, "lest ... they join our enemies and fight against us and escape from the land."
1016. See Exod 1:15-16.
1017. Exod 1:17.
1018. Compare Exod 1:18.
1019. The reason given here differs from that given in Exod 1:19. It is unusual.
1020. At this point, the text makes no distinction between male and female infants, contrast with Exod 1:22 which refers only to male children.
1021. This chronological detail, like those relating to the reigns of a succession of Pharaohs, is not drawn from the biblical text. The totals of Joseph's and the Pharoahs' rule is around 400; see Gen 15:13.
1022. Exod 2:2 says: "she saw that he was a goodly child."
1023. See Exod 2:2.
1024. Exod 2:3.

and gave (it) to Moses' sister. And she took (it) and cast it into the sea and herself watched from afar to see what would befall the infant.[1025]

8/ And at that same time Pharaoh's daughter came to the sea-shore to sport[1026] with women and maidens. And she paid a fisherman[1027] (saying) that whatever he would catch would be hers. And in the course of his fishing, the waves of the sea brought forth the chest to the sea-shore.

9/ And when they opened (it) they saw an infant in it, lively and beautiful.[1028] Pharaoh's daughter rejoiced and said, "I have no child. I will nurture this infant and adopt him, so that I may have a son."[1029]

10/ She saw Moses' sister there, who was watching from afar. She called out to her and said, "Go, see which wet-nurse (will) come, for I will pay her to nurture this infant for me." Then she went and called Moses' mother. She came to Pharaoh's daughter and said, "Pay me (and) I will nurture this child of yours."[1030] Pharaoh's daughter said, "Keep (him) well (and) I will give you two gold pieces[1031] a month." And his mother took and nurtured the boy for three years[1032] and she weaned Moses and gave (him) to Pharaoh's daughter.[1033]

11/ And the child seemed pleasing in Pharaoh's eyes. He took him to (his) bosom to kiss (him). Then Moses scratched Pharaoh's face and beard with his two hands. And Pharaoh wished to kill the child. But the princes and grandees interceded and said, "He acted unknowingly."[1034]

1025. Exod 2:4. In the biblical narrative it is his mother Jochebed who puts the ark into the river, while Israelites in Egypt has Miriam, his sister, put him into the sea. This is odd, since Egypt's river was universally known, but this variation is doubtless part of a literary embellishment that includes the following incident about the fishermen.

1026. Instead of "to bathe." The Arm Bible also has լուանալ "to bathe."

1027. Fishermen fishing in the Nile are known elsewhere in the Hebrew Bible: see Isa 19:8. Yet there is no fisherman mentioned in the Moses story in Exodus. In the legend of Sargon king of Akkad, which is similar to Moses's story in many ways, Aki the water drawer saves Sargon from the river. See Westenholz 1997, 36–50.

1028. Exod 2:2 and 2:6.

1029. Philo, *Mos.* 1.4, Josephus, *Ant.* 2.232 also know stories about Pharaoh's daughter being childless. See further Ginzberg 1909–1938, 5:398.

1030. Perhaps just, "this child (i.e., here)."

1031. Կարմիր «red» in medieval Armenian usage can mean "a gold coin." Nothing is mentioned about payment in the biblical text.

1032. This span of time is not mentioned in Exodus.

1033. Exod 2:9–10.

1034. This story is known in many sources and in varying forms, many of which share two themes: Moses as a baby is suspected to be a threat to Pharaoh and the test of the two bowls that determines whether Moses acted knowingly and this test ends up to be the cause of Moses's

12/ Then the king held a test. He had one bowl[1035] of gold and one bowl of fire brought and he set (them) before Moses. Then Moses quickly took the fire. He thrust it into his mouth (and) it burned his fingers and his tongue. Therefore Moses was heavy tongued.[1036] When Moses broke out weeping and fainted, then Pharaoh believed that he did that innocently. He took pity and did not kill Moses. When Moses grew up, continually he went around with the people of the Israelites and he loved them.[1037]

13/ One day he saw an Egyptian smiting an Israelite. Then Moses killed the Egyptian, and buried him in the sand and effaced the place and went off.[1038] Then one day he went and walked around among the Israelites. And he saw two Israelite men fighting with one another. Moses said, "Brothers, why are you fighting?" Then one of them said, "Who appointed you as a judge and prince over us? Do you wish to kill me just as you killed the Israelite[1039] yesterday?"

14/ When Moses saw that his homicide had become known,[1040] he fled from Egypt and went far off. And going to a place he came upon a well, and the shepherds were drawing water, to water (their) sheep. Two maidens there wanted to draw water for their beasts and the shepherds did not give them water.

15/ Then Moses took water from the shepherds and gave the maidens' sheep to drink.[1041] And they went home and told (their) father, "A man, a foreigner[1042] watered our sheep and our cattle."

"heavy" tongue, i.e., his speech impediment. See Exod. Rab. 1:31 and other midrashim on Exodus. Sources are discussed in Ginzberg 1909–1938, 5:402.

1035. The word is spelt սսկերր here and ակտերր in the next line. The exact form is unclear but we relate it to the word ակունել "bowl, basin."

1036. թլատ is a form of թոյլ meaning "weak, loose"; cf. Exod 4:10.

1037. This addition to the biblical narrative explains how Moses knew that he was a Hebrew despite the fact that he grew up as a child of Pharaoh's daughter.

1038. Exod 2:11–12. The words "effaced the place and went off" is an addition to fill out the narrative, such as we have observed above. It shows a concern for coherence and has no particular conceptual point.

1039. "Brothers" again stresses Moses' consciousness of his Israelite origin. Intriguingly, the biblical text in Exod 2:14 has "Egyptian" and Israelites in Egypt has "Israelite." This seems to be a corruption behind which the graphically similar "Ishmaelite" may have stood. The Armenian text omits the fact that Pharaoh learned of Moses' homicide and sought to kill him.

1040. Exod 2:14.

1041. Exod 2:16–17.

1042. Here the biblical text has "Egyptian" and the Armenian Bible has "Ishmaelite." This seems to be part of a tendency to underplay Moses' Egyptian connection that has been noted above. The story is longer in the Bible.

16/ Their father said, "Go and bring the man so he may break bread (with us)." They honored Moses and prepared a feast.[1043] When he had eaten,[1044] Jethro asked him, "Whom do you have?" Moses said, "I have nobody, neither people nor family." Jethro said, "If[1045] you have nobody, do I not have two daughters,[1046] many possessions and sheep? Take whichever of my daughters you wish. I (will be) a father to you and you (will be) my son."

17/ It pleased Moses and he took the older daughter and made (her) his wife. And he begot two sons.[1047] And one day while he was pasturing the sheep on the mountain,[1048] suddenly fire burned up in the midst of the thorn bush. It burned and heavenly flame went forth and it did not burn up the thorn bush.[1049]

18/ When he wished to draw close to see what it might be, a voice came forth from the fire that said, "Moses, take off your shoes, for this place on which you are standing is holy."[1050] Moses said, "Who are you, Lord?"[1051] The Lord said, "I am the Lord God of your fathers, God of Abraham, God of Isaac, and God of Jacob. I have indeed inspected[1052] my people and I wish to save Israel from the hands of their oppressors.[1053]

19/ And you, go and say before Pharaoh, "Thus says the Lord, God of our

---

1043. We read եղին for the text's եւղին. The word սեղան "table, altar" may also mean "a festive board," and thus, "a feast."
1044. Literally: was full.
1045. Literally: when.
1046. The biblical verse Exod 2:16 says that Jethro had seven daughters, but in our Armenian text, only two daughters are mentioned. The story is reminiscent of Jacob's arrival at Padan Aram and there Laban had two daughters; see Gen 29. There are also similarities with the tale of Eliezer, Abraham's servant in Gen 24.
1047. Exod 2:22 tells of the birth of one son, Gershon. The story in Israelites in Egypt has nothing corresponding to the passage Exod 2:23–25, which relates the death of Pharaoh and God's hearkening to the cry of the Israelites.
1048. The name of the mountain is found in Exod 3:1, "Horeb, the mountain of God."
1049. Exod 3:2.
1050. Exod 3:4–5.
1051. Moses's question is not found in the corresponding biblical passage. However, Moses asks God's name later in the narrative, in Exod 3:14. This question about the name is asked in supernatural encounters, such as in Gen 32:29 and Judg 13:17.
1052. Or: visited. See Exod 3:7.
1053. See Exod 3:8. The biblical text also mentions the promise of the land to the fathers. This omission might be an ideological change caused by the Armenian Christian author's perspective, in which the gift of the land is not a major theme. In a study of Abraham narratives, I observed that all biblical passages specifying the gift of the land have been omitted from the Armenian retellings of the Abraham stories, doubtless because of their connection to the "old Israel"; see Stone 2012, 15.

fathers, God of Abraham, God of Jacob, and God of Isaac. 'Oppress not my people,' and if he does not hearken to you, I will rebuke him with punishment."[1054]

20/ Moses said,[1055] "Lord, since I am heavy of tongue, how can I speak before him?" The Lord said, "I give you a tongue and wisdom to speak before Pharaoh. Take Aaron with you. He will be a mouth for you and will speak on your part."[1056] Moses said, "If Pharaoh will say, 'Which sign do you have from your God?' what shall I say?" The Lord said to Moses, "What is there in your hand?" and Moses said, "A staff." The Lord said, "Cast down your staff!" When Moses cast down his staff it became a serpent.[1057] And the Lord said to Moses, "Strike with your hand, seize the [ ]." When Moses seized the serpent's neck, it became a staff.[1058]

Again the Lord said, "What do you see before you?" And Moses said, "I see water." The Lord said, "Take a portion."[1059] And when he took (it), it became blood. And the Lord said to pour[1060] out the water on the place (ground). And when he poured the water out, again it became water.[1061]

21/ Again the Lord said to Moses, "Put your hand into your bosom and remove it." When Moses put his hand in his bosom and removed it, he saw that it had become leprous and whitened. Again the Lord said to Moses, "Put your hand into your bosom and remove it." And when Moses did thus, again the hand became flesh-colored as at first.[1062]

22/ The Lord said, "Do these three signs before Pharaoh. If he will not hearken to you, then I will reprove him with punishment."[1063] And

---

1054. In Israelites in Egypt, God's speech leaves open the question whether Pharaoh will obey God's command. Exod 3:10–12 implies the success of Moses' mission. Exod 3:19 says, "I know, however, that the king of Egypt will not let you go unless compelled by a mighty hand," thus emphasising Pharaoh's unwillingness to comply.

1055. The order of events here differs from the biblical text as is specified in the coming footnotes.

1056. Exod 4:10–16. This incident is later in the story in Exodus.

1057. Višap, "dragon, serpent."

1058. Exod 4:1–4.

1059. This is the meaning of ḫpg here.

1060. Literally: to cast out.

1061. Exod 4:9. In Exodus God only tells Moses about this sign that he can use, but the text does not say that God demonstrated it to Moses at that time.

1062. Exod 4:6–7.

1063. This is the same formulation as in §19, above.

Moses went in the midst of the people of Israel and he gave them the good news concerning their redemption.

23/ And he took Aaron with him and they went[1064] to Pharaoh. And they spoke before him. And he did the three wonders. Then Pharaoh said, "I do not know your God and I will not let Israel go."[1065] And Moses said, "If you do not let Israel go, you will see great damages and punishments and then you will free (them)."[1066] When Moses and Aaron went forth,[1067] God began to reprove Pharaoh and Egypt by punishment.[1068] As the first punishment he gave ticks,[1069] so that they were unable to open their eyes and (to uncover) their faces. They were bitten[1070] and swollen.[1071]

24/ The second punishment[1072]—he contaminated their houses and residences with frogs.[1073] The third punishment—(the fruit of) their labors was blighted.[1074] Fourth—he gave the remaining (fruit of their) labors to locusts and grasshoppers.[1075] The fifth punishment, he smote

---

1064. Here obviously the immediate subjects of the verb are Moses and Aaron. In the biblical text itself there is some confusion as to who went to Pharaoh. Exod 5:1 clearly says: "And after this Moses and Aaron went in to Pharaoh" despite the fact that in 3:18 God says to Moses: "and thou shalt come, thou and the elders of Israel, unto the king of Egypt" and in 6:27: "It was they (i.e., the heads of Israelite families) that spoke with Pharaoh king of Egypt."

1065. Exod 5:2.

1066. This threat is not found in Exodus, which describes Moses's appeal to Pharaoh very differently; see Exod 5:1, 3.

1067. Israelites in Egypt here omits Pharaoh's further oppression of the Israelites (Exod 5:6–19), God's speech to Moses (6:1–13, 6:27–7:7), and the list of families (6:14–26).

1068. The list of punishments that follows here differs from that in the Bible. Here the list contains only eight punishments, unlike Exodus, which relates ten punishments. The number ten is also found in the independent list of punishments in Armenian, published here as text no. IV.4. Elsewhere in the Bible, Pss 78(77):43–51 and 105(104):28–36 present a list of seven punishments in a different order from that in Exodus, but none of the biblical sources has the same order as here.

1069. In Exod 7:15–21 the first punishment is blood while ticks are the third punishment. In Ps 78 (77) the punishment of ticks does not appear. In Ps 105(104):28 the first punishment is darkness, and ticks are the fourth punishment alongside "wild beasts" (ברע). The Egyptian magicians are not mentioned in Israelites in Egypt.

1070. I.e., bitten.

1071. Exod 8:16–19.

1072. Here it seems that the second punishment starts right away after the first one, and the same style is used in the other punishments. The biblical detail that God hardened Pharaoh's heart is not mentioned here, which of course affects the theological point of the passage.

1073. Exod 7:27–8:9.

1074. The locusts are mentioned in Exod 10:4–15. The grasshoppers are an addition with no parallel in Exodus.

1075. In Exodus the locusts eat the crops remaining after the hail (10:5).

their vineyards with hail and gave their fig-trees to fire.[1076] The sixth punishment, he dried up their remaining plants with frost.[1077] The seventh punishment, he turned their rains to blood;[1078] he changed their waters and rivers to blood, which they could not drink. For the Israelites and the Egyptians drank of one[1079] river: (when) the Israelites drank it was water; and (when) the Egyptians drank it turned into blood. All the punishments appeared in their midst, and not one punishment approached the people of Israel.[1080]

25/ When Pharaoh did not turn away from his wickedness, again the Lord appeared to Moses and said, "Go, instruct your people that this week they should eat unleavened bread and bread with leaven let them not eat.[1081] Let them offer a sacrificial lamb and let them sprinkle the blood of the lamb on the doorposts[1082] in four directions in the likeness of a cross.[1083]

26/ For <in> this night I will send my slaughtering angel into the midst of Egypt, for <on> whichever doorposts he sees a sign (or: a cross),[1084] there the slaughtering angel does not approach.[1085] And thus death was visited[1086] upon Egypt, so that in one night from a one-day old child to a 30 years old and also of the animals, there did not remain either male or female.[1087]

27/ For just as the Lord comman[ded] Moses about the unleavened bread and the sacrifice of the lamb, thus Moses did. And no man lacked of

---

1076. Exod 9:18–26. In the biblical texts there is a mingling of hail and fire. Moreover, Exodus regards the damage to cattle as primary (Exod 9:19), and there is no mention of vineyards and fig trees, but just of "every plant of the field."
1077. There is no punishment in Exodus that is parallel to this.
1078. Exod 7:17–24. In Israelites in Egypt rain is mentioned, though it is not in the Bible where the sign is the turning of the river into blood. In fact, Egypt has a very sparse rainfall, just as frost—the sixth punishment—is also unusual in Egypt.
1079. I.e., the same. This detail is apocryphal.
1080. This is the first mention of the punishment distinguishing between the Egyptians and the Israelites. Exodus mentions the distinction at almost every plague.
1081. Exod 12:15–20.
1082. Exod 12:7.
1083. Observe the Christian influence here.
1084. The Armenian word նշան may be translated "sign" or "cross."
1085. Exod 12:13, 23. In those verses it is God himself who kills the Egyptians firstborn.
1086. Literally: slaughtered.
1087. The formulation is somewhat unclear, though the overall sense is certain. This statement is based on Exod 12:29. The biblical text does not mention firstborn girls explicitly, but does not exclude them.

the people of Israel,[1088] and great fear fell upon Pharaoh and the Egyptians. This was the eight<h> punishment.[1089]

28/ Again the Lord appeared to Moses and said, "Go to Pharaoh and say, 'Free my people!' until they finish making a three-day feast of Passover.[1090] (Afterwards) again they will come and serve you. And if you do not hearken, again punishment will come upon you. And he (i.e., the people of Israel) will leave you. For every man will take ornaments from his master and the women will request ornaments from their mistresses, because you will not see them any more."[1091]

29/ And Moses came and spoke with Pharaoh and said, "Thus says the Lord God of our fathers. 'Let my people go for three days.'" Because fear beset them (the Egyptians), he let the people go. By number and in writing he (Pharaoh) gave (them) into his power and he (Moses) said that after three days that he would bring them and give them into Pharaoh's power, for they were 672 in number.[1092]

30/ When Moses went forth from the city, and all the people with him, they went to the shore of the Red Sea.[1093] And there they were blessing God and were rejoicing. And Moses announced in their midst and said, "Do not enter Egypt again and do not serve Pharaoh." But Pharaoh had secretly sent a spy[1094] with them so that he might know what Moses and the people of Israel wanted to do.

31/ When he heard this speech from Moses' mouth, "You shall no more serve Pharaoh," he came hastily and told Pharaoh. And Pharaoh was

---

1088. I.e., all Israelites did this.
1089. As opposed to the tenth in Exodus.
1090. In the Bible Moses asks permission from Pharaoh to depart for a three-day feast and sacrifice (Exod 5:3), but there is no verse that actually describes God commanding this.
1091. Exod 12:35–36. God had already given this command during the Burning Bush revelation; see Exod 3:21–22. There, however, it was only the women who asked the jewelry from their Egyptian neighbors and the men are not mentioned. In Exod 12:35 "the people of Israel" do this action, with no further specification. In Exodus this act was not part of Moses' threat to Pharaoh, as it is here.
1092. The idea that Pharaoh kept a written record of the Israelites who went away for three days is not paralleled elsewhere. The number 672 for the Israelites must be corrupt, if the numbers that participated in the exodus are recalled. Exodus 12:37 speaks of 600,000 men, apart from women and children, cf. Num 2:32 (603,550), contrast Num 3:34 (600,200) and 11:21 (600,000).
1093. Exodus 13:18 gives the route to the sea as "by the roundabout way of the wilderness toward the Red Sea" (NRSV). JSP gives, "roundabout, by way of the wilderness at the Sea of Reeds."
1094. A tradition about a spy is not known from the Bible, and is probably introduced here to explain the words, "When the king of Egypt was told …" in Exod 14:5. Rabbinic literature also deals with this issue, and comes up with similar solutions: compare Mekh Bešalaḥ 1 (ed. Horovitz-Rabin, 86); Ginzberg 1909–1938, 6:3.

wrath and he issued orders quickly. He assembled all his cavalry and went against the people of Israel and said to his cavalry, "Cut down the men and capture their women and maidens."[1095]

32/ When the cavalry was close, Moses[1096] looked from afar and saw that the cavalry was coming. Moses commanded all the people to beseech God, to take their possessions (and) to enter the sea. And he himself took Joseph's body on his back,[1097] taking his staff in his hand he made the sign of the cross[1098] over the sea, saying:

33/ "Lord, Ahiay Ašrahiay Adovniay Lord. a[ ]ē[1099] Lord help, keep alive, save us." And at once a way was opened and all the people of Israel entered by that maritime way.[1100] When the Israelites had crossed half of the sea, Pharaoh and all the cavalry entered into the midst of the sea so that they might capture the people of Israel.

34/ When Pharaoh assembled his forces and all the Egyptians (were) in the midst of the sea, at once the water of the sea covered them. Pharaoh and all his forces were drowned and suffocated in the waters of the sea, and not one of them was saved.[1101] And the people of Israel crossed through the sea unharmed.

35/ And they encamped at Elim (Ałim).[1102] There stood 72[1103] palm trees

---

1095. This is not based on the Bible.

1096. In Exod 14:10 it is the Israelites who sees Pharaoh coming. There, the Israelites also complain about Pharaoh chasing them, which detail is missing here.

1097. Joseph's body instead of bones, see Exod 13:19. Perhaps the body is mentioned rather than the bones just by a chance of transmission, yet it could also be the author's way of dealing with the fact that Gen 50:26 reports that Joseph was mummified. The Israelites' carrying of Joseph's remains is a well-known tradition with explicit biblical roots and it was the subject of various midrashic exegeses. See, for example, the story of Joseph's body being raised from the Nile; Ginzberg 1909-1938, 6:1.

1098. Note the explicit Christian element.

1099. Moses here invokes magical divine names of power. Some of them are found in early Sinai inscriptions, see H Arm 50 and H Arm 54 and, of course, in amulets. The splitting of the sea is presented as a magical event in Rabbinic literature, see Ginzberg 1909-1938, 3:18-19, 6:6. See also text 4.10 §6 where the same incident is described, and the same names invoked.

1100. This is very different description of the splitting of the sea than that in Exod 14:21.

1101. Exod 14:23-28.

1102. In Exodus the first place the Israelites go to is Marah, there they complain about the lack of water (Exod 15:22-23). Elim is the second place the Israelites reached (Exod 15:27), and see also Num 33:9.

1103. Seventy palm trees are mentioned in Exod 15:27. The alternation seventy/seventy-two occurs in other contexts, such as the number of Christ's disciples, the number of the translators of the Septuagint (which name means "seventy" but who are traditionally six from each of twelve tribes), etc. See Metzger 1958, 299-306; Thomson 2001, §686 210-11; Stone 1982, 112.

and there was a rock from which 12 springs issued forth.[1104] Whatever a man's heart wanted, he consumed of the spring with that taste [ ] whether it was honey, or oil, water, or wine.[1105] He brought down bread from heaven unto them—winged birds, peacocks,[1106] as many as[1107] the sand of the sea.

Again, by means of a golden urn he gave them manna as food.[1108] They were thus for 43 years,[1109] they did not labor and did not toil, they did not buy and did not sell.

36/ Thus, without toil they were eating and drinking; they did not hunger and did not thirst. For when the moon waned, their clothes grew old; when the moon was renewed, their clothes were renewed and shone like before.[1110] In the day a cloud was shading them, and at night, he gave them fire's light,[1111] so that they were not afflicted by sun in the summer or by cold in the winter.[1112]

37/ For Moses always spoke with God concerning[1113] the people of the Israelites, and he asked for the people whatever they wanted. And he brought a book of laws for them written upon a stone tables, five commandments.[1114] Then to the evils, with evil [ ] and they did not accept the commandment.[1115]

1104. Literally: went forth.
1105. This tradition is not mentioned in the Bible. There are similar traditions in Rabbinic sources relating to Elim's palm trees and water wells and to the manna. Compare Ginzberg 1909–1938, 3:40–41, 6:14–16. This is presumably the rock that some Armenian traditions connect with the desert march of the Israelites. See 3.8 §§33–34 above.
1106. The word designates peacocks. The word for "quails" in the Armenian Bible is լորամարգ, which resembles it and the reading "peacocks" is a corruption of "quails."
1107. Literally: like.
1108. On the manna see Exod 16:4, 8 and on its taste, see Exod 16:31. Exodus relates that God commanded an urn of manna to be put "before the Lord" (16:33–34). The "golden urn" comes from Heb 9:4. That Moses fed the people through it is unknown elsewhere, but reminds one of the jars of meal and oil in 1 Kgs 17:14, 16. These items are also listed in the text published above about the Ark (1.5).
1109. Forty years according to Exod 16:35. No reason for the additional three years was discerned.
1110. This tradition about their clothing is an explanation of Deut 8:4 and it appears in Rabbinic literature, see Ginzberg 1909–1938, 3:237, 6:83.
1111. Exod 13:21–22.
1112. Literally: cold's winter.
1113. Or: for the sake of.
1114. This apparently refers to the Pentateuch, for Exod 20 speaks of ten commandments that Moses received. Alternatively, it designates two tablets, each with five commandments.
1115. This sentence is unclear and partly illegible.

Then Moses became angry and smashed the tablet on account of the people's evil.[1116]

38/ For the people said, "Why do you alone go and speak with God and do not take us with you?" They blamed Moses and said, "Why did you bring us forth from Egypt?" In secret they built idols and worshipped (them).

39/ And one night a serpent slithered in and they stung the people.[1117] Then Moses made a bronze serpent and hung it on a pole and all who were bitten by the snakes looked at the bronze snake, so that those who believed in idols, that they are god, were killed, and those who worshipped God, even though the serpent had bitten them, when they looked at the bronze serpent, were immediately cured.

40/ Moses went again to seek a new commandment. When Moses had gone, he stayed for 40 days. The people assembled, they called Aaron and said, "Moses brought us out of the land of the Egyptians and brought us to a foreign land, and he himself has fled. Behold, he has gone for 40 days to speak with God. Why did he not take[1118] us with him? We do not worship his God. Build an idol so that we may worship the (false) god."[1119]

41/ Aaron said, "If you worship an idol, God will be angry with you and dry up the springs.[1120] And they did not listen to Aaron's reproach and the 12 springs dried up.[1121]

42/ They brought Aaron and said, "You brought us to this place and you

---

1116. Exod 32:19. The sequence of events is confused in Israelites in Egypt, for Moses broke the Tablets after the sin of the golden calf. As the text stands, it is not coherent.

1117. The two verbs in this sentence are, the first singular and the second plural. The incident related is drawn from Num 21:6–9. There, however, the people transgress by complaining against Moses. Poisonous serpents attacked them. Moses made a bronze serpent and put it on a pole, and those bitten looked at the serpent were healed (21:6–9). There is no winnowing of the wicked out of the people as described here and, moreover, the incident in Numbers occurs as another point in the narrative.

1118. The verb is actually in the present tense.

1119. In Exod 32:1 the Israelites do not ask Aaron for an idol, but they do complain about the Moses' absence.

1120. Note -pu as accusative plural ending. Aaron's words are not in the Bible and serve to highlight the people's idolatry, as does the people's twice-repeated request that he make them an idol.

1121. Again confusion reigns in the narrative sequence. The twelve springs were at Elim while, according to Exodus, Moses ascended Mt. Sinai after travelling there from Elim. In Exod 15 no mention is made of springs drying up or their renewal. Lack of water is related in Num 20:2. This reflects the tradition of the travelling stone noted in 3.8 §§33–34.

dried up the springs. And if you do not cause the springs to flow, we will stone you."

Then Aaron prayed to God and the springs flowed. Again they accused[1122] Aaron and asked him[1123] to build an idol so that they might worship (it). Then Aaron remained perplexed and said, "Bring gold and silver and precious stones, so that I may build an idol for you."[1124]

43/ He said this for the following reason,[1125] so that perhaps they would not give (them). And in one hour they brought to the place so much gold and silver that it surpassed a man's height. When Aaron saw that he knew [to ..] no other expedient. And he brought the gold and silver and gems, kindled a fire upon a small container[1126] of stone and of sand. And he cast the gold and the silver and the gems into the midst of the fire. They melted, became nothing and perished in the container and the sand.

44/ Then Satan[1127] became like a calf in the midst of the fire and he issued forth. When the people saw (it) they prostrated themselves to the grass-eating <calf>. And they worshipped the false god[1128] until Moses came.[1129]

45/ And God gave stone tablets on which were written ten commandments.

First: You shall love the Lord your God with all your heart and with all your soul and all your mind and all your might.[1130]

1122. Literally: brought into the midst, which means "to accuse" as in court. Perhaps the first verb of this section ("brought") has the same meaning.

1123. Again the people of Israel ask Aaron to build an idol. This is a tendentious change intended to make Aaron's sin less critical and to aggravate the Israelites' sin: see notes 1119 and 1120 above.

1124. Exod 32:2–5.

1125. Literally: on account of that he said. Once more, the latter part of this sentence highlights the people's sin of idolatry.

1126. Not in the dictionaries, the word is derived from stem ընկալ- "contain." The words ընկալիչ and ընկալուչ are attested.

1127. The presence of Satan is not mentioned in Exodus, and this is clearly a later inference.

1128. It seems reasonable to infer from the smelting of gold, silver, and gems related above, that the calf was of gold. The attribute "grass-eating" does not here imply explicitly that it was alive, but that is the case according to the continuation of the text in §46 below. There, Moses slaughtered the calf and it had bones. In Exodus it was of gold (32:4).

1129. Moses's descent from the mountain is drawn from Exod 32:15. The Ten Commandments appear both in Exod 20:2–14 and in Deut 5:6–21.

1130. Although the text says God gave Moses ten commandments, it specifies only eight.

Honor your father and your mother and love your fellow as yourself.[1131]
Do not commit adultery.
Do not steal.
Do not kill.[1132]
Do not swear falsely.
Do not bear false witness.
When he gave the stone tablet through the hand of Moses, his appearance was not [ ] man could [ ]of the face, and a veil [ ] on his face[1133] then that a man could speak with him.

46/ When he came into the camp, great fear fell upon the people. And Moses commanded and he had the calf brought and a bowl. And he destroyed the calf and he separated the flesh and the skin and burnt (them). And he put the ash into the bowl, and he ground up the bones of the calf and made (them) dust with an iron rake and filled the bowl and he added the water and gave (it) to all the people to drink.[1134]

47/ Then all those who had worshipped the calf as a god swelled up[1135] and split open and perished. But those who worshipped Moses' God were not harmed. And they kept the [ ] water until the arrival of Christ. For that was their [ ] which they called "water of testing."[1136] Then those who were without sin it did not hurt at all. Again the people did evil. They forgot the benefits of Moses and were saying, "Why did you bring us out of Egypt, you led (us) to this strange land. We ate and drank sweet things in the midst of Egypt."[1137]

48/ Then Moses asked and quail of the heaven came and showered meat on them, like sand. And he brought down heavenly bread and fed them with manna.[1138] When they ate and were full, the Lord grew wrathful with them.

1131. This phrase, though originally from Lev 19:18, is here quoted from the New Testament: see Matt 22:37–39, Luke 10:27, and Mark 12:32 for this collocation of commandments, and compare also Matt 19:18–19.

1132. See Exod 20:13 and Deut 5:17. Notice that the order of the commandments here is different. In the New Testament Jesus refers to the ten commandments as "the commandments" (Mark 10:19) and he names only six of them and in a different order to Exodus, yet other commandments appear also in various places in NT, see Matt 22:37–40, 1 Cor 10:7.

1133. Compare Exod 34:29–30 and on Moses's luminous face, see Orlov 2007, 327–43.

1134. See Exod 32:20. The description is elaborated in *Israelites in Egypt*.

1135. The meaning of ճưpnuևդիսև is unclear. The word ոռռաև means "swelled."

1136. This passage is clearly based on "the waters of bitterness" (Num 5:18–24).

1137. Compare Exod 17:3 and also Exod 16:3.

1138. See Exod 16:13–14. This is a repetition of statements made above in §35–36. The order of events in this latter part of the work seems almost random.

The earth split open and it swallowed Korah and Dathan and it concealed the camps of Abiron.[1139] And fire burnt in the midst of their people, and flame wore them away. And it destroyed many chosen elect ones of Israel.

And Pinhas, a just man, became an intermediary and beseeched Moses and he was reconciled with the people. Then Moses and Pinhas beseeched God and death was stopped.

49/ Again Moses (went) to God.[1140] Then Eldad and Modad and 72 persons with them also went with Moses,[1141] so that they might see how God speaks with Moses: When they reached Horeb, it thundered and quaked and fire of the Godhead lightened. And all fell upon their faces and became half-dead. When they awoke they saw the mountain,[1142] mist and fog, but they did not see Moses and his disciple. And there they remained for 40 days. And after the 40th day, Moses came forth with a resplendent face and all fell down (and) did Moses obeisance. And they went rejoicing to the camp.[1143]

50/ At the Lord's command a pillar of cloud and of light took up a stand over the camp, (reaching) up to the heavens, and from it was divine speech. And afterwards, the divine speech was behind a curtain of separation. Again at God's command he built[1144] an Ark of wood that did not rot and surrounded it with gold. And he put the stone tablets inside it,[1145] and a golden urn full of manna, and Aaron's censer, which was of copper turned into gold, and the divine speech came from it. And Moses performed many other miracles. We have not written his story completely. And no one knows Moses' tomb. Angels closed it up.

At this point, in col. 1 of fol. 43v a new text starts, which is a typological commentary on the preceding. We resume our edition from fol. 47r.

1139. The text does not provide an explanation of God's anger. See Num 16:24–27.
1140. The sense demands more than has survived in the manuscript.
1141. The text is corrupt here and "them" is surmounted by erasure marks. They signal a dittography.
1142. I.e., covered in.
1143. Compare with Exod 34:28–35. See also §45 above.
1144. The text omits Bezalel and Ahalihav whom according to Exod 36:11 were the men who built the Ark and the Tabernacle.
1145. See 1 Kgs 8:9. See also the text on the Ark, 1.5. The two are closely connected and it may be assumed that a text like 1.5 was taken into *Israelites in Egypt* here.

254 BIBLICAL STORIES

4.9. The Ten Plagues of Egypt

4.9.1. Concerning the Ten Plagues of Egypt 1

This text occurs in numerous copies. We have come across the following, by order of date, but these are far from all the copies.

Manuscript	Date	Sigil
M6897, fol. 413r	1317	M6897
M2188, fol. 244r	fifteenth century	M2188
M2158, fol. 3r	fifteenth century	M2158
M537, fol. 237v	1673	M537
M268, fol. 150v	1697	M268
Galata 154, p. 302	seventeenth century	G154
M605, fol. 25v	seventeenth century	M605
M682, fols. 8–9r	seventeenth century	M682

The earliest copy we have noted is M6897 dated 1317. It was made available to me thanks to the good offices of Dr. Gohar Muradyan. The list of ten plagues was included in Գիրք Հարցմանց (*The Book of Questions*) by Gregory of Tatʻew (1344?–1409; Tatʻewacʻi 1993, 333). Since M6879 was written in 1317, it antedates Gregory of Tatʻew and presumably contains a copy of the text that Gregory included in his work.

It is impossible to conclude whether *The Book of Questions* itself, or the text upon which *The Book of Questions* drew, or still other copies were the source of various of the later rescripts. One instance is clear: M2188, M537 and M2158, also include the discussion of the list of plagues which is found in *The Book of Questions*, which is most likely the discussion's source. So, the copies of the list in these three manuscripts go back to *The Book of Questions*. Moreover, M537 and M2158 are very closely allied textually which fact further strengthens this conclusion.

In some instances, exegetical passages follow the text that are drawn from Grigor Tatʻewacʻi, *The Book of Questions*, 333–34. Such are found in M2188 and M537, showing that these manuscripts are dependent on Tatʻewacʻi. M605, though differing in that it has an expanded text, also follows this list with homiletic material.

The text given below is that of M6897 fol. 413r, with which the other copies, except M605, are compared and their variants recorded in the appa-

PART FOUR

ratus below the text. We do not include those variants involving the notation of the numerals, which are a matter of graphic convention alone. The text of M605 is rather different from the others and is given separately, following the critical text.

Text

1/ Հարուածք Եգիպտոսի
    Առաջինն՝ արիւնն.
    Բ. գորտն.
    Գ. մուն.
5/ Դ. շանաճանճն.
    Ե. մահ անասնոց.
    Զ. կեղն.
    Է. կարկուտն.
    Ը. Մարախն.
10/ Թ. Խաւարն.
    Ժ. մահ անդրանկացն։

Variants

1/   Վասն Ժ հարուածքն Եգիպտացոցն M2188 Վասն Ժ հարուածցն (-ծոց M2158) եգիպտոսի M2158 M537 Այս է. Ժ հարուածն Եգիպտացւոց M268 Այս են Ժ հարուածքն Եգիպտացոց G154
2/   Առաջինն արիւն] Առաջինն. գետն ի յարիւն փոխել M2188 առաջինն է գետն (գէտն M2158) յարիւն փոխիլ M537 M2158 առաջին գետն արիւն փոխիլն M268 Առաջին. գջուրն յարիւն փոխել G154
4/   մուննM2188 M2158 M537 M268 G154
5/   մահ անասնոց] խաշնամահն G154 | անասնոցն M2188 M537 M268
7/   կեղն] կեղն եւ խաղաւարտ M2188 G154 զեղ խաղաւարտ M2158 կեղ եւ խաղաւարտն M537 M268
8/   կարկուտն] + եւ հուրն G154 | կարկուտ M2158
9/   մարախ M2158
10/ խաւարն] + շօշափելի M268 G154
11/ անդրանկաց մահ G154 | + իբր ի փոքունցն (փոքունց M2158) կարգաւ ի խստագոյնսն ելեալ (խստագոյն եղեւ) M537 M2158

Translation

1/ The plagues of Egypt
The first—the blood.[1146]
2. The frogs.[1147]
3. Gnats.[1148]
5/ 4. The dog ticks.[1149]
5. Death of cattle.[1150]
6. The sores.[1151]
7. The hail.[1152]
8. The locusts.[1153]
10/ 9. The darkness.[1154]
10. The death of the firstborn.

4.9.2. Plagues of Egypt 2 (M605)

Text

1 / fol. 25v / Վասն Ժ հարուածոցն եգիպտացոց ձեռամբ Մովսիսի։
Նախ գետն արիւն փոխեալ Ձ աւր։
Բ. Գորտն եռաց յամենայն տունս եւ տեղիս եգիպտացոցն. Գ աւր։
Գ. Մունն շարաւորք։
5 Դ. Շանաձանձն. Բ աւր։
Ե. Մահ անասնացն եւ խաշանց։
Զ. Կեղտն եւ խաղաւարտն։
Է. Կարկուտն սաստիկ։
Ը. Խաւարն շաւշափելի։
10 <Թ>
Ժ. Մահ անդրանկացն։

1146. Exod 9:17–21.
1147. Exod 8:2–7.
1148. Exod 8:16–18.
1149. These are not mentioned by name in Exodus.
1150. Exod 9:3–7.
1151. Exod 9:9–11.
1152. Exod 9:18–25.
1153. Exod 10:12–14.
1154. Exod 10:21–22.

Translation

1/ Concerning the ten Plagues of the Egyptians at Moses<'s>[1155] hands.
First, the river changing into blood for 6 days.
2. Frogs swarmed in all the houses and places of the Egyptians for three days.
3. The gnats stinking.
5/ 4. Dog ticks for two days.
5. Death of the cattle and sheep.
6. The sores and abcesses.
7. The terrible hail.
8. The frightful darkness.
10/ <9.> [1156]
10. The death of the firstborn.

4.10. Concerning Jannes and Mambres

The document is found in a longer work which commences on the last line of fol. 7d[1157] of manuscript M682. It opens with the words վասն Աբրահամու եւ որդոց նորա "Concerning Abraham and His Sons." Here we have edited the text taken from fol. 8v of the manuscript. The material is drawn from the same textual source as Genealogy of Abraham in Galata 154 (Stone 2012, 78–81). In M682 the text is a little longer than the text of Galata 154. It is also presented in an elenchic form, which is not the case in Galata 154.

We have given its copy of the list of Ten Plagues, which is much the same in both manuscripts.[1158] The material on Jannes and Mamres, which comes directly after the list of plagues is not found in Galata 154. Indeed, there were references through the ages to this pair of magicians and their work, but such mentions are rather uncommon in Armenian texts.[1159] They were conceived of as Egyptian magicians, opponents of Moses in the magical contest before Pharaoh. Some years ago, a copy of the lost Book of Jannes and Mambres was discovered on a papyrus, now in Chester Beatty Library in Dublin (Pietersma

---

1155. Apparently the case ending is missing. The biblical references to the plagues are given in the preceding text.
1156. The ninth plague is missing from M605.
1157. On the folio numbers in this manuscript, see part 3, note 86, in 3.7 above.
1158. See also 4.9 above.
1159. James 1920, 31–38. For extensive bibliography DiTommaso 2001, 559–63.

1994). We have, therefore, given the Armenian text in full for its inherent interest. Some of the details seem unparalleled, such as their father's name and their Chaldean origin.

Traditionally the name of Jannes and Mambres' father is Balaam, not Bar Kʻobay as in our text. The Armenian designation calls to mind the Jewish leader Bar Kochba, but there is no mention of this name among the widely scattered literary traditions about Jannes and Mambres, nor any discernable connection.[1160] This seems to be a uniquely Armenian tradition. The legend of their Chaldean origin is mentioned in Jewish sources; Targum Pseudo-Jonathan of Num 22:22 and Yalqut Reubeni waʼera 19a on Exod 7:11 drawing on Zohar Ki Tissa 191a state that they were "chiefs of the Chaldaeans" and expert magicians. This tradition may be influenced by the view that Balaam was the brothers' father and was of Mesopotamian origin (Num 22:5; 23:7; Deut 23:5 [Eng. 23:4]).

Also unique to our text is the legend that they "were stealing the children of the Chaldeans and were sacrificing them to idols who<se> name was their father's." This accusation is reminiscent of the story recorded in Josephus, *Ag. Ap.* 2.83, 93–96, that during the time of Antiochus Epiphanes each year Jews would steal a Greek, fatten and sacrifice him, consume his flesh and then swear hatred towards the Greeks. Josephus states that Posidonius and Apollonius Molon are the source of this calumny, as well as of the remainder of Apion's anti-Jewish bias (*Ag. Ap.* 2.79). The legend in our text also resonates with blood libel accusations of Jews killing Christian children and drinking their blood that arose in the fifth century and became prominent in the Middle Ages. The mention in M682 that demons became obedient to Jannes and Mambres because they sacrificed children to them, is not extant in any other traditions about the brothers. While the brothers' connection with demons is mentioned in extant traditions, and their designation as magicians may engender the conclusion that they would control or be controlled by a demon(s), the reason for the demons' subjugation to Jannes and Mambres, as well as their obedience to the brothers is unique to this text.[1161]

After the material on Jannes and Mambres, and Moses' splitting of the Red Sea, the text continues with questions about subsequent Israelite history, and associated topics, starting with the Golden Calf.

1160. Fragments of the Book of Jannes and Jambres, P Michigan inv. 4925 verso and Targum Pseudo-Jonathan Num 22:22(26) name Balaam as their father. For a summary of scattered literary traditions about Jannes and Mambres, see Pietersma 1994, 25–26.

1161. This and the preceding paragraph embody research by Dr. V. Hillel, to whom hearty thanks are here extended.

Moses splits the sea using divine names and his staff. He calls on God using three names of power, one pronounced forward, one to the right, and one to the left. The same names occur in the same context in 3.8 §§33–34 and in 4.10 §6.[1162] See the discussion there.

Text

1/ Հարց: թէ քանի՞ են հարուածք Եգիպտոսի. Ժ:
Ասա զի գիտացից կարգաւ հակիրճ:[1163]
<Պատասխանի>: Առաջինն գջուրն արինն լինել:
Բ. գորտն:
Գ. մունն:
Դ.[1164] կեղ եւ {խաւարտ}:[1165]
Դ.[1166] շանաճանճ:
Ե. խաշնամահն:
Զ. See above
Է. կարկուտն եւ հուր:
Ը. մարախն:
Թ. խաւար շաւշափելի:
Ժ. անդրանկաց մահն:

2/ Եւ թէ ընդէ՞ր ոչ հաւատային նշանացն. այս է պատճառն: Զի Յանէս եւ Յամրէս որդիք Բարքորայ Քաղդէացոյ կախարդի. գողայնային գոդայս Քաղդէացոցն եւ գոհէին[1167] կռոցն որ անուն հօրն իւրեանց. զոր գիտացեալ քաղդէացւոցն հալածեցին զնոսա. եւ նոքա գնացին յԵգիպտոս:

3/ Որ եւ Մովսէս Ժ ամեայ լեալ ետուն ի նոսա ուսումս. վասն որոյ կախարդութիւն համարէին: Ի ԻԲ ամին Մովսէսի սկսաւ կտուագործութիւնն. ԻԸ ամին իշխան եղեւ. եւ Խ ամին սպան զշարշարիչն Իսրայելի եւ փախեաւ:

4/ Յետ փախչելոյ նորա Յանէս եւ Յամրէս շինեցին զդրախտն

1162. Note that one such name appears in Sinai Armenian inscriptions H Arm 50 and 54.
1163. կ written over ճ, p.m.
1164. Written over another letter. The process seems to have been: (1) plague 6 was written erroneously right after plague 3; (2) then the content of plague 4 was written directly following the end of misplaced plague 6; (3) then Դ, i.e., the numeral "4" was written between the lines at the beginning of the text of plague 4. The original scribe did all this.
1165. This word is corrupt for խաղաւարտ "abscess," found in the other versions.
1166. Numeral *inter lineas* p.m.
1167. For confusion of o/n, see Stone and Hillel, "Index," no. 408 for this phonetic variant.

դիւացյարչարանօքորդոցն Իսրայելի: Եւ արին ՁՉ մանկունս[1168]
ի նոցանէ եւ զոհեցին դիւաց: Եւ յայնմ օրէ հնազանդք եղեն
դեւք կախարդաց:

5/ Հարց. թէ քանի կարք ունէր փարաւն.
Պատասխանի. վեց հարիւր էր կարքն:

6/ ՀՊ.[1169] <հարց>: Որպէս պատառեաց Մովսէս զծովն:
<Պատասխանի>. Զցուպական ձգեաց յառաջն եւ ասէ. Այխա.
այսինքն է Աստուած իմ առաջի իմ: 3աչ կողմն Շրայիա. դու
հանէր զմեզ Աստուած: Ձախ կողմն Ադոնիա. Տէրդ տերացն
ընդ մեզ:

Translation

1/ Question: How many are the plagues of Egypt?—ten.
Say (them) so that I may learn in order, briefly.
<Answer>.[1170] The first, the water becoming blood.
2. The frogs.
3. The gnats.
6. Sores and {darkness.}[1171]
4. Dog ticks.
5. Death of sheep.
(6. see above)
7. The hail and fire.
8. The locusts.
9. Frightful darkness.
10. The death of the firstborn.

2/ <Question>: And, why did they not believe the signs?
<Answer>: This is the reason. Since Yanēs and Yambrēs[1172] sons of Bar K'obay the Chaldean[1173] magician, were stealing the children of the Chaldeans and were sacrificing them to idols who<se> name was their father's. The Chaldeans, learning this, chased them away and they went to Egypt.

1168. This reading is uncertain, particularly of the latter part of the word.
1169. Apparently this is an abbreviation of հարց "question" and պատասխանի "answer."
1170. This might be expected here.
1171. See note 1165 above.
1172. I.e., Jannes and Mambres, perhaps indicating that they played a role in Moses' education. This would be an unusual idea.
1173. See the introductory remarks above.

PART FOUR 261

3/ When Moses was ten years old they gave teaching to them,[1174] on account of which they were reckoned as magic.[1175] And in the 22nd year of Moses he began the fashioning of linen.[1176] In his 28th year he became a prince, and in his 40th year he slew the evil-doing Israelite and fled.
4/ After he fled, Yanēs and Yambrēs built the garden of demons through the sufferings of the children of Israel. And they took 980[1177] children from them and sacrificed to demons and from that day forth the demons became obedient to the magicians.
5/ Question: How many chariots did Pharaoh have?
Answer: The chariots were six hundred.
6/ Question (and) Answer: How did Moses split the sea,?
He held forth his staff before (him) and said, "Ayia," that is, my God (is) before me. To the right side[1178] (he said), "Šrayia," (that is) , God you brought us forth. To the left side (he said), "Adonia," (that is) you, Lord of Lords (are) with us.[1179]

4.11. Story of the Prophet Asaph

This text is found in the *Yaysmaurk'* (Synaxarion) and is devoted to Asaph, presumably meaning the author to whom some Psalms are ascribed.[1180] He is counted among the prophets of David's time also in 4.4 §8 above. We have drawn this document from M724, *Miscellany* of the year 1736 in which manuscript it occurs on fols. 178r–180r. This first part of this compound manuscript was copied in Jerusalem and Bethlehem in 1736 (see Eganyan et al. 2007, 3:485–92). It is inscribed in a rough *notrgir* script and contains a number of diverse texts.

1174. Obscure.
1175. Perhaps this means, "magicians."
1176. Taking the word from կտաւ "linen." It seems that this reference was drawn from Pharaoh's dressing of Joseph in linen (Gen 41:42), and so regarded as a stage on the way to Moses becoming a prince. That is the point of the next clause.
1177. No special significance is attached to this number that I can discover.
1178. I.e., he moved it to the right hand side. And so to the left in the next phrase.
1179. These explanations of divine names sound like onomastic glosses.
1180. See, e.g., Ps 76(77), 79(78:1), 80(79:1), compare 1 Chr 15:19, 16:5, 26:1, and 2 Chr 5:12, etc.

Text

0/   Պատմութիւն Ասափայ Մարգարէի
1/ Արքայն Դաւիթ շինեաց զսուրբն Սիոն. եւ եբեր զտորանն տապանականն. զոր արար զՄովսէս[1181] մեծաւ պատուով, քնարաւ, եւ ձայնիւ փողոյ. եւ կաքաւելով իւր յառաջի տապ/fol. 178v/անակին: Եւ եդ ի սուրբն Սիոն. եհար[1182] անդ զտորանն. եւ կանգնեաց զտապանակ ուխտին: Եւ ած ի տանէն. Ղեւեայ. արս իմաստունս. ուշիմս եւ հանճարեղս. մտացին[1183] փափկածայնս. եւ քաղցրաբարբառս. Եւ ուսոյց նոցա զերգս. սաղմոսացն իւրոց. եւ նոքայ յեղանակս հանէին եւ ի ձայնս բաժանէին:

2/ Որոց յառաջնորդք էին. եւ դասագլուխք Ասափ. եւ Դիթում. եւ որդիքն Կորխեաց. որք եւ յիշատակին ի վերնագիրն սաղմոսին:

3/ Չի էին եւ նոքա շնորհիօք մարգարէք. վասն որոյ եւ գրեաց Դաւիթ զանունանս նոցա ի վերնայգիր սաղմոսին իւրոյ.

4/ Չի ատ յապայս յիշեցին. եւ մի մոռացին անունանք նորայ: Եւ Քրիստոսի յուսույն մերոյ. փառք յաւիտեանս Ամէն:

Translation

0/   Story of the Prophet Asaph
1/ King David built holy Zion and he brought the altar with the Ark, which Moses had made, with great honor and with harp and soundings of trumpet and his dancing before the Ark.[1184] And he set (them) in holy Sion; he fixed the altar there and set up the Ark of the Covenant.[1185] And from the house of Levi he brought wise men, intelligent and skilful. They entered with delicate voice and sweet speech. And he taught them the songs of his Psalms and they brought forth music and were set apart for this singing.[1186]

1181. The prefixed q- is superfluous in standard Ancient Armenian, but many instances of its mistaken insertion are to be observed in medieval manuscripts. See Stone and Hillel, "Index," no. 250.

1182. Literally: smote, struck

1183. This is taken as an odd form of մտանեմ, which should yield մտին.

1184. The incident is described in 2 Sam 6:14, 16 and 1 Chr 15:29. Compare the Armenian text entitled History of the Ark of the Covenant published in Stone in press, 253–66.

1185. 2 Samuel 6:17. This refers to the bringing of the Ark of the Covenant to Jerusalem. It was not put into a building until Solomon built the temple: see 1 Kgs 6:1, 8:6–10, 2 Chr 5:2–8.

1186. This is described in 1 Chr 6:31–33, and Asaph is mentioned in 6:39. Similarly Asaph is

2/ Asaph and Jeduthun (Dit'on)[1187] and the sons of Korah were leaders and heads of ranks, who are also mentioned in the subscription of Psalms.[1188]

3/ For by grace they too were prophets, on account of which David also wrote their names in the superscriptions of his Psalms.

4/ So that in the future their names would be remembered and not forgotten.[1189] And to Christ our hope, eternal glory. Amen.

4.12. Story of the Prophet Nathan

This text is a different composition concerning Nathan from the Life of Nathan, which is part of the Vitae Prophetarum and which I published in Stone 1982, 136–39. A comparison shows that both the order of the incidents and the narrative plot differ from Life of Nathan. It is found directly following the Story of Asaph in M724, fols. 178v–179r. Moreover, both the Story of Nathan and the Life of Nathan contain the apocryphal story explaining how Nathan was delayed en route to rebuke David over the affair of Bathsheba.[1190] The biblical story relates that after David married Bathsheba (2 Sam 11–12), Nathan came to him and rebuked him, using the famous parable of the poor man's lamb (2 Sam 12:1–4). However no incident delaying him and thus foiling his prevention of David's sin is even hinted at in 2 Sam 12:1, which simply says, "And the LORD sent Nathan to David." The incident is also mentioned in the superscription of Ps 51(50).

Text

1/ Այլ եւ զայս եւս Նաթանայ մարգարէին. որ էր ի յաւուրս Դաւ/ fol. 179r /թի եւ որդոյ նորա. Սողոմոնի:

---

included among the Levitical singers in 2 Chr 5:12, together with Heman and Jeduthun. These three singers recur together several time in Chronicles: see e.g., 2 Chr 35:15.

1187. Korah is mentioned in the superscription of various Psalms such as Ps 42(41), 44(43), 46(45), etc. but not associated with Asaph there. Jeduthun is ascribed authorship of Ps 39(38); in Ps 62 (61) he is associated with David and in Ps 77 (76) with Asaph.

1188. Literally: Psalm, but meaning Psalter.

1189. Thus the author systematizes everything. David wrote all the Psalms, but he put the names of Asaph, Jeduthun, and Korah in the superscription of "his Psalms" because, as §3 says, "they too were prophets."

1190. This story is not to be found in 2 Sam 11–12 where the story of David and Bathsheba is recorded. Observe the superscription of Ps 51(50:2).

Եւ էր նա վերակցու եւ խնամածու. տանն Դաւթի. վասն որոյ
յանդիմանեցաւ զԴաւիթ յորժամ յանցեաւն ի կինն Ուրիա: Եւ
յառաջ քան զմեղանչելն Դաւիթի իմացաւ Նաթան որ պիտէր
մեղանչէր արքային:[1191]

2/ Եւ եղեալ զայր ի զզուշուցանել զԴաւիթ. եւ ոչ ժամանեաց
զի յայլում տեղոջ էր. հեռագոյն յարքայէ: Եւ մինչդեռ
զայր հանդիպեցաւ ի ճանապարհին զի երիտասարդ մի
Իսրայելացի յայնմ ժամու սպաննեալ եւ ընկեցեալ էր ի վերայ
ճանապարհին:

3/ Եւ զի ծանօթ եւ սիրելի էր. Նաթան առն սպաննելոյ վասն
այն ոչ կարաց զանց առնել զնդվաւ:[1192] Այլ մինչ բարձեալ
զսպաննեալն զրսպեաց. եւ թաղեաց. մեղաւ Դաւիթ եւ ոչ եհաս
նմա Նաթան:

4/ / fol. 179v / Եւ յետոյ եկեալ յանդիմանեաց զնա առակաւ
դատաստանի: Ճ ոչխարաց. եւ միոյ որոջի: Իբրեւ արքայ ասաց
թէ մահապարտ է այր. ապա ասաց Նաթան թէ դու ես այրն
արքայ: Եւ Դաւիթ ասաց թէ մեղայ Տեառն: Եւ Նաթան ասաց
նմա. Տէր անցոյց զքեւ զմեղդ քո եւ մի մեռցիս:

5/ Սա այս Նաթան մարգարէ խրատեաց զԲերսաբէ զմայրն
Սողոմոնի ի թագաւորէն Ադոնփիա փոխանակ Դաւթի հօրն
իւրոյ: Սորին խրատովս եմուտ Բերսաբէ առ Դաւիթ եւ յիշեցոյց
արքայի ծածուկ երդումն իւր. ընդ նմա:

6/ Ապա եմուտ եւ Նաթան յառաջի արքայի եւ վկայութեամբք
ետ իրաւունս. Բերսաբեայ: Յայնժամ հրաման ետ Դաւիթ
Նաթանայ մարգարէի եւ Բանեայ որդոյն / fol. 180r / Յովիտեայ.
եւ Սադովկայ քահանայի թագաւորեցուցանել զՍողովմոն եւ
այնպես արարին:

7/ Եւ աղաղակեաց յամենայն ժողովուրդն ասելով. Կեցցէ
արքայ. Եւ կեցեալ Նաթան յոլով ժամանակս եւ ապա մեռաւ
խաղաղութեամբք. եւ թաղեցաւ ընդ հօր իւրում փառաւորապէս:

Translation

1/ This is another (text) of Nathan the prophet who was in the days of David and his son Solomon.

He was overseeing and caring for the house of David. For this reason

---

1191. In the manuscript, most occurrences of this word are capitalized.
1192. Observe the deviant orthography: for this see Stone and Hillel, "Index," no. 407.

he reproached David when he sinned with[1193] the wife of Uriah. And before David sinned, Nathan learned that the king was going to sin.[1194]

2/ And going forth he was coming to warn David and he did not arrive in time for he was somewhere else rather distant from the king. And while he was coming it happened on the way that a young Israelite man at that time had been murdered and cast upon the way.[1195]

3/ And because he was known and dear (to him), Nathan was unable to neglect him. But while he took up the murdered man, bound[1196] him and buried him, David sinned and Nathan did not reach him.

4/ And afterwards he came and rebuked him with the parable of the judgement of 100 sheep and one lamb.[1197] When the king said, "The man deserves death," then Nathan said, "You are the man, O king." And David said, "I have sinned against the Lord." And Nathan said to him, "The Lord will make (this) sin of yours pass from you and you will not die."[1198]

5/ This Nathan the prophet advised Bathsheba, Solomon's mother, when Adonia became king instead of David his father. At his counsel, Bathsheba entered in to David's presence and reminded the king of his secret oath with her.[1199]

6/ Then Nathan also entered in before the king and with witness he gave the right to Bathsheba. Then David commanded Nathan the prophet and Banaiah son of Jehoiadea and Sadok the priest to crown Solomon king, and they did so.

7/ And he called out to all the people saying, "Long live the king!"[1200] And Nathan lived a long time and then he died peacefully and he was buried gloriously with his father.

1193. Literally: in.
1194. This incident is discussed in the introductory remarks to this short text.
1195. The same story occurs in the *Life of Nathan* published in Stone 1982, 136–39, but the wording and the order of events are quite different.
1196. I.e., in winding cloths. In *Life of Nathan* §4 he wraps the corpse in his cloak.
1197. 2 Sam 12:1–6.
1198. 2 Sam 12:7–12, 13–14.
1199. 1 Kgs 1:31–35. This incident is not mentioned in the *Life of Nathan*.
1200. 1 Kgs 1:38–39.

4.13. This Is the Story of Nineveh an[d of Jo]nah

This text, found in M6340, fols. 47r–50r retells the Jonah narrative. The manuscript is a rich repository of apocryphal tales, and it is briefly discussed above in connection with text 4.8. As observed in the notes, the author is not familiar with the geography of the Land of Israel.[1201] The retelling reflects consideration of some difficulties in the text, as may be seen in Jonah's concern for his own prophetic standing in §§2–4. He is said to be worried about preaching a destruction which he knows, through his prophetic insight, will not take place.[1202]

Text

1/ / fol. 47r / [Ա]յս է [Պ]ատմութիւն [Նին]վէ ի [ե]ւ [Յ]ունանու: Բ[ազմա]ցան մեղք Նինվեացըն: Եւ ի միում աւուր մինչ աղաւթեր Յունան. ձայն Տեառն եղեւ նմայ եւ ասաց. ո՛վ Ունան գնայ Նինվէ քարոզեայ եւ ասայ. ահա Գ աւր եւ այլ ոչ եւս իցէ Նինվէ. զի բարկացեալ է Տէր եւ կամի կործանել զքաղաքս:

2/ Ասէ Յունան. Տէր գիտեմ զի քաղցր ես եւ ողորմած. երբ քարոզեմ նորա լսեն զքարոզն իմ. դարձ գան ի մեղաց. եւ դու Տէր լսես աղաւթից նոցա. ողորմիս եւ փրկես զնոսա: Եւ սուտ լինի քարոզութիւն իմ. եւ անուն իմ լինի սուտասաց մարգարէ. զի լաւ է ինձ մեռանել քան թէ սուտ ասած լինել:

3/ Դարձեալ ձայն եղեւ առ Ունան եւ ասէ. ո՛չ խնայեմ քակել զՆինվէ. եւ դու Յունան երբ ի Նինվէ. բարձր ձայնիւ գոչեաց եւ ասա. ահա, Գ աւր աւերի եւ կործանի զքաղաքս. այլ ոչ եւս իցէ Նինվէ: Երկեաւ Յունան այլ ոչ կարաց պատասխանի տալ Աստուծոյ. եւ Յունան եւ կամէր երթալ եւ քարոզել Նինվէի. քներ եւ ի միտն ածեր զբազմողորմութիւնն եւ զգութն Աստուծոյ. եւ ոչ հաւատայր զանցումն Նինվէի. քանզի մարգարէ էր գիտեր որ ոչ կործանի Տէր զՆինվէ. եւ սիրտն իւր ոչ վկայեր: Իբրեւ հասաւ եզր ծովուն ի միտն ածեր / fol. 47v / քներ ընդ միտս իւր.

4/ եւ թէ Տէր չկամի զՆինվէ. ընդեր առաքէ զիս ի քարոզութիւն. գիտեմ զի Տէր վասն այն առաքէ զիս ի քարոզել Նինվէ. զի դարձ գան եւ ապաշխարեն եւ ապրեն ի պատուհասէն. բայց անուն իմ սուտասած մարգարէ լինի: Եւ ոչ կարեմ զայդ առնել

1201. See this discussion of this in note 1232.
1202. See the discussion of this in note 1228.

PART FOUR   267

թէ Նինվեացիք մեղք գործեն առանց պատուհասի մնան եւ ես
վասն մեղաց[1203] նոցա սուտասած լինիմ:

5/ Եւ մինչ Ունան զայս խորհէր.[1204] եհաս նաւ մի[1205] զայր մեծ
ի վերայ ծովուն. զի փոքր նաւակն եկն ի եզր ծովուն զի ջուր
քաղցր[1206] առնէ ի գետոյն: Հարցոյց զնոսա Յունան եւ ասաց.
ուր կամի գնալ նաւս. եւ նոքա ասեն Ի Թարս(իս) կամի գնալ
որ Պասրայ ասեն:

6/ Ասէ Յունան. եւ ես կամիմ ի Թարսիս գնալ. առէք զվարձս
նալիդ. եւ զիս ընդ ձեզ առէք: Եւ նոքա առին զՅունան. եւ
տարեալ մուծին ի նա[ւ]ն: Զի կամեցաւ Յունան փախչել ի
Թարսիս. եւ ոչ քարոզել Նինվեացւոցն.

7/ Եւ նոյն ժամայն շարժեցաւ հողմն եւ եղեւ մրրիկ. եւ տապալէր
նաւն մերձ ընկղմիլ: Ամենեքեան աղաղակէին առ աստուածն
իւրեանց: Իսկ Յունան մուշտակն ի գլուխն արկեալ խորթայր
եւ սուտաքուն լինէր. զի գիտէր որ պատուհաս եւ տապալումն
վասն իւրն էր. բայց / fol. 48r / սուտ խորթայր եւ ոչ ինչ ասէր:
Զի առաւել եւս բազմանայր ալիք ծովուն: Իս[կ] մի ումն
զարթուցանէր Ունան եւ ասէր. ընդէ՞ր ննջես. արի աղաչեաց
զԱստուած քո միթէ ապրիմք ի պատուհասէս:

8/ Ել Յունան եւ ասէ. վասն իմ մեղացս է այս շարժմունքս եւ
մրրիկս. եւ թէ կամիք ապրել. արկէք զիս ի ծով. եւ դուք փրկիք:
Եւ եթէ ոչ արկանէք զիս ի ծովդ. դուք ամենայն ընկղմիք ի ծովդ:

9/ Եւ նոքա հարցին թէ ինչ փասա մեղք ես գործեալ որ բարկացաւ
քեզ Աստուած քո: Ասէ Յունան. ստեղծող ամենայնի
երկնաւորն Աստուած. առաքեաց զիս քարոզել Նինվեացոց. եւ
ես ոչ կամեցայ գնալ եւ քարոզել. կամիմ փախչել ի Թարսիս.
վասն այն բարկացեալ է Տէրն իմ. եւ կամի խեղդել զիս: Եւ եթէ
կամիք ապրել արկէք զիս ի ծովդ: Եւ եթէ ոչ արկանէք զիս ի
ծովդ. զի դուք ամենեքեան կորնչիք:

10/ Իբրեւ լսեցին նոքա զբանս Յունանու այլ աւելի երկեան. եւ ոչ
կամէին զՅունան արկանել ի ծովս զի մի բարկասցի Աստուած
Յունանու: Եւ արկին վիճակ թէ ում մեղաց է ալիքն.[1207] եւ
անկաներ վիճակն ի վերայ Յունանու: Եւ Գ անգամ վիճան
արկին. եւ անկաւ ի վերայ Յունանու:

1203. մեղաց om; in marg p.m.
1204. A sign precedes.
1205. Erasure of two letters.
1206. Erasure of one word.
1207. Erasure follows.

եւ քանզ<ի>¹²⁰⁸ եւս բարկանայր եւ զռոայր ալիքն. առինցՅունան
եւ / fol. 48v / արկին ի ծովս. եւ առ ժամայն դատարեցաւ ալիքն:
Չի Յունան զինքն խեղդելն լաւ համարեցաւ. քան թէ քարոզել
Նինվեի անցանել եւ ինքն ոչ սուտ լինել:

11/ Իբրեւ արկին զՅունան ի ծովս. Տէր հրամայեաց ձկան մեծի
կլանել զնա՝ Գ օր եւ Գ գիշեր շրշեցոյց զնա յատակս ծովուն:
Եւ յետ Գ աւուրն հրամանաւն Աստուծոյ տարեալ զՅունան
թքեաց յեզր ծովուն ի կողմն Նինվեի: Դարձեալ ձայն եղեւ առ
Յունան եւ ասէ. Ուր կամիս փախչել¹²⁰⁹ Յունան. երթ ի Նինվէ.
քարոզեայ եւ ասա ահա Գ աւուր այլ ոչ եւս իցէ Նինվէ:

12/ Եւ ելեալ Յունան մտո ի քաղաքն Նինվէացոց. բարձր ձայնիւ
քարոզէր եւ ասէր. Վայ՝ ձեզ Նինվէացիք զի ահա միւսեւ Գ աւր
անցանի քաղաքս եւ կործանի եւ այլ ոչ եւս իցէ Նինվէ: Չի արք
քաղաքին ահագուցանէին զՅունան եւ ոչ ասէլ այնպէս. եւ
Յունան պատմէր նոցա եւ ասէր թէ բարկացեալ է Տէր ի վերայ
ձեր. եւ կամի կործանել զձեզ. զի հրամայեաց Տէր յառաջագոյն
զայս պատմել ձեզ:

13/ Եւ ես կամեցայ փախչել նավով ի Թարսիս. եւ տապալեցոյց
զնավս վասն իմ. ընկեցին¹²¹⁰ զիս ի ծովս: Եւ ձուկն մեծ կլեաց
զիս. պահեաց զիս Գ տիւ եւ Գ գիշեր. եւ բ[ե]րեալ թքեաց
զիս ի յեզր ծովուն. կենդանի պա[հ]/ fol. 49r /եաց զիս Տէր. եւ
առաքեաց զիս կրկին հրամանաւ քարոզել ձեզ զաւերումս
աշխարհիս:

14/ Եւ ես Տեառն հրամանաւ ասեմ ձեզ. ահայ Գ աւուր այլ ոչ եւս
իցէ: Ոչ վախեմ¹²¹¹ ի ձէնջ եւ ոչ երկնչիմ սպանանելըն զիս.
այլ յայտնապէս պատմեմ ձեզ զբարկութիւնն Աստուծոյ թէ
հաւատայք թէ ոչ:

15/ Իսկ իշխանք քաղաքին գնացեալ պատմեցին զբարոզութիւնն
Յունանու եւ զաւերումս Նինվեի: Իբրեւ լուաւ թազաւորն եւ
բերեալ ահացոյց զՅունան եւ ասաց. կտրեմ զլեզուտ մի ասել
այդպէս:

16/ Ասէ Յունան. ոչ կարեմ թագուցանել զբան Տեառն վասն ահէն¹²¹²
քո. զի պատուհասողն ձեր ես չեմ. Աստուած է որ պատուհասէ.
եւ եթէ զիտէք զասացեալն իմ սուտ է զլեզուս իմ կտրեցէք եւ

1208. Clearly a corruption.
1209. Observe the confusion of խ/ղ.
1210. This is a postclassical form. Note also the orthography նաւ.
1211. վախ- above line, p.m.
1212. The case usage is odd.

զիս սպանեցէք: զի բանք Տեառն ոչ է սուտ: Եւ եթէ ոչ դառնայք ի մեղաց եւ ոչ ապաշխարիք. կործանի քաղաքս չնչվիք¹²¹³ եւ կորնչիք ամենեքեան:

17/ Յայնժամ թագաւորն հանեալ զբեհեզն եւ զձիրանին. եւ զգեցաւ խորգ եւ նստաւ ի վերայ մոխրի. ադաւթեր արտասուաւք, ադաչեր զԱստուած զի դարձուցէ զպատուհասն ի քաղաքէն: Եւ պատուիրեաց մեծամեծացն. եւ ամենայն ժողովրդեանն դառնալ ի մեղաց եւ ապաշխարել. Եւ այնմ գիշերի եկն մառախուղ¹²¹⁴ եւ չորք պատեաց զքաղաքն: Երեքեր եւ տապալեր. շարժ / fol. 49v / եւ փլաներ զամենայն շինուածս մինչ զի ոչ մաց բարձր տեղիք շինուածոց. Գ օր եւ Գ գիշեր այնպէս պատեալ էր¹²¹⁵ խոսարն զքաղաքն որ ոչ տիւն գիտին եւ ոչ {գերեկն}¹²¹⁶ գիշերն:

18/ Այնպէս ապաշխարանք մտան. եւ սուք մտան քաղաքն զամենայն. մեծ եւ փոքր. լային եւ ազային. ադաւթէին եւ պադատէին առ Տէր: Իսկ մանկունքն հարցանէին զծնաւղքն¹²¹⁷ իւրեանց եւ ասէին. այլ լոյս տեսանելոց եմք եթէ ոչ: Եւ ծնաւղքն մխիթարէին զորդին իւրեանց եւ ասէին: Ադաչէք զԱստուած. զի դուք մանունք անմեղ էք. թերեւս լսէցէ ադաթից ձերոց. եւ դարձուցէ զպատուհասն. եւ տայ լոյս:

19/ Այնպէս ուղիղ սրտիւ ապաշխարանք մտան պահաւք եւ ծոմովք. մինչ զի անասունս իւրեանց ծոմով պահեցին: Իսկ մարգարէն Յունան չշչեր փողոցն ի վայ բարձր բարբառով ճայներ եւ ասեր. ապաշխարեցէք ապաշխարեցէք. զի յետ Գ աւուրն այլ ոչ եւս իցէ: Եւ յետ Գ աւուրն. դարձեալ եկն Յունան աւետիս ետ քաղաքին եւ ասաց. լուաւ Տէր ադաւթից ձերոց. եւ դարձոյց զպատուհասն. վաղիւն ձեզ լոյս լինելոց է զի առաջաւորի պահոցն էր: Յետ լուսանալ ուրբաթ առաւաւտուն բացաւ զդուռն ողորմութեանն Աստուծոյ. եւ լուաւ Աստուած ճայնի ան/ fol. 50r /մեղաց տղայոցն. Բ-տասան բիւրոցն:

20/ Թող զալեւորսն եւ զկանայան զքիլ անմեղ տղայոցն Բ-տասան բիւրք էին: Յորժամ քաղցրացաւ Աստուած ի Նինվէի. յայնժամ յոյժ տրտմեցաւ Յունան: Եւ երթեալ ի խուչն իւր լայր եւ

1213. This is a postclassical form.
1214. Taken as մառախուղ. For the variant n/ու, see Stone and Hillel, "Index," no. 407.
1215. Above the line p.m.
1216. With deletion marks.
1217. Observe the use of the nominative ending where an accusative would be expected.

աղաւթէր ասելով. զի սուտ մարգարէ եղէ ես ի մէջ Նինվէի. եւ ստեաց Տէր զխաւսս իմ:

21/ Եւ առաւաւտն ելեալ եւտես դրումենի մի մեծ եւ պայծառ կանաչեալ ի գլուխս խցին իւրոյ. որով տեսեալ առաւոտուն ուրախացեալ. եւ բերեալ չոր ծառ գրցեաց ի յատակս դրումենոյն. եւ արկաներ զտերեւսն որ հովանի լինի ի վերայ իւրն: Եւ կայր ուրախութեամբ աւուրս ինչ:

22/ Եւ յետ աւուրց ելեալ առաւատուն եւտես դրումենին չորացեալ յոյժ տրտմեցաւ Յունան: Յայնժամ երեւեցաւ Տէրն մեր Յունանու եւ ասաց. ով Յունան դու որ վասն դրումենոյդ այտչափ տրտմեցար. ապա որչափի տրտմութիւն է կորուստ այտչափ ժողովրդեանտ որ պատկեր եւ հոգի Աստուծոյ են դրքայ:

23/ Յայնժամ անկեալ ի վերայ երեսին դողալով աղաղակեր եւ ասեր. Մեղայ մեղայ կամք քո աւրինեալ եղիցի:[1218]

Translation

1/ [T]his is the [S]tory of [Nin]veh and Jonah.

The sins of the Ninevehites were many.[1219] And one day, while Jonah was praying,[1220] the voice of the Lord came to him and said, "O Jonah, go to Nineveh, preach and say, "Behold, in three days[1221] Nineveh will be no more, for the Lord is wrath and wishes to destroy this city."

2/ Jonah said, "Lord, I know that you are sweet[1222] and merciful. When I preach, will they hearken to my preaching? Will they turn back from sins? And will you, Lord, hear their prayers? Will you have mercy and save them and will my preaching become false and my name will become 'false prophet.' For it is better for me to die than to speak falsely."[1223]

3/ Again a voice came unto Jonah and it said, "I will not pity the destruc-

---

1218. A colophon follows.
1219. Jonah 1:2. The book of Jonah is cited throughout according to NRSV.
1220. In the Bible, Jonah is only said to pray when he is in trouble (Jonah 2:1, 7, 4:2) but here it seems that Jonah's prayer is simple devotion.
1221. Nineveh is granted forty days according to Jonah 3:4. The number "three days" is probably taken from Jonah 3:3, which describes length of a journey the breadth of the city.
1222. An adjective very often used in Armenian texts to describe heavenly beings or states. It has the meaning of "kind" in many contexts.
1223. In the Book of Jonah, this issue only arises in 4:1–3 after Jonah has prophesied to Nineveh. I discuss this sentiment in biblical and apocryphal literature in some detail in Stone 1990a, 86 and see also 256.

tion[1224] of Nineveh. And you, Jonah, go to Nineveh, call loudly and say, 'Behold! In three days this city will be ruined and destroyed. Nineveh will be no more.'"[1225] Jonah was afraid but he was unable to answer God. Jonah set out and wished to go and to preach to Nineveh. He investigated and considered God's great mercy and pity and he did not believe in the passing of Nineveh. Because he was a prophet he knew that the Lord would not destroy Nineveh,[1226] and his heart did not bear witness. When he reached the sea-shore he considered (and) investigated with his mind,

4/ "If the Lord does not desire Nineveh, why is he sending me to preach?[1227] I know that for this reason the Lord has sent me to preach in Nineveh, so that they might turn and repent and be saved from the punishment, but my name (i.e., reputation) will be as a false prophet.[1228] And I cannot do this. If the Ninevehites sinned, they will remain without punishment and I will become a speaker of falsehood because of them."[1229]

5/ And while Jonah thought this, he saw a great ship coming on the sea, for a small boat came to the sea-shore to take sweet water from the river.[1230] Jonah asked them and said, "Where does this ship wish[1231] to go?" And they said, "It wishes to go to Tarshish,[1232] which people call Basra."[1233]

1224. Literally: have pity to destroy.
1225. See §1, above.
1226. Jonah 4:2. Note the late conception of prophet at play in the Armenian document here—a prophet knows the future. We noted the same issue in *The Story of Terah and of Father Abraham* §44 (Stone 2012, 161) and further in that work §45 175, §46 231.
1227. This seems like a philosophical and exegetical question on the original text that was raised in Rabbinic literature as well, see Ginzberg 1909–1938, 4:247, 6:349 where Jonah's fear of giving false prophecy comes from an early event.
1228. Compare with Rabbi Yeshaya of Tirani (twelfth–thirteenth centuries) in his commentary on Jonah 1:3 "to flee to Tarshish That is outside the land of Israel and prophecy does not abide there, so why was he fleeing? As we have heard exegeted, (it was) so that they would not call him a false prophet should they repent and God will repent of the evil."
1229. Jonah seems to be concerned that God will not destroy Nineveh even if the people of Nineveh do not repent.
1230. This expansionary detail shows that the author of this Jonah retelling was not in the least familiar with the actual geographical situation of Jaffa.
1231. I.e., intend.
1232. The port of Tarshish (Tarsus) cannot be identified with any one location, see Gordon, 1962, 517–18. Basra might be an ignorant gloss on the place name made by the author of the Armenian text: see the next note.
1233. There was a city in northern Edom called Bozrah (Gen 36:33, Isa 34:6, Jer 48:24, etc.). Here, however, the intention may well be the city of Basra: see Stone 2012, 245–56, see p. 255, referring to Basrah in Mesopotamia. In fact, the author "knows" Tarshish to be in Babylon, and

6/ Jonah said, "I also wish to go to Tarshish. Receive the ship's fare, and take me with you." And they took Jonah and brought him and boarded him onto the ship, for Jonah wished to flee to Tarshish and not to prophesy to the Ninevehites.[1234]

7/ And at that very time a wind arose and a storm came and the ship was tossed around, close to foundering. All were praying to their gods. Then Jonah put his fur robe on his head, went apart and was feigning sleep, for he knew that the punishment and the ruin were because of him. But he went apart falsely and said nothing.[1235] Because the waves of the sea became even more frequent,[1236] then a certain man[1237] woke Jonah up and said, "Why are you sleeping? Arise, beseech your God so that we may survive this punishment."[1238]

8/ Jonah went forth and said, "These tossings and this storm are on account of my sins. If you wish to live, cast me into the sea and you will be saved. And, if you do not cast me into the sea, you will all drown in the sea."[1239]

9/ And they asked, "Which harmful sin have you done that your God is wrath with you?" Jonah said, "Heavenly God, the Creator of all despatched me to preach to the Ninevehites and I did not wish to go and preach. I wish to flee to Tarshish. Therefore the Lord is wrath and wishes me to drown. And if you wish to live, cast me into the sea. And if you do not cast me into the sea, you all will perish."[1240]

10/ When they heard Jonah's words, they were even more afraid, and (yet) they did not wish to cast Jonah into the sea, lest Jonah's God be wrathful. And they cast lots (to determine) on account of whose sin the waves were. And the lot fell upon Jonah. And they cast lots three times and it fell upon Jonah.[1241] And because the waves grew angrier and more violent,[1242] they took Jonah and cast him into the sea. And at

---

so identified it with Basra, and the goal of Jonah's flight. The actual location of biblical Tarshish is uncertain. See note 1032 above.

1234. Jonah 1:3.
1235. Jonah 1:4–5. That Jonah feigned sleep is an expansion.
1236. Literally: numerous.
1237. Here it is "a certain man," while in Jonah 1:6 it is "the captain."
1238. Jonah 1:6.
1239. Jonah 1:12.
1240. Jonah 1:12. In the biblical story, this incident comes after the sailors draw lots.
1241. The sailors' fear precedes the drawing of lots in Jonah 1:5–7.
1242. Jonah 1:11.

once the waves stopped,[1243] for Jonah reckoned it better that he himself be drowned than that he preach that Nineveh will pass away and he himself become a liar.[1244]

11/ When they cast Jonah into the sea, God commanded a great fish to swallow him.[1245] For three days and three nights (the fish) took him around at the foundations of the sea. And after three days, at God's command it brought Jonah and vomited him up on the sea shore,[1246] in the region of Nineveh.[1247] Again a voice came to Jonah saying, "Where do you wish to flee, Jonah? Go to Nineveh, preach and say, 'Behold! in three days Nineveh will be no longer.'"

12/ And Jonah, going forth entered into the city of the Ninevehites. He preached with a loud voice and said, "Woe to you Ninevehites, for in three days this city will pass away and be destroyed and Nineveh will be no more." [1248] Because the men of the city were intimidating Jonah so that he would not say thus. And Jonah told them and said, "The Lord is wrathful against you and wishes to destroy you. For the Lord commanded me to come to tell you in advance."[1249]

13/ "And I wished to flee by ship to Tarshish and he tossed the ship around on my account. They cast me into the sea and the great fish swallowed me. He kept me for three days and three nights and bringing (me), he vomited me up on the sea shore. The Lord kept me alive and with a second command he sent me to preach to you the destruction of this land.[1250]

14/ "And I say to you at the Lord's command, 'Behold, in three days it will

---

1243. Jonah 1:15.
1244. This additional idea is connected with Jonah's fear that he might be shown to be a false prophet, see above §§3–4.
1245. Jonah 1:17.
1246. Jonah 2:10. Again, the biblical order of events is reversed for there, Jonah prays to God before the fish vomits him ashore.
1247. This does not really make geographical sense because Nineveh does not have a seashore, and the Bible says, "dry land" (Jonah 2:10). The author seems to assume that Tarsus, for which Jonah departed by boat, was near Nineveh. However, even in the book of Jonah this odd assertion is made, for how could the fish deliver him to dry land unless it was by the sea? In Rabbinic literature Jonah's adventure inside the fish is replete with magic and miracles that allow the story to abandon its need for geographical coherence. See Ginzberg 1909–1938, 6:350.
1248. Jonah 3:4. The text here says "three days," but the biblical text says "forty days." See note 1221 above.
1249. Jonah 3:4–5. The reaction of the Ninevehites is added in this text, while in the Bible they believe him straight away. "Previously" could also be translated "in advance."
1250. Or: world. The contents of chap. 2 of Jonah are covered by §13.

be no longer. I am not afraid of you and do not fear my death,[1251] but I will clearly tell you of the Lord's wrath, whether you believe or not.'"[1252]

15/ Then the princes of the city went and related Jonah's preaching and the destruction of Nineveh. When the king heard, having brought Jonah he threatened (him) and said, "I will cut out your tongue. Do not speak thus!"

16/ Jonah said, "I cannot hide the Lord's word on account of fear of you, for I am not the one who punishes you. It is God who punishes (you). And if you apprehend that what I say is false, cut out my tongue and kill me. For the words of the Lord are not false. And if you do not turn away from sin and do not repent, this city will be destroyed. You will all be annihilated and perish."

17/ Then the king put off fine linen and purple and dressed in sackcloth and sat upon ashes.[1253] He prayed, tearfully he beseeched God to turn away the punishment from the city. And he commanded the grandees and all the people to turn away from (their) sins and to repent.[1254] And on that night, fog came and encircled the city. It trembled and was overthrown, [it][1255] shook and knocked down all the buildings until no high spot that was built remained. For three days and three nights in this fashion the darkness surrounded the city so that they did not know day or night.[1256]

18/ Thus all the city, great and small, entered into repentance and entered into mourning. They wept and mourned, they prayed and supplicated to the Lord. Then the children asked their parents and said, "Shall we see light again, or not?" And the parents had pity on their children and said, "Beseech God, for you little ones are without sin. Perchance he will listen to your prayers and turn aside the punishment and give light."[1257]

19/ Thus with upright heart they entered into repentance with fasts and

---

1251. Literally: my being killed.
1252. In the biblical book, the people of Nineveh believe Jonah right after he gives them the prophecy; Jonah 3:4–5.
1253. Jonah 3:6.
1254. Jonah 3:7–9.
1255. ցունդ is at the end of a page, and apparently -ին was not carried over.
1256. This description is not paralleled in the biblical Jonah. Three days' darkness are among the ten plagues of Egypt, see Exod 10:22. In Ps 18:11(17:12) clouds and darkness are elements of a theophany and might have provided inspiration for this Armenian expansion.
1257. The book of Jonah does not have all these details relating to the repentance of Nineveh and the portents that caused the inhabitants to repent.

fasting, to such an extent that they imposed fasting on their cattle.[1258] Then the prophet Jonah went around the streets moaning loudly and said, "Repent, repent! For after the third day (the city) will be no longer." And after the three days, Jonah came again, he informed the city and said, "The Lord has heard your prayers and he has turned aside the punishment. Tomorrow there will be light for you for it was the foremost of the fasts."[1259] After Friday morning dawned the gate of God's mercy was opened and God hearkened to the voice of twelve myriad sinless children.[1260]

20/ Apart from the aged men and the women, the sinless children were 12 myriad in number.[1261] When God relented towards Nineveh, at that time Jonah was exceedingly sad, and he went to his hut.[1262] He wept and prayed saying, "I have become a false prophet in the midst of Nineveh and the Lord has put my pronouncement to the lie."

21/ And in the morning, going forth he saw a great gourd-vine, shining green on the top of his hut.[1263] When he saw this in the morning he rejoiced and brought a dry pole,[1264] he drove it in at the root[1265] of the gourd and he spread its leaves so that there might be shade over him.[1266] And he remained happily for some days.

22/ And after some days, when Jonah went forth in the morning he saw that the gourd-vine had dried up:[1267] he was very sad. Then our Lord appeared to Jonah and said, "O Jonah, you who are so sad on account of this gourd-vine, then how much sadness is the destruction of this many people who are the image and spirit of God?"[1268]

1258. Jonah 3:7.
1259. The translation of this phrase is not certain.
1260. This whole section is an expansion. Note the three days of repentance, which are discussed above: see note 1248. Why Friday should be mentioned is unclear unless it has to do with the day of the Crucifixion, but just what the exegetical logic is remains unclear.
1261. "twelve myriad children" is derived from Jonah 4:11, which speaks of: "more than 120,000 persons who do not know their right hand from their left," the latter phrase being interpreted as innocent children.
1262. See Jonah 4:5.
1263. Jonah 4:6. The author reconciles the gourd vine (§21) with Jonah's hut.
1264. Literally: tree.
1265. Literally: foundation. This again adds a detail to the description in biblical Jonah.
1266. Jonah 4:6.
1267. The worm is omitted here, compare Jonah 4:7. There the withering of the gourd happens at dawn the following day.
1268. This rebuke differs from Jonah 4:10–11.

23/ Then, falling on his face trembling he beseeched and said, "I have sinned, I have sinned. Blessed be your will."[1269]

1269. Jonah's confession of sin and repentance are added in the Armenian document. A scribe's colophon follows.

Bibliography

Ačaṙean, H. 1972. Հայոց Անձանունների Բառարան (*Dictionary of Armenian Proper Names*). Repr. ed. Beirut: Sewan.
Adler, Ada, ed. 1928–1938. Suidae Lexicon. 5 vols. Lexicographi graeci, recognitie et apparati critico instructi. Leipzig: Teubner.
Adler, William. 1989. *Time Immemorial: Archaic History and Its Sources in Christian Chronography from Julius Africanus to George Syncellus*. Dumbarton Oaks Studies 26. Washington DC: Dumbarton Oaks.
Adler, William, and Paul Tuffin. 2002. *The Chronography of George Synkellos*. Oxford: Oxford University Press.
Albrecht, Felix, and Arthur Manukyan. 2014. *Epiphanius von Salamis: Über die zwölf Steine im hohepriesterlichen Brustchild (De duodecim gemmis rationalis)*. Gorgias Eastern Christian Studies 37. Piscataway, NJ: Gorgias.
Amalyan, H. M. 1975. Բարգիրք Հայոց (*Armenian Lexica*). Erevan: Academy of Sciences.
———. 1971. Միջնադարեան Հայաստանի Բառարագրական Հուշարձաններ (XVI–XVII դդ.) (*Lexicographical Monuments of Mediaeval Armenia (XVI–XVII c.)*). Erevan: Academy of Sciences.
Anasyan, H. S. 1959. Հայկական մատենագիտութիւն (Ե-ԺԲ դդ.) (*Armenian Bibliology, 5–18th Centuries*). Vol. 1. Erevan: Academy of Sciences.
———. 1974. "Art. Andeas of Byzantium." P. 1:393 in Հայկական Սովետական հանրագիտարան (*Armenian Soviet Encyclopaedia*). 12 vols.. Erevšan: Academy of Sciences.
Anderson, Gary A. 2000. "The Exaltation of Adam and the Fall of Satan." Pages 83–110 in *Literature on Adam and Eve: Collected Essays*. Edited by Gary A. Anderson, Michael E. Stone, and Johannes Tromp. SVTP 15. Leiden: Brill.
Aptowitzer, V. 1922. *Kain und Abel in der Agada, den Apokryphen, der hellenistischen, christlichen und mohammedanischen Literatur*. Vienna: Löwit.
Aucher, J. B. 1818. *Eusebii Pamphylii Caesarensis Episcopi Chronicum Bipartum*. Venice: Mekhitarist Press.
Bauckham, Richard, James R. Davila, and Alexander Panayotov, eds. 2013. *Old Testament Pseudepigrapha: More Noncanonical Scriptures*, vol. 1. Grand Rapids: Eerdmans.
Blake, Robert P. 1934. *Epiphanius De Gemmis*. Studies and Documents 2. London: Christophers.
Bogharian, N. 1966. Մայր Ցուցակ ձեռագրաց Սրբոց Յակոբեանց (*Grand Catalogue of St. James Manuscripts*). Vol. 1. Jerusalem: Sts. James Press.
———. 1969. Մայր Ցուցակ ձեռագրաց Սրբոց Յակոբեանց (*Grand Catalogue of St. James Manuscripts*). Vol. 4. Jerusalem: Sts. James Press.
———. 1971. Մայր Ցուցակ ձեռագրաց Սրբոց Յակոբեանց (*Grand Catalogue of St. James Manuscripts*). Vol. 5. Jerusalem: Sts. James Press.

———. 1973. Մայր Ցուցակ ձեռագրաց Սրբոց Յակոբեանց (*Grand Catalogue of St. James Manuscripts*). Vol. 6. Jerusalem: Sts. James Press.
Byron, John. 2011. *Cain and Abel in Text and Tradition: Jewish and Christian Interpretations of the First Sibling Rivalry*. Leiden: Brill.
Čemčean, Sahak. 1996. Մայր ցուցակ հայերէն ձեռագրաց մատենադարանին Մխիթարեանց ի Վենետիկ (*Grand Catalogue of the Armenian Manuscripts of the Mekhitarist Library in Venice*). Vol. 6. Venice: Mekhitarist Press.
Conybeare, F. C. 1913. *A Catalogue of the Armenian Manuscripts in the British Museum*. London: British Museum.
Cowley, Roger W. 1988. *Ethiopian Biblical Interpretation: A Study in Exegetical Tradition and Hermeneutics*. University of Cambridge Oriental Publications 38. Cambridge: Cambridge University Press.
Cox, C. 1988. "Review of Zeyt'unian's Edition of Genesis from the Standpoint of Septuagint Criticism." *REArm* 21:87–125.
———. 1993. "A Reply to A.S. Zeyt'unyan's Response." *REArm* 24:313–15.
Cross, F. L., and E. A. Livingstone. 1974. *The Oxford Dictionary of the Christian Church*. 2nd rev. ed. Oxford: Oxford University Press.
Cumont, Franz. 1960. *Astrology and Religion Among the Greeks and Romans*. New York: Dover.
Dan, Joseph. 1986. *Sefer HaYashar*. Mosad Bialik: Jeruselem. In Hebrew.
DiTommaso, Lorenzo. 2001. *A Bibliography of Pseudepigrapha Research 1850–1999*. JSPSup 39. Sheffield: Sheffield Academic.
———. 2010. "Pseudepigrapha Notes III: 4. Old Testament Pseudepigrapha in the Yale University Manuscript Collection." *JSP* 20:3–80.
Eganyan, O. 2009. Մայր ցուցակ հայերէն ձեռագրաց Մաշտոցի անուան Մատենադարանի (*General Catalogue of Armenian Manuscripts of the Maštocʻ Matenadaran*). Vol. 5. Erevan: Nairi.
Eganyan, O., A. Zeyt'unyan, and Pʻ. Ant'abyan. 1965. Ցուցակ ձեռագրաց Մաշտոցի անվան մատենադարանի (*Catalogue of Manuscripts of the Maštocʻ Matenadaran*). Vol. 1. Erevan: Academy of Sciences.
———. 1970. Ցուցակ ձեռագրաց Մաշտոցի անվան մատենադարանի (*Catalogue of Manuscripts of the Maštocʻ Matenadaran*). Vol. 2. Erevan: Academy of Sciences.
———. 1984. Մայր ցուցակ հայերէն ձեռագրաց Մաշտոցի անուան Մատենադարանի (*Grand Catalogue of the Armenian Manuscripts of the Maštocʻ Matenadaran*). Vol. 1. Erevan: Academy of Sciences.
Elliot, J. K. 1993. *The Apocryphal New Testament*. Oxford: Clarendon.
Eynatyan, Juliet. 2002. *The Ancient Armenian Calendar (7th–15th cc.)*. Translated by Gohar Muradyan and Aram Topchyan. Erevan: Matendaran.
Fabricius, J. 1722. *Codex Pseudepigrapha Veteris Testamenti*. Hamburg: Felginer.
Feydit, Frédéric. 1986. *Amulettes de l'Arménie chrétienne*. Bibliothèque arménienne de la fondation Calouste Gulbenkian. Venice: St. Lazare.
Fraade, Steven D. 1984. *Enosh and His Generation: Pre-Israelite Hero and History in Postbiblical Interpretation*. SBLMS 30. Chico, CA: Scholars.
Garitte G. 1958. "La vision de S. Sahak en grec." *Le Muséon* 71:255–78.
Garsoïan, Nina G. 1989. *The Epic Histories attributed to Pʻawstos Buzand. Buzandaran Patmutʻiwnkʻ*. Harvard Armenian Texts and Studies 8. Cambridge MA: Harvard University Press.

Ginzberg, Louis. 1909–1938. *The Legends of the Jews*. 7 vols.. Philadelphia: Jewish Publication Society of America.

Gordon, Cyrus H. 1962. "Art. Tarshish." *IDB* 4:517–18.

Hakobyan, Alexan, ed. 2009. "The Chronicle of P'ilon Tirakac'i." Pages 903–69 in *Armenian Classical Authors*. Vol. 5: *Seventh Century*. Antelias: Armenian Catholicossate of Cilicia.

Harkins, Angela Kim, Kelley Coblentz Bautch, and John C. Endres. 2014. *The Fallen Angels Tradition*. CBQ Monographs 53. Washington: Catholic Biblical Association.

Harutyunyan, Sargis. 2006. Հայ հմայական եւ ժողովրդական աղօթքներ (*Armenian Incantations and Folk Prayers*). Erevan: Erevan University Press.

Heist, W. W. 1952. *The Fifteen Signs before Doomsday*. East Lansing, MI: Michigan State College.

Herbert, Máire, and Martin McNamara. 1990. *Irish Biblical Apocrypha*. Edinburgh: T&T Clark.

Issaverdens, J. 1934. *The Uncanonical Writings of the Old Testament Found in the Armenian MSS. of the Library of St. Lazarus*. 2nd ed. Venice: Mekhitarist Press.

James, Montague Rhodes. 1920. *The Lost Apocrypha of the Old Testament: Their Titles and Fragments*. Translations of Early Documents 1. London: SPCK.

———. 1924. *The Apocryphal New Testament*. Oxford: Clarendon.

Karst, J. 1901. *Historische Grammatik des Kilikisch-Armenischen*. Strassburg: Trübner.

Kirschner, Robert S. 1981. "Maimonides' Fiction of Resurrection." *HUCA* 52:163–19.

Kiwleserian, Babgen Coadj. Catholicos. 1961. Յուցակ ձեռագրաց Ղալաթիոյ Ազգային Մատենադարանի Հայոց (*Catalogue of the Manuscripts of the Armenian National Library of Galata*). Calouste Gulbenkian Armenian Library. Antelias: Catholicossate.

Kugel, James. 1990. "Why Was Lamech Blind?" *HAR* 12:91–103.

Kvam, K., L. Schearing, and V. Ziegler. 1999. *Eve and Adam: Jewish, Christian, and Muslim Readings on Genesis and Gender*. Indianapolis: Indiana University Press.

Lipscomb, W. L. 1978. "A Tradition from the Book of Jubilees in Armenian." *JJS* 29:149–63.

———. 1990. *The Armenian Apocryphal Adam Literature*. UPATS 8. Atlanta: Scholars.

Loeff, Yoav. 2002. "Four Texts from the Oldest Known Armenian Amulet Scroll: Matenadaran 115 (1428) with Introduction, Translation." MA thesis, Hebrew University of Jerusalem.

Malan, S. C., ed. and trans. 1882. *The Book of Adam and Eve, also Called The Conflict of Adam and Eve with Satan, A Book of the Early Eastern Church*. London: Williams & Norgate.

Malkhasyan, Armen. 2007. Յուցակ ձեռագրաց Մաշտոցի անուան մատենադարանի (*Catalogue of Manuscripts of the Maštocʻ Matenadaran*). Vol. 3. Erevan: Erevan State University Press.

McNamara, Martin. 1975. *The Apocrypha in the Irish Church*. Dublin: Institute for Advanced Studies.

Metzger, Bruce M. 1958. "Seventy or Seventy-Two Disciples." *NTS* 5:299–306.

Muradyan, Gohar. 2014. "The Vision of St. Sahak in the History of Łazar Pʻarpecʻi." Pages 313–25 in *The Armenian Apocalyptic Tradition: A Comparative Perspective*. Edited by Kevork Bardakjian and S. La Porta. Leiden: Brill.

Nersoyan, Tiran. 1984. *The Divine Liturgy of the Armenian Apostolic Church*. New York: Delphi Press.

Nickelsburg, G. W. E. 2001. *1 Enoch 1: A Commentary on the Book of 1 Enoch Chapters 1–36; 81–108*. Hermeneia. Minneapolis: Fortress.

Orlov, Andrei A. 2007. *From Apocalypticism to Merkabah Mysticism: Studies on the Slavonic Pseudepigrapha*. JSJSup 114. Leiden: Brill.

Pietersma, Albert. 1994. *The Apocryphon of Jannes and Jambres the Magicians: P. Chester Beatty XVI* (with new editions of Papyrus Vindobonensis Greek inv. 29456+29828 verso and British Library Cotton Tiberius B. v f. 87). Leiden: Brill.

Reed, Annette Yoshiko. 2005. *Fallen Angels and the History of Judaism and Christianity: The Reception of Enochic Literature*. Cambridge: Cambridge University Press.

Russell, James R. 2011. "The Armenian Magical Scroll and Outsider Art." *Iran and the Caucasus* 15:5–47.

Sargisian, Barseł. 1898. Ուսումնասիրութիւնք Հին Կտակարանի Անվաւեր գրոց վրայ (*Studies on the Uncanonical Books of the Old Testament*). Venice: Mekhitarist Press.

———. 1904. Անանուն Ժամանակագրութիւն (*Anonymous Chronicle*). Venice: Mekhitarist Press.

Stone, Michael E. 1978. "The Penitence of Solomon." *JTS* 29:1–19.

———. 1981. *Signs of the Judgment, Onomastica Sacra and The Generations from Adam*. UPATS 3. Chico: Scholars Press.

———. 1982. *Armenian Apocrypha Relating to Patriarchs and Prophets*. Jerusalem: Israel Academy of Sciences.

———. 1988. "The Months of the Hebrews." *Le Muséon* 101:5–12.

———. 1989. "An Armenian Epitome of Epiphanius de gemmis." *HTR* 82:467–76.

———. 1990a. *Fourth Ezra. A Commentary on the Book of Fourth Ezra*. Hermeneia. Minneapolis: Fortress.

———. 1990b. *Textual Commentary on the Armenian Version of IV Ezra*. SCS 34. Atlanta: Scholars Press.

———. 1992. "Some Armenian Angelological and Uranographical Texts." *Le Muséon* 105:147–57.

———. 1996a. *Armenian Apocrypha relating to Adam and Eve*. SVTP 14. Leiden: Brill.

———. 1996b. "The Armenian Apocryphal Literature: Translation and Creation." Pages 611–46 in *Il Caucaso: Cerniera fra Culture dal Mediterraneo alla Persia. Secoli IV–XI*. Spoleto: Presso la Sede del Centro.

———. 2000. "The Bones of Adam and Eve." Pages 241–45 in *For a Later Generation: The Transformation of Tradition in Israel, Early Judaism, and Early Christianity*. Edited by R. A. Argall, B. A. Bow, and R. A. Werline. Harrisburg, PA: Trinity Press.

———. 2002. *Adam's Contract with Satan: The Legend of the Cheirograph of Adam*. Bloomington, IN: Indiana University Press.

———. 2006a. *Apocrypha, Pseudepigrapha and Armenian Studies: Collected Papers*. 2 vols.. OLA 144–45. Leuven: Peeters.

———. 2006b. "Some Further Armenian Angelological Texts." Pages 427–35 in *Apocrypha, Pseudepigrapha and Armenian Studies: Collected Papers*. Leuven: Peeters.

———. 2007. *Adamgirk': The Adam Book of Aŕak'el of Siwnik'*. Oxford: Oxford University Press.

———. 2010. "Some Texts on Enoch in the Armenian Tradition." Pages 517–30 in *Gazing on the Deep: Ancient Near Eastern and Other Studies in Honor of Tzvi Abusch*. Edited by Jeffery Stackert, B. N. Porter, and P. D. Wright. Bethesda, MD: CDL.

———. 2012. *Armenian Apocrypha relating to Abraham*. EJL 37. Atlanta: Society of Biblical Literature.
———. 2013. *Adam and Eve in the Armenian Tradition, Fifth through Seventeenth Century*. EJL 38. Atlanta: Society of Biblical Literature.
———. 2015. "Enoch and The Fall of the Angels: Teaching and Status." *DSD* 22:342–57.
———. in press. "Two Stories about the Ark of the Covenant." Pages 253–66 in *Sion, Mère des Églises. Mélanges liturgiques offerts au Père Charles Athanase Renoux*. Semaines d'Études Liturgiques Saint-Serge S1. Münster: Aschendorff.
Stone, Michael E. and R. R. Ervine. 2000. *The Armenian Texts of Epiphanius of Salamis De mensuris et ponderibus*. CSCO 583. CSCO Subsidia 105. Leuven: Peeters.
Stone, Michael E. and M. E. Shirinian. 2000. *Pseudo-Zeno, Anonymous Philosophical Treatise*. Philosophia Antiqua 83. Leiden: Brill.
Stone, Michael E., and Th. M. van Lint. 2000. "The Armenian Vision of Ezekiel." Pages 144–58 in *The Apocryphal Ezekiel*. Edited by Michael E. Stone, B. G. Wright, and D. Satran. EJL 18. Atlanta: Society of Biblical Literature.
Stone, Michael E., Aryeh Amihai, and Vered Hillel. 2010. *Noah and His Book(s)*. EJL 28. Atlanta: Society of Biblical Literature.
Tatʿewacʿi, Grigor. 1993. Գիրք Հարցմանց (*Book of Questions*). Constantinople 1739. Repr. Jerusalem: St. James Press.
Ter-Ghewondyan, Aram. 1976. *The Arab Emirates in Bagratid Armenia*. Trans. Nina G. Garsoïan. Armenian Library of the Calouste Gulbenkian Foundation. Lisbon: Livraria Bertrand.
Tēr-Vardanean, Gēorg. 2012. Մայր ցուցակ հայերէն ձեռագրաց Մաշտոցի անուան Մատենադարանի (*General Catalogue of Armenian Manuscripts of the Maštocʿ Matenadaran*), vols. 6 and 7. Erevan: Nairi.
Theodor, J., and Ch. Albeck. 1929. *Bereschit Rabba*. Berlin: Akademie Verlag.
Thomson, Robert W. 1970. *Teaching of St. Gregory*. Harvard Armenian Series. Cambridge: Harvard University Press.
———. 2001. *The Teaching of St. Gregory*. Rev. ed. Avant 1. New Rochelle: St. Nersess Seminary.
———. 1995. *A Bibliography of Classical Armenian Literature to 1500 A.D.* Corpus Christianorum. Turnhout: Brepols.
———. 2006. *Movsēs Khorenatsʿi History of the Armenians*. Rev. ed.. Ann Arbor: Caravan Books).
VanderKam, James C., ed. 1989. *The Book of Jubilees*. CSCO 511. Scriptores Aethiopici Tomus 88. Leuven: Peeters.
Walraff, Martin, and William Adler. 2007. *Iulius Africanus Chronographiae: The Extant Fragments*. GCS NF 15. Berlin: de Gruyter.
Westenholz, Joan G. 1997. *Legends of the Kings of Akkade*. Winona Lake, IN: Eisenbrauns.
Wutz, F. X. 1915. *Onomastica Sacra: Untersuchungen zum Liber Interpretationis Nominum Hebraeorum des Hl. Hieronymous*. Texte und Untersuchungen 41.1–2. Leipzig: Hinrichs.
Yacoubian, N. 2003. "The Twelve Gifts Lost by Adam and a List of Ideograms." *Le Muséon* 116:45–52.
Yovsēpʿianc‛, Sargis. 1896. Անկանոն Գիրք Հին Կտակարանաց (*Uncanonical Books of the Old Testament*). Venice: Mekhitarist Press.

Zeyt'unyan, A. 1985. Գիրք ծննդոց (*The Book of Genesis*). Monuments of Ancient Armenian Translations. Erevan: Academy of Sciences.

Subject Index

Abraham, descendants of, 41, 46, 49
Adam, no repentance of, 105
Adam, place of creation of, 91, 97
allegory, 1
altars in Temple, ten, 151
anachronism, geographical, 135, 150, 271–73
angel(s), fall of, 66, 72, 73, 97, 102, 104
angelology, 65,
angels, day of creation of, 89, 90
angels, fiery, 108,
angels, functions of, 65, 67–70
angels, names of, 66, 67
angels, nine classes of, 66, 77–79, 87, 82, 104, 106
angels, numbers of, 106, 107
angels, praise of, 77, 79
angels, prayer to, 108–10
angels, prophecies about, 86
angels, twelve guardian, 110–11
Antichrist, 7
Antioch, 150
apotropaic texts, 65, 109, 111–12
Arabs, conquest of Armenia, 26
archangels, seven, 67
Ark of the covenant, 253
Ark of the covenant, contents of, 254
Ark of the covenant, dimensions of, 16
Ark, Noah's, 99
Armenian Catholic manuscript, 76

banking image, 21
blindness, of Jacob, 224
blood, commandment concerning, 99
book of the Law, second, 161
buildings, destruction of, 9

Cain, death of, 92, 93
Cain, mark of, 18, 92

calendar, calculations of, 55
calendar, Jewish, 55
calendarical text, 2
camel, Joseph rides, 208
cavalry, Pharaoh's, 248
censer, turned into gold, 16, 17, 253
census, Pharaoh's of departing Israelites, 247
chiliasm, 34
Christian touches, 228, 229, 248
chronography, 25, 26
chronological summaries, 27, 30
chronology, of Septuagint, see dates, Septuagint tradition of
clothes, renewed during desert period, 249
corrupted image, Enoch restores, 170
creation, by God's hand, 13

darkness at Nineveh, 274
dates, Armenian, two years variation in, 32, 45, 169,
dates, lists of, 25, 45, 46
dates, Septuagint tradition of, 29, 41, 56, 138, 147
David, King, 262
dew, bloody, 9
Dionysius Areopagiticus, pseudo-, 66, 77, 81, 84, 88
displacement, 80
dittography, 6
dragon, 67, 105

earth, renewal of, 101
earthquake, at Nineveh, 274
Eden, 172
Eden or Paradise, on mountain, 115
Eden, length of protoplasts' stay in, 61, 97–98

embroideries of biblical traditions, 10
Enoch, reasons for the translation of, 172
ephod, 22, 23
era, seventh, 38

fast, 105
fisherman, 241
flood, 8
flood, fiery, 174
fog, at Nineveh, 274
forty, typological number, 7
four hundred horsemen, Esau's, 128
freedom, 211–12
fruit, Enoch refrains from, 98

garden, Enoch planted, 172
gems. *See* jewels
Genesis, commentaries on, 28, 93
gifts, 10, given to Adam, 10
gifts, 12, lost by Eve, 13
God, vision of, 14, 15
graves, opened, 9
Grigor Tatʻewacʻi, *Book of Questions*, 11, 14, 18, 70, 72, 73, 77, 78, 254

heavens, fiery, 8
heavens, looking at, 171–72
heavens, tent, 8
Hebrew ʻayin, transliteration of, 47
Hebron, cave of, in Shechem, 137
heifers, four yokes of, 150
homiletic passages, 217–18, 227–28, 203–4
hope, associated with Enosh, 170–71
horn, Cain's, 18
hours, names of, 1

incantations, 65

Jacob, sons of, 49
Jannes and Mambres, Chaldean origin, 258
Jannes and Mambres, garden of, 261
jawbone, water flows from, 51
Jesus genealogy of, 41
Jethro, two daughters of, 243
jewels, 12, 22, 23
Jonah, and false prophecy, 266, 270–71, 274

Jonah, reason for flight, 101
Joseph, beauty of, 202
Joseph, body of, 248
Joseph, bones of, 138, 210
Joseph, three years in prison, 213
Joseph, transgression of, 132–33
Judges, list of, 41, 49

Kenan (Kaynan), 46, 53, 54, 62, 148
kingdom, Adam's, 13, 14

Lamech, Cainite, kills Cain, 18, 92–93
lament, Joseph's at Rachel's tomb, 208–10
land, gift of, 243
languages, seventy-two, 27
Lent, 7, 10, 25
limp, Jacob's, 128
linen, 261
lists, chronological, 25, 27
literate nations, 27
Lucifer. *See* Satan
luminaries, mode of creation of, 90
luminous garment, 14, 15
lunar zone, 115

magic, 1, 261
Mary, women called, 48, 49
mercy, as bird, 21
mercy, oil of, 22
Michael, archangel, 109
month name, replaces number, 161
Moses, incantation by, 248
Moses, infant, trial of, 241–42
Moses, speech impediment, 241–42
Moses, tomb closed by angels, 253
mourning, 7

Nablus, name of Samaria, 153
names, Divine, invocation of, 248, 259
names, of all things, true, 170–71
names, etymologies of. *See* onomastic material
names, Syriac forms of in Armenian, 50–51
narrative anomaly, 218
narrative line, confusion of, 209
Nathan, delay of by corpse, 265
Nativity, date of, 34

SUBJECT INDEX

Noah, wife of, 61, 62

olive tree, 21
onomastic material, 70, 71, 169, 170, 175, 207, 228, 261

P'ilon Tirakac'i, *Chronography*, 115–16
Parousia, 9
Parousia, date of, 34
patience, virtue of, 207
patriarchs, names of wives of, 56
payment, to Zipporah, 241
penitence, Enoch's, 171–72
Pharaoh's daughter, name of, 41
Pharaohs, additional, 239
phonetic confusion, 6
plagues, lists of, 245–46, 254–57
planets, 8
polemics, Armenian church, 11, 30, 72
portents, lists of, 5, 8, 274
possession, demonic, 98, 211
potions and spells, 130
priesthood, 79–81
priesthood, Adam's, 13, 14
prophecy, Adam's, 13, 14
prophet, understanding on, 271
prophetic power, Jacob's, 221
Psalms, attribution of, 263
punishments of Cain, seven, 18

queen of the Ethiopians, name of, 41
questions and answers, literature of, 72, 83, 92

Rachel, tomb of, 208
Rahab, husband of, 149
Red Sea, splitting of, 8, 259
righteous, become start, 21
rivers, fiery, 8
rock, followed Israelites, 100
rock, twelve springs from, 249
rocks split, 9
rulers, of Jews, 51

Sadayēl. *See* Satan
Satan, 67, 72, 211
Satan, day of fall of, 91

Satan, in Eden, 211
Satan, is the golden calf, 251
Satan, pride of, 104
sea shore, Pharaoh's daughter at, 241
seal, 22
seas, level of, 8
Sebastia, name of Samaria, 153
serpent, 98, 211
Sethites, on Mt. Hermon, 174
seven years' slavery, Joseph's, 210
seventy, palm trees, 248
seventy and seventy-two, alternation of, 248
seventy-five, go down into Egypt, 136
seventy-two, 116, 253
seventy-two builders of Tower, 114, 115
silver, pillars of, 163
Solomon, sins of, 100–101
Sons of God, 67
souls, fate of, 21
spy, planted by Pharaoh, 247
staff, Aaron's, 17
stars, 8
stars, identified with righteous, 21
stelae, Enosh writes on, 167

talismans, 1
thirty, silver coins, 205, 223
thirty coins, Joseph's price, 130
thirty years, ideal age, 132
tithes, Jacob gives, 127
Tower of Babel, 99, 114
Tower of Babel, dimensions of, 115–16
Triahagion, 104
twelve springs dry up, 250
typology, 37, 78, 86–88, 90, 205, 239

urn, golden, 16, 17, 249

virgins, 77

waters, of testing, 252
wings, hiding under, 21
word play, 22
wrestling with God, 128

Xēms, city of, 150

Index of Persons and Places

Aaragiēl, 111
Aaron, 17, 22, 23, 138, 149, 244, 245, 250, 251,
Abdon, 50
Abel, 19, 98, 168, 206
Abiathar, 150
Abijah, 47, 54
Abijam (Abihu), 151
Abimelech, 50
Abiron, 253
Abiron, 153, 253
Abiud, 48, 54
Abraham, 22, 27, 32, 33, 35, 36, 37, 40, 41, 46, 49, 53, 54, 56, 60, 62–64, 83, 116, 125, 129, 137, 148, 163, 210, 216, 224–26, 243, 244, 257
Abusakʻ, Cain's sister, 168
Ačaṙean, H., 33
Achim, 48
Achin, 54
Adam, 1, 10, 11, 13, 14, 26, 27, 31, 32, 35, 37, 39, 45, 51–56, 60–63, 83, 91, 92, 97–99, 102, 105, 106, 115, 147, 150, 163, 168–71, 211
Adler, A., 27
Adler, W., 25, 41, 73
Adonia, 265
Adoniel, 66, 72
Agathangelos, 13, 106
Ahab (Ahaiab), 47, 153–55, 159
Ahaliav, 253
Ahaz, 48, 150, 158
Ahaziah, 47, 57, 154, 155, 159
Ahiab (Ahab), 153
Ahijah, 151, 152
Aki the waterdrawer, 241
Albeck, Ch., xi, 62
Albertus Magnus (Albert), 76

Alexander the Great, 25, 48
Amalek, 149
Amalyan, 71
Amazia, 47, 156
Aminadab, 47, 149
Ammon, 48
Amos, 48
Amram, 49, 54, 138
Amzara, 62
Anael, 66
Anania (Hanani), 153
Anania Širakacʻi, 25
Anasyan, H. S., 10, 32
Anayel, 71
Anderson, G. A., 73
Andreas, 26, 33
Andreas of Byzantium, 32
Andreas of Cappadocia, 76
Antʻabyan, Pʻ., 1, 2, 16, 18, 19, 22, 27, 30, 34, 38, 51, 76, 116, 229, 261
Antichrist, 7
Antioch, 150
Antiochus the Great (Epiphanes), 38, 258
Apion, 258
Apollonius of Tyana, 1
Aptowitzer, V., 93
Aram (Paddan), 47, 149, 155, 243
Arameans, 154, 155, 158
Arpachshad, 46, 53, 54, 57, 62, 148
Artapanus, 41
Asa, 54, 152, 153
Asaph, 261, 263
Asaph, 47, 54, 132, 150, 261–63
Asenath, Aseneth, 225
Asher, 202
Asher, 49, 202
Asl-amanos, 70
Assyria, 157–60

288 INDEX OF PERSONS AND PLACES

Assyrians, 157
Astarte, 152
Athaliah, 47, 155
Aucher, J. B., 25
Augustine, 76
Azaria, 152, 156, 157
Azariel, 70
Azor, 48, 54
Azovra, Seth's wife, 61, 169

Baal Peor, 229
Baasha, 152, 153, 159
Babylon, 114, 162, 163, 271
Balaam, 258
Banaiah, 265
Bar Kʻobay the Chaldean, 258, 260
Barak, 50
Barakʻael, 66
Barakʻa, 61
Barlaam, 116
Baronian,, 116
Bartikian, Hŕach, 25
Basil, 22
Basra, 271, 272
Bathsheba, 263, 265
Bauckham, R., 66, 92, 99, 115
Bautch, K. C., 66, 73
Bedrossian, M., 204
Bēl of Ham, 114
Benjamin, 49, 128, 133–35, 151, 183, 202, 203, 209, 210, 219–21
Benjamin (tribe of), 149
Bethel, 128, 151, 153
Bethlehem, 48, 128, 208, 261
Bezalel, 253
Blake, R. P., 23
Boaz, 47, 54, 149
Bogharian, N., ix, 1, 5, 65, 67, 68, 110, 138
Bovatʻael, 66
Bozrah, 271
Bozrah, 271
Budayel, 69
Butʻayēl, 69
Byron, J., 93

Cain, 18, 19, 22, 39, 92, 93, 98, 168, 170, 172, 173, 205

Cain, descendants of, 173
Canaan, land, 226
Canaanites, 63, 217
Cedrenus, George, 25
Čemčean, S., 39
Chalcedon, 33
Chaldean, 258
Cleopas, 48
Constandianos (Constantine), 31–33
Constans, 26
Constantinople, ix, 33
Conybeare, F. C., 27, 116
Cornelius, 22
Cowley, R. W., 93
Cox, C., 177, 225
Cross, F. L., 34, 36
Cumont, F., 21

Daksiel, 72
Daksuel, 69
Dakuēl, 66, 69
Dan, 49, 130, 151, 202
Dan, J., 208
Daniel, 76, 85, 86, 162
Darius, 31
Dathan,, 253
David, 46, 47, 54, 100, 132, 138, 149–51, 154, 161, 216, 261–64, 265
Davila, J., 66, 92, 99, 115
Deborah, 128
Devil, 67
Dinah (Dina), 49, 61
Dionysius, 81–83, 88
DiTommaso, L., 4, 257
Dizeykłibad(a), 62
Dothaim, 129
Dothan, place, 203
Dragon,, 67
Dublin, 257
Dvin, 26, 33
Eber, 46, 53, 57, 63, 148

Ebrem, 132
Eden, 172, 211
Edna, 61, 63
Edni, 61
Edom, 49, 101, 128, 271

Eganyan, O, 1, 2, 16, 18, 19, 22, 27, 30, 34, 38, 51, 76, 92, 116, 229, 261
Egypt, 32, 35, 40, 54, 100, 107, 130, 134–37, 149, 150, 161, 163, 176, 177, 205, 206, 210, 216, 217, 219, 224, 226, 227, 229, 241–47, 250, 252, 254, 256, 260, 261, 274
Egyptian(s), 99, 100, 135, 151, 210, 216–19, 225, 242, 245–47, 250, 257
Ehud, 49
Elah, 153, 158, 159
Eldad, 253
Eleazar, 48, 54
Eli, 51
Eliakim, 48, 54, 162
Eliezer, 243
Elijah, 172
Elim, place, 248–50
Eliud, 48, 54
Elizabeth, 40
Elkʻos, 70, 111
Elliot, J. K., 48
Elon, 50
Emran, 49
Emzara, 62
Endres, J.C., 66, 73
Enoch, 29, 31, 35–37, 39, 46, 53, 56, 57, 61, 62, 92, 98, 105, 147, 169, 171–73
Enoch, Cainite, 172
Enosh, 29, 45, 56, 61, 147, 169–71
Ephesus, 30, 33
Ephraim, 132, 137, 151, 175, 176, 225, 226
Ephrath, 128, 208
Epiphanius of Salamis, 19, 23, 38, 258
Erevan, ix, 5
Esau, 64, 127, 128, 210
Esbok, 49
Êsr, 153
Euphrates River, 161
Eusebius of Caesarea, 25, 32, 41, 56, 57, 69
Eve, 13, 61, 92, 105, 106, 168–70, 211
Exile, 41, 51, 54
Exodus, 17, 32, 35, 40, 54, 149, 150, 163, 239
Eynatyan, J., 1, 2, 27, 28, 30, 32–34, 38–40
Ezekiel, 21, 86

Fabricius, A., 27
Feydit, F., 65, 80, 110, 111

Gabriel, 66, 69, 71, 86, 111
Gad, 202
Gad, 49, 130, 150, 202
Garden (of Eden), 13–16, 32, 39, 60, 91, 97, 98, 105, 115, 164, 168, 171–73, 211. *See also* Eden
Garitte, G., 38
Garsoïan, N., 99
Gershon, 243
Gideon, 50
Gilead, person, 226
Ginzberg, L, 41, 100, 149, 208, 241, 242, 247–49, 271, 273
Godołia, 155
Goliath, 149
Gordon, C. H., 271
Goshen, 136
Gregory Thaumaturgus, 69
Gregory, Tatʻewacʻi (of Tatew), 10, 11, 14, 18, 55, 70, 72, 73, 77, 78, 254

Hagar, 41, 49, 64
Hakobyan, A. (Hagopian), 25, 26
Ham, 57, 62,
Haran, 63
Hargeł, 70
Harkins, A. K., 66, 73
Harutyunyan, S., 65
Hayk of Japheth, 114
Hazael (Azayēl), 154, 155
Hebron, 128, 129, 137, 149
Heist, W. W., 4, 5
Helkiah, 161
Hell, 104
Heman, 263
Heraclius, 26
Herbert, M., 4
Herclius Constantinus, 26
Hermon, Mt., 173
Heron, 149
Hezekiah, 48, 158–60
Hezron, 37
Hiel (Ahiel), 153
Hillel, 50, 258

290 INDEX OF PERSONS AND PLACES

Hillel, V., 9, xii, 6, 41, 45, 52, 56, 74, 81, 99, 178, 186, 201, 231, 259, 262, 264, 269
Homer, 151
Horeb, Mt., 243, 253
Horeb, Mt., 243, 253
Horovitz, H. S., 247
Hosea, 158, 159, 160

Ibzan, 50
Ignatius, 49
Isaac, 46, 49, 54, 63 64, 128, 137, 148, 210, 217, 224–26
Isaiah, 77, 82, 207
Iscah, 63
Ishmael, 49, 64
Ishmaelite, 242
Isidoros, 151
Israel, 40, 99, 100, 137, 151–60, 229, 239–51, 258, 261, 265
Israel (Jacob), 221, 226
Israel (land), 35, 137, 154, 177, 210, 266, 271
Israel, New, 176
Israelites, 100, 136 229, 239–53, 258, 261, 265
Issachar, 49, 202
Issaverdens, J., 41

Jabesh, 157
Jabin, 50
Jacob, 41, 46, 48, 49, 54, 64, 127–30, 132–34, 136–38, 148, 149, 175, 202, 203, 205, 209, 217–19, 221, 222, 224–26, 243, 244
Jaffa, 271
Jair, 38, 50
James, M.R., 27, 257
Jannes and Mambres, 258, 260, 261
Japheth, 37, 57, 62
Jared, 29, 46, 57, 61, 147, 171
Jechoniah, 48, 54, 162
Jeduthun, 263
Jehoahaz, 161
Jehoiadea, 265
Jehoiakim (Yovakim), 48, 162
Jehoida, 155
Jehoikim, 162

Jehoram, 54, 154, 155, 158, 159
Jehoshahat, 52, 54, 153, 154
Jehosheba (Yovsabēē), 155
Jehu (Esu), 153, 155, 157, 159
Jektan, 49
Jeohahaz, 159
Jepthah, 50
Jereboam, 151, 152, 159
Jeroboam, 157, 158
Jerusalem, 5, 9, 65, 86, 91, 105, 150, 151, 153–56, 158, 161, 162, 261, 262
Jesse, 47, 54, 149
Jesus Christ, vii, 9, 26, 32, 33, 40, 41, 45, 48, 51, 54, 55, 70, 72, 78, 90, 100, 101, 111, 128, 130, 138, 163, 176, 205, 207, 212, 225, 229, 252, 263
Jethro, 243
Jews, 5, 9, 51, 55, 176, 206, 207, 212, 258
Jezreel, 155
Joad, 54, 152
Joasaph, 116
Joash, 155, 156, 159
Job, 22
Jochebed, 49, 138
Joel, 152
John, 86, 101
John Chrysostom, 21, 49
Jonah, 101, 229, 266, 270–75
Jonathan, 149
Jorah, 46
Joram, 47
Jordan, 14, 70, 111, 127, 149
Joseph, 48, 49, 54, 129, 130–38, 175–77, 202–29, 239, 248, 261
Joshua, 35, 49, 138, 149, 153
Josiah, 48, 161
Jotham, 47, 54
Judah (person), 46, 47, 49, 130, 133, 135, 149, 151, 202, 221
Judah (place), 152, 153, 155, 156, 158–60, 225, 226
Judea, 48

Karst, J., 82
Kenan, 171
Kenan (Kaynan), 29, 45, 46, 53, 54, 56, 57, 61, 62, 147, 148, 171

INDEX OF PERSONS AND PLACES 291

Keturah, 41, 49
Khosrow II, 38
Kishon, 50
Kiwlesarian, B. C., 16
Kohath, 49, 54
Korah, 229, 253, 263
Kugel, J., 92, 93
Kvam, K., 211

Laban, 243
Lamech, 29, 46, 57, 61, 62, 92, 93, 147
Lamech, Cainite, 172, 173
Lamech, Sethite, 173
Lamur, 114
LaPorta, S., 33
Lazar P'arbec'I, 21
Lazarus, 49
Leah, 49, 129, 137
Levi, 49, 54, 134, 202, 262
Levites, 155
Lipscomb, W .L., 18, 61, 73, 98, 164, 171, 172
Livingstone, 34, 36,
Loeff, Y., 65
Loma, 63
Lucifer, 67
Łukiēl, 111

Mahalalel (Małałiēl), 29, 45, 53, 57, 61, 147, 169, 171
Małałeda, 61
Malan, S. C., 93
Malkhasyan, A., 10, 11
Mambrē, 128
Manasseh, 48, 132, 137, 160, 161, 175, 225, 226
Manoah, 51
Marah, place, 248
Mari, 41, 49
Marutha of Maipherkat, 19
Mary (Virgin), 36, 37, 40, 41, 49, 90, 101, 109
Mary Magdalene, 41, 43, 48
Mary mother of James and Joses, 41, 48
Mary the Cleopite, 41, 48
Mary, sister of Lazarus, 41, 49
Masis, Mt., 99

Matenadaran, ix, 5, 35
Mattan, 48
Matthan, 54
Mazis, 99
McNamara, M., 4
Mdasayēl, 69
Mdasuēl, 66
Medan, 49
Mełk'ion, 68, 70
Mełkisn, 70
Melkizedek, 80
Melqos, 111
Menahem (Manayēm), 157, 160
Meroïs, 41
Merris, 41
Mesopotamia, 271
Methusaleh, 29, 46, 53, 56, 57, 61, 62, 98, 147, 173
Micaiah b. Imla, 76
Michael , 66, 69, 70, 71, 109, 111
Michiah, 154
Midian, 49
Midianites, 49, 130
Milcah, 63
Miria, 241
Moab, 49, 226
Modad, 253
Mohammed, 19, 51, 54
Moses, 7, 33, 41, 49, 54, 99, 100, 107, 137, 138, 150, 161, 229, 238, 240–53, 257–62
Mount Seir, 128
Movsēs Xorenac'i, 25, 26
Muk'a, 63
Muradyan, G., 2, 21, 30, 32–34, 38, 254
Mxit'ar Ayrivanec'i, 14

Nablus, 153
Nabot (Nadab), 152
Naboth, 151, 152, 159
Nachshon, 54
Nadab, 159
Nahor, 46, 53, 58, 63, 148
Nahshon, 149
Nahson, 47
Naphtali, 49, 157, 202
Nathan, 263, 265

292 INDEX OF PERSONS AND PLACES

Nathan, 150
Nebuchadnezzar, 162, 163
Nebuzadran, 163
Neco, 161
Nersoyan, T., 83
Nicea, 30, 33
Nickelsburg, G. W. E., 73
Nile, river, 241
Nile, river, 241
Nineveh, 101, 270–75
Noah,, 173
Noah, 8, 26, 27, 29, 37–39, 46, 53, 57, 61, 62, 98, 99, 115, 116, 148, 173
Noam, 61
Noyem Zara, 62
Nuena, 61
Nuriēl, 111
Nuriel, 66, 69

Obed, 47, 149
Okʻozia, 154
Omri, 153, 155, 159
Oreb, 50
Othniel, 49

Pʻawstos Buzand, 99
Pʻutʻayēl, 66
Padan Aram, 243
Panayotov, A., 66, 92, 99, 115
Paul, 212, 223, 226
Pedaja, 48
Pekah, 158, 160
Pekah(iah) (Pʻakēē), 157, 160
Peleg, 46, 53, 57, 63, 148
Pentapʻrēs, 130, 132
Perez, 46, 148, 149
Phanuel, 66, 72
Pharaoh, 41, 49, 100, 107, 130–32, 135–37, 161, 210, 214, 216, 239–48, 257, 261
Philip, 32, 33
Pietersma, A., 257–58
Pilon (Philo) of Tirak, 25–27
Pinhas (Phineas), 238, 253
Potiphar, 130, 210, 211, 213, 225
Ps. Dionysius, 66, 76, 81
Pseudo-Zeno, 90
Ptolemy, 38

Pua, 157
Pul, 157

Rab-Shakeh (Rapakʻ), 160
Rabin, I., 247
Rachel, 128, 202, 208–10
Rahab, 149
Ram, 149
Ramot Gilead, 154, 155
Raphael, 66, 69–71, 111
Rasueya, 62
Rebecca, 128, 208
Red Sea, 138, 229, 247
Rehoboam, 47, 54, 151, 152, 156, 159
Remaliah, 157, 158, 160
Reu, 46, 53, 58, 63, 148
Reuben, 49, 129, 134, 202, 219, 221, 258
Rezin (Hṙasim), 158
Runia, 8
Russell, J. R., 65, 134
Ruth, 46, 149, 226

Sabbath, 34, 38, 55
Sadayēl, 91
Sadok, priest, 265
Sahak, St., 21, 33, 38
Salathiel, 47, 48, 54
Salmon, 47, 149
Sama, Abel's sister, 168
Samaria, 151, 153–56, 158, 159
Samaritans, 158
Samea, 151, 152
Samson, 51
Samuel, 51, 149
Saragiēl, 111
Sarah, 129, 137
Sararad (Sararat), 99
Sargisean, B., 25
Sargon, king of Akkad, 241
Satan, 67, 72, 73, 91, 92, 97, 98, 101, 104, 173, 211, 212, 251
Satanayēl, 102, 104
Saul, 51, 149
Schearing, L., 211
Sebastia, 153
Sedeqtelebab, 62
Sela, 57, 62, 63, 148, 171

INDEX OF PERSONS AND PLACES

Selah, 46
Sennacherib, 146, 160
Serpent, 67, 73, 75, 98, 106, 211, 244, 250
Serug, 38, 46, 53, 58, 63, 148
Seth, 29, 39, 45, 53, 56, 61, 92, 147, 164, 168, 169, 171–73
Seth, descendants of, 173
Sethite(s), 73, 92, 172, 173
Sextus Iulius Africanus, 25
Shallum (Sellum), 157, 160
Shalmaneser, 158
Shamgar, 50
Shechem, 128, 129, 137, 138, 203, 226
Shelah, 53, 54
Shem, 26, 45, 46, 53, 56, 57, 62, 114, 147, 148
Shemer (Samiron), 153
Shirinian, 90
Shishak (Sosakim), 151, 152
Shomron (Somron), 153
Shua, 49
Simeon, 49, 133, 134, 202, 218, 219
Sinai, Mt., 250
Sisera, 50
Sokʻayēl, 70
Solomon, 32, 33, 36, 37, 40, 47, 54, 100, 101, 150, 151, 163, 262, 264, 265
St. Gregory, 33, 34, 106
Stone, M.E., 1, 4, 5, 8–10, 13, 16, 19, 21, 23, 26–28, 34, 38, 41, 45, 51, 61, 62, 65–67, 71, 73, 74, 81, 89–91, 97, 98, 101, 104, 105, 110, 113–16, 137, 138, 150, 163, 164, 168
Sukʻiēl, 111
Sura, 63
Susanna, 207
Syncellus, 41

Tʻesbi (Ethiopian Queen), 41, 49
Tʻomas (priest), 138
Tʻutʻayel, 66
Tarmuth, 41
Tarshish, city, 271–73
Tēr Vardanean, G., ix, 2, 10, 15, 30, 34, 41, 163
Ter-Ghewondyan, A., 26
Terah, 46, 53, 58, 63, 148, 271

Thaddeus, 33
Theodor, J., xi, 62
Thermuthis, 41
Thomson, R. W., 19, 25
Three Young Men, 162
Tiglath Pileser, 157
Tikorecʻi, J., 33
Toal, 50
Tomer Doitch, 9, 56
Topchyan, A., 2, 34, 38
Tower (of Babel), 16, 32, 35, 36, 63, 83, 99, 113–15
Trdat (Tiridates III), 106
Tuffin, P., 25, 41

Uriah, 265
Uriel, 66, 72
Uzziah, 47, 54, 156–58

Van Lint, Th., 19
VanderKam, J. C., 41, 46
Vahram, 38

Walraff, M., 25
Westenholz, J. G., 241
Wutz, F. X., 71, 175, 176

Xēms, 150
Xosraw son of Hormizd, 38

Yacoubian, N., ix, 10
Yadnera, 61
Yanes and Yambres. See Jannes and Mambres
Yazdekert II, 38
Yeshaya of Tirani, Rabbi, 271
Yovēl, 70
Yovhannēs Erznkacʻi Corcorecʻi, 14
Yoviēl, 111
Yovsēpʻiancʻ, S., 41
Ysaburia, 62

Zadok, 48, 54, 151, 152
Zakʻaria Katʻołikos, 91
Zalmunna, 50
Zebee, 50
Zebulun, 49, 202

Zechariah, 82, 157, 159
Zecharias, 86
Zedekiah, 162
Zeeb, 50
Zerubbabel, 31, 40, 48, 51, 54
Zeytʻunyan, A., 1, 2, 16, 18, 19, 22, 27, 28, 30, 34, 38, 51, 76, 116, 177, 229, 261
Ziegler, V., 211
Zikayēl, 111
Zimri (Zambri), 153, 159
Zion, 91, 150, 262
Zitʻayel, 66
Zitʻayēl, 69
Ziura, 63
Zohrab, 80
Zuba, 63
Zuriel, 66

Ancient Sources Index

Hebrew Bible

Genesis
1:1–3	89
1:3	89
1:6–8	90
1:11–12	90
1:14–18	90
1:20–22	90
1:24–25	90
1:27	13
2:7	13
2:8	91, 97
2:16–17	97
2:17	14
2:19–20	91
3:7	14
3:9	105
3:12	106
3:12–19	106
3:13	106
3:18	14
3:19	14
3:22	14
3:23	105
3:23–24	14, 39
3:24	98
4:2	115
4:12	19
4:15	18, 92
4:16–26	39
4:22	62
4:23–24	98
4:24	18, 98
4:25	61
4:26	169
5	45, 61, 147
5:5	45
5:5–32	55
5:6	45
5:6–7	29
5:6–28	29
5:8	169
5:8–11	29
5:11	45, 171
5:12–14	29
5:14	45
5:15–17	29
5:17	45
5:18–20	29
5:20	46
5:21–24	29
5:22–24	35–37, 39
5:23	46
5:24	105
5:25–27	29
5:27	46
5:28–31	29
5:31	46, 147
5:32	98
6–9	35–37, 39
6:1–2	173
6:1–4	67, 73
6:9	173
6:10	45
7:4	99
7:10	62
7:12	99
7:17	99
7:191–20	8
8:11	225
9:4–5	99
9:20–21	99
9:24	62

Genesis, cont'd.

9:29	46, 148	37:2–50:25	177
11	147	37:3	129, 202, 204
11:1–9	35–37 114	37:6–7	120
11:3	114	37:6–8	203
11:3–9	63	37:8	129, 203
11:4	115	37:9	203
11:10	62	37:9–11	129
11:10–11	46, 148	37:11	129, 203
11:10–27	45	37:12	203
11:12–13	46	37:12–17	129
11:13	148	37:14	204, 205
11:14–15	148	37:18	129 205
11:16–17	148	37:21–22	129
11:18–19	46, 148	37:22–24	130
11:20–21	148	37:23	205 206
11:22–23	46, 148	37:25	206
11:24–25	148	37:26–27	130
11:26	40	37:27	206
11:29	63	37:28	130, 205 206
12:1	63	37:31–33	130, 206
12:1–3	35–37	37:36	130, 210
15:13	240	38:29	47
16:15	49, 64	39:1	210
17:11	64	39:2–4	211
21:1–3	64	39:2–5	130
24:64	208	39:6	202
25:7	148	39:7	212
25:25–26	64	39:7–20	130
27–33	210	39:12	213
30:4	228	39:17–18	213
30:21	49	39:21–23	131, 213
30:24	207	40:1–4	131
32:24–25	128	40:2–3	213
32:28	221	40:6–7	131
32:30	72	40:6–8	214
33:1	128	40:8–10	131
33:4	128	40:9–13	214
33:5–14	128	40:12–13	131
33:16	128	40:14–15	131
35:6	128	40:16–19	131, 214
35:7	128	40:20–22	131
35:19	202, 208	41:1	214
35:22	202	41:1–4	132
35:22–26	49	41:1–24	215
35:28	46, 128, 148	41:6–7	133
36:33	271	41:8	133
		41:14–45	133

41:33–39	216	44:13–14	135
41:39–41	216	44:16	221
41:42	261	44:17	135, 221
41:45	225	44:18–34	135, 221
41:46	132	44:30	202
41:48	216	45:1–2	135
41:48–49	133	45:2	135
41:50	225	45:3–13	135, 221
41:50–52	133	45:6	137
41:51	175	45:15	223
41:52	176	45:16–20	224
41:57	217	45:17–21	136
42:1–3	217	45:21–23	136
42:1–9	133	45:22–23	224
42:6	218	46:8–12	225
42:7	133, 218	46:12	46, b148
42:8	218	46:20	225
42:13–20	218	46:26	225
42:18–20	133	46:26–27	136
42:24	218	46:27	136
42:25–27	134	46:29	224
42:30–34	218	47:8–9	136
42:35	218	47:10	136, 221
42:36	133, 219	47:11–12	136
42:37	219	47:28	46, 136, 148
43:2	133	47:31	137
43:3	133	48:1	137, 176
43:8–9	133, 219	48:2	137, 226
43:11–14	134	48:10	226
43:15	134	48:13–14	175, 226
43:16	219	48:15–16	226
43:20–22	134	48:17	175
43:23	134	48:18	175
43:27–28	134	48:19	175
43:29	134	49:8	225
43:30	134, 219	49:8–12	225
43:30–31	134	49:1–27	137
43:32	219	49:9	225
43:33–34	135	49:22–26	226
43:43	219	49:31	130, 137
44:1–2	135	49:33	137
44:2	219	50:2	226
44:4	135, 220	50:5–10	226
44:4–6	220	50:7–13	137
44:5	134	50:12–13	226
44:5–6	135	50:24–25	137
44:12	135, 220	50:25	227, 210
		50:26	137, 248

Exodus		9:18–25	256
1:5	136, 224	9:18–26	246
1:6	239	9:19	246
1:7	239	10:5	245
1:9	240	10:12–14	256
1:15–16	240	10:21–22	256
1:17	240	10:22	274
1:18	240	12:3–4	206
1:22	240	12:13	246
2:2	240, 241	12:23	246
2:3	240	12:15–20	246
2:4	241	12:29	246
2:6	241	12:30–42	35
2:9–10	241	12:35	247
2:11–12	242	12:35–36	247
2:14	242	12:37	107, 247
2:16–17	242	13:18	247
2:23	239	13:19	177, 210, 248
3:10–12	244	13:21–22	248
3:18	243, 245	14:5	247
3:19	244	14:10	248
3:21–22	100, 247	14:21	248
4:1–4	244	14:22	8
4:6–7	244	14:23–28	248
4:8	18, 205	14:29	9
4:9	244	15:10	248
4:10	242	15:19	100
4:10–16	244	15:22–23	248
5:1	243, 245	15:27	248
5:2	243, 245	16:3	252
5:3	245, 247	16:4	249
5:6–19	243, 245	16:8	249
6:1–3	245	16:13–14	252
6:14–16	245	16:31	249
6:16–20	49	16:32–34	17, 249
6:23	149	16:36	249
6:27	243, 245	17:3	252
6:27–7:7	245	17:6	100
7:15–21	245	20:2–14	251
7:17–24	246	20:12	228
7:27–8:9	245	20:13	252
8:2–7	256	23:19	250
8:16–18	256	24:18	7
8:16–19	245	25:10	16
9:3–7	256	25:21	16
9:9–11	256	25:22	172
9:17–21	256	28:18	24

ANCIENT SOURCES INDEX

28:19	24	4:13	50
28:20	24	4:17–22	50
32:1	250	4:24	50
32:2–6	251	5:24–27	50
32:4	251	6:11	50
32:15	251, 252	6:37–39	50
32:20	252	7:24–25	50
34:28–35	253	8:5–12	50
36:11	253	8:29–9:56	50
38:26	107	10:1	50
40:2	17	11:1	50
		11:34	50
Leviticus		12:8–10	50
8:35	17	12:11–12	50
9:34	17	12:13–15	50
		13:24	51
Numbers		15:4–5	51
2:32	247	15:15–19	51
3:34	247	15:19	51
5:18–24	252	16:3	51
7:89	172		
11:1	247	Ruth	
16:4–27	253	4:18–22	46, 148
17:8	17	4:19	47, 149
21:6–9	250	4:20	149
26:21	148	4:21	149
26:59	49	4:22	149
40:2	17		
		1 Samuel	
Deuteronomy		10:20–21	149
1:8	100	15:3–9	149
5:6–21	251	17	149
5:16	228	25:1	149
5:17	252	28:3	149
11:4	100	31:1–6	149
31:7	100		
		2 Samuel	
Joshua		2:11	149
2:10	9	5:4	149
4:23	9	5:5	149, 150
15:17	49	6:2	172
24:32	210	6:2–12	150
		6:14	262
Judges		11–12	263
3:9	49	12:1	263
3:15–30	49	12:1–4	263
3:31	50	12:1–6	265

2 Samuel, cont'd.

12:7–12	265
12:13–14	265
12:24	47
22:8	9
22:11	172

1 Kings

1:17	151
1:20	151
1:21	151
1:33–35	150
2:11	149
4:2	152
5:3	100
6:1	54, 150, 163
6:1–9	36, 37, 40
6:2	151
6:20	151
6:38	150
7:15–22	151
7:48	151
7:49	151
10:1–10	150
10:10	151
11:1–6	150
11:2	150
11:3	159
11:13	151
11:29–36	151, 159
11:42	150, 151
11:42–43	151
11:43	47
12:16	151
12:20	151, 159
12:28–29	151
12:30–33	151
13:10	156
13:11	156
14:1	156
14:2	156
14:4–55	152
14:11–13	156
14:14	156
14:17	156
14:19	156
14:20	156
14:21	151, 152
14:23	156
14:24	156
14:25	151
14:25–26	151
14:29	156
14:31	152
15:1	152
15:2	152
15:1–2	156
15:3	152, 157
15:4	157
15:5	157
15:8	47, 152, 157
15:9	157
15:10	152, 157
15:11–12	152
15:12	157
15:13	152, 157
15:16–21	152
15:17	157
15:19	157
15:20	157
15:22	157
15:23	157
15:25	152, 157, 159
15:27	158
15:28	152, 158
15:29	152, 158
15:32	152
15:33	152, 159
15:34	152
16:1–4	153
16:6	153
16:8	153, 155, 159
16:9–13	153
16:15	159
16:17–18	153
16:23	153, 159
16:28	153
16:29	153, 163
16:30	153
16:34	153
17:1	153
17:14	249
17:16	249
21:1	151

22:15–22	154	16:5	158
22:34–38	154	16:6	158
22:41	154	16:7–8	158
22:42	154	16:9	158
22:50	154	17:1	158, 160
22:51	154, 159	17:3–6	158
		17:6	158, 159
2 Kings		17:6, 23	160
1:3	151	18:10–11	158, 159, 160
1:10, 13	160	18:13	160
1:17	151, 154	18:13–19:26	159
2:9	106	18:17	160
2:10	106	19:23–24	160
2:11	105	19:35	160
2:13	106	20:1	160
2:17	163	20:6	160
3:1	154, 159	21:11	160
8:16	154	21:13–15	160
8:25	47, 154	21:18	161
8:26	155	21:21	160
8:28	155	21:24	161
8:29	155	22:1	161
9:24	155	22:2	161
9:27	155	22:3	161
10:35	156	22:4, 8	161
10:36	155, 159	23:21–22	161
11:1	155	23:29	161
11:1–3	48	23:30	161
11:2	155	23:31	161
11:4–6	155	23:34	161, 162
11:12	47	23:35	162
12:1–2	155	23:37	162
12:2	155	24:1	162
12:28–29	151	24:6	162
12:30–33	151	24:8	162
13:1	155, 159	24:12	162
13:2	155	24:12–15	162
13:3	155	24:12–16	162
13:10	159	24:17	162
14:23	159	24:18	162
15:3	47	24:20	162
15:14, 17	160	25:1–2	162
15:23	160	25:6–7	163
15:25, 27	160	25:8	163
15:32–33	158		
16:1	158	1 Chronicles	
16:2	158	1:4–6	149

1 Chronicles, cont'd.

1:32	49
2	46, 148
2:9	47
2:10	149
2:12	149
3:10	49
3:11	47
3:14	48
3:17	48
6:31–33	262
11:5	150
11:7	150
13:6–14	150
15:3–16:1	150
15:29	262
23:1	150
25:1–2	150
26:1	47
29:29	150
29:27	150

2 Chronicles

2:5–6	158
5:2	262
5:12	261
9:1–32	151
9:30	150
21:4	154
21:6	154
21:12–15	154
21:12	154
22:11	155
26:1	47
33:20	161
34:19	161
35:1	161
35:15	263
35:17–18	161
35:20–24	161
35:23	161
36:5–6	162
36:6	162
36:21–23	163

Ezra

3	40
3:2	48

Nehemiah

1:12	48

Job

12:10	21

Psalms

2:8	78, 85
18:11(17:12)	27
18(17):8	9
22:15(21:16)	222
24(23):8	80, 82, 84
27(26):10	210
39(38)	263
42(41)	263
44(43)	263
45:6(44:7)	79, 82, 84
46(45)	263
51(50)	263
52:8(51:10)	21
60:6 (59:8)	226
62(61)	263
66(65):6	8
68:8(67:9)	9
76(77)	261
78(77):43–51	245
79(78):1	261
80(79):1	261
90(89):4	169
91(90):1, 4	111
105(104):17–22	189
105(104):28–36	245
105(104):39–41	216
108(107:8)7	226
110(109):4	82
110(109):4–5	79, 81, 85
118(117):9	132
137(136):6	222
145(144):13	80, 82, 85
147(146):4	21

Proverbs

2:16	150
14:20–21	22

ANCIENT SOURCES INDEX

Isaiah
- 3:6 — 83
- 6:3 — 81, 82, 84, 104
- 7:17 — 151
- 14:12–15 — 67, 73
- 14:13–14 — 97
- 19:8 — 241
- 34:6 — 271
- 50:2 — 9
- 51:10 — 9
- 63:1 — 101
- 66:8 — 91
- 66:24 — 105

Jeremiah
- 48:24 — 271

Ezekiel
- 1:24 — 86
- 3:12 — 79, 84
- 17:9 — 225
- 37 — 21
- 38:20 — 9

Daniel
- 1:2, 6 — 162
- 4:31–32 — 106
- 5:2–4 — 162
- 7:10 — 86
- 8:10–12 — 21
- 8:16 — 86
- 9:21–24 — 86
- 9:27 — 38
- 11:31 — 38
- 12:7 — 38

Hosea
- 5:3 — 151

Joel
- 2:10 — 9
- 2:30 — 8

Jonah
- 1:2 — 270
- 1:3 — 272
- 1:4–5 — 272
- 1:6 — 272
- 1:12 — 272
- 1:11 — 272
- 1:15 — 273
- 1:17 — 273
- 2:1 — 270
- 2:7 — 270
- 2:10 — 273
- 3:3 — 270
- 3:4 — 273
- 3:4–5 — 273, 274
- 3:6 — 274
- 3:7 — 275
- 3:7–9 — 274
- 4:1–3 — 270
- 4:2 — 270
- 4:6 — 275
- 4:7 — 275
- 4:10–11 — 275
- 4:11 — 275

Nahum
- 1:6 — 9

Haggai
- 1:1 — 48

Zechariah
- 1:12 — 80, 82, 86

New Testament

Matthew
- 1 — 41–48, 54
- 1:5 — 149
- 1:9 — 47
- 1:10 — 48
- 1:11 — 48
- 1:12 — 48, 54
- 1:16 — 48
- 1:17 — 53
- 1:18 — 36, 40
- 3:6 — 111
- 3:17 — 14, 45
- 4:2 — 7
- 5:3 — 176
- 5:7 — 227

ANCIENT SOURCES INDEX

Matthew, cont'd.
- 5:11–12 — 228
- 10:22 — 227
- 11:11 — 101
- 13:8 — 101
- 13:23 — 101
- 19:18–19 — 252
- 19:19 — 227
- 22:37–39 — 252
- 22:37 — 252
- 24:7 — 9
- 24:15 — 38
- 25:32 — 176
- 25:34 — 176
- 26:15 — 130, 205
- 26:64 — 80
- 27:3 — 130, 205
- 27:9 — 130
- 27:51 — 9
- 27:52 — 9
- 27:61 — 48

Mark
- 1:9 — 41
- 1:10 — 111
- 1:11 — 14
- 8:3 — 48
- 10:18 — 252
- 12:31 — 227
- 12:32 — 252
- 13:13 — 227
- 15:24 — 41
- 15:40 — 48
- 16:9 — 48

Luke
- 1:24 — 40
- 1:30–36 — 40
- 2:6–7 — 36, 37, 40
- 2:14 — 81, 82, 85
- 3:22 — 14, 111
- 3:23–38 — 46, 148
- 3:36 — 54
- 6:36 — 227
- 7:28 — 111
- 8:2 — 48
- 10:8 — 67
- 24:10 — 48
- 10:27 — 252
- 16:19 — 175
- 21:19 — 200
- 23:33 — 41

John
- 1:14 — 36, 37, 40
- 1:32 — 111
- 8:34 — 212
- 8:44 — 212
- 11:2 — 49
- 12:3 — 49
- 12:25 — 175
- 13:35 — 22
- 19:18 — 41

Acts
- 10 — 22
- 12:12 — 48

Romans
- 1:28–29 — 212
- 12:17 — 223
- 12:20–21 — 223
- 15:2 — 225

1 Corinthians
- 10:4 — 100
- 10:7 — 252

Ephesians
- 3:10 — 88
- 6:12 — 88

Colossians
- 2:14 — 105

1 Thessalonians
- 5:15 — 223

1 Timothy
- 6:20 — 21

2 Timothy
- 1:12 — 21

Philemon		LAE	
3:18–19	212	41:2	22
9:4	229	42:3	22
11:20	226	Lives of the Prophets	138, 147, 163
11:21	226	Life of Joad	152
9:4	16, 17	TPatr	
		T. Jos 6	130
James		T. Levi 18:3	21
37:18	205	1QGenesis Apocryphon	
		6:7	62
1 Peter		2.23	115
3:9	223		
3:22	88	**ARMENIAN APOCRYPHA**	
Revelation		Abel and Cain	
12:9	67	38–45	18
14:2–3	86	50–58	19
		Adam and His Grandsons	
APOCRYPHA		1	168
		23	54
4 Ezra		Adam, Eve, and the Incarnation	211
4:42	21	Biblical Paraphrases	27, 113, 138,
5:5	9		150, 163
6:14	9	Bones of Adam and Eve	19
10:53–54	9	Chariot of the Divinity	19
		Chronological Summary down to	
Susannah		Christ	27
1:42–43	207	Concerning the Tower 1 and 2	99
		Concerning the Tower 2	114
PSEUDEPIGRAPHA AND QUMRAN		Concerning the Weights	19
		Dates	27, 138, 163
2 Apoc Bar 70:8	9	Dimensions of the Ark	16–17, 113
1 Enoch		Enumeration of the Generations	46
6	73	Fifteen Signs of the Judgement 1	
6:6	173	and 2	8, 9
43:4	106	Fifteen Signs of the Judgement III	4–9, 5
	21	From the Wisdom of Solomon	19
Jubilees		Genealogy of Adam	16
3	61	Generations of Adam	26
4:14	61	Good Tidings of Seth	164
4:27	61	12–35	171
4:31	92	History of Adam and His Grand-	
4:33	62	sons 23	150, 163
7:16	62	History of Moses	41
8:1	62	History of the Forefathers, Adam and	
8:5	62	His Sons and Grandsons	164
10:18	63	16	172
LAB 33:5	21		

History of the Forefathers, Adam and His Sons and Grandsons, *cont'd.*		Story of Father Abraham	16, 113
		Story of Terah and Father Abraham	
27	168	§4	271
28	169	§45 175	271
29	169	§45 231	271
30	169	Ten Plagues of Egypt	16
31–32	169	This Is the Story of Nineveh and of Jonah	101
33	169	Third Story of Joseph 54	71, 117, 130
34	169	Twelve Gifts lost by Adam	10–15
35–41	169	Twelve Hours of the Night	1
35b	170	Twelve Hours of the Night 2	1–4
37	170	Years and Lives of the Forefathers	138
38	170	Years and Names of the Forefathers in Order	46
39	170		
40	170		
41–43	171		
45	171	OTHER ARMENIAN SOURCES	
History of the Forefathers to Abraham, and Their Years	55–64	*Adamgirkʻ*, Aṙakʻel Siwnecʻi 1.24.87	9
41	114	*Life and History of St. Gregory*, Agathangelos 2, 17	13
Hours of the Day and Night	1	212	106
Life of Nathan (Armenian) 4	265	*Anonymous Philosophical Treatise*, Pseudo–Zeno 1.0.1	90
Memorial of the Forefathers	128		
Miracles (Wonders) of Solomon's Temple	19	*Book of Questions*, Grigor Tatʻewacʻi	11, 14, 15
Names of the Forefathers	138	144	77–78
Names of the Jewels	22–24	287	18
Peoples of the Sons of Noah	27	*Book of Sermons*, Grigor Tatʻewacʻi	55
Praise of the Angels	77	144	70
Question		1.3.7, 152–153	72–73
4–6	73	*Pʻawstos Buzand* 3:10	99
5.3	172	*Chronography*, Pʻilon of Tirak	25–27, 116
Questions and Answers from the Holy Books	92	57–60	27
Question concerning the Archangels	72–75	68	27
		89	27
Questions of Ezra B6	21	103	27
Ranks of the Angels who Rebelled	106	*Commentary of Genesis*, Vardan Arewelcʻ1	28
Repentance of Adam and Eve 50–58	19		
Sermon concerning the Flood 2–6	73	*History of the Armenians*, Łazar Pʻarbecʻi	
Sethites and Cainites 10–11	73	16:8	21
Seven Punishments of Cain	18–19, 22	16:17	21
Seventy-Two Languages	27	*History of the Armenians*, Movsēs Xorenacʻi	25
Short History of the Holy Forefathers	71		
28–29	73	*Onomastica Sacra*	207, 221
Short Questions Selected and Assembled from Books	77		

ANCIENT SOURCES INDEX

Sources in Greek and Latin

Acts of Paul	163
Acts of Pilate	27, 54
Aetius, *Plactia* 2.11	8, 9
1.70–71	170
Ascension of Isaiah	66
Celestial Hierarchy, Pseudo-Dionysius Areopagiticus	77, 81, 83, 88
Chronographiae, Sextus Iulius Africanus	25
Chronography, George Cedrenus	25
Chronicle, Eusebius of Caesarea	25, 56, 57
De gemmis, Epiphanius	23
Historia Scholastica, Petrus Comestor	9
Hypomnesticon of Josephus	27
Infancy Gospel of Ps.–Matthew 42	48
Josephus	
A.J. 1.70–71	170
A.J. 2.232	242
Palaea Historica (Bauckham) 604–5	92
Philo, *Mos.* 1:4	241
Suda (ed. Adler, 1:450)	27
Testament of Adam	66

Rabbinic Sources and Targum

Genesis Rabba	18
23.3	62
Exodus Rabba 1:31	242
Tanḥuma Berešit	
10–11	18
on Gen 11	92
Targum Pseudo-Jonathan	
Num 22:22(26)	258

Other Sources

Cave of Treasures, Syriac	66, 92
18:13, 19:4 (Bauckham)	115
Conflict of Adam and Eve with Satan (Malan) 122–123	94
Sefer HaYashar, Hebrew	208

www.ingramcontent.com/pod-product-compliance
Lightning Source LLC
Chambersburg PA
CBHW031545300426
44111CB00006BA/183